Oxford EAP

A course in English for Academic Purposes

INTERMEDIATE / B1+

Edward de Chazal & Louis Rogers

OXFORD
UNIVERSITY PRESS

Contents

		LISTENING	SPEAKING

READING	WRITING	VOCABULARY

Textbooks (7)
Evaluating different sources
Taking notes on detailed information
Using notes to write a summary
Identifying and referencing source material
Noun phrases (5): Expressing key information using complex noun phrases

Introductions
Analysing essay titles
Identifying the features of an introduction
Evaluating thesis statements
Writing an introduction
Stating aims and purpose

Essay verbs
Identifying essay focus
Using essay verbs

Textbooks (8)
Recognizing objectivity in a text
Identifying and understanding references in a text
Using source texts in writing
The passive (1): Understanding the use of active and passive forms

Referencing
Identifying and analysing types of citation in context
Paraphrasing ideas from a source
Planning and writing an accurately-referenced paragraph
The passive (2): Using active and passive forms to change the focus of a sentence

Cohesive language
Selecting and using linking expressions
Using cohesive language in texts

Textbooks (9)
Analysing models and theories in a text
Understanding comparison in text
Identifying and evaluating authorial stance
Comparison and contrast (2): Understanding longer phrases or structures

Comparison essays
Introduction to essay writing
Writing an effective conclusion
Planning and organizing comparison essays
Comparison and contrast (3): Referring to similarity and difference

Comparing and contrasting
Identifying comparing and contrasting language
Using comparative and contrasting structures

Textbooks (10)
Identifying main arguments
Understanding and using evaluative language
Evaluating premise and conclusion in an argument
Evaluative language: Adjectives

Argument Essays
Planning, organizing, and writing an argument essay
Incorporating evidence in an essay
Making a text more cohesive by varying vocabulary
Cohesion (4): Using synonyms and other cohesive language in a written text

Argument
Presenting and assessing views
Noticing and interpreting arguments

Textbooks (11)
Identifying supporting detail and evidence in a text
Identifying problems, solutions, and evaluation in a text
Understanding how meanings are expressed through prepositional phrases
Prepositions (2): Expressing meaning using complex prepositions

Problem-solution essays
Effectively evaluating solutions
Planning and organizing problem-solution essays
Evaluating your own work
Evaluative language: It and There structures

The language of problems and solutions
Recognizing problems
Introducing and responding to problems

Textbooks (12)
Identifying cause and effect relationships in a text
Identifying stance in cause and effect relationships
Noticing and using prepositional verbs
Prepositional verbs

Cause and effect essays
Planning and structuring a cause and effect essay
Stating cause and effect connections through appropriate language
Writing and evaluating a cause and effect essay
Cause and effect language

Cause and effect
Identifying cause and effect language
Identifying causes in a text and revising

Introduction

Welcome to *Oxford English for Academic Purposes* – a complete course for anyone preparing to study in English at university level.

What is Oxford EAP?

Oxford EAP is designed to improve your ability to study effectively in English, whether you are planning to study on an undergraduate or postgraduate programme. Whatever your academic background, and whatever your chosen subject, *Oxford EAP* will help you develop your knowledge and skills in all of the following areas:

- reading and understanding authentic academic texts
- listening to lectures and presentations
- writing sentences, paragraphs, and different essay types
- participating in seminar and group discussions
- preparing and giving simple presentations
- improving your study skills such as note-taking, critical thinking, and working independently
- recognizing and using academic grammar and vocabulary.

What is in a unit?

Oxford EAP has twelve units. Each unit starts with a preview page which shows the learning objectives for that unit, plus a short discussion task to get you thinking about the unit theme.

The **academic focus** of each unit covers an important aspect of academic study relevant to all subject areas – for example, definition and explanation, description, using sources, comparison and contrast, argument and evidence, and cause and effect. This focus is maintained throughout the unit.

The units are divided into four main modules – Listening, Speaking, Reading, and Writing – plus a one-page Vocabulary module. Each module starts with a rationale (a short text explaining what happens in the module), and includes a number of carefully sequenced tasks which help you to meet the learning objectives for that module.

Listening focuses mainly on listening to lectures and presentations. It uses short video extracts from lectures to help you understand key information and language, as well as how the lecturer's material is organized. Note-taking is a key part of most modules, and the module usually ends with a critical thinking task which asks you to respond to some questions about the content of the lecture or presentation.

Speaking includes participating in seminars and discussions, and giving presentations. It covers communication strategies for these situations, and presents and practises useful language. Usually you will do a short listening or reading task to introduce the context and present examples of useful language. At the end of the module there is normally an opportunity to think about and evaluate your own performance in the discussion or presentation task.

Reading uses extracts from authentic academic textbooks. It usually starts with a short task to get you thinking about the topic, or to predict the content of the text. Further tasks will help you to identify important features of the text, such as the main ideas or specific language, and demonstrate how you can read and understand an academic text even if you don't understand every word. This module often ends with a task where you respond critically to what you have read.

Writing focuses on some of the most important aspects of academic writing in the first four units, such as writing sentences, descriptions and simple paragraphs. Later in the book you move on to analyse paragraph structure, learn how to write summaries and citations, and introductions and conclusions to essays. In the last four units, you will look at different types of essay (e.g. argument, problem-solution, cause and effect), looking at key aspects of organization, style, and use of language. You will also be helped to check and evaluate your writing.

Vocabulary looks at key aspects of academic vocabulary using the content of each unit, and covers useful vocabulary-learning strategies.

What else is included?

Each unit includes:

- **Academic language** (grammar, vocabulary, and useful phrases) related to the academic focus of the unit, with examples taken from the texts or video / audio transcripts. Where necessary, there is a cross-reference to the Language reference at the back of the book.
- **Critical thinking** tasks encourage you to think about the content of each module, and about your own performance in writing and speaking tasks.
- Independent study tips suggesting how to transfer the skills from the course to your own studies.

At the back of the book there is:

- **Glossary** of grammatical and academic terms used in this book
- **Language reference** with more detailed information on the language covered in the units
- **Additional reference material** with information of plagiarism, citation, and proofreading and self-editing
- **Sample essays** and examples of academic writing
- **Video and audio transcripts**.

UNIT 1 Knowledge

ACADEMIC FOCUS: UNDERSTANDING AND PRESENTING INFORMATION

LEARNING OBJECTIVES

This unit covers:

Listening
- Understanding main ideas in a presentation
- Identifying word class to assist note-taking
- Recognizing signposting in a presentation

Speaking
- Talking about experiences using the past simple and present perfect
- Structuring and signposting a short presentation
- Presenting information about your academic experience and aims

Reading
- Gaining an overview of an academic text
- Identifying topics and main ideas
- Building word families

Writing
- Expanding notes into sentences
- Correcting and evaluating sentences
- Writing simple and compound sentences

Vocabulary
- Identifying and using general, academic, and technical vocabulary

Discussion

1 Think about how knowledge is transferred and how you learn things. Put the following sources in order from 1 (most important) to 5 (least important).

the internet   in lectures   textbooks
the media (e.g. television, newspapers)   other students

2 Work in groups and explain why you chose your particular order.

Example: *The internet is very important because you can search for a wide variety of information, but you can't believe everything you read ...*

3 Discuss how you use the sources in 1 in your own area of study. Which are the most useful? Give reasons.

Example: *I read the relevant part of the textbook, and make brief notes on the most important points. I revise from these notes later, which helps me to remember the information in the longer term.*

4 Briefly present your group's ideas to the whole class. Use the following phrases to help you.

We discussed ...

Our group think that ...

1A Listening Short presentations

During your course, you may have to listen to presentations by other students, by professional people, or by experts from your area of study. Presentations usually contain language that tells you how the information in the talk is organized - in other words, it signposts the structure of the talk. You can use this **signposting language** to help you follow a presentation and to take notes.

This module covers:
- Understanding main ideas in a presentation
- Identifying word class to assist note-taking
- Recognizing signposting in a presentation

TASK 1 Thinking about listening

1 **Read questions 1–4 and think about your own answers. Give reasons and examples.**
   1 What do you listen to in English?
   2 How often do you do this in a typical week?
   3 What do you find most difficult about listening to English?
   4 How can you improve your listening skills?

2 **Discuss your answers with a partner.**

TASK 2 Previewing the topic

1 **You are going to watch three people presenting their experiences of educational courses. Work in pairs and discuss the main differences between courses 1–3.**
   1 A pre-sessional course (a language course before university study)
   2 A Bachelor's degree (an undergraduate course)
   3 A Master's degree (a postgraduate course)

2 **What are some of the reasons for taking each of these courses?**

TASK 3 Understanding the introduction to a presentation

1 ▶1.1 **Watch Extract 1 and complete the table.**

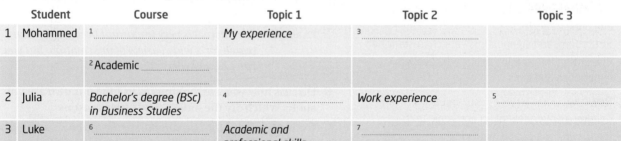

	Student	Course	Topic 1	Topic 2	Topic 3
1	Mohammed	1	My experience	3	
		2 Academic			
2	Julia	Bachelor's degree (BSc) in Business Studies	4	Work experience	5 ....
3	Luke	6	Academic and professional skills	7	

2 ▶1.1 **Watch Extract 1 again and complete sentences 1–5.**
   1 OK. My name's Mohammed. I'm ....
   2 So, firstly, ... my experience of the course itself and then .... how the course ...
   3 I'm here today ....
   4 I've .... three main parts ...
   5 Just to .... overview ...

TASK 4 Understanding the main ideas in a presentation (1)

1 ▶1.2 **Watch Extract 2 and take notes on topics 1 and 2.**

Presentation 1 (Mohammed)

1 Academic reading – differences

2 Useful things learnt

2 **Which words helped you to identify the presenter's main ideas?**

ACADEMIC LANGUAGE   ▶Language reference page 185 45

Word class Using word class to identify main ideas

When you are listening or reading it is important to identify the main ideas. This helps you to take notes on the most important information. The words that carry most of this information are often nouns, verbs, and adjectives. For example:

To give you an idea of what I mean, in academic situations you are always reading for a reason, for example, to write an essay, to give a presentation, to prepare for a test.

You also need to understand the writer's opinion, so you can use it to support your argument.

TASK 5 Identifying word class

1 **Underline the words in sentences 1–4 that express the main idea.**

Example: *In <u>academic situations</u> you are always <u>reading for</u> a <u>reason</u>, for example, to <u>write</u> an <u>essay</u>, <u>give</u> a <u>presentation</u> or <u>prepare</u> for a <u>test</u>.*

1 It can be difficult to decide what you need to read and what makes a good source.

2 So you have to learn to challenge ideas and not just accept everything you read …

3 Your dissertation is a real test of your academic abilities and it will probably decide the degree classification you get.

4 Another 30% of you probably come from different education systems.

2 **Look back at the words you underlined. Identify the word class for each word.**

TASK 6 Understanding the main ideas in a presentation (2)

1 ▶1.3, 1.4 **Watch Extracts 3 and 4 and take notes on topics 3–7 for both presentations.**

3 Getting good marks

4 Work experience – importance

5 Dissertation

6 Professional and academic skills – importance

7 Students' backgrounds

2 **What actual words did you note down? Which word class are they?**

TASK 7 Recognizing phrases for signposting a presentation

1 **Match each phrase 1–5 to functions a–e.**

1 To give you an idea of what I mean

2 To go back to what I was saying earlier

3 OK, let's move on and talk about

4 As you all know

5 So, to sum up

a to return to an important point ....

b to summarize the main idea ....

c to change the subject ....

d to give an example ....

e to refer to the audience's knowledge ....

2 ▶1.5 **Watch the five short clips and check your answers to 1.**

TASK 8 Responding to a presentation

1 **Look back at your notes from Tasks 4 and 6. Work in pairs and discuss these questions.**

1 Is getting work experience important to your future success? Why / Why not?

2 What skills can your area of study give you that will help in your future career?

> **INDEPENDENT STUDY**
>
> The classroom provides only some of your opportunities for learning. You need to practise listening outside the classroom too - for example, by watching online lectures or presentations.
>
> ▶ Next time you have the chance to listen to English outside the classroom, note down what, and how much, you understood.

Presentation skills are important in many academic contexts. You may have to give a short presentation in a seminar, or a more formal presentation to a particular audience. You need to think about what to say, and what language to use. This module helps you to prepare a short presentation about yourself, your experiences, and your aims or ambitions. It also reviews language for talking about past and recent experiences.

This module covers:

- Talking about experiences using the past simple and present perfect
- Structuring and signposting a short presentation
- Presenting information about your academic experience and aims

TASK 1 Preparing personal information

1 **Make brief notes on the following points. Then answer questions 1 and 2 for each point.**

- Your education experience in the last 1–2 years: for example, where you studied, the main subjects you studied, any inspiring teachers.
- Your recent experience: for example, work experience, places you have travelled to, new skills you have learnt.

1 What did you learn from the experience?

2 What difficulties did you have? How did you overcome these difficulties?

ACADEMIC LANGUAGE   ▸Language reference page 184 41

Tense and aspect Talking about experiences

Past simple

Use the past simple to talk about what you did in the past, especially with a time reference (e.g. *last year / in 2012 / when I was at school*):

   Last year I **studied** English and Business.

Also use the past simple to talk about a sequence of events:

   On the course I **learnt** how to give a presentation; then I **focused on** research skills.

Present perfect

Use the present perfect to talk about things that were completed in the past but are also relevant now, especially experiences and achievements:

   The course **has helped** me to develop core academic skills. I**'ve researched** and **written** three long essays. It **has** also **given** me greater confidence.

Questions

In a conversation, follow-up questions are often in the past simple:

   Did you **learn** anything new?   How **did** it **help** you do this?

TASK 2 Using questions to discuss experiences

1 **Complete questions 1–5 below using question words (*how, what, when, why*) and/or *did*.**

1 .... is the most useful thing you learnt? How .... you learn it?

2 .... you decide to go there?

3 .... you spend most of your free time when you were studying?

4 .... you ever think about studying something different?

5 .... this experience help you?

2 **Discuss your own experiences with another student. Ask and answer follow-up questions.**

   Example: *So you've been to Russia. Why did you decide to go there?*

TASK 3 Understanding a short presentation

1 ▶ 1.6 **Watch a short presentation by a Japanese student and complete the notes.**

Example: Focus of presentation: *educational experience and aims*

1 Aim of presentation: ....
2 Ryo's first main aim: ....
3 Ryo's university: ....
4 Ryo's chosen department: ....
5 Ryo's second main aim: ....
6 Ryo's main message: ....

2 ▶ 1.6 **Watch the presentation again and notice the language Ryo uses to organize his ideas. Tick the phrases in each column (A, B, or C) that you hear.**

A	B	C
Today I'd like to talk to you about ...	OK, so first let me tell you about ...	My first main aim was to ...
What I want to talk about today is ...	The next stage of my presentation is ...	I plan / hope / aim / want to...
The focus of this presentation is ...	And this brings me on to my second main point.	What I would really like to do is ...
	I'd like to finish my presentation by ...	My main aim / ambition is to ...

3 **Match headings 1–3 with the appropriate column A–C in 2.**

1 Talking about plans, aims, and ambitions
2 Introducing the topic of your presentation
3 Moving on to the next point

TASK 4 Evaluating a presentation

1 ▶ 1.6 **Watch the presentation again, and evaluate it using the checklist on page 195.**

2 **Compare your evaluation with another student.**

TASK 5 Preparing and giving a personal presentation

INDEPENDENT STUDY

Other students' input can be very useful in developing your presentation style.

▶ Next time you give a presentation, ask other students to evaluate it, then agree at least two things you could improve on.

1 **Prepare a short presentation of about two minutes, talking about your own experience of education or work. Use guidelines 1–4 to plan your ideas.**

1 Decide on a maximum of <u>three</u> points that you want to make. Note them down in order. For example: your recent experience; your present situation; your future plans, aims, and ambitions (academic / other).

2 Think of a way of introducing yourself and your presentation.
Today I want to talk about ...
In this presentation I'd like to tell you about ...

3 Think about the language you will use to:
• talk about your experiences in the past
• move from one point to the next
• talk about your future plans, aims, and ambitions.

4 Think of a phrase to end your presentation. For example:
I'd like to finish my presentation by saying ...
The main thing I learnt from this experience was ...

2 **Work in pairs and practise your presentation. Aim to speak clearly and not too fast. Give each other feedback and suggest improvements.**

3 **Work in groups and take turns to give your presentations.**

1 Aim to speak for about two minutes, and respond to any questions at the end.
2 While you listen, note down any main points and key information, as in Task 3.1.
3 Think of a question to ask after each presentation.
4 Give feedback to the other presenters in your group using the checklist on page 195.

4 **Evaluate your own presentation, using the checklist on page 195. Note down two things you would like to improve.**

Understanding textbooks can be difficult, because they often express complex concepts or ideas, and use specialized vocabulary. This module shows that by developing some simple reading strategies, you can get the information you need even from a difficult text. When you read academic texts, you will need to skim, scan, or close read. **Skimming** means reading quickly for the general meaning, or gist. This is useful when you have large amounts of text. **Scanning** is reading for specific information or details. **Close reading** is when you read line by line, and every word. This is useful when concentrating on a short, specific piece of text.

This module covers:

- Gaining an overview of an academic text
- Identifying topics and main ideas
- Building word families

TASK 1 Thinking about reading

1 **Note down short answers to questions 1–4 about your own reading.**

1 Do you enjoy reading texts in English?

2 What sorts of texts have you read in English recently?

3 Where do you find the texts that you read?

4 What do you find difficult about reading texts in English?

2 **Compare your answers. Discuss what you can do to be a better reader in English.**

TASK 2 Preparing to read

1 **Work in pairs. Explain an idea related to your area of study to your partner.**

Example: ***Aerobic exercise*** *is moderate exercise which you do over a long period of time, like jogging or swimming. It increases the amount of oxygen your body takes in.*

2 **How easy or difficult was it to (a) give your explanation, and (b) understand your partner's explanation?**

3 **Read the two definitions from the *Oxford Advanced Learner's Dictionary*.**

> **psychology** /saɪˈkɒlədʒi/ *noun* [U] the scientific study of the mind and how it influences behaviour
> **cognitive** /ˈkɒgnətɪv/ *adj* connected with mental processes of understanding

1 What do you know about psychology? Have you ever studied it?

2 What do you think cognitive psychology is?

TASK 3 Understanding a text: topic, purpose, and main idea

1 **When you read part of a textbook, you need to understand the *topic*, the *purpose* of the text, and the *main idea or ideas*. Match terms 1–3 with the best description a–c.**

1 topic   a the most important thing that the author wants to communicate

2 purpose   b what the text is about

3 main idea   c the reason for writing

2 **Look at Text 1 from a psychology textbook, paying attention to the title and any words that are highlighted in bold. Select the best answer to Question 1.**

Question 1: *What is the text about?*

1 people's experiences

2 cognitive processing and psychology

INDEPENDENT STUDY

When approaching a new academic text, it is useful to gain an overview by quickly looking at key parts of the text, starting with the title and any headings and words highlighted in bold or italics.

▶ **Find a textbook extract from your own area of study and look at it in this way.**

3 Read Text 1 quickly and select the best answer to Question 2. Use the glossary to help you.

Question 2: *What is the purpose of the text?*

1 To introduce the concept of cognition and some of the ideas related to it.

2 To explain how and why people behave as they do.

4 Read Text 1 again and decide which of the following two statements best expresses the main idea.

Question 3: *What is the main idea?*

1 People process information about the world in different ways, and this has an effect on how they think about things.

2 People need to understand cognitive psychology in order to understand the world.

5 Compare your answers to Questions 1–3 with another student.

Principles that define the cognitive level of analysis

TEXT 1

1 When people are thinking about how best to solve a mathematical problem, trying to remember the title of a book, observing a beautiful sunset, telling a joke they have heard, or thinking about what to do tomorrow, they are involved in cognitive processing. **Cognitive psychology** is concerned with the structure and functions of the mind. Cognitive psychologists are involved in finding out how the human mind comes to know things about the world and how it uses this knowledge. **Cognitive neuroscience** combines knowledge about the brain with knowledge about cognitive processes.

2 The mind can be seen as a set of mental processes that are carried out by the brain. Cognitive processes include perception, thinking, problem-solving, memory, language, and attention. The concept of **cognition** refers to such processes. Cognition is based on a person's **mental representations** of the world, such as images, words, and concepts. People have different experiences and therefore they have different mental representations – for example, of what is right or wrong, or about what boys and girls can or cannot do. This will influence the way they think about the world.

SOURCE: Crane, J. & Hannibal, J. (2009). p.67. *IB Psychology: Course Companion.* Oxford: Oxford University Press.

GLOSSARY

analysis *(n)* the detailed study or examination of sth in order to understand more about it

cognition *(n)* the process by which knowledge and understanding is developed in the mind

influence *(v)* to have an effect on the way that sb behaves or thinks

mental representation *(n)* an image or idea in the memory

TASK 4 Reading in detail to understand key information

1 Read Text 1 carefully and find the key terms or concepts 1–6 related to the word *cognitive*. Complete the notes for items 2–5.

1 Cognitive processing: *involves* problem-solving, remembering something, thinking

2 Cognitive psychology: *is concerned with* ....

3 Cognitive psychologists: *are interested in* finding out ....

4 Cognitive neuroscience: *concerns* knowledge of ....

5 Cognitive processes: *include* ....

6 Cognition, i.e. cognitive processes: *are based on* how the human mind represents the world (e.g. images, words, concepts)

TASK 5 Explaining key terms

1 Work in pairs. Use the words / phrases below to explain or give more information about key terms or concepts from your own area of study.

are based on   involves   is concerned with

Examples: *Civil engineering **involves** building bridges, roads, canals, and other structures.*
*Plate tectonics **is concerned with** the movement of the earth's surface.*

2 How might cognitive psychology be useful in your area of study? Give examples.

TASK 6 Predicting the content of a text

1 You are going to read another extract from the same textbook. Read the title and decide which *four* of items a–e you would expect the text to include.

a An explanation of what *schemas* are.

b An example to show what *schema theory* is.

c Information about how *schema theory* is used.

d Information about how psychologists define *schema theory*.

e A comparison of *schema theory* and other academic theories.

2 Read Text 2 quickly and check which of your predictions in 1 were correct.

3 Match one item from 1 to each paragraph of Text 2. There is one item you do not need to use.

A theory of cognitive process: schema theory

TEXT 2

1 When an expert football player kicks the ball directly into the goal for a penalty, it may look like any other goal. However, this particular kick is the result of many hours of practice, combined with an adjustment to the challenges of the particular situation. The player needs to think about the position of the goalkeeper and predict the goalkeeper's possible reactions, as well as determining how he should kick the ball. This is done based on his previous experience, which is stored in his memory as knowledge – but there is more to it than this. The most successful players have learnt this behaviour to perfection, but they need to modify it to fit the particular situation. The player must respond to visual information about the goalkeeper's position and movement, and its possible consequences. This is based on the recognition of patterns. This 'how-to-score knowledge' will help a player decide what aspects of the situation he needs to pay attention to in order to place the ball accurately between the goalposts. Specialists in a certain field have expert knowledge that comes from hours of practice. This means that to some extent they can do the right things at the right time more or less automatically, but they always need to be able to analyse each individual situation.

2 Cognitive psychologists would call this 'how-to-score knowledge' a **schema**, and **schema theory** is a cognitive theory about information processing. A **cognitive schema** can be defined as networks of knowledge, beliefs, and expectations about particular aspects of the world.

3 Schemas can describe how specific knowledge is organized and stored in a person's memory so that it can be accessed and used when it is needed – as in the example of the expert footballer. It is not possible to see a schema inside someone's head, but using concepts like schemas help psychologists – and all of us – to understand, and discuss, what it would otherwise not be possible to do.

4 Schema theory suggests that what we already know will influence the outcome of information processing. This idea is based on the belief that *humans are active processors of information*. People do not passively respond to information. They interpret and integrate it to make sense of their experiences, but they are not always aware of it. If information is missing, the brain fills in the blanks based on existing schemas, or it simply invents something that seems to fit in. Obviously this can result in mistakes – called **distortions**.

SOURCE: Crane, J. & Hannibal, J. (2009). pp.70–1. *IB Psychology: Course Companion.* Oxford: Oxford University Press.

GLOSSARY

determine *(v)* to calculate sth exactly

integrate *(v)* to combine two or more things so that they work together

interpret *(v)* to explain the meaning of sth; to decide that sth has a particular meaning and to understand it in this way

modify *(v)* to change sth slightly

outcome *(n)* the result or effect of an action or event

recognition *(n)* the act of remembering or identifying what sth is

TASK 7 Identifying the topic and main idea in a paragraph

1 Each paragraph of an academic text typically has a topic and a main idea. Look at paragraph 3 of Text 2 below and match items a–d to parts 1–4.

a an example ....   c information about schemas and how they are used ....

b the topic ..1..   d an explanation of what schemas do ....

> [1]Schemas [2]can describe how specific knowledge is organized and stored in a person's memory so that it can be accessed and used when it is needed – [3]as in the example of the expert footballer. [4]It is not possible to see a schema inside someone's head, but using concepts like schemas help psychologists – and all of us – to understand, and discuss, what it would otherwise not be possible to do.

2 Which part of paragraph 3 includes the main idea?

3 Read paragraphs 1, 2, and 4 of Text 2 again and identify the topics and the main ideas. Write the number of each paragraph next to the notes in the table.

Paragraph	Topic	Main idea
3	Schemas	Schemas help us understand and discuss knowledge.
	Schema theory	In cognitive psychology, schema theory explains how we do things.
	'How-to' knowledge	Experts and specialists use their experience, 'how-to' knowledge, and analysis to do difficult things.
	Human information processing	How schema theory explains how people process information using experience and knowledge.

ACADEMIC LANGUAGE   ▸Language reference page 185 45 / page 177 4

Academic vocabulary (1) Building word families

By learning word families, you will greatly increase your vocabulary. Word families are groups of words based on the same root word, but with different forms, for example:

Noun	Adjective	Adverb	Verb
theory	theoretical	theoretically	theorize

Some words within a word family may be more common than others – for example, the noun *theory* is more frequent and more useful than the verb *theorize*. Not all forms of the word are found in all word families.

Suffixes

Suffixes are a group of letters added to the end of a word to change the form of that word. For example:

Noun suffixes include: -tion, -ity, -ism, -ness (*cognition, reality, criticism, happiness*)

Adjective suffixes include: -al, able, -ive, -ful (*critical, memorable, informative, successful*)

Adverbs typically take the suffix -ly: (*critically, successfully*)

The verb suffix -ize is very frequent: (*criticize, theorize*)

TASK 8 Choosing the right word form

1 Complete the table with the correct forms of the words from Texts 1 and 2. Use your dictionary to help you.

Noun	Adjective	Adverb	Verb
theory	theoretical	theoretically	theorize
			base (on)
	cognitive		–
information			
		–	involve
knowledge			
memory			
	possible		–
	–	–	process
representation			

2 Complete the sentences with the correct form of the word in brackets.

1 The .... theory is that people choose how they behave. (base)

2 This latest piece of research .... a significant achievement. (representation)

3 There seems to be no .... that the research can be successfully completed. (possible)

4 In a presentation it's important to speak .... about your subject. (knowledge)

5 In order to learn new information, try representing it as a picture, and then .... it. (memory)

6 It's difficult to complete a group assignment without the .... of the whole team. (involve)

3 Look at how words from the table in 1 are used in Texts 1 and 2 on pages 013 and 014. Select three or more words from the table and use them to write your own sentences.

TASK 9 Reflecting on your learning

1 Look back at Task 1.1, question 4 on what you find difficult about reading in English. Think of at least one way that this module has helped you.

Example: *The technical terms in the texts looked difficult, but I now realize that they are explained in the text with examples. In this kind of text, if I focus on the explanations, I should be able to understand the concepts.*

2 Note down two or three aims for improving your reading. Think of strategies for achieving these aims.

Example: **Aim:** *By the end of the academic year I want to be able to read textbooks in my subject and understand the main points.*
Strategies: *I can do this by setting myself short tasks, such as reading two pages from a textbook, with deadlines. Then I can increase the difficulty by adding another page, and taking less time.*

1D Writing Simple & compound sentences

From a simple summary to a dissertation, your academic writing needs to express your ideas clearly. It is important be able to write **simple sentences** in English, containing a single idea. From simple sentences you can build longer, **compound sentences** that contain more than one closely related idea. This module gives you practice in writing and evaluating simple and compound sentences.

This module covers:
- Expanding notes into sentences
- Correcting and evaluating sentences
- Writing simple and compound sentences

TASK 1 Thinking about your writing

1 **Look at the statements about writing. Rate your ability for each aspect of writing.**

	Very strong	Strong	OK	Weak	Very weak
1 I can use a wide range of vocabulary.					
2 I can use a variety of grammatical structures accurately.					
3 I can structure a paragraph and an essay well.					
4 I can understand and answer a variety of essay questions.					

2 **Compare your answers with a partner. Discuss why you think you have these strengths and weaknesses.**

TASK 2 Understanding simple sentence structure

1 **Work in pairs and discuss questions 1–3.**
  1 What do you know about how sentences are structured in English?
  2 Do you know what a *subject*, *verb*, and *object* are in a sentence?
  3 Identify the subject, verb, and object of the sentence below.
     Motivated learners make fast progress.

ACADEMIC LANGUAGE   ▸Language reference page 183 35

Sentence structure (1) Writing simple sentences

Simple sentences in English must have a subject (**s**) and a verb (**v**). Most sentences also include an object (**o**). The subject is a noun or noun phrase, and tells you what or who the sentence is about. The verb tells you what the subject is or does. The object is also a noun or noun phrase, and is affected by the action of the verb.

Psychologists study human behaviour.
   s   **v**   **o**

People have different experiences of studying.
  s   **v**   **o**

Cognitive processes include thinking and problem-solving.
     s   **v**   **o**

---

2 **Identify the subject, verb, and object in sentences 1–5.**
  1 Researchers use a variety of methods.
  2 The human mind understands many different ideas.
  3 A specialist has expert knowledge in a particular field.
  4 Different kinds of motivation affect people's performance.
  5 A Master's degree improves your career prospects.

TASK 3 Expanding notes into complete sentences

1 **Notes often include key words instead of complete sentences. Look at notes 1–5 and decide which of the following they include: a subject, a verb, and an object.**

1 have different experiences of education

2 some students not motivated by languages

3 contribute billions of dollars to the global economy

4 Dubai an example of a knowledge economy

5 awards degrees in four classifications

2 **Expand the notes in 1 into sentences by using subjects and verbs from the list. Compare your answers with a partner.**

~~People~~   The university   is   International students   are

Example: ***People*** *have different experiences of education.*

3 **Notes often miss out other 'non-essential' words such as determiners (*the, a/an, many*), prepositions (*for, in*), and adverbs (*very*). Compare notes and sentences 1–6. Which words are missing from the notes in each case?**

Example: *Notes: Psychologists – see mind as complex machine.*
    *Sentence: Psychologists see **the** mind as **a** complex machine.*

1 *English: subject-verb-object sentence structure*
English follows a subject, verb, object sentence structure.

2 *People study – different reasons*
People study for many different reasons.

3 *Feedback students learn*
Feedback helps students to learn.

4 *Work experience important getting job*
Work experience is important for getting a job.

5 *Korea: students study hard*
In Korea students study hard.

6 *university – excellent business school*
The university has an excellent Business School.

4 **Expand notes 1–6 into complete sentences.**

1 office open 9.00 to 5.00

2 UK: international students pay higher fees

3 tests main method of assessment

4 students take maximum six modules

5 good presentation skills – important (!) in workplace

6 dissertation – 30% final mark – this degree programme

TASK 4 Correcting run-on sentences

1 **Run-on sentences are a common mistake in writing. They happen when two simple sentences are joined together without the correct punctuation. Read run-on sentences 1–4 and identify the two simple sentences.**

Example: *People do not passively respond to information, they interpret and integrate it to make sense of their experiences.*

1 The long-term memory is like a big store of information, this store has no size limit.

2 There are many different ways of doing market research, the use of questionnaires and holding focus groups are two examples.

3 The world's oceans contain hundreds of thousands of life forms with many not yet discovered, there could be millions of life forms according to scientists.

4 There are two main types of exercise, many people prefer aerobic exercise (e.g. jogging, swimming) to anaerobic exercise (e.g. lifting weights, running fast over short distances).

2 **Rewrite the run-on sentences in 1 as two simple sentences.**

Example: *People do not passively respond to information. They interpret and integrate it to make sense of their experiences.*

> **INDEPENDENT STUDY**
>
> Checking your work for mistakes is an important part of the writing process. Run-on sentences are a common error, but each student makes different kinds of mistakes, so it is important to pay attention to teacher feedback.
>
> ▶ Next time you receive teacher feedback on your writing, look for the language errors they highlight and try to correct them.

Sentence structure (2) Writing compound sentences using coordinators

Two closely related simple sentences can be joined together to make a compound sentence. Three of the most common words (or *coordinators*) for joining simple sentences together are *and, but,* and *or.* Each simple sentence then becomes an independent part (or *clause*) of a compound sentence. For example:

> *Cognitive psychologists call 'how-to-score knowledge' a schema,* **and** *schema theory is a theory about how we process information.*

> *Science is continually exploring how memory is organized in the human brain,* **but** *it is still not possible to say how memory works.*

> *Research findings can change original models,* **or** *a model can be rejected because of the evidence.*

Run-on sentences can also be corrected by adding a coordinator such as *and, but,* and *or.*

TASK 5 Writing compound sentences

1 Match each coordinator 1–3 to its function a–c.

1	and	a	to introduce a contrast or different idea
2	or	b	to add information
3	but	c	to connect different possibilities / alternatives

2 Match the beginning of sentences 1–6 with the correct ending a–f.

1 It is not possible to see a schema inside someone's head,

2 People interpret information to make sense of their experiences,

3 This model is based on the idea of information processing,

4 Psychologists observe real life,

5 The short-term memory is limited to around seven items,

6 Research data supports existing theories and models,

a but they are not always aware they are doing it.

b or create situations similar to real life in a laboratory.

c but using concepts like schemas helps psychologists.

d and only a very small part of this information will stay in the long-term memory.

e or it may create new models.

f and it is one of the most important models in use.

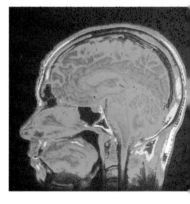

3 Join the two simple sentences together with the correct coordinator, *and, but,* or *or.*

1 The human mind contains many ideas which are stored in the memory. These ideas are organized in categories.

2 Science explores the way the human brain organizes memory. There are still many questions to answer about the biological origins of memory.

3 People can choose to remember information. They can choose to forget it.

4 Some people use automatic processing to help them remember things. Some use different techniques.

5 Pickering and Gathercole (2001) used the Test for Children. They found an improvement in the working memory of the children they tested.

6 The material is not an exact copy of events or facts. It is stored in outline form.

4 Write at least two simple sentences for each of the following topics.

1 Previous courses you have studied

2 Your strengths and weaknesses in English

3 Some interesting things you know about your school/college/university

4 Information connected to your area of study

5 Connect your simple sentences from 4 to make compound sentences.

6 Compare your sentences with another student and ask follow-up questions.

Academic texts in English use a large number of words to present information and express meaning. Such texts typically contain about 80% *general* vocabulary. The remaining 20% is divided into *academic* and *technical* vocabulary, less frequent words, and proper nouns (e.g. *Oxford*). Academic vocabulary items can be found in texts from all subjects: *result in*, *concept*, and *significantly*. Technical vocabulary is specific to one or more disciplines, e.g. *schema* in Psychology. It is useful to be able to identify whether a word is general, academic, or technical, in order to use it in the appropriate context.

TASK 1 Identifying general, academic, and technical vocabulary

1 **Read the descriptions of types of words a–f. Decide if they are examples of *general*, *academic*, or *technical* vocabulary.**

   a grammatical words: determiners (e.g. *the*), pronouns (e.g. *it*) and prepositions (e.g. *as*)

   b adjectives and nouns relating to subjects and perspectives, e.g. *psychology*

   c adjectives expressing familiar qualities / characteristics / time, e.g. *possible*

   d names of familiar concepts, e.g. *information*

   e descriptions of specific concepts, e.g. *top-down, cognitive*

   f adverbs used to show sequence, e.g. *finally*

2 **Read the text, which illustrates the use of general, academic, and technical vocabulary. Check your answers to 1 and find one further example for categories a–e in 1.**

> One of the most fundamental principles of cognitive psychology is that human beings are information processors and that mental processes guide behaviour. One goal of cognitive research is to discover possible principles underlying cognitive processes. Psychologists see the mind as a complex machine – rather like an intelligent, information-processing machine using hardware (the brain) and software (mental images or representations). According to this line of thinking, information input to the mind comes via bottom-up processing – that is from the sensory system. This information is processed in the mind by top-down processing via pre-stored information in the memory. Finally, there is some output in the form of behaviour.
>
> SOURCE: Crane, J. & Hannibal, J. (2009). pp.67-8. *IB Psychology: Course Companion.* Oxford: Oxford University Press.

3 **Decide on the word class for each academic word 1–5. Then match the words with definitions a–e.**

   1 fundamental   a series of things that are done in order to achieve a particular result

   2 process   b a law, a rule, or a theory that sth is based on

   3 principle   c a careful study of a subject, especially in order to discover new facts or information about it

   4 research

   5 complex   d serious; affecting the most central and important parts of sth

                   e difficult to understand

TASK 2 Selecting and using academic vocabulary

1 **Complete the text with the most appropriate words / phrases from the list.**

models   demonstrated   deal with   challenges   complexity   theories

> Psychologists recognize the importance of cognition in understanding the ¹............... of human behaviour. Cognitive ²............... and ³............... are applied to real-world scenarios. Health and sports psychologists have ⁴............... that there is a subtle relationship between how people *think* about themselves and how they *behave* – for example, how they manage to ⁵............... ⁶.............. .
>
> SOURCE: Crane, J. & Hannibal, J. (2009). p.68. *IB Psychology: Course Companion.* Oxford: Oxford University Press.

2 **Select at least five of the academic words from the texts in this module, and write sentences containing the words. If possible, relate the sentences to your own area of study.**

   Example: *The **theory** that supply affects prices is a **fundamental principle** of economics.*

UNIT 2 Organization

ACADEMIC FOCUS: PERSPECTIVE AND STANCE

LEARNING OBJECTIVES

This unit covers:

Listening
- Understanding and taking notes on key information
- Understanding the language of perspective
- Identifying perspectives in a lecture

Speaking
- Identifying perspective and stance in a discussion
- Using perspective to inform stance
- Expressing and responding to stance in a discussion

Reading
- Understanding main ideas in paragraphs and longer texts
- Identifying perspective and stance in a text
- Responding critically to stance in a text

Writing
- Analysing paragraph structure
- Recognizing cohesion in a paragraph
- Writing topic sentences and concluding sentences

Vocabulary
- Identifying common academic nouns
- Understanding stance

Discussion

1 **Read the definitions.**

   A *perspective* is a way of looking at or thinking about an idea, fact, or situation. You can look at the same thing from different perspectives – for example, political, economic, ethical.

   Your *stance* is the position you take on an idea, issue, or situation. It is essentially a more personal view which is influenced by different information and evidence.

2 **Read the situation below and match statements 1–4 to perspectives a–d.**

   Situation: A company is deciding whether to move its manufacturing base from the UK to India.

   1 'We are unlikely to locate to India as it's too far away from our main markets.'

   2 'We might move to India because the labour costs are lower.'

   3 'We might need to work in a different way to be successful in India.'

   4 'It could be a good idea because manufacturing methods are very advanced in India.'

   a economic   b geographical   c technological   d cultural

3 **Underline the words in each statement that show the speaker's stance.**

4 **Work in pairs. Discuss the issue of deciding where to study abroad from each of perspectives a–d in 2.**

5 **Using the perspectives you discussed in 4, discuss your stance on studying in an English-speaking country like the UK.**

Listening Lectures (1)

Lectures are an important part of many academic courses. They provide an opportunity to gain a large amount of key information for your own area of study. Sometimes the transcript of a lecture will be made available online to help you understand the content. The lecturer may give information on a topic from different **perspectives**. This module helps you to focus on key information about the topic, and to understand the language for referring to different perspectives.

This module covers:
- Understanding and taking notes on key information
- Understanding the language of perspective
- Identifying perspectives in a lecture

TASK 1 Understanding the introduction to a lecture

1 You are going to watch the introduction to a lecture about the United Nations. Discuss what you know about the United Nations – for example, its purpose and its activities around the world.

2 ▶2.1 Watch Extract 1 and note down (a) the aim of the lecture, and (b) the three things the lecturer will talk about.

TASK 2 Taking notes on key information

1 Work in groups. Look at these four main organs of the UN and discuss what you think is the role of each one.

1 the Security Council
2 the General Assembly

3 the Secretariat
4 the Economic and Social Council

2 ▶2.2 Watch Extract 2 and note down two pieces of information for each of the four UN organs in 1.

Example: **Security Council:** *five permanent members; main responsibility – to maintain international peace & security*

3 Compare your notes with another student, and check your predictions in 1. Help each other complete any missing information.

TASK 3 Understanding the language of perspective

1 Use a dictionary to find the noun and adverb forms of the adjectives in column 1 and add them to the table.

1 Adjective	2 Adverb	3 Noun	4 Collocation
historical			
geographical			–
international	–		
military			*military power, military law*
political			
legal			
economic			*economic power, economic institution*
social			
ethical			
financial			

2 Match the nouns below to an adjective in column 1 to make collocations like those in column 4. Some words can be used more than once.

court   institution   law   power   society   work

3 Check your answers against the transcript on page 207.

TASK 4 Identifying perspectives in a lecture extract (1)

1 Which perspectives in Task 3 were discussed in the introduction to the lecture?

2 ▶2.1 Watch Extract 1 again. Listen for any words from the table in Task 3.1 and note down the perspectives that the lecturer mentions.

ACADEMIC LANGUAGE

Talking about perspectives: using contextualizing language

To talk about perspectives, you can use phrases based on an adjective, adverb, or noun. For example:

From a political perspective, the UN is arguably not very powerful. (adjective)

Politically speaking, these institutions are independent. (adverb)

As far as geography is concerned, the UN Security Council appears to cover a lot of the globe. (noun)

TASK 5 Using language to talk about perspectives

1 Complete sentences 1–5 using phrases from Academic Language, and the perspective in brackets.

1 The proposal is a good one, but ...., it's not affordable. (financial)

2 ...., this sum is equivalent to ten new fighter planes. (military)

3 ...., the UN has more influence in the northern hemisphere. (geographical)

4 Military action is permitted, but ...., it's not advisable. (ethical)

5 ...., the council needs the support of all members before acting. (political)

INDEPENDENT STUDY

Speakers can introduce perspectives explicitly by using the word itself e.g. *financially*, or implicitly, e.g. by using a phrase like *What will this cost us?*

▶ When you listen to presentations, note down the perspectives mentioned explicitly and implicitly, and the language used to express them.

TASK 6 Identifying perspectives in a lecture extract (2)

1 ▶2.3 Watch Extract 3. Tick the perspectives that are mentioned.

historical   military   political   ethical   legal   financial   geographical

2 ▶2.3 Watch Extract 3 again and note down any information about the UN that you used to identify the perspectives in 1.

Example: **Historical perspective:** *UN established 24 Oct 1945 / historically – replaced League of Nations / aim – ensure future wars impossible*

3 Use the information you noted in 2 to write one sentence on each perspective mentioned. Refer to the transcript on page 207 if necessary.

Example: *The UN was established on 24 October 1945 to replace the League of Nations – its aim was to ensure that future wars were impossible.*

TASK 7 Critical thinking – evaluating the content of a lecture

1 Work in groups. Discuss questions 1–3.

1 What did you learn about the UN from the lecture?

2 What was the most interesting thing you heard?

3 What are the most positive things about the UN? What are the negative things?

TASK 8 Evaluating listening strategies

1 Evaluate the strategies for listening to a lecture, using the checklist on page 195.

2B Speaking Seminar discussions (1)

In seminars, you will have the opportunity to discuss a variety of theories and ideas. You may be asked to give examples using real-life events and scenarios. When you make or support a point during a discussion, you may need to consider different perspectives on the topic you are discussing. Thinking about different perspectives can also help to make your own **stance**, or supported opinion, more academic.

This module covers:
- Identifying perspective and stance in a discussion
- Using perspective to inform stance
- Expressing and responding to stance in a discussion

TASK 1 Preparing for a discussion

1   **Discuss the following statement. Do you agree or disagree? Give reasons.**

   'It is the government's job to manage pollution, not the job of individuals or companies.'

2   ◀)) **2.4 You are going to listen to two students discussing the statement in 1. Listen to Extract 1 and decide:**
   1   who agrees with the statement
   2   what reason(s) each person has for their opinion.

TASK 2 Identifying different perspectives in a discussion

1   **You are going to listen to two other students discussing different perspectives on the statement in Task 1.1. Predict which perspectives below they might discuss.**

   commercial   environmental   geographical   historical   political   social

2   **Select two perspectives and add more details.**

   Example: *Environmental – people who cause pollution should have to manage their impact*

3   ◀)) **2.5 Listen to Extract 2 and check your predictions in 1.**

TASK 3 Listening for more detail

1   ◀)) **2.5 Listen to Extract 2 again and make notes on the different perspectives.**

2   **Compare your notes with another student and help each other complete any missing information.**

3   **How is this discussion better than the one you listened to in Task 1? Give examples.**

TASK 4 Discussing different perspectives

1   **You are going to discuss the following statement. Think about the different perspectives that could be used and add one more perspective of your own to the table.**

   'University education should be provided for free by governments.'

Moral	Economic	Political	
All people are equal and this is a policy of equality.			

2   **Work in groups. Discuss the statement and make notes on the different perspectives.**

3   **Report your discussion to the class. Use some of the phrases below.**

   From an economic perspective, ...   *If we look at this from a social perspective, ...*

   Politically speaking, ...   *As far as politics are concerned, ...*

TASK 5 Using perspectives to inform your stance

1 Use your notes from Task 4.1 to write a sentence showing your own stance on the statement about university education.

Example: *I think university education should be free because an educated workforce benefits the whole of society, and that's good from an economic perspective.*

2 Explain your stance to other students in the group.

TASK 6 Identifying stance in a discussion

1 ◀))2.6 Listen to two students in a seminar discussing the statement in Task 4.1. Are they *for* or *against* the statement? Note down each student's stance.

2 ◀))2.6 Listen again and complete extracts 1–7.

1 So come on, then, Dan. ....? I mean, should university education be provided for free by the government?

2 Er ... well, yeah. ...., it should be.

3 I mean ... .?

4 .... it shouldn't be free ... . if you want to go to university you should be, well, you know, ... prepared to pay for it.

5 OK, ..., but in most countries people pay their taxes ...

6 Mm ... . I don't know, I'm not sure that's the case.

7 .... if they have to pay, that means only people with money will get to go to university.

<hr>

ACADEMIC LANGUAGE

Expressing stance (1) Useful phrases

To take part in a seminar effectively, you need to be able to say what you think, ask other people what they think, and respond appropriately.

Giving an opinion	**Asking for an opinion**	**Responding**
I think (that)	*What do you think?*	*I can see what you're saying*
In my view	*What are your views on ...?*	*I see what you mean*
From my point of view		*But surely ...*

TASK 7 Taking part in a discussion

1 You are going to take part in a discussion on the following statement. Think about questions 1–3 to prepare for the discussion.

'School should not be compulsory because not everyone needs an education.'

1 What different perspectives can you think of on this statement?

2 What is your own stance on the statement?

3 What different stances might people take and how could you respond to them?

2 Work in groups and discuss the statement in 1. Make sure you give your opinion, and listen and respond to other people.

3 Evaluate your contribution to the discussion. Think about how well you did the following things.

- Give your opinion
- Use different perspectives to inform your opinion
- Listen and respond to other people

4 Select one thing to improve next time you take part in a discussion.

INDEPENDENT STUDY

It is important that your stance is informed by a number of perspectives as this will making your thinking more academic.

▶ Next time you take part in a seminar or discussion, try to consider different perspectives on the issue before you give your opinion.

Academic texts usually consist of paragraphs containing one or more **main ideas**. As shown in Unit 1, when you read a text it is important to focus on the main idea or ideas before you look at the detail. It is also useful to try to identify the writer's stance, which is usually informed by different perspectives – for example, political, economic, or cultural perspectives.

This module covers:
- Understanding main ideas in paragraphs and longer texts
- Identifying perspective and stance in a text
- Responding critically to stance in a text

TASK 1 Preparing to read

1 **Discuss who controls each of these things in your country. Is it the government, private business, or both?**

1 Education (schools, universities)

2 Health care (hospitals)

3 Energy supplies (electricity, gas, oil)

4 The supply of goods (food, consumer products, etc.)

5 Transportation (roads, railways, etc.)

2 **The items in 1 are part of a country's *infrastructure*. What are the advantages and disadvantages of government or private business controlling the infrastructure?**

TASK 2 Understanding the main idea in a paragraph

1 **You are going to read an extract from an economics textbook. Read Text 1 and match statements 1–4 to each type of economy – a *planned economy* and a *free market economy*.**

1 All decisions are made by one organization.

2 There is a lot of competition between organizations.

3 Prices and wages tend to be fixed.

4 Prices vary depending on how much people need or want a product.

TEXT 1

Planned economies In a planned economy, sometimes called a centrally planned economy or a command economy, decisions about what to produce, how to produce, and who to produce for, are made by a central body, the government. All resources are collectively owned. Government bodies arrange all production, set wages and set prices through central planning. Decisions are made by the government on behalf of the people and, in theory, in their best interests.

Free market economies In a free market economy, sometimes called a private enterprise economy or capitalism, prices are used to ration goods or services. All production is in private hands and demand and supply are allowed to set wages and prices in the economy. The economy should work relatively efficiently and there should be few cases of surplus and shortages.

SOURCE: Blink, J. & Dorton, I. (2006). pp.9–10. *IB Economics companion*. Oxford: Oxford University Press.

2 **Which of these statements best describes the author's stance on planned economies?**

1 In a planned economy, government decisions are always for the benefit of people.

2 In a planned economy, government decisions may be for the benefit of the government.

3 **Which of these statements best describes the author's stance on free market economies?**

1 Free market economies always have a steady supply of goods.

2 Free market economies normally have a steady supply of goods, but not always.

4 **Which words or phrases in each paragraph helped you answer 2 and 3?**

5 **Do you think the author believes one system is better than the other? Give reasons.**

TASK 3 Understanding the main ideas in a longer text

1 **You are going to read a longer text about the free market approach. Discuss the following questions.**

1 The USA and the UK are examples of *developed* countries. Think of some examples of *developing* countries.

2 What are some of the advantages and disadvantages of a free market economy for developing countries?

2 **Read the first paragraph of Text 2 and identify the main idea, a or b.**

a A free-market economy is best for both developed and developing countries.

b Ideas about the best ways to achieve economic growth have changed over time.

3 **Read the rest of Text 2 and match paragraphs 2–8 to ideas a–g.**

a Developing countries need governments to help in areas such as transportation, energy supply, and health care. ......

b A free market economy can cause problems for the poorest people. ......

c A free market economy can cause different problems in cities than in rural areas. ......

d A combination of planned and free market policies is the most effective approach. ......

e It is difficult for developing countries to compete with developed countries. ......

f Other countries may not invest in a developing country for political reasons. ......

g Government intervention has helped some countries to be successful. ......

4 **Identify the key words that helped you match each idea to a paragraph.**

TEXT 2

1 In the 1980s, there was a movement towards more free market, supply-side-oriented governments in developed countries such as the USA and the UK, which saw a shift of emphasis in government policy. This resulted in a change in direction in thinking on the best way to achieve growth and development in developing countries. However, as we have moved into the new century, a number of concerns have been raised about the value of adopting a pure market-led approach.

2 Infrastructure is unlikely to be created through a market-based approach and developing countries simply do not have sufficient infrastructure to adopt a free market approach. Thus, this requires planning for the future and government intervention.

3 Although the more developed countries promote trade liberalization, they themselves do not liberalize all their trade. Protectionism in developed countries makes it very difficult for the developing countries to compete on a fair basis. In recent years, led by the larger developing countries such as Brazil and India, developing countries have been cooperating with each other to have more influence in trade negotiations.

4 The success of the export-led Asian Tigers did not happen without government intervention. The governments in question were very interventionist in specific areas, especially in product markets that needed help and protection before they were able to export. They also were able to place great emphasis upon education and healthcare.

5 Although a more free market approach may lead to economic growth in the long term, there are without doubt short-term costs to the poorest people. In the short term, unemployment rises, as do the prices of essential products, and the provision of public services also falls. This will hit the poorest sector of the population more than anyone else, causing greater income inequality.

6 The adoption of free market strategies tends to concentrate attention and activities on the urban sectors of an economy. This tends to increase the divide between rural and urban areas, increasing the levels of poverty in rural areas and also leading to migration from rural to urban areas. This has created large areas of slums on the edge of many major cities in developing countries.

7 Governments may adopt the concept of liberalized flows of capital, but a lack of political stability means that many countries are not in a position to attract the foreign investment necessary to achieve growth.

8 In the end, it is clear that solutions will lie in a combination of the different approaches and that the combination will need to be tailored to suit the needs of each individual country. Adopting a 'one size fits all' policy will not be effective, as the IMF discovered in the 1980s.

SOURCE: Blink, J. & Dorton, I. (2006). pp.401-4. *IB Economics companion*. Oxford: Oxford University Press.

GLOSSARY

IMF *(n)* the International Monetary Fund

interventionism *(n)* a policy where the government influences the economy

protectionism *(n)* protecting your country's businesses and economy

slums *(n)* areas where poor people live

supply-side oriented policy *(n)* policies that try to increase efficiency and competition

trade liberalization *(n)* buying and selling with very few rules

TASK 4 Identifying perspective and stance in a text (1)

1 Read paragraph 2 of Text 2 again. What is the topic of the paragraph?

2 Look at the words or phrases that are circled and underlined in paragraph 2 below.

 1 Which words / phrases are related to a perspective?

 2 Which words / phrases indicate the author's stance, or opinion?

> Infrastructure is <u>unlikely</u> to be created through a market-based approach and developing countries <u>simply do not have</u> <u>sufficient</u> infrastructure to adopt a free market approach. Thus, this <u>requires</u> planning for the future and government intervention.

3 Which of the following perspectives are referred to by the author in Text 2?

political   environmental   social   economic

4 Complete the sentence to summarize the author's stance on the topic.

Developing countries .... governments to develop an infrastructure – a free market approach .... work.

ACADEMIC LANGUAGE   ▸Language Reference page 183 36

Expressing stance (2) Adverbials and verbs

Stance is the personal position that an author takes on a particular topic. It is often based on a number of perspectives. Authors use a variety of language to show what they think about an issue, rather than just presenting the facts.

To express certainty or add emphasis:

*Developing countries **simply** do not have sufficient infrastructure to adopt a free market approach.*

(the author is emphasizing a statement)

*There are **without doubt** short-term costs to the poorest people.*

(the author is expressing certainty about this)

To express uncertainty or reduce emphasis:

*Decisions are made, **in theory**, in the people's best interests.*

(the author is not sure that this really happens)

*Infrastructure **is unlikely to be** created through a market-based approach.*

(the author does not think this will work)

TASK 5 Using adverbials to express stance

1 Complete the sentences using an appropriate adverbial from the list.

apparently   clearly   generally   in theory   without doubt

 1 .... the company is in a difficult situation – the share price has dropped by 50% in the last month.

 2 .... the country is in recession, but a large number of people feel positive about their financial situation.

 3 There are .... signs of improvement in the labour market, as unemployment figures decline.

 4 While it may be .... true that urbanization brings problems, it is not always the case.

 5 The policies were made, ..., to support greater economic growth.

2 Compare your ideas with a partner.

TASK 6 Identifying perspective and stance in a text (2)

1 Read paragraphs 3–8 of Text 2 again and complete the table.

	Main perspective	Vocabulary related to perspective	Phrases for expressing stance
2	Political, economic	*market-based approach, free market approach, government intervention*	*unlikely, simply do not have, sufficient, requires*
3			
4			
5			
6			
7			
8			

2 Complete the sentences to summarize the author's stance in paragraphs 3, 5, and 7.

1 Developed countries create rules that they _____ follow, making it _____ for developing countries. (paragraph 3)

2 Free markets _____ create social and economic divides, and are not always _____ for the poorest sector of a society. (paragraph 5)

3 Without political stability, it is more _____ for governments to attract investment. (paragraph 7)

3 Write three sentences to summarize the author's stance in paragraphs 4, 6, and 8.

4 Read statements 1–3. Which one best summarizes the author's overall stance in Text 2?

1 Free market economies are superior.

2 Planned economies are superior.

3 Economies need to adapt to their own needs.

> **INDEPENDENT STUDY**
>
> Being able to identify a writer's stance will help you to understand a text more easily.
>
> ▶ Find a text or texts related to your area of study and, as you read, try to identify the writer's stance.

TASK 7 Critical thinking – responding to the content of a text

1 Work in groups and discuss the following questions. Give reasons or examples where possible.

1 Do you think governments should be responsible for developing a country's infrastructure?

2 Is inequality between individuals normal in any society? Is it a cause for concern?

3 Do you think the benefits of economic growth outweigh the negatives (e.g. poverty, poor health conditions, pollution)?

A paragraph is a key part of most academic essays. Each paragraph in an essay normally develops a single topic, or idea. Usually, you start a paragraph with a **topic sentence** which states the topic or main point. You can end your paragraph with a **concluding sentence**, which refers back to the topic and states the main point again. You also need to make sure your paragraph has **cohesion** - in other words, that all the parts are connected and fit together well.

This module covers:
- Analysing paragraph structure
- Recognizing cohesion in a paragraph
- Writing topic sentences and concluding sentences

TASK 1 Understanding and analysing a paragraph

1 **Read the paragraph from an essay – the first sentence is missing. Decide which of the following items is the topic of the paragraph.**

universities   pharmaceutical and agricultural companies   research

> [1] .... [2]Universities do research in all academic subject areas, such as medicine, and companies carry out research into a wide range of products and services, from new models of cars to what people buy in supermarkets. [3]For example, research by pharmaceutical companies leads to the development of new medicines, and agricultural companies research new varieties of vegetables and grains to provide better quality food for our tables. [4]However, universities are essential for research, because they are where students learn research methods. [5]These examples show that research is a widespread and essential activity in universities and in the business world.

2 **Read the paragraph again and select the best topic sentence from 1–3. Say why you selected this sentence.**

1 Fast-changing markets mean that companies have to respond to new demand.

2 Research today is carried out by both universities and companies.

3 Today's companies are heavily involved in research.

3 **Match features a–d to sentences 1–5 in the paragraph.**

a rationale: to explain why the topic is important

b concluding sentence: to restate the main point and evaluate briefly

c development: to develop the main point with examples and explanation

d topic sentence: to introduce the topic of the paragraph

Sentences: 1 ....   2 ....   3 and 4 ....   5 ....

TASK 2 Writing a topic sentence

1 **Read the paragraph and identify the topic. Sentence 1, the topic sentence, is missing.**

> [1] .... [2]It is important because it allows the assessor to see the employee working and interacting with other employees, and to decide how effective they are at carrying out their duties and responsibilities. [3]Unlike other methods of assessment, such as psychometric tests and interviews, observation is simple and direct. [4]Psychologically, observation is less threatening, and in terms of cost, it is also likely to be cheaper than other methods. [5]For these reasons, observation is a very practical and effective assessment method for people at work.

2 **Match sentences 2–5 to features a–d.**

a development   b rationale   c concluding sentence   d perspectives

3 Write a topic sentence to start the paragraph in 1. Include the topic and a related idea, for example, where the topic takes place or why it is important.

> Example: *Research today is carried out by both universities and companies.*
> (topic)   (related idea)

4 Work in pairs. Compare and evaluate your topic sentences using questions 1–3.

1 Does the sentence introduce the topic of the paragraph?

2 Does it also mention a related idea?

3 Is the language in the sentence accurate?

TASK 3 Recognizing cohesion in a paragraph

1 Read the paragraph below and work out what the words in bold refer to.

> Example: *Universities do research in all academic subject areas such as medicine, and companies carry it out – 'it' refers back to 'research.'*

> Universities do research in all academic subject areas, such as medicine, and companies carry **it** out into a wide range of products and services, from new models of cars to what people buy in supermarkets. For example, **it** can lead to the development of new medicines, and **they** also research new varieties of vegetables and grains to provide better quality foods for **them** to eat. **This** is very important.

2 Work in pairs. For each word in bold, decide if the word it refers to (its *referent*) is clear and certain.

3 Read the paragraph below. Underline the words and phrases which match the words in bold in the paragraph in 1. The first is done as an example.

> Universities do research in all academic subject areas, such as medicine, and companies carry out <u>research</u> into a wide range of products and services, from new models of cars to what people buy in supermarkets. For example, research can lead to the development of new medicines, and agricultural companies also research new varieties of vegetables and grains to provide better quality foods for people to eat. This type of research is very important.

ACADEMIC LANGUAGE   ▸Language Reference page 180 24.1

Cohesion (1) Pronouns and determiners

Cohesion is how parts of a text are connected through meaning and language. One way you can make your writing cohesive is by using pronouns (*it, they*) and determiners (**this** *problem*, **the** *research*). For example:

> *However, universities are essential for research, because **they** are where students learn research methods.* (the pronoun *they* refers back to universities)

> **These** *examples show that research is a widespread and essential activity.* (*these examples* refers back to information in earlier sentences)

You need to make the referent of a pronoun clear to your readers. For example, if you write *This is important*, your readers will ask the question 'What is important?', so they need to know exactly what *this* refers to.

TASK 4 Cohesion – using pronouns and determiners

1 Look again at the paragraph from Task 2.1. Decide what each word in bold refers to.

> [1]Observation is an important way for employers to assess their workforce. [2]**It** is important because it allows the assessor to see the employee working and interacting with other employees, and to decide how effective **they** are at carrying out their duties and responsibilities. [3]Unlike other methods of assessment, such as psychometric tests and interviews, observation is simple and direct. [4]Psychologically, observation is less threatening, and in terms of cost, **it** is also likely to be cheaper than other methods. [5]For **these** reasons, observation is a very practical and effective assessment method for people at work.

2 Complete the paragraph using the words in the list. You need to use some words more than once.

they   their   them   this   some   it   who

> One of the major health challenges facing developed countries today is that increasing numbers of people are doing little or no exercise. Recent research indicates a growth in the number of people [1]................. appear to spend most of their day sitting down. As a result, [2]................. are becoming more at risk of serious illness, including heart disease. [3]................. people report that [4]................. long working hours do not allow [5]................. enough time for exercise, while others admit that [6]................. prefer to do sedentary activities like watching television. The problem is serious from a number of perspectives. It has been estimated to cost national health services up to 10% of [7]................. entire budgets in related treatment. For the people concerned, [8]................. lack of exercise is likely to have a negative effect on [9]................. overall quality of life. Exercise is also a social activity, so a lack of [10]................. can result in fewer opportunities for social interaction. The lack of exercise among certain groups of people is a very serious problem today with significant health, financial, and social impacts.

TASK 5 Linking topic sentences and concluding sentences

1 Read topic sentences 1–3. Decide which concluding sentence, a or b, is more likely to end the paragraph.

Example: Organized tourism is becoming more personalized with the growth of individual trip advisers.
   a In short, the development of trip advisers meets the needs of individual tourists who want a specific holiday which can only be delivered on an individual basis.
   b Mass-market tourism has developed rapidly since the 1960s.
   Sentence a refers back to the paragraph topic of individual trip advisers, and seems to state the main point. Sentence b does not seem relevant to the topic.

1 Continuing professional development, or CPD, is becoming more important in the workplace.
   a These examples show that CPD is increasing in importance in both public and private companies.
   b Workplace environments vary greatly across different cultures and countries.

2 Recent research suggests that smart phones are being used by children at younger ages, even at pre-primary school age.
   a This research shows that smart phone technology has been developing rapidly for several years, and has greatly helped people of all ages.
   b The increasing use of smart phones among very young children is not risk-free, and can lead to children using dangerous websites.

3 Another cause of unemployment is poor personal organization.
   a This discussion shows the importance of personal organization in finding a job.
   b Therefore, unemployment has at least three main causes, including poor government planning, economic uncertainty, and poor organization by individual people.

2 Work in pairs. Discuss your answers and give reasons.

3 Look again at the topic sentences and concluding sentences in 1. Note down words and phrases from each sentence that you can use in your own writing on any topic.

Examples: *1   [topic] is becoming more important in [place].*
   a   These examples show that [topic] is developing in importance in [place].

INDEPENDENT STUDY

Good writers clearly signal the start of each paragraph by stating the topic, and end the paragraph with a brief conclusion of the main point.

▶ Find at least three paragraphs in different textbooks related to your area of study. Identify and evaluate the topic sentences and concluding sentences.

TASK 6 Analysing concluding sentences

1 Read the guidelines below. Evaluate the concluding sentences from the paragraphs in Tasks 1.1 and 4.1. using guidelines 1–3.

Guidelines – a concluding sentence should:

1   restate the topic and main point of the paragraph
2   summarize the information in the body of the paragraph
3   give a brief evaluation of the main point.

> These examples show that research is a widespread and essential activity in universities and in the business world. (Task 1.1)

> For these reasons, observation is a very practical and effective assessment method for people at work. (Task 4.1)

2 Read the paragraph in Task 1.1 again. Decide if each sentence 1–3 below could replace the concluding sentence in the paragraph. Use the guidelines in 1.

1   A further key point about research is that it can be extremely expensive.
2   These examples show that research takes place in a range of educational and commercial settings.
3   Universities, however, focus not only on research but also teaching.

TASK 7 Writing a concluding sentence

1 Read the paragraph below from another essay and write a concluding sentence.

> [1]Computer files can be organized in a number of different ways. [2]The first choice for the user is to decide how many folders to have. [3]Most users choose between organizing data into either a very small number of folders, each containing a large number of files, or a very large number of folders, each containing very few files. [4]Other choices include how many folders to present at the highest level of the 'tree', and the number of levels. [5]This means that the user either has to navigate a large number of folders at the start, or work their way down through a 'deep' number of levels. [6] ....
> ....

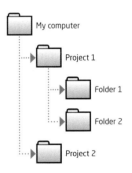

2 Evaluate your concluding sentence using the guidelines in Task 6.1. Compare your sentence with a partner, and evaluate each other's sentences.

2E Vocabulary Expressing stance

In Academic English texts there are a number of key nouns that can be used to describe a range of academic concepts, e.g. *theory* and *approach*. These often appear in frequent word combinations known as collocations. Authors often indicate their stance on concepts by collocating them with a modifying adjective. The adjective-noun collocations highlight stance by showing the position authors take, and the strength of their opinion.

TASK 1 Identifying common academic nouns

1 **Match academic nouns 1–8 to meanings a–h.**

1	strategy	a	an idea or a principle that is connected with something abstract
2	approach	b	an opinion on or an attitude towards a particular subject
3	concept	c	a plan that is intended to achieve a particular purpose
4	solution	d	the general way in which a person or thing develops
5	position	e	a way of solving a problem or dealing with a difficult situation
6	policy	f	a formal set of ideas that is intended to explain why something happens or exists
7	direction	g	a way of thinking about a problem or task
8	theory	h	a plan of action agreed or chosen by a political party, a business, etc.

TASK 2 Understanding stance

1 **Look at the collocations in italics and decide what stance the author is taking.**

1 Reducing interest rates became a *central strategy* in stabilizing the economy.
  a The strategy is important   b The strategy is unimportant

2 The government was accused of lacking *transparent policies* on immigration.
  a The policies were easily understood   b The policies were not easily understood

3 It is considered one of the *major theories* in the development of the field.
  a The theory is the most important   b The theory is the least important

4 The *likely approach* to success is a mixture of both a planned and controlled economy.
  a The approach is probable   b The approach is improbable

5 It is a *basic concept*, but plays a key role in the understanding of the subject.
  a It is a simple idea   b It is a complex idea

6 *Practical solutions* averted catastrophe in the recent recession.
  a The solutions are sensible, and easily manageable
  b The solutions are risky, and hard to implement

7 Their *influential position* within the organization gave them significant control.
  a Their position was weak   b Their position was powerful

8 The leadership took the organization in an *unsuitable direction* that diminished its power.
  a The direction was right   b The direction was not right

2 **Complete the paragraph with the collocations in the list.**

central strategy   practical solutions   basic concept   influential position
transparent policies   unlikely approach   suitable direction

While government control is a ¹............................... in stabilizing economics, political parties have to accept that big business now has an ²............................... when it comes to guiding economic growth in a ³............................... . ⁴..............................., such as the minimum wage, have been supported by companies wanting to give workers a fairer deal. This, and ⁵............................... to reducing working hours, have had major impacts on the way we work and spend. However, recent market turmoil has shown that following business completely is an ⁶............................... to economic success. Perhaps a better solution is for governments to align the best of business ideas with ⁷............................... for growth.

3 **Use collocations from 2 to write three sentences about key concepts in your own area of study.**

UNIT 3 Motivation

ACADEMIC FOCUS: DEFINITION AND EXPLANATION

LEARNING OBJECTIVES

This unit covers:

Listening
- Listening for the main points
- Recognizing signposting language
- Taking detailed notes on explanations and examples

Speaking
- Understanding written and spoken definitions
- Asking for and giving definitions and short explanations
- Participating in a seminar discussion

Reading
- Predicting the purpose of a text
- Understanding main ideas
- Recognizing cohesive language
- Recognizing definitions, explanations, and examples

Writing
- Writing definitions using prepositional phrases
- Writing definitions using relative clauses
- Writing a paragraph that includes definition

Vocabulary
- Understanding and using evaluative adjectives
- Understanding and using classifying adjectives

Discussion

1 **Work in pairs. Look at the following careers and discuss questions 1–3. Give reasons and examples where possible.**

   teacher or professor   professional footballer
   business person   health worker

   1 What motivates people in these careers? Note down at least three different ideas.

   2 Which of the following items are the most important motivating factors for each career?

   achieving success in your field   making money
   becoming famous   having power   making changes
   helping people

   3 Which of the items above are important motivating factors for other careers? Why?

2 **Note down your answers to the following questions.**

   1 Are successful people always motivated?

   2 How can people motivate themselves to do something they don't want to do?

   3 What motivates you personally? Is it an idea not listed in 1.2?

3 **Work in groups and discuss your answers in 2. Then present them to the class. Use the following phrases to help you.**

   We discussed ...

   Our group think that ...

   We came to the conclusion that ...

When listening to a lecture, you need to be able to recognize the main points and supporting details. It is also important to understand how information and ideas are organized. Lecturers may use signposting expressions to show how their lecture will be organized - recognizing these expressions will help you understand what you are going to hear and the order in which you will hear it. Lectures also often include **definitions** and **explanations** of key terms and ideas. It is important to recognize these in order to take effective notes.

This module covers:
- Listening for the main points
- Recognizing signposting language
- Taking detailed notes on explanations and examples

TASK 1 Using your knowledge to prepare for a lecture

1 **Work in pairs. Discuss how the following factors are linked to motivation at work.**

praise from your boss	earning a lot of money	your job title
being creative	having power	doing challenging work
respect from colleagues	a good pension	a sense of achievement

2 **Which factors in 1 do you think are the most motivating?**

TASK 2 Understanding the main points of a lecture

1 **You are going to listen to extracts from a lecture about motivation at work. Look at slides A–C from the start of the lecture and decide which order they will appear in.**

2 ▷**3.1** **Watch Extract 1 and check your prediction in 1. Make brief notes on the main points the lecture will cover.**

3 **Work in pairs. Use your notes to tell each other what you understood from Extract 1.**

TASK 3 Understanding the organization of a lecture

1 ▷**3.1** **Watch Extract 1 again and complete the expressions in sentences 1–5 that show how the lecture will be organized.**

1 .... I'd like to look at a number of theories related to motivation ...

2 ...., we'll look .... at Taylor's idea that money is the key motivator in the workplace.

3 Then, we'll .... look at one of the most famous theories of motivation, which is Maslow's hierarchy of needs.

4 ...., we're .... how Maslow's ideas influenced the work of Douglas McGregor ...

5 And ...., I want to .... at a slightly different view of motivation developed by McClelland and Burnham ...

ACADEMIC LANGUAGE

Signposting language (1) Giving an overview, sequencing

Lecturers often use different expressions to show the organization of the lecture. For example:

Giving an overview	**Sequencing points**
As we'll see from today's lecture ...	*First, we'll look in more detail at ...*
In today's lecture I'd like to look at ...	*Then, we'll move on to look at ...*
In this lecture, I'll be focusing on ...	*After that, we're going to see ...*
	And then finally, I want to take ...

Slide A

> 1 What motivates people?
> 2 How have theories developed?
> 3 How have they influenced each other?

Theories of motivation
- Taylor
- Maslow
- McGregor
- McClelland & Burnham

Slide B

The history of motivational theories at work

Dr David Hughes
Institute of Psychology

Slide C

TASK 4 Taking notes on key information

1 ▶3.2 Watch Extract 2 and label the timeline with the people behind the theories of motivation.

1 McClelland and Burnham   2 Taylor   3 Maslow   4 McGregor

Early 20th Century	1940s/1950s	1960s	1970s

2 ▶3.2 Watch Extract 2 again and complete the notes.

1 Taylor: _____ motivates everyone

2 Maslow: motivation = _____ main areas

3 McGregor: management styles = _____ groups: _____ and _____

4 McClelland and Burnham: studied _____ main motivator = _____

TASK 5 Taking detailed notes on explanations and examples

1 ▶3.3 Watch Extract 3 of the lecture. Complete the notes on each level of Maslow's hierarchy of needs.

	Explanation	Example related to work
Self-actualization	7	8
Esteem	Status – being accepted and respected	6
Belonging	4	5
Security	2	Job security and 3
Physiological	Basic survival needs – food, water, etc.	1

2 ▶3.3 Watch the last part of Extract 3 again and answer questions 1-4.

1 Which need is fulfilled first?

2 Can you move from security needs straight to esteem needs?

3 What happens when one need is met?

4 Does everyone have to reach the top of the pyramid to be satisfied?

3 Compare your answers in 1 and 2 with another student. Help each other to complete any missing information.

TASK 6 Recognizing phrases for signposting a lecture

1 Match the following phrases the lecturer uses with functions a–c.

As I said   So for example   this can be understood as   In other words
An obvious example of this is   How that works is   As we've already seen

a giving an example   b giving an explanation   c referring to something said earlier

2 ▶3.3 Watch Extract 3 again and check your answers.

TASK 7 Critical thinking – responding to the content of a lecture

1 Look back at your notes from Tasks 4 and 5. Work in groups and discuss questions 1–3. If possible, give reasons for your answers.

1 Think of a job you have done, or a job you would like to have. Where on Maslow's hierarchy would you place that job?

2 Would you need to reach the level of self-actualization to be satisfied in your work?

3 Do you agree that everyone is motivated by money (Taylor), and managers are motivated by power (McClelland and Burnham)?

INDEPENDENT STUDY

Lecturers often use diagrams or images in their slides, and you can use them as a starting point for further research.

▶ Next time you are given a handout with diagrams, try to find the original source for the diagram and note down any key information.

3B Speaking Seminar discussions (2)

In a seminar, you will often be asked to discuss a particular topic, text, or question. To prepare for the seminar, you will normally have to do some specific reading. You may have to evaluate the material and discuss it with other students. You may also have to give definitions and explanations of key terms and concepts. During the seminar, it is important to contribute your own ideas, to listen to other students, and respond to what they say.

This module covers:

- Understanding written and spoken definitions
- Asking for and giving definitions and short explanations
- Participating in a seminar discussion

TASK 1 Reading to prepare for a discussion

1 **Read the text and decide if items 1–4 are examples of *intrinsic* or *extrinsic* motivation.**

> ### Intrinsic and extrinsic motivation
>
> **Intrinsic** motivation occurs when someone gets satisfaction from an activity itself without threats or rewards from outside. People are more likely to be intrinsically motivated if they:
> - can see that their success is a result of something they have done – if they have put in more work they will achieve more positive outcomes
> - have some control over their results – they are given a degree of freedom
> - are interested in what they are doing.
>
> Rewards are **extrinsic** motivators – motivators that come from outside the individual. In the workplace, pay is an obvious example. Extrinsic motivators provide satisfaction that the job itself may not provide and may compensate workers for the 'pain' or dissatisfaction that they may experience at work.
>
> ─────────────────────────────────
> SOURCE: Clark, P., Golden, P., O'Dea, M., Weiner, J., Woolrich, P. (2009). p.124. *IB Diploma Programme - Business and Management Course Companion.* Oxford: Oxford University Press.

1 a bonus (extra money) paid by a company to employees for good performance
2 an invitation for the best students to meet senior university professors at a party
3 wanting to write a bestselling book
4 asking for extra time to study for a qualification in first aid

2 **Work in pairs. Compare your answers and explain your decision.**

TASK 2 Thinking about learning

1 **What are the most important qualities you need to be a good language learner? Put qualities a–f in order from 1 (most important) to 6 (least important).**

a enthusiasm, resulting in full attendance in all classes

b being open to new technologies and methodologies

c an analytical mind

d a strong interest in learning languages

e good organizational skills

f a clear focus on the learning tasks

2 **Work in pairs. Compare your answers and explain your selection. Are there any other qualities you would add?**

TASK 3 Listening to a seminar discussion

1 ◀)) 3.4 **Listen to an extract from a seminar discussion and complete notes 1–4.**

1 topic of discussion: ....
2 two qualities of a language learner: ....
3 definition given for the first quality: ....
4 definitions given for the second quality: ....

2 ◀)) **3.4 Listen again and complete sentences 1–8.**

1 Well, yes. I think _____ I'm concerned, it's about focus.

2 Focus _____ have a clear idea what you want to achieve, and why.

3 I see. And so _____ that focus is the most important thing?

4 And what about you, Carina? What _____ makes a good language learner?

5 Well, _____ motivation.

6 Can you explain _____ by intrinsic and extrinsic motivation?

7 _____ intrinsic motivation is motivation that comes from inside you.

8 Look, to put it _____, if you're intrinsically motivated, then you'll do it because you really want to do it.

ACADEMIC LANGUAGE

Spoken definitions

Taking part in a seminar discussion may involve asking for and giving definitions of key terms. You may need to give more explanation if people don't understand your first definition.

Asking for a definition / explanation
Can you explain what you mean by intrinsic and extrinsic motivation?

Introducing a definition / explanation
Focus is when you have a clear idea what you want to achieve.
What I mean by intrinsic motivation is …

Defining a term using a relative clause with that or which
Intrinsic motivation is motivation that comes from inside you.
Motivation can also be extrinsic, which means it comes from outside.

TASK 4 Preparing and presenting definitions

1 **Select at least two of the following nouns. For each noun, write a definition and a short explanation using a relative clause.**

achievement   focus   goals   motivation   results   success

Example: *Motivation is the reason why someone does something.* (definition)
*It can involve hard work, and may be **extrinsic**, which means coming from outside, or **intrinsic**, which means coming from inside.* (explanation)

2 **Work in groups. Take turns to ask for and give your definitions and explanations.**

TASK 5 Taking part in a seminar discussion

1 **Work in groups. You are going to take part in a seminar discussion on what makes a good language learner. Make sure you:**

- ask for and give definitions based on the topic
- listen actively to what other students say
- respond to what other students say and ask for more information if necessary.

2 **Evaluate your contribution to the discussion. Think about how well you did the following things.**

- asked for definitions or explanations
- defined or explained your key terms
- listened and responded to other people

3 **Select one thing to improve next time you take part in a discussion.**

INDEPENDENT STUDY

The topic of a seminar is normally given in advance.

▶ Ask your tutor for a list of useful texts on the topic before your seminar. Read some of these and note down ideas to contribute.

Reading Textbooks (3)

Reading an academic text involves understanding different kinds of information, including the main ideas, definitions of key terms, explanations, and examples. Taking notes on this information will help you to remember it and to use it later, in discussions or in your writing. Recognizing how key information and ideas are introduced and organized will help you to understand. You also need to be able to recognize language in texts for defining, explaining, and giving examples of key terms and ideas.

This module covers:

- Predicting the purpose of a text
- Understanding main ideas
- Recognizing cohesive language
- Recognizing definitions, explanations, and examples

TASK 1 Discussing the theme of a text

1 **Work in groups. Select three scenarios from 1–5 and discuss how you motivate yourself.**

Example: *When I take part in a sporting event, I imagine myself at the end with everyone cheering. This helps me to get up early to go training.*

1 Training for a sporting event
2 Preparing for an important examination
3 Practising for a musical performance
4 Giving a presentation
5 Writing a long essay (e.g. 1,000–2,000 words)

2 **Discuss some possible goals you can set yourself, which can help with motivation for the scenarios in 1. For example:**

- to improve your time for a 10-kilometre run
- to get a better grade in your next essay.

3 **Present your ideas to the class. Use the phrases below to help you.**

Our group discussed ...
One way of motivating yourself is to ...

An example of a goal you can set yourself is ...

TASK 2 Predicting the main purpose of a text

1 **You are going to read an extract about motivation from a psychology textbook. Look at Text 1 on page 041, paying attention to the title, the photo, and the words highlighted in bold. Is the writer's purpose:**

1 to discuss how motivation varies across different cultures?
2 to explain how setting goals can help motivation?
3 to argue that some people are more motivated than others?

2 **Work in pairs. Compare your predictions. How did you decide on your answer?**

TASK 3 Understanding the main ideas in a text

1 **Read Text 1 and check your prediction in Task 2.1.**

2 **Use information from the text to complete the table.**

Type of goal	Main focus	Example
Outcome goal	*the competitive results of the game*	
Performance goal		*setting a better time for a 10km run*
Process goal		

> **INDEPENDENT STUDY**
>
> You can improve the effectiveness of your reading if you try to predict the content of the text.
>
> ▶ Next time you are given a reading text, use the title, headings, and any visuals such as pictures and diagrams to help you predict the content.

Goal setting

1 Every year, more than 50,000 people run in the London Marathon. Most of them have no expectation of winning the race. The same can be said for any marathon. It is clear that the runners must have different goals for the same event, although this does not seem to influence their motivation to participate.

2 Psychologists identify three types of goals. **Outcome goals** focus on the competitive results of the game. If your goal is to win the bowling tournament, you may bowl your best night ever, and still not win – and thus not reach your goal. As it is competitive, you do not have total control, since your success is based on your opponent's ability. **Performance goals** focus on achieving objectives independent of other competitors. Setting a better time for a 10km run, or improving the percentage of successful tennis serves from 50 per cent to 70 per cent are performance goals. **Process goals** focus on the actions one must take to be successful in a sport and improve performance – for example, a basketball player releasing the ball at the peak of his or her jump. Studies have shown that using a combination of these three types of goals produces better performance than focusing on just one.

3 Much of today's research on goal setting is based on the original theory of goal setting established by Locke and Latham (1981). They argue that performance is regulated by the conscious goals that individuals attempt to achieve on a task.

4 To be effective, goals should be specific, measurable, and related to behaviour. An ineffective goal is 'to improve my golf game'. An effective (and achievable) goal is 'to lower my golf handicap from 14 to 11 by improving the accuracy of my approach shots to the green'.

SOURCE: Crane, J. & Hannibal, J. (2009). pp.302-3. *IB Psychology: Course Companion.* Oxford: Oxford University Press.

GLOSSARY

expectation *(n)* a belief that sth will happen because it is likely

handicap *(n)* (in golf) an advantage given to a weaker player so that competition is more equal when they play against a stronger player

regulate *(v)* to control sth by means of rules or laws

---

3 **Read sentences 1–3 from the text. Select the option, a or b, which is most similar in meaning to each sentence.**

Example: The same can be said for any marathon. (paragraph 1)
   a All marathons have runners who have different goals for the same event.
   b In other marathons most people have no expectation of winning the race.

   *Option **b** is most similar in meaning, because the expression 'the same can be said' refers back to the sentence before. The authors are saying that in any marathon most people know they won't win the race, but they still take part.*

1 It is clear that the runners must have different goals for the same event, although this does not seem to influence their motivation to participate. (paragraph 1)
   a Competitors take part in a race for different reasons, but this does not affect their motivation.
   b Different levels of motivation mean that competitors in an event have different goals.

2 Studies have shown that using a combination of these three types of goals produces better performance than focusing on just one. (paragraph 2)
   a Research shows that people achieve better results when they follow outcome, performance, and process goals.
   b It is not clear which type of goal – outcome, performance, or process – is the most effective for competitors.

3 They argue that performance is regulated by the conscious goals that individuals attempt to achieve on a task. (paragraph 3)
   a Locke and Latham (1981) say that successful performance is achieved by strong individuals.
   b The research by Locke and Latham (1981) shows that there is a link between performance and setting goals.

4 **The sentences in 3 all express main ideas. Answer questions 1–3.**
   1 What is the position of the sentences in each paragraph?
   2 Why are the sentences in this position?
   3 How do the sentences relate to the rest of the paragraph? Select one option.
      a they introduce the topic of the paragraph
      b they refer back to the rest of the paragraph
      c they express the writers' stance

Cohesion (2) Introducing key information

Authors use cohesive language to show how information in a text is connected, and introduce key information. In the examples, the phrase *focus on* tells the reader that key information about outcome goals comes next. The phrase is repeated for other types of goal.

> Outcome goals **focus on** the competitive results of the game.

To report key information about other people's research, the writers use the following phrases:

> Studies **have shown that** using a combination of these three types of goals produces …

> Much of today's research on goal setting **is based on** the original theory of goal setting established by Locke and Latham (1981). **They argue that** performance is regulated by …

TASK 4 Identifying and using cohesive language in sentences

1 Identify the phrases for introducing key information in 1 and 2.

1 Many of today's ideas about sports psychology are based on the work of Rainer Martens (1979). Martens argued that researchers needed to study sports people in the field, rather than the laboratory.

2 The practice of visualization focuses on the idea that athletes and sports people can improve their performance by imagining themselves achieving their goals. Studies show that visualization can improve performance in many different sporting situations.

2 Complete the text with the phrases in the list.

They argue that   focuses on (x2)   is based on

Motivation can be divided into two types. **Extrinsic motivation** [1] .... outside factors such as rewards. **Intrinsic motivation** [2] .... internal factors which come from inside the individual, such as the enjoyment of doing something. Recent research on motivation [3] .... the important work done by Taylor et al. (1979). [4] .... a combination of both types of motivation is likely to work most effectively.

TASK 5 Identifying definitions, explanations, and examples

TEXT 2

[1]**Motivation** is defined as the direction and intensity of one's effort (Sage 1977). The direction of one's effort refers to whether an individual seeks out or is attracted to certain activities. The intensity of one's effort refers to how much effort a person puts into a task or situation. [2]Going to the gym three times a week is not enough; one actually has to put in some effort to undertake a regime of exercise. Do you seek the lowest amount of exercise so that you can simply say, 'I go to the gym'? Or do you work with a trainer and then follow the regime closely? Or do you push yourself too hard, often resulting in fatigue and personal injury? Intensity also includes one's persistence in the face of failure or adversity.

One way of looking at motivation is to discuss intrinsic versus extrinsic motives. [3]**Intrinsic motives** are those that come from within the individual. This could be the fun of being with the team, the satisfaction of a faster finishing time in a 100m race, enjoying the competition, or improved well-being after an hour in the gym. Intrinsic motivation depends on the individual's own attitudes and perceptions, and it involves thinking carefully about situations. Intrinsic motivation does not have to be provided by others, and serves as a continuous drive towards satisfying individual needs. [4]This means that intrinsic motivation can be very persistent.

[5]**Extrinsic motives** are the external rewards that we can gain from taking part in sport or exercise. [6]This could be praise from your coach, the chance to be with your friends, a major contract with a professional sports team, or the status that follows from being famous.

Both intrinsic and extrinsic motives are important in sport and exercise. Psychologists can target both intrinsic and extrinsic motives to improve the performance of the individual.

SOURCE: Crane, J. & Hannibal, J. (2009). pp.304–5. *IB Psychology: Course Companion.* Oxford: Oxford University Press.

GLOSSARY

adversity *(n)* a difficult or unpleasant situation

intense *(adj)* very strong

intensity *(n)* the state or quality of being intense

persistence *(n)* the fact of continuing to try to do sth despite difficulties, especially when other people are against you

regime *(n)* a set of rules about food, exercise or medical treatment that you follow in order to stay healthy

status *(n)* the social or professional position of sb / sth in relation to others

well-being *(n)* general health and happiness

1 **Read Text 2 quickly and find:**

  1 a definition of *motivation*

  3 two examples of *extrinsic motives.*

  2 two examples of *intrinsic motives*

2 **Read Text 2 again. Decide whether each underlined sentence 1–6 is:**

  1 a definition

  2 an explanation or example.

3 **Identify the phrases in sentences 1–6 of Text 2 that introduce a definition, an example, or an explanation.**

ACADEMIC LANGUAGE   ▶Language Reference page 178   14

Definitions Definitions, explanations, and examples

Authors of academic texts often use certain typical phrases for giving definitions, explanations, and examples - especially when they are linked.

Definitions

Motivation **is defined as** the direction and intensity of one's effort.

Intrinsic motives **are those that** come from within the individual.

'The intensity of one's effort' **refers to** how much effort a person puts into a task.

Success **can be defined as** achieving your goals.

Explanations

This means that intrinsic motivation can be very persistent.

Intrinsic motivation **depends on** the individual's own attitudes and perceptions.

Examples

This could be the fun of being with the team ...

An example of extrinsic motivation **could be** praise from your coach.

TASK 6 Writing definitions

1 **Read the example and write similar definitions for terms 1–3.**

  Example: goal / an objective you set for yourself
               A goal can be defined as an objective you set for yourself.

  1 exercise psychology / the study of psychological theories related to exercise

  2 the term 'goal setting' / the process of planning ways to achieve better results

  3 team cohesion / the way a group sticks together while working towards its objectives

2 **Select three of the following terms. Write a sentence which defines the term, and adds an explanation or example. Use phrases from Academic Language.**

  Example: **Success** *is when you have achieved something. An example of* **success** *could be winning a race or meeting your personal fitness goal.*

  success   failure   attitude   performance   praise   adversity   status

3 **Think of some key terms from your own area of study. Write a definition for each one, with an explanation or examples. Compare your definitions with other students.**

> **INDEPENDENT STUDY**
>
> Recognizing language used for defining and explaining key terms or ideas will help improve the effectiveness of your reading.
>
> ▶ **Find a text related to your own area of study and try to identify definitions, explanations, and examples of key terms.**

TASK 7 Critical thinking - responding to the ideas in a text

1 **Work in groups. Read the main points from Texts 1 and 2 below and discuss whether you agree. Give reasons and examples.**

  1 To be effective, goals should be specific, measurable, and related to behaviour. (Text 1)

  2 Both intrinsic and extrinsic motives are important in sport and exercise. (Text 2)

2 **Discuss what you think are the best ways to achieve (a) success in sport, and (b) academic success.**

3 **Think of a future event in your life. Discuss how you can improve your own motivation in order to achieve a better result.**

Writing clear definitions is an important part of academic writing and will show your tutor that you understand key terms and ideas related to your subject. Using different structures to write definitions is also important, especially when there are different possible definitions of a term. This will show your tutor how you are interpreting a particular idea or concept in your writing.

This module covers:

- Writing definitions using prepositional phrases
- Writing definitions using relative clauses
- Writing a paragraph that includes definition

TASK 1 Defining key terms

1 **Read essay titles 1–3. Underline any words that are important to define in each essay.**

Example: *Compare and evaluate two theories of <u>motivation</u> in the workplace.*

1 Identify three factors which affect motivation. Explain the reasons for your choice.

2 To what extent does motivation have an impact on performance in sport?

3 'Instrumental motivation has a more positive effect on language learning than integrative motivation.' Discuss.

2 **Compare your answers with another student and give reasons for your selection.**

3 **Complete definitions 1–3 with key terms you underlined in 1.**

Example: <u>*Instrumental motivation*</u> *is the motivation for achieving concrete goals such as getting a job.*

1 _____ is the motivation that comes from wanting to be part of a community.

2 _____ is a measure of how someone or something is doing a task.

3 _____ is the need or reason for doing something.

ACADEMIC LANGUAGE ▶Language Reference page 181 24.3

The structure of definitions (1) Noun + prepositional phrase

One of the most common ways to define something in academic writing is to use a prepositional phrase. For example:

A meeting is an event for making decisions.
Psychology is the scientific study of the mind.

The sentences can be divided into four main parts.

Term being defined	verb	determiner / adj + head noun	prepositional phrase to show specific feature
A meeting	is	an **event**	for making decisions.
Psychology	is	the scientific **study**	of the mind.

TASK 2 Recognizing the structure of definitions

1 **Read sentences 1–5 and identify:**

a the term being defined   b the head noun   c the prepositional phrase.

1 A wrench is a metal tool for holding and turning objects.

2 Persistence is the state of continuing to try to do something despite difficulties.

3 A pension is a financial product for saving and investing money for old age.

4 Physiology is the scientific study of the normal function of living things.

5 Efficiency is the quality of doing something well with no waste of time or money.

TASK 3 Writing definitions with a prepositional phrase

1 Match 1–5 with a–e to complete the definitions of the words in bold.

1	A **marathon** is a long race	a	of doing something.
2	A **regime** is a method or system	b	for operating a computer.
3	**Enthusiasm** is a strong feeling	c	of excitement and interest.
4	**Software** is the program	d	of related steps to deal with a specific problem.
5	A **procedure** is a series	e	of about 42 kilometres or 26 miles.

2 Write definitions for terms 1–4.

1 biology ....

2 a conference ....

3 a salary ....

4 ambition ....

3 Think of at least two terms from your area of study. Write a similar definition for each one.

TASK 4 Identifying definitions using relative clauses

1 Read this extract from an essay about motivation and answer questions 1–3.

> There is strong evidence from many fields, such as business and sport, that motivation is a key factor in achieving success. In business, studies have shown that managers who understand what motivates their employees usually have a better success rate. Companies whose managers are not aware of employee motivation are less likely to be successful. Also companies that use money as a sole means to motivate their staff may find it difficult to keep them. Similarly, high levels of motivation are essential to success in sport. Teams which use a sports psychologist often have a more positive mental attitude. Athletes that set achievable goals typically enhance their performance. The situation is similar in education. For example, people who are motivated to learn are often the most successful language learners.

1 What kinds of companies are likely to be (a) more successful, and (b) less successful?

2 What kinds of sports teams often have a more positive attitude?

3 Who are often the most successful language learners?

2 Compare your answers with another student. Identify the phrases that helped you answer the questions in 1.

ACADEMIC LANGUAGE ▸ Language Reference page 181 24.4

The structure of definitions (2) Noun + relative clause

In academic writing, relative clauses are often used in definitions. The relative pronoun (*who, whose, which, that*) can change depending on what you are defining.

For people, use *who* or *that*:

*People **who** are motivated to learn are often the most successful language learners.*

*Athletes **that** set achievable goals typically enhance their performance.*

For most things or ideas, use *that* or *which*:

*Also companies **that** use money as a sole means to motivate their staff may find it difficult to keep them.*

*Teams **which** use a sports psychologist often have a more positive mental attitude.*

For people and certain things, use *whose* (possessive):

*Companies **whose** managers are not aware of employee motivation are less likely to be successful.*

TASK 5 Writing definitions using relative clauses

1 Read sentences 1–6 and identify the relative clause.

Example: *Students <u>who read a lot</u> often increase their vocabulary quickly.*

1 A psychologist is a scientist who studies and is trained in psychology.

2 A hierarchy is a system which organizes people into different levels of importance from highest to lowest.

3 Management that is effective includes everyone in the decision-making process.

4 Learners who are not motivated are likely to progress more slowly.

5 An opponent that is weaker than you is unlikely to motivate you to win.

6 A goal is something which you hope to achieve.

2 Match 1–5 with a–e to make a sentence including a relative clause.

1 I need to borrow the book about motivation

2 An employee

3 Strangely, a member of staff

4 Sports psychology is a topic area

5 The learner

a **whose** job is under threat is unlikely to work harder.

b **who** has both intrinsic *and* extrinsic motivation is more likely to succeed.

c **which** involves analysis of how the mind affects performance.

d **that** our tutor recommended.

e **who** feels no motivation to do well will usually underperform.

3 Think of an example for options 1–3. Write a definition for each using a relative clause.

Example: *A lecturer is someone who teaches and researches in a university.*

1 A person (e.g. an athlete, a lecturer) ....

2 An academic subject (e.g. psychology) ....

3 A place (e.g. a university) ....

4 Compare your sentences with another student. Evaluate each other's sentences and rewrite them if necessary.

TASK 6 Recognizing definitions in paragraphs

1 Read paragraph 1 and match items a–c to sentences 1–3.

a an example .... b a definition .... c an explanation ....

Paragraph 1

Herzberg (1957) developed a two-factor theory of motivation based on hygiene needs and motivational needs. [1]Hygiene needs are those factors **which** create dissatisfaction at work if they are not attended to. [2]At school you will probably be demotivated if the classrooms are not clean, or if the heating is not working properly. If these things are satisfactory, however, it is unlikely to lead to motivation. [3]Hygiene factors are the things that are necessary for you to get started, but they don't motivate you to succeed.

2 Read paragraph 2 and match items a–d to sentences 1–4.

a an example ....   c a definition ....

b development including explanation ....   d topic sentence ....

Paragraph 2

[1]The difference between job enrichment and job enlargement is the difference between quality and quantity. [2]Job enrichment **is a way to give employees opportunities for using** the different skills they have, while job enlargement **means** simply increasing the range of tasks a worker has to do. [3]So, for instance, job enlargement could involve replacing an assembly line with modular work where an employee (or group of employees) carries out a job from start to finish. [4]An enriched job differs from an enlarged job in that it involves a range of tasks and challenges of varying difficulty, as well as a complete unit of work, so that an employee has a sense of achievement. On top of this, a manager will offer feedback, encouragement, and support.

TASK 7 Writing a paragraph with a definition

1 Read the following essay title. Answer questions 1 and 2.

> **TITLE:** *Describe a theory of motivation that you know about, and show how the theory can be applied to work, or a sport.*

1 Underline words or terms you might need to define.

2 Think of examples, further details, or specific information to include.

2 Write a paragraph of about 100 words, including <u>at least</u> three sentences. Use paragraphs 1 and 2 in Task 6 to help you. Make sure your paragraph includes:

a topic sentence

a definition of the key term or terms

an example

an explanation

3 Exchange your paragraph with another student and evaluate each other's paragraph using questions 1 and 2.

1 Does the paragraph contain:
- a topic sentence?
- a definition of the key term or terms?
- an example?
- an explanation?

2 Is the definition clear? What language is used to write the definition?

Sample answer
page 189

3E Vocabulary Adjectives

Adjectives are widely used in academic texts when describing, classifying, and evaluating concepts. Classifying adjectives are generally objective, e.g. *individual* and *behavioural*, and are used to classify, categorize, or limit the meaning of a noun. For example *behavioural psychology* is limited to the study of people's behaviour, rather than their thoughts or beliefs. In contrast, evaluative adjectives are subjective, e.g. *achievable*. Choice of evaluative adjectives depends on how you perceive something, e.g. a specific goal may be *achievable,* or *challenging*.

TASK 1 Understanding and using evaluative adjectives

1 **Decide which evaluative adjective in lines 1–4 has a different meaning from the others.**

  1 important   significant   intense   major

  2 successful   effective   positive   unbelievable

  3 specific   achievable   feasible   attainable

  4 accurate   original   correct   precise

2 **Select the two evaluative adjectives which best collocate with each noun.**

Adjectives: *rewarding, major, achievable, satisfying, influential*
Nouns: *experience, goal, theory*

3 **Complete the examples from the *Oxford Advanced Learner's Dictionary* with adjectives from 1.**

  1 Large or important enough to have an effect or to be noticed: *a highly _____ discovery*
     a significant   b major

  2 Directed at dealing with sth or producing a successful result: *It will require _____ action.*
     a effective   b positive

  3 That is possible and likely to be achieved: *a _____ target*
     a specific   b feasible

  4 Correct and true in every detail: *an _____ description / account / calculation*
     a accurate   b original

4 **Write three sentences using a selection of nouns and adjectives from 2.**

TASK 2 Understanding and using classifying adjectives

1 **Complete sentences 1–4 with the correct adjective from each pair.**

  1 Learning outcomes and objectives can be expressed in either _____ or _____ terms, i.e. what a student needs to do, or think. (cognitive / behavioural)

  2 When formulating a personal action plan, goals should be as _____ as possible. Goals that are too _____ are harder to define, or achieve. (general / specific)

  3 Examples of _____ motivation include praise from tutors and coaches, and rewards for success. _____ motivation includes the 'love of learning'. (extrinsic / intrinsic)

  4 _____ approaches are best understood by stating _____ examples. (practical / theoretical)

2 **Complete the text using appropriate classifying and evaluative adjectives.**

attainable   individual   personal   unrealistic

Burton (1989) argues that goal setting has a psychological effect in that setting goals may affect cognitive processes. This is known as the **indirect thought process view**. This argues that failing [1] _____ goals leads to changes in psychological factors that can influence performance. [2] _____ outcome goals can raise anxiety and harm performance, whereas [3] _____ performance goals can lower anxiety and boost confidence. Setting [4] _____ goals is useful, but these must be done carefully.

3 **Write a short paragraph describing and evaluating an aspect of your own area of study. Include some of the adjectives from this module.**

UNIT 4 **Nature**

ACADEMIC FOCUS: DESCRIPTION

LEARNING OBJECTIVES

This unit covers:

Listening
- Preparing to listen to a seminar presentation
- Identifying context
- Using noun phrases in descriptions

Speaking
- Identifying main points and descriptive language
- Referring to numerical information
- Giving a short presentation and providing peer feedback

Reading
- Predicting the content of a text
- Identifying the main ideas
- Identifying and evaluating supporting evidence
- Using progressive forms to refer to change

Writing
- Analysing, planning, and using notes to build up a paragraph
- Using adverbials to add context and supporting information to a sentence
- Writing a descriptive paragraph

Vocabulary
- Identifying adverbial meanings
- Using adverbials for cohesion

Discussion

1 **Work in groups. Take turns to describe an area of natural interest in your country – for example, an area with mountains or lakes, or a part of the coast. Answer questions 1–4.**

   1 Where exactly is the area situated?

   2 Is it typical, or unusual, within your country?

   3 Has it changed in the last fifty years? If so, how?

   4 Are there any threats to it? If so, what?

2 **Select an area from 1 and analyse it from at least three of these perspectives:**

   commercial, cultural, ecological, environmental, geographical, historical, political, technological.

3 **Note down any themes, such as changes created by human activity. Compare your themes with the other students in your group. Is there anything that you found particularly interesting or surprising?**

4 **Briefly describe the area to the class.**

   Example: *The Lake District is situated in the north-west of England. There are lakes in other areas of England, but in the Lake District there are many lakes close together, so it's quite an unusual part of the country (geographical). The area is a national park, so it's protected by the government (political). Any forestry work is sustainable – meaning it's well managed to protect the environment – and the region's safe from development (environmental / ecological).*

4A Listening Seminars (1)

A common activity in seminars is to present information you have read about or researched. This is a way of sharing information about the seminar topic. As well as preparing what you will say, you need to listen carefully to other students' presentations. As you listen, try to identify (1) **contextualizing information**, such as where something is and what it looks like, and (2) the speaker's main points. You may have an opportunity to ask questions, but it is also useful to make brief notes on this information so that you can refer to them later.

This module covers:
- Preparing to listen to a seminar presentation
- Identifying context
- Using noun phrases in descriptions

TASK 1 Preparing to listen to a seminar presentation

1 **You are going to watch extracts from a seminar where two students give presentations on the topic of eco-cities. Decide which definition a–c best defines an eco-city.**

a a city which has very little industry and does not allow the use of cars

b a city which is planned to have low energy use and low emissions

c a city which has lots of green, open spaces and plenty of trees

2 **Which perspectives (e.g. political) are likely to be discussed in the seminar?**

TASK 2 Understanding the context

1 ▶4.1 **Watch Extract 1 and complete the notes.**

Seminar topic: *Eco-cities*

Definition: ....

Contextualizing questions:

a What *is an eco-city?* .... d Why ....

b Where .... e How ....

c When .... f Evaluation: ....

2 **Compare the definition you noted down with your selection in Task 1.1.**

TASK 3 Identifying context and description

Tianjin

Masdar

1 ▶4.2 **Watch Extract 2 where Tianjin eco-city is described. Complete column A of the table with the speaker's main points.**

	A Presentation 1: main points	B Presentation 1: signalling phrases	C Presentation 2: main points
What	*a modern, environmentally-friendly city*	*So, what is Tianjin eco-city?*	
Where			
When			
Why			
How			
Evaluation			

2 ▶4.2 **Watch Extract 2 again and complete column B with the phrase the speaker uses to signal each main point.**

3 ▶4.3 **Watch Extract 3 where the speaker describes a different eco-city, Masdar. Complete column C in the table in Task 3.1 with the speaker's main points.**

4 ▶4.3 **Watch Extract 3 again and complete sentences 1–5 with the descriptive phrases the speaker uses.**

1 Basically, Masdar is a _____.

2 It's been described as an _____.

3 They're based around clean technology like _____.

4 So, as I said, Masdar is this new development for _____.

5 It uses solar energy, and _____.

5 **Compare your answers with another student. Help each other complete any missing information.**

ACADEMIC LANGUAGE   ▶Language Reference page 181

Noun phrases (1) Adjective + noun, adverb + adjective + noun

In a description, you can add detail to a noun by putting an adjective before the noun, for example: *an **old** city, a **new** project, a **low** impact.*

You can extend the simple adjective + noun phrase by adding another adjective or an adverb.

   *First of all, it has **high-level political** support. (adjective 1 + adjective 2 + noun)*

   *This has been a **really important** factor in getting the project off the ground. (adverb + adjective + noun)*

You can add more detail by joining two or more adjectives, or adverb + adjective combinations, with a conjunction (*and, but, or*).

   *... to discuss the building of a **new sustainable but efficient** city.*

   *... and today it's an **increasingly important and fast growing** city.*

TASK 4 Using noun phrases in descriptions

1 **Rewrite expressions 1–6 as more concise noun phrases, making any necessary changes in word class.**

   Example: an achievement which is significant in political terms
          *a **politically significant** achievement*

1 a country whose importance is increasing

2 a company that is expanding rapidly

3 an organization which is international but little known

4 a building that is modern, and that is environmentally friendly

5 a solution that is practical and has a low impact on the environment

6 a city which is developing rapidly and whose influence is increasing

2 **Describe three items related to your area of study, using similar noun phrases.**

TASK 5 Critical thinking – evaluating presentations

1 **Work in pairs. Using your notes in the table in Task 3.1, discuss questions 1–3.**

1 Do you agree with the speakers that eco-cities like Tianjin and Masdar City are always a good thing? Give reasons.

2 The speakers say that the reason for creating eco-cities is to benefit the environment. What other reasons could there be for creating them?

3 What possible problems might be associated with eco-cities?

> **INDEPENDENT STUDY**
>
> You can listen more effectively to seminar presentations if you have the contextualizing questions in mind.
>
> ▶ **Next time you listen to a presentation of information in a seminar or lecture, listen carefully for the main point connected to each question.**

Giving a presentation in a seminar may involve presenting factual and numerical information, as well as different perspectives on an issue. Often the perspectives you choose will influence the way your presentation is organized. When a presentation includes numbers, it is important to be able to say these clearly and correctly. When giving each other feedback on a presentation, try to be as constructive as possible and make specific suggestions for improvement.

This module covers:

- Identifying main points and descriptive language
- Referring to numerical information
- Giving a short presentation and providing peer feedback

TASK 1 Previewing the topic of a presentation

1 **Work in groups and discuss questions 1–4.**

1 Do most people in your country live in rural or urban areas?

2 Has the number of people living in rural and urban areas changed in recent years?

3 What causes people to move from rural to urban areas?

4 List at least three advantages and disadvantages of living in (a) a rural area, and (b) an urban area.

2 **Briefly explain your answers to the class.**

TASK 2 Taking notes on the main points of a presentation

1 ▶4.4 **You are going to watch a short presentation on *urbanization* – the growth of towns and cities and the movement of people from rural to urban areas. Watch the presentation and note down key information under headings 1–4.**

1 Urbanization since 1900

2 Urbanization in the newly industrialized countries

3 The economic impacts of urbanization

4 The environmental impact of urbanization

2 **Work in pairs and discuss questions 1 and 2.**

1 Which perspectives did the speaker mainly use to organize her presentation?

2 What do you think is the speaker's stance on urbanization? Does she think it is mainly positive or negative?

TASK 3 Taking notes on numerical information

1 ▶4.5 **Watch an extract from the presentation again and complete the table.**

World's urban population		Urbanization in China and the US	
1900: .... million or .... per cent		1978: Urban population China .... Urban population USA	
1950: .... million or .... per cent		2011: Urban population China .... Urban population USA	
2005: .... billion or .... per cent		2030: an extra .... million urban residents in China	

2 **Compare your answers with another student. Help each other complete any missing information.**

Numbers Large numbers, percentages, fractions, decimals

When presenting numerical information, large numbers are often expressed as decimals, and are usually rounded up or down.

> ... greater Tokyo is currently around thirty-five point six (35.6) million (compare: 35,682,460 thirty-five million, six hundred and eighty-two thousand).
>
> ... in 1900 it stood at just two hundred and twenty (220) million
>
> ... this figure is likely to rise to four point nine (4.9) billion

When talking about large numbers, it's usual to use approximation.

> ... **almost** half the world's population living in major towns and cities
>
> ... **around** 50,000 new skyscrapers will be built
>
> ... with **just over** 5 billion urban residents

Slide 1 World urban population since 1900

Slide 2 Urbanization in China and the US

TASK 4 Presenting numbers

1 Look at slides 1 and 2. How would you say the numbers?

2 Practise presenting the numerical information on slides 1 and 2.

TASK 5 Recognizing and using signposting language

1 Match the phrases from the presentation in Task 2 with functions 1–5.

For instance   As you can see   So moving on to look at   Next I'd like to look at ...
In my presentation today I'm going to look at   OK, that was ...   For example
I'll then move on to look at firstly ..., and secondly ...   So if we look at the slide

1 introducing the structure of the presentation
2 introducing a new point
3 referring to a visual
4 moving on to a new point
5 giving an example

2 ▶4.6 Watch eight clips from the presentation and notice how the phrases in 1 are used.

3 Use slides 1 and 2 to practise signposting language for introducing a new point and moving from one point to another.

TASK 6 Preparing a short presentation describing change

1 Work in groups. Think of a key change that your countries are facing (for example, the move from rural to urban population) and discuss:

1 the reasons why the change is happening (e.g. why people migrate from rural to urban areas)

2 problems associated with the change (e.g. problems with overcrowding in cities, lack of jobs in rural areas).

2 Prepare a short presentation on the change you discussed in 1. Use the guidelines on page 195.

TASK 7 Giving and evaluating a presentation

1 Work in groups and take turns to give your presentations.

2 Evaluate each other's presentations using the guidelines on page 196. Give each other feedback. Try to make at least one suggestion for improvement.

INDEPENDENT STUDY

In your academic study you will encounter a wide range of data and figures and it is important for you to be able to discuss or present these clearly.

▸ **Research some figures or data related to your area of study. Practise saying them out loud and check against the rules provided in Language reference page 181.**

Reading Textbooks (4)

You can use headings, pictures, and diagrams to predict the content of an academic text. It is also important to use your own knowledge of a topic. This can help to identify the main ideas in a text, and key details and evidence which support these ideas. Taking clear notes on main ideas and supporting evidence will enable you to use the information from the text in your own writing later.

This module covers:

- Predicting the content of a text
- Identifying the main ideas
- Identifying and evaluating supporting evidence
- Using progressive forms to refer to change

TASK 1 Predicting the content of a text

1 **You are going to read a text describing *desertification* – the process by which lands is changed into desert. Is desertification mainly (a) a natural process, or (b) a man-made process?**

2 **Read the section headings in the text and questions 1–4. Predict what information or evidence you think the text will include for each heading.**

1 What is desertification?

2 How widespread is the risk of desertification?

3 What are the natural causes of desertification?

4 What are the human causes of desertification?

3 **Read the text quickly and check your predictions from 2.**

Figure 4.31

TASK 2 Identifying the main ideas in a text

1 **Identify where in the text the authors express the main ideas 1–6.**

1 The areas most at risk of desertification are near existing deserts.

2 Climate change is a current concern and is happening now.

3 It is not known whether temperature and rainfall are a direct cause of desertification.

4 Human damage is an accident.

5 There is a limit to how much farming an area of land can support.

6 Using too little or too much water can contribute to desertification.

2 **Note down the evidence in the text that helped you identify each of the main ideas in 1.**

Example: Main idea – *Natural processes were causing desertification before humans started to have an effect.*
Evidence from text – *'Natural climate change turned this region into desert thousands of years ago – long before humans had any major impact.'*

Desertification

What is desertification?

At first glance, figure 4.31 looks just like any other desert photo – lots of sand. But if you look more closely, you can see signs of change in this environment. In the recent past, this landscape looked very different to the way it looks today. As you can see, there is plenty of dead vegetation, plus the remains of animals that once grazed the area. The land in the photo is turning into a desert. This is called **desertification**.

How widespread is the risk of desertification?

Figure 4.32 shows the location of land vulnerable to desertification across the world. The most vulnerable areas tend to be located on the margins of the hot deserts. The UN estimates that roughly a third of the world's land surface is currently affected by desertification.

Figure 4.32

What causes desertification?

Natural causes

The main natural cause is connected to climate, which has changed throughout geological time – altering global temperature and rainfall patterns. For instance, there is evidence that – as recently as 8000 years ago (around the age of the last Ice Age) – the climate in North Africa and the Middle East was much wetter than it is today. This evidence includes large aquifers (groundwater reserves) lying beneath desert countries like Egypt and Jordan, as well as fossil plant remains and archaeological evidence (such as ancient rock art). Natural climate change turned this region into desert thousands of years ago – long before humans had any major impact.

Climate worldwide is still changing today, but now there is serious international concern that human actions are worsening natural global warming and climate change. For example, serious droughts have become more common in many parts of Africa over the last few decades.

Temperature and rainfall patterns worldwide have certainly been changing. But the changes have not been gradual or consistent - they have been erratic, and have involved extremes of drought and flood. The climate is becoming more unpredictable and more variable. Only time will tell how much of this is a direct cause of current and future desertification.

Human causes

People are not likely to deliberately damage the land on which they depend on for their survival. However, circumstances can lead to people's actions tipping the delicate balance and inadvertently contributing towards the process of desertification. Most commonly, this involves:

- **over-cultivation**. Intensive farming on marginal land can reduce soil fertility and damage its structure. The lack of organic matter makes it crumbly and more likely to be washed or blown away. It also reduces its capacity to retain moisture.
- **over-grazing**. Marginal grassland has a sustainable carrying capacity - the number of animals that can be supported without causing long-term damage. If this number is exceeded, the system becomes unsustainable and the vegetation and soil deteriorate. If it continues, desertification can result.
- **over-irrigation**. If plants are appropriately irrigated, little water should be wasted. However, if land is over-irrigated, salinization can occur. This creates an impermeable and infertile salty crust on the surface, which (according to UNESCO) is a key feature of desertification.

Other human activities that can damage the soil and vegetation (leading to soil erosion and ultimately desertification) are: road building, deforestation, and inappropriate tourism.

SOURCE: Ross, S., Digley, B., Chapman, R. & Cowling, D. (2011). pp.146–7. *AQA Geography*. Oxford: Oxford University Press.

GLOSSARY

climate change *(n)* changes in the earth's weather, especially the rise in temperatures caused by the increase of particular gases

cultivation *(n)* the preparation and use of land for growing plants or crops

drought *(n)* a long period of time without rain

grazing *(n)* land with grass that cows, sheep, etc. can eat

irrigation *(n)* the supply of water to an area of land through pipes or channels for growing crops

marginal *(adj)* on the edge

sustainable *(adj)* involving the use of natural products and energy in a way that does not harm the environment

TASK 3 Identifying and evaluating supporting evidence

1 **Work in pairs. Read the essay title and discuss questions 1 and 2.**

> **TITLE:** *'Desertification is a natural process and is not caused by man.' Discuss.*

   1 From your reading, do you think desertification is (a) a natural process, (b) a man-made process, or (c) both natural and man-made?

   2 Do you think the writers of the text would agree with the statement in the essay title?

2 **Find examples of evidence in the text on page 055 that is both *for* and *against* the statement in the essay title.**

For	Against
8,000 years ago the climate in North Africa and the Middle East was much wetter	Intensive farming can damage soil

3 **Look at the arguments for and against the statement in 1. Do the authors provide strong evidence to support both arguments?**

4 **What other evidence could you offer to support either argument?**

TASK 4 Using evidence from the text in writing

1 **Read the extract from the text on the *natural* causes of desertification. Match items a–c to sentences 1–3.**

   a examples of evidence   b a statement of evidence   c the main idea

> [1]The main natural cause is connected to climate, which has changed throughout geological time – altering global temperature and rainfall patterns. [2]For instance, there is evidence that – as recently as 8,000 years ago (around the age of the last Ice Age) – the climate in North Africa and the Middle East was much wetter than it is today. [3]This evidence includes large aquifers (groundwater reserves) lying beneath desert countries like Egypt and Jordan, as well as fossil plant remains and archaeological evidence (such as ancient rock art).

2 **Using your notes from Tasks 2 and 3, write three similar sentences about the *human* causes of desertification.**

   1 The main human cause is connected to farming ....

   2 For instance, there is evidence that ....

   3 This evidence includes ....

INDEPENDENT STUDY

You might already have an opinion on an assessment topic before you do any reading or research. Try to stay open to adapting your position depending on what you find out while researching.

▶ Next time you are given an assessment topic, make a note of your stance at the start. As you do your research, add to your notes to see if, and how, your stance changes.

ACADEMIC LANGUAGE   ▶ Language Reference page 183 **31**

Progressive forms Referring to change in progress

Progressive forms are often used to refer to change. They use the auxiliary verb *be* to indicate the tense (present or past), plus the *-ing* form of the main verb.

> The land in the photo **is turning into** a desert.
>
> Climate worldwide **is** still **changing** today, but now there is serious international concern that human actions **are worsening** natural global warming and climate change.
>
> The climate **is becoming** more unpredictable and more variable.

The present perfect progressive can be used to show that, although the event is still in progress, there is a sense of completion:

> Temperature and rainfall patterns worldwide **have** certainly **been changing**.

This example shows that some changes in temperature and rainfall patterns already exist. Notice that an adverbial can be added for extra meaning, e.g. *still, certainly*.

TASK 5 Identifying and using progressive forms

1 Complete the text with the correct form of the *present progressive* or *present perfect progressive*.

The world's climate [1] .... (change) for centuries. However, not everyone is convinced that climate change [2] .... (actually happen) because the data is sometimes misleading or inaccurate. Ice caps and glaciers [3] .... (get) smaller across the world, although some predictions and estimates have not been very accurate. Glaciers and ice caps outside of the Antarctic and Greenland [4] .... (melt) at half the rate previously thought. Jacob et al (2011) found that glaciers in the Himalayas [5] .... (not shrink) as fast as was predicted; in fact, there has been very little change at all. While their research overturned some previous ideas, in general it supported the overall view that sea levels [6] .... (rise) every year. Although some recent findings seem to contradict previous research, the vast majority of it supports the idea that the climate [7] .... (change) and that human activity [8] .... (cause) it.

2 Think about three changes in your country that are currently happening. Write a sentence to describe each of these changes.

1 ....

....

2 ....

....

3 ....

....

TASK 6 Critical thinking – reflecting on ideas for writing

1 Which of the following 1–5 do you think are the authors' aims in the text on page 055?

1 To inform the reader about causes of desertification

2 To describe where desertification is happening

3 To evaluate the causes of desertification

4 To argue that man is the main cause of desertification

5 To argue that desertification is a natural and unstoppable process

2 Which essay title 1–3 do you think the text might be the most useful source for?

1 Describe the stages and process of desertification.

2 Compare and contrast the different causes of desertification.

3 Evaluate the most effective way to manage the impact of human activity on desertification.

3 Work in pairs. Discuss which parts of the text you could use for each essay title in 2.

Writing Paragraphs (2)

A paragraph develops a topic or an idea, using supporting information such as examples, explanations, and evidence. Some paragraphs may also include analysis from different perspectives. When you write a paragraph, you need to use appropriate words or phrases to connect the ideas or add information. These will also help the reader to navigate your text.

This module covers:
- Analysing, planning, and using notes to build up a paragraph
- Using adverbials to add context and supporting information to a sentence
- Writing a descriptive paragraph

TASK 1 Analysing the structure of a paragraph

1 **Work in pairs. Read the paragraph from an essay and match features a–f to sentences 1–6.**

[1]There has been increasing interest in sustainable development in recent years. [2]Sustainable development can be defined as 'development which meets the needs of the present without affecting the ability of future generations to meet their own needs' (United Nations, 1987). [3]For example, in the UK a Sustainable Development Commission has been set up to advise on such matters. [4]Similarly, in many countries, including newly industrialized countries such as China, many businesses now have sustainable development policies. [5]In other words, businesses are working to improve the sustainability of the natural world. [6]These examples show that sustainable development is increasingly important globally in political and economic terms.

a the topic sentence ....   c an explanation ....   e another example ....

b the concluding sentence ....   d an example ....   f a definition ....

2 **Which sentence includes both the main point and evaluation?**

3 **Find words / phrases 1–6 below in the paragraph and decide what kind of information they introduce.**

Example: *'There has been increasing interest in' – introduces a new topic*

1 [...] can be defined as   3 Similarly,   5 In other words,

2 For example,   4 such as   6 These examples show

ACADEMIC LANGUAGE ▸Language Reference page 179 21

Cohesion (3) Using adverbials to introduce supporting information

Adverbials are used to introduce supporting information. They help to make your paragraph cohesive by showing the reader how ideas are connected.
- To connect two similar ideas or examples, use *Similarly, In the same way,* or *Likewise*:
  China's urban population has increased dramatically since the 1970s. **Similarly**, *India's cities have grown in the last thirty years.*
- To introduce explanations, use *In other words (i.e.)* or *To put this another way*:
  Countries like China, South Africa, and Brazil are considered newly industrialized countries (NICs). **In other words**, *they are no longer seen as developing countries.*
- To introduce an example, use *For example (e.g.), For instance,* or *such as*:
  For example, *there are several famous cold deserts,* **such as** *the Gobi and the Atacama deserts.*
- To introduce evaluation or indicate your personal stance, use adverbs like *Basically, Interestingly, Significantly, Surprisingly*:
  Significantly, *a number of emerging economies are introducing new environmental laws.*
- To summarize or restate a key point, use phrases like *To summarize,* or *Essentially*:
  To summarize, *it's clear that sustainable development is increasingly important.*

TASK 2 Using adverbials to make a paragraph cohesive

1 **Complete the paragraph using the words / phrases in the list. Use the prompts in brackets to help you.**

For example   such as   In other words   Essentially   Similarly   Interestingly

It's clear that economic growth and development need to be sustainable. ¹_____, (*explanation*) growth and development need to have an effect on nature which is not too negative or damaging. There are several ways to help this to happen. ²_____, (*example*) non-governmental organizations and charities need to put pressure on businesses to operate cleanly. In the same way, governments across the world need to bring in new laws to protect the natural world. ³_____, (*evaluation*) in countries where laws like this have been introduced, environmental damage has fallen. ⁴_____, (*similarity*) people's attitudes need to change so that they see the world as an interconnected system rather than a limitless resource which humans can exploit. This can be done in a number of ways, ⁵_____ (*example*) through education and advertising. ⁶_____, (*evaluation*) the future of our world depends on people changing the way they think and behave.

2 **Compare your answers with another student. Explain why you put the words / phrases in these positions.**

TASK 3 Expanding notes into sentences

1 **Read the notes for a paragraph. Work out the topic and the main idea.**

Notes

a   Environmental damage – serious / overlooked effect of driving – locally & globally

b   Driving – releases different pollutants → air, e.g. greenhouse gases, e.g. CO_2

c   Oil production, i.e. drilling – harmful to local environment → pollutes deserts, oceans

d   Use / sourcing fuels, i.e. petrol / diesel – affects air quality – damages human health & surrounding ecosystem

e   Need – look for different / more sustainable kinds of fuel

2 **Study the example, where the notes in 1 are expanded into a complete sentence. Look at the annotated example to see which words were added.**

Example: Notes: *Environmental damage – serious / overlooked effect of driving – locally & globally*
Complete sentence: *Environmental damage **is a** serious **but** overlooked effect of driving, **both** locally **and** globally.*

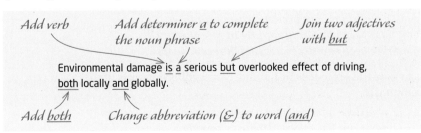

3 **Follow a similar process for notes b–e. You may not need to make exactly the same changes, but you may need to make grammatical changes to some words.**

4 **Compare your complete sentences with another student.**

TASK 4 Connecting sentences to form a paragraph

1 **Join your sentences from Task 3.3 to create a single paragraph. Use steps 1–3 to guide you.**

   1 Decide on a logical order for your sentences.

   2 Include a topic sentence and a main point based on your answer to Task 3.1.

   3 Include adverbials from Academic Language to make your paragraph cohesive.

2 **Compare your paragraph with another student. Explain why you chose the particular order of sentences.**

ACADEMIC LANGUAGE   ▸Language Reference page 176

Sentence structure (3) Adding further information using adverbials

As shown in Unit 1, the basic structure of simple sentences in English is subject (S) + verb (V) + object (O). These parts are known as *clause elements*. For example:

People talk about the cost of motor transport.

You can add more detail to this basic sentence structure using adverbs or adverbial phrases:

*People **often** talk about the cost of motor transport.*

*People **often** talk about the cost of motor transport, **mainly in financial terms**.*

*People **often** talk about the cost of motor transport, **mainly in financial terms such as the cost of fuel and insurance**.*

TASK 5 Adding detail to sentences

1 **Identify the different clause elements (subject, verb, object) in sentences 1–6. Not all the sentences have an object.**

   Example: CO_2 emissions have been increasing. (in recent years / rapidly)
                (S)   *(V)*

   1 Manufacturing companies should be regulated. (more strongly)

   2 Pollutants damage the natural environment. (seriously / in almost every country)

   3 These examples suggest that the damage is considerable. (strongly / to our environment)

   4 Businesses need more research on their environmental impact. (in simple terms)

   5 Researchers are focusing on extinction. (increasingly)

   6 We need solutions to the destruction of natural habitats. (urgently / from politicians and business leaders)

2 **Rewrite the sentences in 1 to include the additional information (adverbials) in brackets. The position of the adverbials in some sentences can vary.**

   Example: CO_2 emissions have been increasing (in recent years / rapidly)
            *In recent years, CO_2 emissions have been increasing **rapidly**.*
            *OR CO_2 emissions have been increasing **rapidly in recent years**.*
            *OR CO_2 emissions have been **rapidly** increasing **in recent years**.*

3 **Work in pairs. Take turns to read the sentences in 1 aloud. Stress different parts of the sentences to change the emphasis.**

   Example: *In recent years, <u>CO_2 emissions</u> have been increasing rapidly.*
            In <u>recent</u> years, CO_2 emissions have been increasing <u>rapidly</u>.

TASK 6 Planning and writing a paragraph

1 Work in groups. Discuss ways that nature or the environment are related to different academic disciplines – for example, technology, medicine, or business. For each idea, think of an example or explanation, and an additional point.

Example: Idea: *Nature relates to technology because many technological devices such as mobile phones affect the environment.*
Example: *For example, phone masts can spoil the beauty of the local environment.*
Additional point: *When researchers are considering designing a new piece of technology, they should think about its impact on nature.*

2 You are going to write a paragraph describing the relationship between the environment and one or more academic disciplines. Note down ideas for stages 1–5.

	Stage	Example
1	Select an idea to write about from those you discussed in your groups.	The relationship between technology and the environment.
2	Decide on the topic of your paragraph.	The effect of technology on the environment.
3	Decide on the main point you want to make.	Students need to understand that technology has a negative impact as well as benefits.
4	Think of some examples and/or explanations to support your main point.	Mobile phone masts and wind turbines; toxic materials in things like mobile phones
5	Identify any terms that need a definition.	*toxic materials*

3 Using your notes in 2, write a paragraph of about 120–150 words. Follow guidelines 1–5. You may find it helpful to refer back to the sample paragraph in Task 1.

1 Write your topic sentence.

2 Decide where to state your main point – after the topic sentence or near the end of the paragraph.

3 Add sentences which include examples and explanation.

4 Make sure your paragraph is cohesive: check your use of pronouns (*it, its, they, their*) and adverbials such as *Similarly* and *In other words*.

5 Write a concluding sentence to state or restate the main point and, if necessary, give a brief evaluation.

Sample answer
page 189

TASK 7 Critical thinking – evaluating your writing

1 Use the following checklist to evaluate your paragraph.

Check the paragraph structure. Does it contain …	Yes	No
a topic sentence?		
a clear statement of the main point?		
examples and/or explanations?		
definitions if necessary?		
a concluding sentence?		

Check your language	Yes	No
Does each sentence have a subject, verb, and object?		
Is each verb in the right tense and form?		
Do you use adverbials and pronouns to make the paragraph cohesive?		

2 Read at least two other students' paragraphs. Evaluate their paragraphs using the checklist in 1 and give feedback.

4E Vocabulary Adverbials

You can introduce supporting information using adverbials. These guide your reader through your text and help to make it cohesive. For example, you can use adverbials at the start of your sentence to introduce a comparison with something similar: *Similarly* ... . For explanations, you can use *In other words* (sometimes abbreviated to *i.e.*), and to introduce an example you can use an adverbial like *For example*. You can introduce evaluation using adverbials which signal your stance, e.g. *Significantly*. Finally, you can introduce the main point, summarize, or conclude: *In brief* ... .

TASK 1 Identifying adverbial meanings

1 **Match these adverbials to functions 1–5.**

basically   essentially   for example   for instance   in brief   in conclusion   in other words
in short   interestingly   in the same way   likewise   surprisingly   to conclude

1 Comparing with something similar: ....

2 Offering explanation: ....

3 Introducing an example: ....

4 Showing stance: ....

5 Signalling main point / summary / conclusion: ....

TASK 2 Using adverbials for cohesion

1 **Complete sentences 1–6 with an appropriate adverbial from the list.**

for instance   in conclusion   in other words   likewise   surprisingly

1 There are several extensive deserts, ... the Sahara in North Africa.

2 ...., very little of the sun's energy is currently used for desalination of water.

3 ...., this essay has argued that consumption rather than production needs to be evaluated.

4 Standards of living have risen in line with increased urbanization; ...., there is arguably a direct correlation between these two factors.

5 China has shown vast urban and economic development in recent years; .... there has been considerable growth in India.

2 **Complete the text with an appropriate adverbial from each pair.**

While often criticized for their ecological impact, cities are sources of ideas, creativity, and technology. [1].................................... (For instance / Essentially) humans are social animals and require a place to exchange knowledge and socially interact. [2].................................... (In other words / Significantly) economic opportunity has been a driver behind urban growth – [3].................................... (in other words / essentially) there is more chance of employment in cities despite widespread economic problems. [4].................................... (To conclude / Similarly) opportunites for education in cities are greater than elsewhere. [5].................................... (For instance / In other words) in Senegal the urban literacy rates for males is 80.6%, compared to 45.2% in rural areas (UNESCO, 2011). [6].................................... (Significantly / To conclude) by 2030 approximately two thirds of the global population will be urban. Although there are definite disadvantages, we must also look at the benefits of city living.

3 **Decide on the function of each adverbial in 2. Choose from the five options in 1.1.**

4 **Write a brief paragraph describing a theory or ideas from your own area of study. Include one or two linking adverbials to guide your reader.**

UNIT 5 Power

ACADEMIC FOCUS: REPORTING AND SUMMARIZING

LEARNING OBJECTIVES

This unit covers:

Listening
- Identifying different positions in a lecture
- Identifying supporting arguments
- Using present and past tenses to report findings

Speaking
- Taking notes on a student presentation
- Using reporting verbs to refer to points in a presentation
- Participating in a seminar discussion

Reading
- Identifying the main ideas and key information in a text
- Identifying key features of a summary
- Using noun phrases to summarize ideas
- Evaluating summaries of a text

Writing
- Analysing and using active note-taking strategies
- Identifying and using summarizing words and phrases
- Writing a summary of a short academic text

Vocabulary
- Using suffixes to recognize word families
- Building word families using affixes

Discussion

1 **Work in groups. Discuss how each of the two groups in 1–4 can influence the other. Give examples.**

   1 Private companies and ordinary people

   2 Social media and society in general

   3 The media and ordinary people

   4 Managers and employees

   Example: *Private companies influence what ordinary people buy through advertising and marketing. Ordinary people can influence companies to stop making certain products through boycotts or protests.*

2 **Present your group's main ideas to the class. Use the following phrases to help you.**

   Our discussion focused on …

   The main points we discussed were …

   We feel that …

   We came to the conclusion that …

Lectures do not simply give information on a topic; they also present different positions on an issue from individual groups of people, or organizations. It is important to identify and understand these different positions, as you may need to discuss them in a seminar or write about them in an assignment. To argue for or against a particular position, a lecturer will often refer to a study on the topic. Identifying references to these studies can help you to research further examples to support your own ideas in your written assignments.

This module covers:

- Identifying different positions in a lecture
- Identifying supporting arguments
- Using present and past tenses to report findings

TASK 1 Thinking about note-taking styles

1 **Look at the different ways of organizing lecture notes a–d. Which style of notes would be best for showing:**

   1 arguments *for* and *against* a particular point?

   2 different positions in a debate?

   3 a process or a sequence of events?

   4 connections between ideas?

a Mind map

b Two-page split

c Page split into four

d Linear notes

2 **Work in pairs and discuss how you like to organize your notes.**

3 ▶ 5.1 **Watch the introduction to a lecture about the advertising industry. As you watch:**

   1 predict what the lecturer will talk about in the rest of the lecture

   2 think about how the lecture will be organized, and what note-taking style you could use to organize your notes on the rest of the lecture.

TASK 2 Thinking about stance to prepare for a lecture

1 **Work in pairs and discuss questions 1 and 2.**

   1 Is there much advertising aimed at children in your country?

   2 Do you think advertising to children should be regulated?

2 **Discuss what stance you think the following groups might take on advertising to children: doctors, parents, advertisers, the government.**

   Example: *Doctors – advertising unhealthy foods and drinks to children should be banned. (stance) It can lead to childhood obesity. (reason)*

   ***obesity** (n) a condition where someone is so fat it is a danger to their health*

TASK 3 Identifying positions within a debate

1 ▶ 5.2–5.5 **Watch Extracts 2–5 of the lecture. Complete the first two columns of the table with (a) the interested group, and (b) their position.**

Extract	Group	Position	Supporting argument
2	Advertisers		
3			
4			
5			

2 **Compare your notes on Extracts 2–5 with another student. Help each other to complete any missing information.**

INDEPENDENT STUDY

The introduction to a lecture usually gives an indication of how it will be organized.

▶ Watch the opening minutes of a lecture related to your area of study on your institution's Virtual learning environment (VLE), or an external website. Decide how you would take notes for this lecture.

TASK 4 Identifying supporting arguments

1 ▶5.2–5.5 Watch Extracts 2–5 again. Complete column 3 of the table in Task 3 with the argument(s) that support(s) each group's position, and the source it comes from.

2 Compare your notes with another student. Discuss questions 1–3.

  1 What information did the lecturer give to support each position?

  2 Which position do you most agree with? Give reasons.

  3 What did you find most interesting about the lecture?

ACADEMIC LANGUAGE

Present and past tenses Referring to research findings

The present simple, present perfect, and past simple can all be used to refer to research findings. The speaker's choice of tense may depend on whether the research is past or current, but may sometimes be a question of style.

The **present simple** is used to make general statements about research findings where time is not relevant.

> Marketresearch.com **estimates** that children in the US directly spend $51.8 billion each year.
> McNeal **puts** this figure at around $670 billion, and these figures **continue** to rise annually.

The **present perfect** is used when the findings are new or still relevant today.

> One study by the Australian consumer group CHOICE **has shown** that …
> The same study **has also highlighted** the fact that 86% of parents would …

The **past simple** is normally used when a specific date in the past is mentioned.

> In 2007, CBS **reported** that the amount of money spent on advertising to children in the US was $17 billion.

TASK 5 Using past tenses to refer to research findings

1 Complete sentences 1–4 with an appropriate past tense form of the verb in brackets.

  1 Harris (2009) _____ (estimate) that fast food companies spent $4 billion in 2009 on advertising in the US.

  2 CBS _____ (put) the figure at around $17 billion on advertising to 8- to 12-year-olds, and these figures continue to rise annually.

  3 According to Halford et al. (2007), children's food intake _____ (increase) 100% after watching food advertising.

  4 The World Health Organization _____ (judge) that advertising is a probable cause of obesity.

2 Work in groups. Select one of the interested groups from the table in Task 3.1 and summarize their position and supporting argument. Which position is most similar to your own?

TASK 6 Critical thinking – responding to a lecture

1 Look at the slide featuring the lecturer's discussion questions. Think about your own position and what you heard in the lecture extracts. Work in pairs and discuss the questions.

2 Think of a similar issue in your own area of study, or another field that you are familiar with. Work in pairs, and give a brief summary of the different positions. Say which position you agree with, and why.

> 1 Do you believe that advertising influences children's demands?
>
> 2 Do you think it can be connected to issues such as obesity or smoking?
>
> 3 Should governments limit or control what can be advertised to children?

When you take part in a seminar, you will normally need to prepare by reading a text, or attending a presentation or lecture. In this module you will listen to a student presentation, and then discuss ideas from this presentation in the seminar. During the discussion, you will need to refer to points that the presenter made, so it is important that you take good notes as you listen.

This module covers:
- Taking notes on a student presentation
- Using reporting verbs to refer to points in a presentation
- Participating in a seminar discussion

TASK 1 Discussing a topic to prepare for a presentation

1 Work in groups. Decide which of the following media are the most powerful, and why.

social media (e.g. Facebook)   television   the internet   newspapers

2 Discuss the effect of these media on you personally, on business, and on society in general.

TASK 2 Predicting the content of a presentation

1 Read the speaker's slides 1–4, and check the meaning of any unknown words.

The power of social media

Twitter   Facebook

Jamila Khan

Slide 1

The purpose and possibilities of social media
- Changes in use
- Allow people to network
- Bypass* traditional media
- Unexpected outcomes

Slide 2

Advantages and limitations of social media
1 Easy to access
2 Equality
3 Cost
4 Bypass governments
5 'Safety in numbers'
6 Social media vs. real-life chat

Slide 3

Next steps for social media
- Are the real-life social skills of users declining?
- How many real friends have you got?
- Are you tweeting or working?
- Will everyone use social media?

Slide 4

GLOSSARY
bypass (v) to go around, or avoid something

2 Work in pairs and predict one or two points that the speaker might make for slides 2–4.

TASK 3 Taking notes on key information

1 ▷5.6 Watch Extract 1 of a presentation on the power of social media. For each social media company mentioned, note down the following information.
- company name
- launch date
- who it was launched for, and why
- approximate number of users

2 ▷5.7 Watch Extract 2 and note down the main points relating to slides 2 and 3.

Example: The purpose and possibilities of social media
change in focus from small local groups → global mass-market use (allows people to network, chat, & exchange personal info worldwide)

3 Compare your notes with your predictions in Task 2.2. Did you predict any points mentioned by the speaker?

Reporting verbs Referring to points in a presentation

When you report what a speaker says, you can select from a number of verbs to show different meanings.

Reporting a statement neutrally

*The speaker **says** / **states** that ...*

Reporting the presentation of examples or evidence

*The speaker **shows** / **demonstrates** that ...*

Reporting a speaker's position or stance

*The speaker **argues** / **believes** / **suggests** that ...*

When you respond to what someone says, it is more common to use a different verb.

*The speaker **suggests that** social media sites limit the way we communicate, but I **believe that** they can help us to communicate better.*

TASK 4 Using reporting verbs

1 **Read statements 1–5 made by the speaker, and report what she says. Select a different reporting verb for each statement.**

Example: 'What's interesting is that social media can often bypass the traditional media.'
*The speaker **states** that social media can often bypass the traditional media.*

1 '... There have been some unexpected outcomes of using social media.'

2 'They're easy to access, easy to use, and almost anyone can get their message out there.'

3 'Most governments find that they're almost impossible to regulate.'

4 'Some users have even been convicted of crimes, ... like the recent case where a student was sent to prison for writing racist Tweets about a public figure.'

5 'In theory, everybody can access social media. But in reality, they can't.'

INDEPENDENT STUDY

Presenters and lecturers use a range of reporting verbs, depending on their purpose and their audience.

▸ Find a lecture online related to your discipline, and note down any reporting verbs. If possible, also read the transcript.

TASK 5 Preparing for a seminar discussion

1 **You are going to take part in a seminar discussion based on the presentation in Task 3. Prepare for the discussion using stages 1–4.**

1 Read the headings on the slides and your notes from Task 3. Decide which of the speaker's points you agree with.

2 Note down your own views on the points on slides 2 and 3.

3 Work out how you will refer to these points using reporting verbs.

4 Think of answers to the questions in slide 4.

2 **Work in pairs and explain your ideas.**

TASK 6 Taking part in a seminar discussion

1 **Work in groups. The purpose of the discussion is for you to raise the points you prepared in Task 5, and respond to other students' points.**

1 Select a point from the presentation to begin with.

2 Take turns to make the points you prepared. Try to use a good range of reporting verbs and respond to what other people in your group say. Try to include your own views.

3 Continue the discussion until everyone has contributed. Then move on to the next point.

2 **Evaluate your own performance in the discussion using questions 1–3.**

1 Did you make the points you prepared?

2 Did other students understand and respond to your points?

3 Did you participate effectively by listening to and responding to other students' points?

When you are preparing for an assignment, such as an essay, textbooks are useful **sources** of information. You need to be able to select those parts of the text which are relevant to the topic of your assignment. It is important to identify and note down the main ideas from the text. You can then use your notes on these main ideas to write a **summary** of the text, which you can include in your own writing.

This module covers:

- Identifying the main ideas and key information in a text
- Identifying key features of a summary
- Using noun phrases to summarize ideas
- Evaluating summaries of a text

TASK 1 Discussing reading to prepare for writing

1 **Work in pairs. Think of an academic project you have done which involved reading and writing, and discuss points 1–3.**

   1 How much reading did you have to do to prepare for the writing? How long did it take?

   2 What sorts of texts did you have to read?

   3 How much material from the texts did you use in your writing?

2 **Imagine you have to prepare to write an essay on individual power and social power. Decide the order in which you would do the following.**

   a Search for key words such as *power* in the title, index, and contents pages of textbooks, or online

   b Study the essay title carefully and make sure you understand it

   c Read selected extracts from your sources

   d Use material from the notes and summaries in your essay

   e Think of ideas to use in the essay

   f Make notes and summarize key information from your sources

   g Search for relevant sources of information, such as textbooks or online articles

3 **Compare your ideas with another pair, and give reasons for your selection. Are there any other stages you would include?**

TASK 2 Identifying the main ideas in a text

1 **Work in groups. Read Text 1 and discuss questions 1–3.**

> TEXT 1
>
> Social class has traditionally been divided into three broad categories: an *upper class* that owns property, land, and investments and is wealthy and powerful; a *middle class* made up of professional workers such as managers and owners of small businesses; a *lower class* of people who have low-paid jobs or who are unemployed.

   1 To what extent is this *stratification* (i.e. the division of something into different layers or groups) of society into three classes accurate?

   2 What other factors can determine a person's class?

   3 How easy is it for someone to change classes, and how long might this take?

2 **Read Text 2, which is the opening part of a longer section in a sociology textbook. Identify the three aspects of power mentioned in the text.**

Class and status

1　The German sociologist Max Weber (1864–1920) saw social stratification as a central feature of social life, and it figured in all his sociological studies. Yet his theoretical discussions of it were very brief. These discussions have, however, been enormously influential. The distinctions that he made between class, status, and party have become commonplace in sociology, as has his related definition of authority. Here we will review Weber's key ideas, building on them where necessary, in order to provide a comprehensive framework for understanding social stratification. (See J. Scott 1996 for a fuller discussion.)

2　Weber identified three distinct aspects or dimensions of the distribution of power within societies. These can be called the economic, the communal, and the authoritarian. Each of these aspects of power has a separate effect on the production of advantaged and disadvantaged life chances. In summary, he holds that:

- *economic* power is the basis of class relations;
- *communal* power is the basis of status relations;
- *authoritarian* power is the basis of authority relations.

　　We will look at each of these, concentrating on class and status, and we will show how other writers have helped to develop ideas about these issues.

SOURCE: Fulcher, J. & Scott, J. (2011). p.746. *Sociology* 4th ed. Oxford: Oxford University Press.

GLOSSARY

authority *(n)* the power or right to do sth, or to influence people

communal *(adj)* involving different groups of people in a community

distinction *(n)* a clear difference or contrast

status *(n)* a person's social position

3　**Complete the notes using information from Text 2.**

Paragraph 1

Weber's theories:
1　social stratification
- central to social life
- only discussed briefly, but ....
2　Class, status, and party
- these distinctions common in sociology
- Weber's .... also common in sociology

Paragraph 2

Weber identified three distinct .... of .... in societies
- economic power – class relations
- ....
- authoritarian power – authority relations

4　**Based on the completed notes, identify the main points that could be included in an essay on individual and social power.**

TASK 3　Identifying the key features of a summary

1　**Read the summary of Text 2, and evaluate it using the '4Cs' criteria below.**

In their text on class and status, Fulcher and Scott (2011, p.746) report the work of Weber. They state that Weber's theory of social stratification is brief but highly influential, with his distinctions of class, status, and party being widely accepted. Weber proposed three key aspects of power in society: economic, communal, and authoritarian.

An effective summary is:

1　Complete: it includes all the main ideas, but *not* supporting details or examples
2　Concise: it is as brief as possible, and shorter than the original text
3　Clear: it is easy to understand
4　Creative: it uses some key terms from the text, but mainly uses the summary writer's own language.

2　**Compare the summary to the notes in Task 2.3. Find one example of information that is included in the summary, and one example of information that is not included.**

Noun phrases (2) Summarizing ideas

Summaries need to be concise and information-rich. Noun phrases are useful for writing summaries because they can express complex ideas in just a few words. Three typical patterns of noun phrase are:

1 Adjective + noun

 ... and it figured in **all his sociological studies**.

2 Noun + prepositional phrase (beginning with a simple preposition like *of* or *for*)

 Weber saw social stratification as a central feature of social life ...

 ... in order to provide a comprehensive framework for understanding social stratification.

3 Noun + relative clause (part of a sentence that provides extra information, often starting with *that, which,* or *who*)

 The distinctions that he made between class, status, and party have become ...

TASK 4 Writing noun phrases from notes

1 Use notes 1–4 to write noun phrases including all the information given. Add grammatical words such as prepositions (*of*) and determiners (*a, the*) if necessary.

 Example: *Adorno's theory*
  Identity = key idea
  → *Identity is a key theory in Adorno's theory*

 1 Leaders = *people – high status – in their community*

 2 Durkheim's study: social roles = important!!!

 3 'The masses' = people (low economic status)

 4 This = important concept – sociological & political

2 Match your noun phrases to one of the patterns from Academic Language.

Class and economic power

TEXT 3

Class relations and class divisions have an economic basis because they result from the distribution of property and other resources in the capital, product, and labour markets. It is possession and non-possession of economic resources that give people their power to acquire income and assets from their involvement in market relations. What Weber called **class situation** is a person's position in the capital, product, and labour markets as determined by the kinds of resources that they have available to them. People occupy a similar class situation whenever they have similar abilities to secure advantages and disadvantages for themselves through the use of their marketable resources. Someone who owns company shares, for example, will earn an investment income on them and may be able to sell them for a profit on the stock market. Similarly, someone with educational qualifications and a particular technical skill may be able to demand a higher income in the labour market than someone without this skill. A carpenter and an electrician both have skills that allow them to earn higher wages in the labour market than an unskilled labourer.

A person's economic power is, Weber said, a factor resulting in the determination of their life chances. What he means by this is that the inequalities in life chances that we examine in Chapter 18 are determined, to a greater or lesser extent, by differences in property and market position. A person's class situation not only determines his or her life chances; it also determines the interests that he or she has in protecting and increasing these life chances. This is very important, as Weber held that people are often likely to act, individually or collectively, in pursuit of their class interests.

SOURCE: Fulcher, J. & Scott, J. (2011). pp.746–7. *Sociology* 4th ed. Oxford: Oxford University Press.

GLOSSARY

acquire *(v)* to gain sth by your own efforts

asset *(n)* something of value, especially property

capital *(n)* a large amount of money that is invested or used to start a business

company shares *(n pl)* units of equal value which a company is divided into

determine *(v)* to make sth happen in a particular way

investment income *(n)* money earned from investments

TASK 5 Identifying key information in a text

1 Work in pairs. Decide which *three* characteristics are most associated with a person's individual power.

money   qualifications   status / official position in society   job title

2 Read Text 3, *Class and economic power*, which follows on from Text 2, *Class and status*. Which characteristics in 1 are mentioned in the text?

3 Find other words and phrases in the text related to each characteristic.

Example: *money – economic basis / assets / property / economic resources / investments*

TASK 6 Evaluating summaries of a text

1 Read the two summaries of Text 3 and decide which is the better summary.

Summary 1

In their text on class and economic power, Fulcher and Scott (2011, pp.746–7) state that class and economic power come from property and other resources, so they are economically-based: people's power comes from their economic resources. Weber's term 'class situation' refers to a person's economic position. This reflects how they use their economic resources, whether financial, professional, or educational. Weber also argues that a person's economic power affects their 'life chances' and the actions they take to maintain these life chances.

Summary 2

Fulcher and Scott's (2011, pp.746–7) text on class and economic power explains that a person's class status is brought about by what they possess in terms of property and other assets; whether they own something or not, or how much they own, means that they have a particular status and class. People can change what they have by gaining assets through the market. This is an interesting observation, which Weber calls 'class situation'. This includes various assets such as financial assets, and these affect them in different ways, whether through the ownership of stock market shares or the possession of a specific skill such as electrical skills. These allow a person to hold different positions socially, financially, and economically.

2 Work in pairs and evaluate the two summaries using the '4Cs'. Is each summary:
   - Complete?
   - Concise?
   - Clear?
   - Creative?

3 Identify the weaknesses and possible areas for improvement in the less effective summary. Discuss how to improve these areas by deciding what to add, delete, or change.

4 Look back at the better summary you selected in 1. Match each sentence in the summary to the part of Text 3 it refers to.

TASK 7 Critical thinking – responding to ideas in a text

1 Work in groups. Discuss whether you agree with ideas 1–3 from the texts. Give reasons and examples.

   1 A person's power comes from their economic resources.

   2 A person's economic power affects their life chances.

   3 People are often likely to act, individually or collectively, in pursuit of their class interests.

When taking notes from a text, it is important that you have a clear purpose for the notes. This may be preparing for a seminar or finding information for a written assignment. It is also important to be **active** in your note-taking as this will help you to think critically about the ideas in the text. You can then use your notes to write a summary of the text which includes all the key information.

This module covers:
- Analysing and using active note-taking strategies
- Identifying and using summarizing words and phrases
- Writing a summary of a short academic text

TASK 1 Critical thinking – discussing the features of a summary

1 **Work in pairs. Discuss items 1–6 and decide which you agree with. Give reasons.**

A summary ...

1 includes your own ideas
2 is much shorter than the original text
3 includes all main and supporting details

4 includes all minor details
5 helps you to understand a text
6 is useful for future activities.

TASK 2 Analysing note-taking strategies

1 **Work in pairs. You are going to read a short text about leadership. Before you read, discuss questions 1–3.**

1 Do you think a leader should have a lot of power and make most of the decisions?
2 When might it be a good idea for a leader to share power with other people?
3 Would you rather work for:
  a a leader who controls everything?
  b a leader who shares power and responsibility?

2 **Read the following statement and answer questions 1 and 2.**

'One style of leadership is suitable for all situations.'

1 Work in pairs and discuss your initial response to the statement.
2 What areas might you need to research in order to prepare for a seminar discussion on this statement?

3 **Read the text and the notes. Identify which note-taking strategies 1–8 on page 073 are used.**

Research questions: How many leadership styles are there? Are different styles better for different situations?

Autocratic leadership

A strong hierarchy

traditional command / control leadership

Autocratic leaders hold on to as much power and decision-making as they possibly can. There is likely to be minimal consultation and employee input into decision-making. Orders should be obeyed and employees should welcome the structured environment and the rewards they receive.
   This style of leadership is most likely to be used when subordinates are unskilled, not trusted, and their ideas are not valued. It is also more likely in an organization that focuses on results and has to make urgent decisions that depend highly on the manager. The style is likely to be accompanied by very detailed instructions and close supervision. In some situations subordinates may expect – and like – to be told what to do since there can be no second guessing or uncertainty.

could be useful in manufacturing

Would this work in all cultures?

Not good for creative industries?

Note: no evidence provided for any of the claims

Note-taking strategies

1 underlining or highlighting words
2 translating words you do not understand
3 making notes mainly in your own words
4 writing down a lot of direct quotations
5 highlighting anything useful for your research aims
6 writing notes on everything you read
7 evaluating and criticizing a source
8 thinking about and planning your research aims

4 Look at each note-taking strategy in 3 and decide if they are *passive* or *active*.

Passive note-taking – accepting what you read or hear, and writing it down without reacting or thinking critically about what you are writing, or why.

Active note-taking – having a clear purpose for note-taking, evaluating what you read or hear, and thinking critically about what you are writing down, and why it is useful.

5 A key idea in the first sentence of the text is *holding on to power and decision-making*. Find words in the rest of the text that are related to this idea.

6 Read the notes summarizing the main ideas from the text. How might this person be planning to use their reading of the text in a seminar discussion?

Autocratic leaders = control and power – useful in unskilled non-creative job sectors – employees expect and are given instructions and supervision.

TASK 3 Using active note-taking strategies

1 Read the text on a different leadership style. Take notes using the approach in Task 2.3 as a model. As you take notes:

1 try to use *active* note-taking strategies
2 remember your response to the statement in Task 2.2.

Laissez-faire leadership

Laissez-faire means to 'leave alone'. In this leadership style the manager gives employees considerable freedom in how they do their work. Employees can set their own goals, make their own decisions, and resolve problems as they see fit.

   This may be an appropriate management style to use when employees can be trusted to do their job because they are motivated, skilled, and educated. It may be appropriate when working with a culture based around the individual, and where people can work successfully on their own.

2 Compare your notes with another student. Which active skills did you use?

3 Look back at the summary notes in Task 2.6. Write similar notes summarizing the main ideas from the text on laissez-faire leadership.

4 How are the ideas in the two texts connected? How could you link your notes on each text?

> **INDEPENDENT STUDY**
>
> Try to be active in your note-taking by using your own words, thinking critically about the text, and keeping in mind your research aims.
>
> ▶ Find two texts from your area of study and take notes using active note-taking strategies.

ACADEMIC LANGUAGE	▶ Language Reference page 180 24.1

Noun phrases (3) Summarizing ideas using key nouns and determiners

Key nouns and a related determiner can be used to summarize the main ideas within a text or section of the text.

Use definite determiners to refer to a specific example.

   The rewards … ***This*** style of leadership … ***These*** studies … ***His*** ideas … ***Their*** own decisions …

Use indefinite determiners to refer to an idea in general.

   An organization … ***A*** culture …

One use of determiners is to summarize ideas within or outside a text.

   Employees are motivated by ***the benefits*** a company provides.

The benefits are not actually mentioned in the text, but they are specific and will include things like paid holidays, pensions, bonuses, etc.

TASK 4 Identifying and using summarizing words and phrases

1 **Look back at the texts in Tasks 2.3 and 3.1 and find the phrases below. Do they summarize an idea within the text or outside the text?**

the structured environment   the rewards   this style   their own goals
their own decisions

2 **Replace the phrases in italics in the text below with a suitable summarizing phrase.**

the structured environment   the rewards   the relationships   the working process
the personal characteristics

> ¹*A strong, determined, and decisive personality* traditionally associated with a good leader
> is perhaps more associated with ²*a setting in which there is a strong hierarchy and chain
> of command* found in traditional manufacturing contexts. ³*The role of individuals and their
> position* within the hierarchy clearly determine how an individual is expected to behave in
> an organization. Employees were not expected to demand anything more than ⁴*the salary,
> holidays, pension, and bonuses* associated with their role. Today, however, ⁵*the way in which
> people are expected to work* plays a much more important role in determining managerial style.

ACADEMIC LANGUAGE ▸ Language Reference page 181 24.5

Noun phrases (4) Paraphrasing longer structures

To avoid using exactly the same words to repeat an idea, lecturers and textbook writers often
use a noun phrase instead of a longer structure (a clause or sentence). The noun phrase says
the same thing in a different, more concise way. Two typical patterns of noun phrase are:

1 Determiner + noun + prepositional phrase
2 Determiner + adjective(s) + noun

Compare these examples:

1 Clause: *In some situations employees may expect to be told what to do …*
  Noun phrase: *This expectation of being told what to do …*
2 Sentence: *It may be appropriate when working with a culture based around the individual …*
  Noun phrase: *Such individualized cultures …*

Using noun phrases in this way often involves changing the class of a word. For example:

individual → *individualized* (noun → adjective), *expect* → *expectation* (verb → noun)

TASK 5 Paraphrasing longer structures using noun phrases

1 **Rewrite sentences 1–4. Use one of the noun phrase patterns in Academic Language to
rephrase the underlined words, with the word in brackets as the head noun.**

Example: *Chapter 12 looks at how business became more global. (globalization)*
            → *Chapter 12 looks at the globalization of business.*

1 The following chapter examines how a laissez-faire business style has come to be
  adopted. (adoption)

2 The arguments for a laissez-faire business style lack a sufficient amount of evidence to
  support it. (evidence)

3 An important aim of a successful business is to build trust among its employees.
  (building)

4 This discussion in this essay is limited to what has caused this worrying situation to
  arise. (cause)

1 Read the paragraph on democratic leadership and the summary that follows. Identify the parts of the original paragraph that are included in the summary.

Democratic leadership

The democratic leadership style may not always work out, though. It is likely to be most effective when used with skilled, free thinking, and experienced subordinates who enjoy the relationships and chaos that can result from belonging to a highly effective team. Nevertheless, the democratic process may slow down decision-making and may prove costly. The style also requires a positive chemistry in the team and if this is absent, no amount of democracy can make the style work.

Summary: Experienced, skilled, and open-minded employees work well in a team when relationships are good. However, democratic leadership can be slow and costly, and can fail without an effective team.

2 Look back at your own notes from Task 3.3. Write summaries of autocratic and laissez-faire leadership styles using the summary in 1 above as a model.

3 Read the paragraph on trait theory and write notes on the main ideas. Use your notes to write a summary of the paragraph.

Sample answer
page 189

Trait theory

'She's a born leader' encapsulates the idea behind trait theory, which argues that some individuals are born with the characteristics that make them natural leaders. Trait theory suggests that leaders are different from other groups of individuals in that they consistently demonstrate the following characteristics: intelligence, self-confidence, determination, integrity, sociability. Interestingly, height and fluency in speech were often found to be common traits too, as were flat feet. Critics of trait theory believe that it fails to take into account the life experiences that can affect leadership.

4 Compare your summary with a partner. Use questions 1–4 to evaluate (a) your own summary, and (b) your partner's summary. Is the summary:

1 Complete (does it include the main idea from the original text)?
2 Concise (is it significantly shorter than the original text)?
3 Clear (is it easy to understand)?
4 Creative (does the writer use their own language)?

5E Vocabulary Affixes

Affixes include both prefixes, e.g. *un-*, *dis-*, and suffixes, e.g. *-tion*. Many affixes are grammatical, and do not have much 'meaning', for example the prefix *-un* shows an opposite, and the suffix *-ity* shows that the word is probably a noun. Sometimes a suffix can be taken away to leave the root word, e.g. *intensity → intense*, but sometimes this does not work, e.g. *capacity*. Affixes can help you recognize word class, which in turn can help you understand wider meanings and sentence structure.

TASK 1   Using suffixes to recognize word families

1 Match each group of suffixes to their typical word classes.

1 -tion, -sion, -ity, -ment, -ism, -ness   Nouns: ....

2 -ly, -ily   Verbs: ....

3 -ify, -ize, -ate   Adjectives: ....

4 -al, -ous, -ent, -ive   Adverbs: ....

2 Choose one group, and give at least one example word for each suffix.

Example: *-ity: authority, intensity*

3 Write a sentence related to your own area of study using each example word from 2.

TASK 2   Building word families using affixes

1 Decide on the word class for words 1–8. Then write in the remaining forms where possible. The first is done as an example.

		noun	verb	adjective	adverb
1	centre	centre	centralize	central	centrally
2	divide				–
3	discuss				
4	category				
5	theoretical				
6	similar		–		
7	differentiate				
8	collectively				

2 Add the word class to words 1–8. Then complete the second column with the word class given.

1 involve (   ) .... (n)

2 similar (   ) .... (n)

3 market (   ) .... (adj)

4 intense (   ) .... (adv)

5 summary (   ) .... (v)

6 division (   ) .... (adj)

7 equal (   ) .... (n)

8 resource (   ) .... (adj)

3 Complete the sentences with the appropriate form of the word given.

1 UN .... in recent elections has helped stabilize the region. (involve)

2 Life on other planets is .... possible, but highly unlikely. (theoretical)

3 The .... between rich and poor has increased with each generation. (divide)

4 Researchers noted a .... in responses from male and female test groups. (similar)

5 Attempts to .... the flora and fauna of rainforests have been limited. (category)

4 Write a short paragraph related to your own area of study using at least three of the words from 2.

UNIT 6 Growth

ACADEMIC FOCUS: USING SOURCES

LEARNING OBJECTIVES

This unit covers:

Listening
- Completing notes on the main points of a lecture
- Identifying and discussing stance in source material
- Summarizing stance and perspective of source material

Speaking
- Referring to the main ideas in a text
- Forming a stance based on a reading
- Offering and responding to opinions

Reading
- Identifying and evaluating sources for an essay
- Identifying author stance on main ideas
- Identifying details and examples from sources to support an argument

Writing
- Analysing the use of sources in a text
- Understanding and using ways of referring to sources
- Selecting and synthesizing sources to use in a paragraph

Vocabulary
- Identifying form in reported structures
- Using reporting structures

Discussion

1 **Work in pairs and decide which area 1–4 is the most important for the growth of a country. Give reasons and examples.**

   1 technology and industry
   2 education
   3 natural resources (e.g. oil, forests)
   4 government policy

2 **Which of the following are likely to be the *causes* of growth, and which are more likely to be the *results* of growth?**

   a higher standard of living   a more powerful country
   innovation   environmental problems

3 **Work in groups. Identify the most effective ways of promoting the growth of a country. Briefly present these to the whole class.**

Lecturers are likely to use a number of **sources**, such as textbooks or articles, to inform their lectures. They will often use these to support their argument. Reading the sources either before or after the lecture will help you to understand the topic of the lecture more fully. While listening to a lecture, you need to be able to identify the sources that the lecturer refers to, so that you can follow up by reading any useful extracts.

This module covers:

- Completing notes on the main points of a lecture
- Identifying and discussing stance in source material
- Summarizing stance and perspective of source material

TASK 1 Discussing a topic to prepare for a lecture

1 Read the definition of the Industrial Revolution. Work in groups and make a list of the *three* most important technological developments since the Industrial Revolution.

> **the Industrial Revolution** *(n)* [sing.] the period in the 18th and 19th centuries in Europe and the US when machines began to be used to do work, and industry grew rapidly

2 Discuss what you know about these key terms. Say how they can be connected, for example, as a cause and effect.

globalization capitalism the Industrial Revolution political theories technological growth

3 You are going to watch the first part of a lecture on 'the globalization of business'. The lecturer refers to two sources which her students will need to read during the course. Look at the contents page of one of the books on page 196 and answer questions 1 and 2.

1 Which *three* chapters relate to the worldwide growth of industry and technology?

2 How could you use the book to prepare for the lecture?

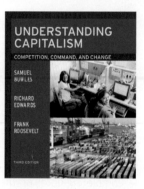

TASK 2 Completing notes on the main points of a lecture

1 ▶6.1 Watch Extract 1 and complete the notes on the lecture overview.

Course module: [1]*The Globalization of Business*

Main topic: [2]

Focus: [3]

Key question: [4]

2 Compare your answers in 1 with another student, and identify the language that helped you complete the notes.

3 ▶6.2 Watch Extract 2 and complete the notes on the Industrial Revolution. The symbol → means *causes* or *leads to*.

Contextualizing the Industrial Revolution:

[1]*advances in technology & inventions* → *the Industrial Revolution* [2]
(date) → [3]*growth in*

[4]*the Industrial Revolution is permanent (evaluation)*

Major areas of 19th century technological advance:

[5]*agriculture* [6] [7]

Major areas of 20th century advance:

[8]*transport (highways / cars and trucks)* [9]
[10] [11] [12]

4 ▶6.3 Watch Extract 3 and note down the information given by the lecturer relating to points 1–4.

1 Examples of 21st C technological growth

2 The impact of 20th C technological growth

3 The buying power of Americans

4 The cause of this increase in buying power

5 The lecturer says that there have been 'significant increases in people's consumption standards'. Whose stance is this?

    1 the lecturer's   2 the authors' (i.e. Bowles, Edwards, and Roosevelt)

6 Work in pairs. Use your notes on Extracts 1–3 to answer questions 1 and 2.

    1 Why was the Industrial Revolution such an important social and historical event?

    2 What are some of the benefits of industrialization and economic growth?

TASK 3 Critical thinking – offering an opposing stance

1 ▶6.4 Watch the last part of Extract 3 again. Read statements 1–3 and decide if they represent the stance of (a) the lecturer, or (b) the authors (Bowles, Edwards, and Roosevelt).

    1 The 'unprecedented growth in the availability of material goods' is universally beneficial.

    2 Everyday life was also made better through changes in diet and housing.

    3 Industrial and technological growth is a positive development.

2 Work in groups. Write one sentence expressing an *opposing* stance to each statement in 1.

    Example: *The 'unprecedented growth in the availability of material goods' can cause both unhappiness and environmental damage.*

3 Compare your answers with another group.

> **INDEPENDENT STUDY**
>
> Lecturers often present opposing stances so that the information is not one-sided.
>
> ▶ In a lecture, listen out for evaluative words like *beneficial* and *positive* and think of critical questions, e.g. *How beneficial? Beneficial for whom?*

TASK 4 Listening for stance and perspective

1 ▶6.5 Watch Extract 4, where the lecturer refers to a second source. Read sentences 1 and 2 and decide if they represent the stance of (a) the lecturer, or (b) the authors (Wetherly and Otter).

    1 'So we might expect a more critical stance than the one we looked at earlier, put forward by Bowles, Edwards, and Roosevelt.'

    2 'So essentially, the Marxist view is anti-capitalist – it sees the effect of capitalism as increasing poverty among the majority of the population.'

2 ▶6.5 Watch Extract 4 again. Make brief notes about:

    • the Marxist perspective as presented by the authors, Wetherly and Otter

    • Adam Smith's perspective as presented by the authors, Wetherly and Otter.

3 Read summaries 1 and 2. Which summarizes (a) the Marxist perspective, and (b) Adam Smith's perspective on capitalism?

Summary 1

This perspective accepts that capitalism can bring about economic growth. However, it recognizes a major weakness in capitalism: it results in inequality, with a small number of rich people owning a very large amount of a country's wealth.

Summary 2

This perspective accepts that capitalism can bring about economic growth. It believes that capitalism, and in particular international free trade and open markets, are positive forces for economic development.

TASK 5 Critical thinking – responding to the content of a lecture

1 Work in groups and discuss questions 1 and 2.

    1 Is continued economic growth always a good thing?

    2 Does economic growth lead to increased wealth for everyone, or to increased inequality?

2 Write a short paragraph summarizing your own stance on the Industrial Revolution. Choose from one or more of the following perspectives.

    social   political   financial   technical   environmental

> **INDEPENDENT STUDY**
>
> Find a source from your own area of study.
>
> ▶ What's the stance of the author? What perspectives are covered?

Speaking Seminar discussions (4)

A common seminar task is to discuss a text that you have read in advance. You will be expected to read and think about the text before the seminar. You will need to check that you understand the main points and arguments in the text. You will also have to think about your own stance and your reaction to the points in the text, and be prepared to discuss them with other students.

This module covers:

- Referring to the main ideas in a text
- Forming a stance based on a reading
- Offering and responding to opinions

TASK 1 Previewing the topic

1 **Work in groups and discuss questions 1–4.**

  1 How do you do most of your travelling? By car, bus, train, or another method?

  2 Look at the graph. Is there a similar pattern in your country?

  3 What are the advantages and disadvantages of car use in your country?

  4 Has your government taken steps to solve the problems caused by cars in your country? Explain what these steps are and whether or not they have been effective.

2 **Briefly present your answers to the class.**

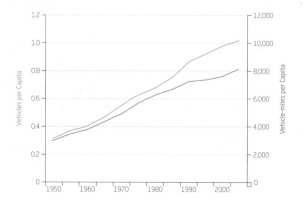

TASK 2 Referring to the main ideas in a text

1 **Read Text 1 and underline the main ideas.**

> **TEXT 1**
>
> Can the planet sustain two billion cars? Not as we know them. Today's one billion vehicles are already releasing extraordinary quantities of greenhouse gases into the atmosphere. They are using up the world's conventional petroleum supplies, starting political arguments over oil, and putting pressure on the roads of today's cities. Billions of hours are wasted stuck in traffic, and billions of people are sickened by pollution from cars. From Paris to Fresno, and Delhi to Shanghai, conventional motorization, conventional vehicles, and conventional fuels are polluting cities. Cars are arguably one of the greatest man-made threats to human society.
>
> Yet cars aren't going to go away. The desire for personal vehicles is powerful and everywhere. Cars offer unprecedented freedom, flexibility, convenience, and comfort, unmatched by bicycles or today's public transport. Cars have many benefits for those fortunate enough to own them. They have transformed modern life and are one of the great industrial success stories of the twentieth century. What, then, should be done about the soaring vehicle population? Radical changes are called for. Vehicles need to change, as do the energy and transportation systems in which they are embedded. Even according to the most conservative scenarios, dramatic reductions in oil use and carbon emissions will be needed within the next few decades to avoid serious economic and climate change.
>
> SOURCE: Sperling, D. & Gordon, D. (2009). pp.1–2. *Two Billion Cars: Driving towards sustainability.* Oxford: Oxford University Press.

GLOSSARY

conservative *(adj)* an estimate lower than what is probably the real sum or amount

conventional *(adj)* normal and ordinary; (of fuels) not nuclear

sustain *(v)* to provide enough of what sb/sth needs in order to exist

2 ◀))6.6 **Listen to an extract from a seminar discussion. Identify which ideas from Text 1 the speakers refer to. Do they agree or disagree with these ideas?**

3 ◀))6.6 **Listen again and note down the phrases the speakers use to:**

  1 refer to the text

  2 respond to a point in the text

  3 respond to each other's points.

Referring and responding to points of view

In a discussion, it is important to make clear whether you are referring or responding to the content of a source (e.g. a text or lecture), or putting forward your own points.

Referring to a source

It says in the text that …

the text talks about …

according to the text …

if you look at … it suggests …

the authors also suggest that …

Responding to a point in a source

I have to agree that …

I think that's pretty clear.

I don't necessarily agree with that point.

Responding to another speaker

Exactly, yes.

I understand what you're saying, but …

I suppose so, but …

TASK 3 Using phrases to refer to points in a source

1 **Complete the discussion extract using phrases from Academic Language.**

A So do you think the situation is really that bad?

B Well, [1]................................ the first paragraph, I think it's difficult to argue with the points. I mean, [2]................................ the number of cars is increasing, which means the problem will only get worse.

A [3]................................ it seems to me that there are more serious threats to society than cars. I mean, over-population, water supply … there are other things to worry about.

B [4]................................ , but isn't it all connected? I mean, the authors [5]................................ that there's a connection with climate change.

A But … well, yes, [6]................................ with that. But [7]................................ that we need a radical solution, we need to make big changes in the technology and the infrastructure. [8]................................ with that point.

2 🔊 6.7 **Listen and check your answers.**

TASK 4 Reading to prepare for a seminar

1 **You are going to take part in a seminar discussion. Read the statement and think about questions 1–3.**

'Most people aspire to improve their standard of living. It is therefore understandable that the number of cars worldwide is growing rapidly. However, this aspiration will cause increasing demand for limited resources that could ultimately lead to conflict.'

1 What is your opinion on this statement?

2 What are other possible opinions?

3 What arguments could you use to counter these opinions?

2 **Read Text 2 on page 197 and follow the instructions.**

> **INDEPENDENT STUDY**
>
> Whenever you discuss a topic based on a text or other source, always try to move beyond just understanding the ideas in the text. Try to think about your reactions, and the reactions other people may have, in order to discuss the ideas more effectively.
>
> ▶ **Find a short text or lecture related to your area of study. Make notes on two different ways you could respond to it.**

TASK 5 Taking part in a seminar discussion

1 **Work in groups and discuss the statement from Task 4.1. During the discussion, make sure you:**

- refer to points from the text
- respond to the points from the text
- respond to points made or referred to by other people.

2 **Evaluate your own performance in the discussion using questions 1–3.**

1 Did you make the points you prepared?

2 Did other students understand and respond to your points?

3 Did you participate effectively by listening to and responding to other students' points?

Reading an academic text often informs another task such as taking part in a seminar, writing an essay, or sitting an exam. When using a text to inform your writing, it is important to think about *how* you can use the material from that text - for example, do you want to include summaries of large quantities of material, or specific details to support your stance or argument? This module helps you to evaluate and select relevant material from a longer text in preparation for a piece of writing.

This module covers:
- Identifying and evaluating sources for an essay
- Identifying author stance on main ideas
- Identifying details and examples from sources to support an argument

TASK 1 Previewing the topic of a text

1 Work in pairs and discuss questions 1–3. Give reasons and examples.

1 Think of three increasing demands that humans are placing on the Earth (e.g. the demand for oil), and discuss which has the greatest impact.

2 At the same time as the world's population has grown, incomes in many countries have also risen. How might this add to the pressure on the Earth?

3 Is quality of life increasing around the world? Is it increasing equally everywhere?

2 Compare your ideas with another pair.

TASK 2 Analysing essay titles

1 Read the essay title. Decide which of the research questions 1–5 it would be useful to answer in preparing for this essay.

> **TITLE:** *'Current levels of food consumption are unsustainable.' Discuss.*

1 What are the levels of food consumption?

2 What are the most popular foods in the world?

3 Are any countries self-sufficient in food production?

4 What evidence is there to show that the world is consuming too much?

5 Is consumption the same everywhere in the world?

2 Read the essay title. Work in pairs and discuss what background information would help you prepare for the essay.

> **TITLE:** *'Population growth is placing immense pressure on the world's resources and humans need to adapt their lifestyle to maintain the planet's existence.' To what extent do you agree?*

TASK 3 Understanding a longer source text

1 Read the text quickly and decide how you could use it as a source for the essay in Task 2.2.

2 Match sentences a–h with the paragraph (1–8) they summarize.

a Incomes have risen dramatically, by 700% in fifty years. ....

b Food supplies are most likely to suffer first: grain stocks fell for three years in a row. ....

c The world's population has grown rapidly in the last fifty years, faster than in the four million years before it. *1*........

d In the past, farmers increased production when there was a shortage of food, but now it is not clear if they can do so. ....

e It was the goal of the UN to halve levels of world hunger by 2015. ....

f We are using more water than is being replaced by the natural environment, causing significant ecological damage. ....

g Income and population growth have increased food demand so much that farmers are now farming land that is not sustainable. ....

h Nature is struggling to cope with CO_2 emissions, which are up from 316ppm to 369ppm in just over forty years. ....

3 **Identify the specific words or phrases in the text that helped you to match each paragraph to its summary.**

4 **Highlight the main ideas in paragraphs 9 and 10. Use these to write a one-sentence summary of each paragraph.**

A Planet Under Stress

1   Humanity's demands on the Earth have multiplied over the last half-century as our numbers have increased and our incomes risen. World population grew from 2.5 billion in 1950 to 6.1 billion in 2000. The growth during those 50 years exceeded that during the 4 million years since we emerged as a distinct species.

2   Incomes have risen even faster than population. Income per person worldwide nearly tripled from 1950 to 2000. Growth in population and the rise in incomes together expanded global economic output from just under $7 trillion (in 2001 dollars) of goods and services in 1950 to $46 trillion in 2000, a gain of nearly sevenfold.

3   Population growth and rising incomes together have tripled world grain demand over the last half-century, pushing it from 640 million tons in 1950 to 1,855 million tons in 2000. To satisfy this swelling demand, farmers have plowed land that was highly erodible – land that was too dry or too steeply sloping to sustain cultivation. Each year billions of tons of topsoil are being blown away in dust storms or washed away in rainstorms, leaving farmers to try to feed some 70 million additional people, but with less topsoil than the year before.

4   Demand for water also tripled as agricultural, industrial and recreational uses climbed, out-stripping the sustainable supply in many countries. As a result, water tables are falling and wells are going to dry. Rivers are going to be drained dry, to the detriment of wildlife and ecosystems.

5   Fossil fuel use quadrupled, setting in motion a rise in carbon emissions that is overwhelming nature's capacity to fix carbon dioxide. As a result of this carbon-fixing deficit, atmospheric CO_2 concentrations climbed from 316 parts per million (ppm) in 1959, when official measurement began, to 369ppm in 2000.

6   The sector of the economy that seems likely to unravel first is food. Eroding soils, deteriorating rangelands, collapsing fisheries, falling water tables, and rising temperatures are converging to make it more difficult to expand food production fast enough to keep up with demand. In 2002, the world's grain harvest of 1,807 million tons fell short of world grain consumption by 100 million tons, or four percent. This shortfall, the largest or record, marked the third consecutive year of grain deficits, dropping stocks to the lowest level in a generation.

7   Now the question is, can the world's farmers bounce back and expand production enough to fill the 100-million-ton shortfall, provide for the more than 70 million people added each year, and rebuild stocks to a more secure level? In the past, farmers responded to short supplies and higher grain prices by planting more land and using more irrigation water and fertilizer. Now it is doubtful that farmers can fill this gap without further depleting aquifers and jeopardizing future harvests.

8   In 1996, at the World Food Summit in Rome, hosted by the U.N. Food and Agriculture Organization (FAO), 185 countries plus the European Community agreed to reduce hunger by half by 2015. Using 1990-92 as a base, governments set the goal of cutting the number of people who were hungry – 860 million – by roughly 20 million per year. It was an exciting and worthy goal, one that later became one of the U.N. Millennium Development Goals.

9   But in the late 2002 review of food security, the United Nations issued a discouraging report: 'This year we must report that progress has virtually ground to a halt. Our latest estimates, based on data from the years 1998-2000, put the number of undernourished people in the world at 840 million ... a decrease of barely 2.5 million per year over the eight years since 1990-92.'

10   Since 1998-2000, world grain production per person has fallen five per cent, suggesting that the ranks of the hungry are now expanding. As noted earlier, life expectancy is plummeting in sub-Saharan Africa. If the number of hungry people worldwide is also increasing, then two key social indicators are showing widespread deterioration in the human condition.

source: Brown, L. in Dryzek, J.S. and Schlosberg, D. (2005). pp.38-9. *Debating the Earth: the Environmental Politics Reader.* Oxford: Oxford University Press.

TASK 4 Identifying author stance on the main ideas

1 Highlight the sentences in the text where the authors express their stance on points 1–5 below. Complete column A of the table with notes on the authors' stance.

		A Authors' stance	B Evidence used to support the stance
1	The part of the economy most under pressure	*The sector of the economy that seems likely to unravel first is food.*	
2	The ability of farmers to increase food production		*None provided*
3	Reducing world hunger by 50%		
4	The success of the World Food Summit's goal		
5	The standard of living for humans		

2 Identify the evidence the authors use to support their stance on each point and complete column B of the table.

3 Use your notes from the table to summarize the authors' stance on each point.

   Example: *Food supplies are the area most likely to collapse first, because of our continuing over-use of resources.*

TASK 5 Identifying details in a text to support an argument

1 Work in pairs. Discuss whether you agree with the statement in the essay title.

> **TITLE:** *'The world has a maximum number of people that it can support, and we have already passed that point.' Discuss.*

2 Read the essay plan. Does the writer plan to agree or disagree with the statement?

   1 Introduction: main stance – The world has reached maximum capacity because resources are being used so quickly that they are not naturally being replaced.

   2 Paragraph 1 – The growth in population and demand on resources

   3 Paragraph 2 – Growth is good for economic prosperity and ultimately for standards of living, especially in areas such as health and education.

   4 Paragraph 3 – The environment is being destroyed by human activity.

   5 Paragraph 4 – We are no longer able to support everyone on the planet with the amount of food we produce.

   6 Conclusion – Consumption patterns or the overall population size need to change in order for human existence to continue.

3 What is going to be the writer's main line of argument, a or b?

   a The effect of humans on the world's resources means that future growth is not sustainable.

   b The demand for resources needs to change to ensure sustainable growth.

4 Read the text on page 083 again and identify any details that the writer of the essay could use to support their main argument.

5 Compare the details you identified with another student. Give reasons for your selection.

> **INDEPENDENT STUDY**
>
> When you are preparing an essay, think about your stance on the issue, and what type of information you need to find in order to support your argument.
>
> ▶ Identifying your stance will give you a purpose for reading, and guide you to the sources you need to use.

Prepositions (1) Referring to time and quantity

Prepositions have many different functions in academic texts. Many of the prepositions in the text on page 083 refer to different periods of time or to changes in quantity. For example:

* *over* and *during* both refer to periods of time; *over* can also mean *more than* (quantity)
* *in* refers to a fixed period of time such as a particular year, month, or century
* *from* and *to* are used together to indicate a starting and finishing point
* *by* indicates the latest time something can happen (time) or the amount of change (quantity)

> *Population growth and rising incomes together have tripled world grain demand **over** the last half-century, pushing it **from** 640 million tons **in** 1950 **to** 1,855 million tons **in** 2000.*

> *World population grew **from** 2.5 billion **in** 1950 **to** 6.1 billion **in** 2000. The growth **during** those 50 years exceeded that **during** the 4 million years since we emerged as a distinct species.*

> *... 185 countries plus the European Community agreed to reduce hunger **by** half **by** 2015.*

TASK 6 Using prepositions to refer to time and quantity

1 Find other examples of the prepositions from Academic Language in the text, and notice how they are used.

2 Use the prepositions in the list and notes 1–5 to write complete sentences showing a change in time or quantity.

Example: China's livestock population / tripled / 1950 / 2002
          *China's livestock population tripled **from** 1950 **to** 2002.*

over   from   to   in   during   by

1 grain harvest / fall / 10 per cent / 2050
2 Californian population / increase / 26 million today / 40 million / 2030
3 the last 50 years / Gobi desert / expanded / 52,400 square kilometres
4 global temperatures / higher / the last century
5 1972 / wheat prices / went up / $70 / $181 per tonne

TASK 7 Reflecting on reading for a purpose

1 Work in pairs and discuss questions 1–3.

  1 Which of these specific skills are practised in this unit?
    * Understanding essay questions
    * Identifying the relevance of a text to a writing task
    * Understanding main ideas in a text
    * Understanding supporting details in a text
    * Understanding key terms in a text
    * Using a text to support your stance in a writing task

  2 How can you continue to practise these skills?

  3 What makes this way of reading a text more challenging than the skills you practised in earlier units?

2 Read statements 1–5 and discuss which you agree with. Give reasons and examples.

  1 I know a lot about my subject area so I don't need to support my ideas.
  2 Using sources such as texts makes an essay stronger.
  3 Essays are just a way of showing the teacher you have learnt something from your research.
  4 You can use any source you find in an essay.
  5 Using sources such as texts helps you write a more complete and balanced essay.

Writing Using sources

When you write an academic assignment such as an essay, you will need to use material from other sources, such as textbooks and academic articles. The material from these sources adds details and evidence that support your main points. You need to select the source material carefully so that it is useful, relevant, and coherent (clear and well-organized). Each use of a source is known as a **citation**. You need to include a reference for each citation, to make clear where the material is from, and to avoid plagiarism (see page 186).

This module covers:
- Analysing the use of sources in a text
- Understanding and using ways of referring to sources
- Selecting and synthesizing sources to use in a paragraph

TASK 1 Analysing the use of sources in an essay extract

1 **Work in pairs. Read the essay title and note down at least two 'challenges' that you could include in this essay.**

> **TITLE:** *What are the main challenges facing the world today as a result of economic and technological growth?*

2 **Read the paragraph from an essay on this title and answer questions 1–4.**
   1 Is this paragraph from the beginning of the essay, or near the middle?
   2 How many different sources are used?
   3 What are the two main views discussed in the paragraph?
   4 What is the main idea of the paragraph?

> [1]As we have seen, recent economic and technological growth has led to a number of environmental problems. [2]However, it has also led to a number of social challenges, the most important of which is inequality. [3]One view is that in capitalist countries people's incomes have risen steadily (Bowles, Edwards, and Roosevelt, 2005, p.8). [4]This means that countries have become richer over the past two hundred years. [5]However, an opposing view is that some people have become richer very quickly while others have not. [6]In other words, inequality has increased. [7]A Marxist perspective supports this view. [8]As reported by Wetherly and Otter (2011, p.341), Marx believed that 'the social system of capitalism is very unequal'. [9]It seems that although incomes have risen generally, the gap between rich and poor people has increased.
>
> **References:**
> 1 Bowles, S., Edwards, R., and Roosevelt, F. 2005. *Understanding Capitalism: Competition, Command, and Change*. Oxford: Oxford University Press.
> 2 Wetherly, P. and Otter, D. 2011. *The Business Environment: Themes and Issues* 2nd ed. Oxford: Oxford University Press.

3 **Match the sentences with features a–d.**

Sentence 2:	a a citation
Sentences 3 and 8:	b an explanation
Sentences 4 and 6:	c the concluding sentence, including evaluation
Sentence 9:	d the topic sentence

4 **Look at the two citations in the paragraph and answer questions 1–4.**

   Which citation ...
   1 is a *direct quotation*, using exactly the same words as the source?
   2 is a *paraphrase* of an idea in the source, using the student's own language?
   3 is a statement followed by a reference to the authors of the source text?
   4 refers to the authors of the source text, followed by a statement?

5 **Underline the language that introduces each statement in the two citations.**

Referring to sources (1) Using reporting verbs and verb structures

When referring to sources, you can use more than one style of citation.

1 Statement + reference (This style means that the reader focuses on the statement first)

Marx believed that 'capitalism is very unequal' (Wetherly and Otter 2011, p.341).

Marx believed that 'capitalism is very unequal', **as stated by** *Wetherly and Otter (2011, p.341).*

2 Author-focus (This style puts the author names first)

As reported by / According to *Wetherly and Otter (2011, p.341), Marx believed that 'capitalism is very unequal'.*

Wetherly and Otter (2011, p.341) **state** *that Marx believed 'capitalism is very unequal'.*

You can also select from a number of verbs within specific structures. For example:

Taylor **argues / believes / says / states / suggests that** *…*

Brennan and Walsh **define / describe** *X* **as** *…*

As described / reported / shown / stated by *Gonzalez and Friel …*

According to *Baker and Walsh …*

TASK 2 Using reporting verbs and verb structures

1 Read the text and complete citations 1–4 using the reporting verb structures.

> But wherever and whenever capitalism took hold, people's incomes and consumption levels began to rise in a sustained way. [...] In the U.S. the buying power of the average income in 2002 was 32 times what it was in 1789 (the year the U.S. Constitution was adopted). This does not mean, of course, that Americans are now 32 times happier than they were in 1789, but does indicate an unprecedented growth in the availability of material goods.
>
> SOURCE: Bowles, S., Edwards, R., & Roosevelt, F. (2005). p.8. *Understanding Capitalism: Competition, Command, and Change.* Oxford: Oxford University Press.

GLOSSARY

unprecedented *(adj)* that has never happened, been done, or been known before

state that   as reported by   describe   according to

1 The buying power of the average American rose by an extraordinary 32 times between 1789 and 2002, _____ Bowles, Edwards, and Roosevelt (2005, p.8).

2 Bowles, Edwards, and Roosevelt (2005, p.8) _____ the 200-year growth of material goods in the US as 'unprecedented'.

3 Bowles, Edwards, and Roosevelt (2005, p.8) _____ capitalism led to an 'unprecedented growth' in the US economy after 1789.

4 _____ Bowles, Edwards, and Roosevelt (2005, p.8), there is a clear link between capitalism and growth.

TASK 3 Understanding references

1 A reference in a text is known as an *in-text reference*. The full reference is also given at the end of a text, in the References section. Look at the two examples of these references below and answer questions 1–3.

In-text reference: (Bowles, Edwards, and Roosevelt, 2005, p.8)

Entry in References section: Bowles, S., Edwards, R., and Roosevelt, F. 2005. *Understanding Capitalism: Competition, Command, and Change.* Oxford: Oxford University Press.

1 Which of the following pieces of information are included in each reference?

	Publisher	Year of publication	Place of publication	Authors' surnames	Authors' initials	Title of the book	Page number(s)
In-text reference		✓					
Reference section							

2 Why do you think page numbers are included in a reference?

3 What is the order of the items of information in each reference?

2 Look again at the first citation from the paragraph in Task 1, and answer questions 1–4.

> One view is that in capitalist countries people's incomes have risen steadily (Bowles, Edwards, and Roosevelt, 2005, p.8).

1 Which part of the sentence is the statement, and which part is the reference?
2 Does the citation focus on the statement or the authors?
3 Does the student use a reporting structure to introduce the reference?
4 Is the 'view' mentioned in the sentence
  a the view of the student writing the essay?
  b the view of the authors named in the reference?

INDEPENDENT STUDY

When you are writing, academic referencing conventions can be quite complicated, for example how to use the right punctuation.

▶ Locate the referencing guide used by your institution and use it to help you write accurate references for your citations.

TASK 4 Using summary in citations

1 In order to write a correct citation, you need items a–c. Match these items with extracts 1–3 from an essay.

a the author's original words
b the writer's summary of the original words
c the References section entry for the original source

1 People have become richer as technology has grown.
2 Bowles, S., Edwards, R., and Roosevelt, F. 2005. *Understanding Capitalism: Competition, Command, and Change.* Oxford: Oxford University Press.
3 'The technological changes of the past five centuries have been accompanied by significant increases in people's consumption standards.'

2 Read the citation from an essay based on the material in 1. Complete citations 1–5 using the same material.

> Bowles, Edwards, and Roosevelt (2005, p.8) argue that people have become richer as technology has grown.

1 Bowles, Edwards, and Roosevelt (2005, p.8) state that ....
2 .... (Bowles, Edwards, and Roosevelt, 2005, p.8).
3 As stated by .... , ...
4 .... , according to ....
5 As .... argue, ...

TASK 5 Using direct quotation

1 If you think the original words in a source are particularly interesting, you can use them as a direct quotation rather than a summary. Complete the table using material from the essay extract in Task 1.

> As reported by Wetherly and Otter (2011, p.341), Marx believed that 'the social system of capitalism is very unequal'.

The quotation	
The reporting verb structure	
The author(s) of the quotation	
Who the quotation concerns	
The reference	

2 Complete the citations using the appropriate material from the table on page 088.

1 Marx believed that ....(Wetherly and Otter 2011, p.341).

2 The Marxist view is that 'capitalism is very unequal' ....

3 According to ...., ... 'capitalism is very unequal.'

4 Wetherly and Otter (2011, p.341) describe Marx's view on capitalism as ....

5 Capitalism is seen by Marx as ...., according to ....

TASK 6 Analysing sources to use in citations

1 Read Texts 1 and 2 on page 198, and complete the table. Try to summarize the main point of Text 1 in one sentence. Select a useful quotation from each text.

		Text 1	Text 2
1	In-text reference (following the statement)	(Bowles, Edwards, and Roosevelt, 2005, p.8)	
2	In-text reference (author-focus style)		Wetherly and Otter (2011, p.341)
3	Stance of authors in text (pro-capitalism, anti-capitalism, or neutral)	Pro-capitalism	
4	Main point		The Marxist view is that the growth of capitalism and wealth leads to income inequality.
5	Useful quotation		

2 Compare your answers to points 3–5 in the table with another student.

3 Write one citation for each source. Use two different ways of referencing.

TASK 7 Selecting sources to use in a paragraph

1 Read the essay title and decide whether it is asking you to:

a compare the importance of economic and technological growth with equality and quality of life

b argue for and against the importance of equality and quality of life rather than economic and technological growth.

> **TITLE:** 'Equality and quality of life are more important than economic and technological growth.' Discuss.

2 You are going to write a paragraph for the essay in 1. Your paragraph should present reasons why quality of life is *more important* than growth. Follow steps 1–3 to select material from different sources to use in your paragraph.

1 Turn to page 198 and read Text 3. Identify any useful and relevant material from this text to include in your paragraph. Repeat this process for Text 1 and Text 2 on page 198.

2 Organize the material you have selected using the headings in the table in Task 6.1.

3 Select material from at least two of these sources to use in your paragraph.

TASK 8 Writing a paragraph incorporating citations

1 Plan and write a 120–150 word paragraph using guidelines 1–4.

1 Review the sample paragraph in Task 1, in particular the reporting structures and the use of sources.

2 Write one or two sentences expressing the topic and main point of your paragraph.

3 Select supporting material from your sources in Task 7, and incorporate these into your paragraph. Write at least one sentence for each.

4 Write a concluding sentence.

Sample answer
page 190

2 Evaluate your paragraph using the checklist of questions on page 199.

Vocabulary Reporting structures

When incorporating sources into your work it is important that you use an appropriate reporting verb or structure. Choice of reporting verbs can indicate the strength and position of the stance that the source provides. Using a range of reporting verbs also shows that you are including a variety of stances, or a broad selection of relevant quotations to illustrate your point. Each verb is followed by a particular structure that you will need to learn. Many of the verbs are similar in their meaning and use but there are slight variations depending on whether the source is used in a neutral manner, or is for or against the issue being discussed.

TASK 1 Identifying form in reported structures

1 Put the words in the correct column.

according   as stated   asserts   as reported   contends   is~~ defined~~
describe sth   disputes   maintains

followed with *as*	followed with *by*	followed with *that*	followed with *to*
defined			

2 Compare your answers with a partner.

3 Which phrases are used in a neutral way, which to argue for an issue, and which to argue against an issue?

For	Neutral	Against
Maintains that		

TASK 2 Using reporting structures

1 Complete sentences 1–4 with the most appropriate reporting verb.

1 Even though much research has shown it to be flawed, Krashen (contends / maintains) that his theory holds true today.

2 As (asserted / stated) by Maslow, his theory was never grounded in scientific research.

3 Friedman (reports / disputes) that businesses have an ethical role in society; he believes that they are there solely to make money.

4 Johnson (contends / asserts) that the population will reach levels the planet cannot cope with. Unlike many other forecasters, he believes that population levels will fall again in the next 40 years.

2 Complete the gaps with an appropriate phrase from below.

describe as   as reported by   maintains that   according to

[1] .... Brown (2005), population growth is placing significant demands on the planet as people consume more and more food, water, and fossil fuels.
[2] .... the UN in 1996, there were around 860 million people in the world that were hungry. The world food summit [3] .... this .... a catastrophic situation and set the goal of cutting the numbers by 20 million for the next twenty years. Brown [4] .... while this was a good goal to set out to achieve, they have so far failed in doing so.

3 Write a short paragraph using two different sources to report on a key issue in your own area of study.

UNIT 7 **Networks**

ACADEMIC FOCUS: CONTEXTUALIZING

LEARNING OBJECTIVES

This unit covers:

Listening
- Using abbreviations and symbols to take notes
- Identifying support for a position
- Identifying examples and explanations

Speaking
- Discussing and evaluating learning and assessment methods
- Listening for and comparing specific context
- Identifying explaining and rephrasing language

Reading
- Evaluating different sources
- Taking notes on detailed information
- Using notes to write a summary
- Identifying and referencing source material

Writing
- Analysing essay titles
- Identifying the features of an introduction
- Evaluating thesis statements
- Writing an introduction

Vocabulary
- Identifying essay focus
- Using essay verbs

Discussion

1 The world is now more interconnected than at any time in the past. Work in pairs and put items a–e in a logical order, based on which items have had the greatest impact on connecting different parts of the world.

- .... a transport
- .... b radio and television
- .... c the telephone
- .... d the internet
- .... e business

2 Compare your order with another pair, giving reasons and examples.

3 Present your group's main ideas to the class. Use the following language to help you.

The main points we discussed were …

We feel that …

Our discussion focused on …

7A Listening Lectures (5)

Lectures contain a large amount of information delivered over a long period of time, so it is useful to develop note-taking strategies that mean you can write quickly while listening. One method is to use **abbreviations** and **symbols** as you take notes. It is important to identify different positions being presented in a lecture. You also need to recognize any supporting explanations and examples, so that you can evaluate the strength of an argument.

This module covers:
- Using abbreviations and symbols to take notes
- Identifying support for a position
- Identifying examples and explanations

TASK 1 Using background knowledge to prepare for a lecture

1 **Work in pairs and discuss questions 1–3.**

   1 What do you know about the history of the internet?

   2 What do you know about cloud computing?

   3 How have cloud computing and the internet affected the way companies work?

2 **You are going watch a lecture that presents arguments *for* and *against* the use of cloud computing. How might you organize your notes?**

TASK 2 Using symbols and abbreviations to take notes

1 **Symbols and abbreviations can help you to take notes more effectively. Decide which items 1–12 are abbreviations and which are symbols.**

1 #	4 &	7 info.	10 →
2 =	5 x	8 etc.	11 adv.
3 i.e.	6 e.g.	9 ↗/↘	12 disadv.

Robert Cailliau

2 **Match the symbols and abbreviations in 1 to the correct meaning a–l.**

...... a for example, for instance

...... b disadvantage

...... c an increase / a decrease

...... d information

...... e leads to (cause and effect)

...... f in other words

...... g and

...... h advantage

...... i a number or amount

...... j number of times

...... k and other things

...... l equals, is

Tim Berners-Lee

3 **Use the symbols and abbreviations in 1 to make notes on sentences 1 and 2.**

   Example: For instance, an advantage of cloud computing service providers is that they can control and monitor communication and data at will.
   e.g. adv = cloud computing provides & monitors communication & data

   1 In other words, they can lawfully or unlawfully access confidential information and this allows them to do what they wish with the data.

   2 In an article about the web, Tim Berners-Lee wrote 'collaborators welcome'. So many people took up this invitation that by 2009 there were 230 million websites and an average of six million new ones being added every month.

4 ▷7.1 **Watch Extract 1 of the lecture and complete the notes using these symbols.**

   → = ↗ & = ↗

   1 Cloud computing .... biggest creator of wealth in history

   2 Berners-Lee .... Robert Cailliau: document .... growth of the web

   3 User .... Internet .... size of 'cloud'

TASK 3 Taking notes on advantages and disadvantages

1 ▶7.2 **Watch Extract 2 of the lecture and take notes on:**

a what cloud computing is

b the advantages and disadvantages of cloud computing (use symbols and abbreviations where appropriate).

Advantages		Disadvantages
1		1
2		2
		3

2 **Work in pairs. Discuss whether the lecturer thinks cloud computing is mainly a good thing or a bad thing.**

TASK 4 Recognizing support for a position

1 ▶7.3 **Read the lecturer's statement. Watch the first part of Extract 2 again and note down information from sources 1 and 2 that the lecturer uses to support her statement.**

'However, there's still some debate about what cloud computing is, exactly.'

1 William Gibson has argued that ...   2 Larry Ellison has argued that ...

2 **Why does the lecturer use the two quotations? What point is she trying to make?**

TASK 5 Identifying supporting points

1 **Read the statement below. Select the point (1–3) which best supports the main point.**

'The internet has led to significant changes in how businesses work in the last fifty years.'

1 For example, businesses have been transformed by transportation methods, working practices, and the development of the knowledge economy.

2 In other words, it has changed the way businesses trade, the way people shop, and the very products and services that are offered.

3 For instance, there has been a rapid growth in the number of users, particularly from China and India.

2 **Which of the supporting points in 1 give (a) an example, and (b) an explanation?**

TASK 6 Recognizing examples and explanations

1 **Lecturers often use examples and explanations to support or clarify what they say. Which of these phrases are used to (a) give an example, and (b) give an explanation?**

For example   Let me clarify that   If we take X as an example
Let me explain what I mean by ...   Let's look at a couple of examples
What I mean by this is ...   For instance   In other words   By way of illustration
One scenario is   To put it another way   Think of it like ... , say   such as

2 ▶7.4 **Watch the second part of Extract 2 again. For each advantage and disadvantage you noted in Task 3, note down the example or explanation given by the lecturer.**

3 **Work in pairs and discuss:**

• how you identified the examples and explanations

• how the examples and explanations help you to understand each of the main points.

TASK 7 Critical thinking – responding to the content of a lecture

1 **Work in groups and discuss questions 1 and 2.**

1 What have you learned about cloud computing that you didn't know before?

2 Do you think cloud computing has more advantages or disadvantages for business users?

You are likely to spend time at university speaking in informal contexts – for example, discussing an assignment with other students, planning your work, or collaboratively working out difficult concepts. To do this, it can be very useful to form **study groups** or **networks**. These can be simple face-to-face meetings, virtual networks, or a combination of both. The aims of such groups or networks is to share ideas and materials, offer support and advice, and help you study more effectively.

This module covers:

- Discussing and evaluating learning and assessment methods
- Listening for and comparing specific context
- Identifying explaining and rephrasing language

TASK 1 Evaluating learning and assessment methods

1 **Work in groups. Discuss which teaching, learning, and assessment methods 1–9 you have experienced. Say what you know about each one.**

1 face-to-face learning	4 online discussion groups	7 lectures
2 e-learning	5 group presentations	8 role plays
3 blended learning	6 seminar discussions	9 self-study quizzes

2 **Decide the extent to which each item in 1 is:**

a individual   c interactive (who with?)

b face-to-face   d virtual

3 **Use questions 1–3 to evaluate the effectiveness of each method. Give reasons and examples.**

1 Does the method help most students to learn effectively, or only some?

2 Is the method interesting and engaging for you personally?

3 Are there any weaknesses with any of the methods, and how could these be improved?

TASK 2 Listening for context

1 🔊 **7.5 You are going to listen to a discussion about ways of working together. Listen to Extract 1 and make notes on:**

- who the speakers are
- where they are
- what they have been doing
- what they decide to do next.

TASK 3 Listening for and comparing specific content

1 🔊 **7.6 Work in pairs. Select *one* listening task, A or B. Listen to Extract 2 and make notes *only* on the points related to your selected task.**

Task A: Based on what the students say, note down the points that Professor Chapman made in his presentation.

Task B: Note down the questions asked by the students to plan their study network, e.g. *What is a study network exactly?*

2 **Compare the information you noted down in 1.**

3 **Use questions 1–2 to evaluate the effectiveness of the discussion.**

1 How well did the students understand each other?

2 How relevant and useful were the students' questions about their proposed study network?

4 **Which teaching and learning methods in Task 1 do the speakers talk about?**

TASK 4 Identifying language for explaining and rephrasing

1 ◄))7.7 **Listen to Clips 1–5 and tick the expressions (a–g) you hear.**

a You know what I mean. What I meant was …

b Well, basically what it means is …

c My point is …

d What I'm trying to say is …

e So that means …

f Let me rephrase that …

g What I'm saying is …

2 **Which expressions include an element of repetition and rephrasing?**

ACADEMIC LANGUAGE

Explaining and rephrasing

In discussions, speakers often use a range of expressions to make their message clear.

Explaining (adding information)

__But I meant__, you know, about the information on learning and assessments.

__So that means__ obviously our assignments and assessments.

Well, __basically what it means is__ that we have to take responsibility.

Rephrasing (saying the same thing in different words)

__What I meant was__ … basically, we've got to work together and study together.

__What I'm trying to say is__, in France we worked together a lot.

__What I'm saying is__, how does a study network add to all that?

INDEPENDENT STUDY

Using rephrasing and explaining expressions can make the conversation 'flow' more easily, and help you to sound more natural.

▶ Listen to online discussions and debates, and note down the most frequent expressions used.

TASK 5 Using explaining and rephrasing language

1 ◄))7.7 **Work in pairs. Listen to Clips 1–5 again and note down the words that the speakers stress. What types of words are these (verbs, nouns, etc.)?**

2 **Think of a method or concept you are familiar with from your area of study. Explain it to your partner using expressions from Academic Language.**

TASK 6 Preparing for and taking part in a seminar discussion

1 **Work in groups. Discuss how you would set up a study network to help you improve your EAP skills and language. Follow guidelines 1 and 2.**

  1 Before the discussion, decide who is going to note down the main ideas.

  2 During the discussion, try to reach agreement on the following points:
  - the type of network and its aims
  - the benefits of the network
  - how the group will work together
  - roles and responsibilities of each student
  - any challenges and how to overcome these
  - the resources needed.

2 **Take turns to explain your decisions to the class. Make sure each point in guideline 2 is included. After each presentation, ask questions to check your understanding.**

TASK 7 Critical thinking – evaluating the discussion

1 **Use the checklist to evaluate your performance.**

Questions	Yes	No
Did you contribute to the discussion?		
Did other students understand and respond to your points?		
Did you listen and respond to other students' points?		
Were you happy with the decisions made by the group?		

2 **Work in pairs. Discuss questions 1 and 2, giving reasons.**

  1 Do you think study networks are an effective way of studying?

  2 Would you be happy to take part in one?

Textbooks are one important source for both written assignments and presentations, but there are a wide range of other sources available. Two important reasons for reading textbooks are that they are generally seen as informative and reliable. When using textbooks and other sources, you need to evaluate them, for example by working out how useful, complete, and reliable they are. You also need to identify information which is relevant to your **purpose**; that is, what you are searching for and what you want to use the information for.

This module covers:
- Evaluating different sources
- Taking notes on detailed information
- Using notes to write a summary
- Identifying and referencing source material

TASK 1 Critical thinking – evaluating different sources

1 **Look at the types of source 1–6 and say which ones you (a) have used for your written assignments, and (b) might use in the future.**

   1 A page from a company website

   2 An article from an academic journal

   3 A textbook for university students

   4 An article from a national newspaper or news website

   5 A comment or thread on a blog

   6 An encyclopaedia entry

2 **Add any further sources that you might use.**

3 **Work in groups and discuss questions 1–4. Give reasons and examples where possible.**

   1 Which sources are most likely to be *accurate* and *reliable* – i.e. you can trust what they say?

   2 Which sources can be the most *current* – i.e. the information is recent and up-to-date?

   3 Which sources offer the most *depth* and *coverage* – i.e. are comprehensive and detailed?

   4 Which sources are the most *factual* – i.e. mainly present facts rather than opinion or interpretation?

4 **Look at the essay title and select sources from 1 that you could use in the essay.**

> **TITLE:** *'The more traditional sources of information such as textbooks are less relevant to students today than newer sources such as blogs.'* Discuss.

INDEPENDENT STUDY

Asking evaluative questions is a key academic skill.

▶ Search for examples of key words from your own area of study in a variety of sources, and evaluate the information using the four questions in Task 1.3.

TASK 2 Reading to build context

1 **Before you read, note down what you know about points 1–4.**

   1 The definition of a blog

   2 The history of blogging

   3 What bloggers do

   4 The relationship between companies and bloggers

2 **Read Text 1 and make notes on points 1–4 in 1 using information from the text.**

3 **Compare your answers in 1 to your notes in 2. What additional information is included in the text?**

4 **Who is the main audience of the text (i.e. who is the text mainly written for)?**

   a students

   b business people

   c bloggers

Blogging

One of the latest developments suitable for use by the online marketers is the 'weblog' or 'blog' – a kind of online personal journal. Although the term 'weblog' was first used by Robot Wisdom in December 1997, with the term 'blog' being introduced in 1999, the practice dates back to the early 1990s. At that time there were far fewer web sites, but without search engines it was not so easy to find them. Bloggers were individuals who surfed the web and listed, or logged, what they found interesting. When the bloggers added their own comments or reviews of the sites other web users would then access influential bloggers' pages for their opinions on those web sites. The focus of the blogs very quickly moved on beyond other web sites to encompass any and all subject areas that took the interest of the bloggers. Webopedia (www.webopedia.com) defines a blog as 'a web page that serves as a publicly accessible personal journal for an individual. Typically updated daily, blogs often reflect the personality of the author'. The last six words of this definition are the key to blogging. Bloggers have attitude. They have an opinion on everything, or a specific subject, and they are not shy about letting others know their views. Companies upset bloggers at their peril – a blog is another example of consumer generated media.

The boom year for blogging was 2002 as it moved from minority interest into the mainstream of the Internet. Setting up a blog also became easier as online hosts, for example, www.blogger. com, provided would be bloggers with a free web-based tool and web space. 2005 saw a boom in commercial organizations using blogs as part of a marketing strategy.

SOURCE: Gay, R., Charlesworth, A., & Esen, R. (2007). p.426. *Online Marketing: A Customer-Led Approach.* Oxford: Oxford University Press.

GLOSSARY

at their peril *(IDM)* to do sth that may be dangerous or cause them problems

encompass *(v)* to include a large number or range of things

ACADEMIC LANGUAGE ▸Language reference page 180

Noun phrases (5) Expressing key information using complex noun phrases

In academic texts, authors often use complex noun phrases to express concepts and ideas which include several different pieces of information. Many complex noun phrases use this pattern:

determiner (e.g. *the, their, one of the*) ➜ adjective(s) or noun(s) to modify the head noun ➜ the head noun ➜ extra information following the head noun.

The following example is built round the head noun *developments*:

One of the latest developments suitable for use by the online marketers

Understanding how complex noun phrases work will help you to understand academic texts. Using complex noun phrases helps you to write more clearly and concisely.

| determiner |
| adjective |
| head noun |
| information following the head noun |

TASK 3 Analysing complex noun phrases

1 Read sentences 1–4 from Text 1. The complex noun phrase in each sentence is underlined. For each noun phrase, identify the features a–d it includes.

a head noun

b determiner

c adjective / noun modifying the head noun

d extra information following the head noun

1 Bloggers were <u>individuals who surfed the web and listed, or logged, what they found interesting</u>.

2 When the bloggers added <u>their own comments or reviews of the sites</u> other web users would then access influential bloggers' pages for their opinions on those web sites.

3 The focus of the blogs very quickly moved on beyond other web sites to encompass <u>any and all subject areas that took the interest of the bloggers</u>.

4 Webopedia defines a blog as '<u>a web page that serves as a publicly accessible personal journal for an individual</u> […].

2 Write a two-word noun phrase to start the next sentence following each sentence (1–4) in 1. This two-word noun phrase should refer back to the complex noun phrase in the first sentence. This technique helps to make a text more cohesive.

Example: *One of the latest developments suitable for use by the online marketers* is the *'weblog' or 'blog' – a kind of online personal journal.* **These developments** …

TASK 4 Taking notes on detailed information

1 Read a later extract from the same text. Which *three* items from 1–5 are discussed?

1 the content of blogs
2 advice on how to write blogs
3 costs relating to blogs
4 advantages and disadvantages of commercial blogs
5 technical information for bloggers

TEXT 2

1 [1]As with web content in general, e-mail marketing and newsletters, the content of any organizational blog must be considered carefully, and this is the main problem for organizations considering this form of marketing communication. [2]Blogs are easy to start, but difficult to maintain. [3]Writing coherently is a difficult and time-consuming task. [4]Writing with a passion is even more so and blogs should show 'attitude' or they are simply press releases. [5]A comprehensive blogging strategy is not, therefore, a cheap option. [6]For the commercial organization, a blog would be a permanent, almost full-time job for a member of staff - plus back-up to cover holidays, illness, etc. [7]In some organizations, outsourcing the blog to a professional might be the best option. [8]Any expense comes from the marketing budget. [9]As with web content, the commercial blog should also be part of a managerial process in its publishing, with some kind of editorial control included. [10]After all, like a web site, for the customer the blog *is* the organization. [11]Leaving the global reputation of the organization to an unskilled member of staff is not good business.

2 [12]As with chat-rooms and bulletin boards the e-marketer can use blogs as a source of information. [13]Bloggers are usually enthusiasts on their own chosen subject, but they are also very often early adopters who spread the word on new products. [14]Offline market researchers spend a lot of time and money identifying and finding out the views of early adopters. [15]Online they identify themselves and make their opinions freely available.

SOURCE: Gay, R., Charlesworth, A., & Esen, R. (2007). p.429. *Online Marketing: A Customer-Led Approach*. Oxford: Oxford University Press.

GLOSSARY

early adopters *(n pl)* people who start to use a new technology or product as soon as it is available

outsource *(v)*, **outsourcing** *(n)* (*business*) to arrange for sb outside a company to provide goods or services for that company

press release *(n)* an official statement made to journalists by a large organization, a political party, or a government department

2 In paragraph 1 of Text 2 the main point is that blogs are 'easy to start, but difficult to maintain'. This is shown as being a *problem*. Work in pairs and complete the table using information from paragraph 1 (sentences 1–11).

Sentence	Main point	Type of information (explanation, evaluation, problems, solution)
1	• The content of a blog can be a problem	topic sentence
2–4	• Blogs – easy to start / hard to maintain	problems
	•	
	•	
5	• Blogging is expensive	explanation
6	•	
7	• Outsource the blog	
8–10	• Marketing budget covers the cost	
	•	
	•	
11	• Don't make unskilled staff responsible for an organization's reputation	

TASK 5 Using notes to write a summary

1 Look at the summary of sentences 1–6 from Text 2, paragraph 1. It uses the following structure:

   a an opening sentence with reference to the source text

   b a statement of the main point (problems) + evaluation + explanation

   Summary

   [a]In their text on blogging, Gay, Charlesworth, and Esen (2007, p.429) discuss various aspects of commercial blogging. [b]They identify several problems associated with blogging: working out the content; maintaining and writing appropriate content for a blog; the high costs involved as blogs need to be permanent, which is a full-time job.

2 Use your notes from the table in Task 4.2 to complete the summary of Text 2, paragraph 1. Write one sentence summarizing sentences 7–11. Use the following structure:

   statement of main point (solution) + explanation + evaluation

3 Take notes on the main point and explanations in paragraph 2 (sentences 12–15) using the same approach as in Task 4.2.

4 Use your notes to write a summary of paragraph 2 with the following structure:

   statement of main point (solution) + explanations.

TASK 6 Identifying and referencing source material

1 Read Texts 1 and 2 on pages 097 and 098 again. Note down:

   • all the types of source mentioned

   • any specific sources mentioned (e.g. titles of sources).

2 Work in groups. Identify information in Texts 1 and 2 which you could use to answer the essay title below.

   > TITLE: 'The more traditional sources of information such as textbooks are less relevant to students today than newer sources such as blogs.' Discuss.

3 Select two pieces of information that you identified in 2, and write a reference for each one.

   Example: *Gay, Charlesworth, and Esen (2007, p.426) argue that bloggers have 'attitude' and 'an opinion on everything'.*

4 What other sources could you use for the essay, and where could you find them?

TASK 7 Critical thinking – reviewing learning and planning

1 Work in groups and discuss questions 1–4.

   1 How has your reading helped your understanding of blogs?

   2 How has working in groups with other students helped you develop ideas for the essay?

   3 If you were going to write the essay, what would be your next steps in reading for and planning the essay?

   4 How can you record the sources you have used, in order to use them in a later piece of work?

When you are first given an essay question it is important to analyse the question and check your understanding. You can then move on to plan the three main elements of most essays – the **introduction**, the **main body**, and the **conclusion**. An introduction has a number of important roles. Firstly, it should gain the interest of the reader – this can be done by using an interesting fact, a quotation, or statistic. The introduction should also give a clear statement of your argument and explain exactly how you are going to answer the question (the **thesis statement**). It may also indicate the structure of the essay.

This module covers:

- Analysing essay titles
- Identifying the features of an introduction
- Evaluating thesis statements
- Writing an introduction

TASK 1 Analysing essay titles

1 **Look at the following essay title and the features that are highlighted. Identify similar features in essay titles 1–3. Not all titles have the same four features, but most will have at least two.**

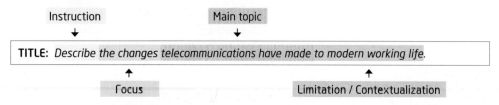

1 Evaluate the effects of telecommuting on family life.

2 To what extent has telecommunications enhanced company productivity?

3 Face to face communication is the most effective communication method. Discuss.

2 **Work in pairs. Read essay titles 1 and 2 and discuss the difference in focus.**

1 Evaluate the effects of telecommuting on family life.

2 Describe the effects of telecommuting on family life.

3 **Match the common essay verbs 1–7 to meanings a–g.**

1 analyse
2 compare
3 discuss
4 illustrate
5 justify
6 describe
7 evaluate

a to look at two or more things in order to show how they are similar to or different from each other

b to talk or write about something in detail and consider different ideas and opinions about it

c to say what someone or something is like by giving details about them

d to examine something closely, in detail

e to think about the positive and negative aspects of something and give an opinion about it

f to give a good and acceptable reason for something

g to make the meaning clear by giving examples

> **INDEPENDENT STUDY**
>
> Essay titles can include many different verbs but they can usually be divided into two groups: (1) those with an element of evaluation such as *discuss, evaluate,* and *justify*; and (2) those with an element of description, such as *explain* and *describe*.
>
> ▶ Next time you get an essay question, analyse the question to make sure you understand what is expected.

TASK 2 Identifying the features of an introduction

1 **Look at the tutor's comments on the introduction to this essay on the next page. Use the comments to complete the criteria (1–6) for writing a good introduction.**

> **TITLE:** *'Improving telecommunications networks are a positive development for human impact on the environment.' Discuss.*

gets the reader's interest well

Some of the fastest-growing economies in the world have recently achieved these levels of growth based mainly on their export trade. While this has brought many positive effects in the development of a number of societies, at the same time there has been widespread environmental damage. One significant positive development in recent years is in the vastly improved telecommunications sector; using this development to reduce man's negative impact on the environment is a key step towards reversing current global trends that harm the environment. This essay will look firstly at some key impacts man has had on the environment, followed by an analysis of the positive effect telecommunications can have in reducing this.

good contextualization moving towards more specific information

clear thesis statement giving position

aims clearly stated to show how the essay will be structured

A good introduction usually includes:	It may also include:
1 a statement to get the reader's interest	5 a definition
2	6 a citation.
3	
4	

2 Look at the essay title and answer questions 1–3.

> **TITLE:** *'Globalization would not have been possible without the development of the internet and telecommunications.' Discuss.*

1 What is the main topic of the essay?
2 What is the specific focus?
3 Does the question require evaluation?

3 Read the introduction to the essay in 2 and match features a–d with the highlighted sections 1–4.

[1]International trade, travel, and communications have been part of life for centuries; however, the speed of growth in the internet and telephony has significantly transformed the world. [2]In the 1930s in the UK it cost nearly a week's wages to make a three-minute phone call; today it is around one penny to make a one-minute call from the UK to India. More recently, internet usage has exploded, from 100 million users worldwide in the early 1990s to more than a billion in 2006 (Webster and Hamilton, 2009). [3]Were it not for the growth and falling costs of telecommunications then globalization is unlikely to have happened at the rate it did. [4]This essay will look first at the historical growth of the internet and telecommunications, followed by an assessment of their impact on the world.

a thesis statement ....
b rationale ....
c background information ....
d a citation ....

4 Sentences a–d form an introduction to the following essay question. Put the sentences in the correct order moving from general to specific information.

> **TITLE:** *'To what extent has the internet helped developing countries to progress?' Discuss.*

a This essay will argue that only a few developing countries have been able to progress beyond that status due to the effects of the internet. ....

b The internet has clearly transformed both the professional and private lives of the developed world, but the key question is how far it has impacted on the developing world. ....

c While some countries have been able to take full advantage of the advances in the reliability and reductions in the cost of communications, a great many more have been left behind. ....

d Former developing countries such as India have benefited from the growth and development of communications technology, with more than fifty per cent of the world's top 500 companies outsourcing IT and other parts of business there. (Hamilton and Webster, 2009). ....

TASK 3 Critical thinking – evaluating an introduction

1 Work in pairs. Look at the essay question and the introduction below. Evaluate the introduction using the criteria in Task 2.1.

> **TITLE:** *'Improving telecommunications networks are a positive development for human impact on the environment.' Discuss.*

> Companies would have faced numerous challenges when working internationally only thirty years ago. Today cultural issues still play a great role a company's potential for global success and trade barriers still mean that trade within a country is easier than international trade (Hamilton and Webster, 2009). Whilst the globalization of business has transformed the world for both businesses and consumers it is debatable to what extent this has been positive or negative, in particular for areas such as the environmental impact.

2 Rewrite the introduction so that it meets all the criteria in Task 2.1.

TASK 4 Evaluating thesis statements

1 A thesis statement usually carries the main argument of your essay. It should:
  - include a reference to the topic and focus of the essay
  - indicate your stance or position on the main question
  - makes your approach clear.

Look at the thesis statement from the essay introduction in Task 2.1 and identify the (a) writer's position, and (b) the main argument.

> One significant positive development in recent years is in the vastly improved telecommunications sector; using this development to reduce man's negative impact on the environment is a key step towards reversing current global trends that harm the environment ...

2 Read essay titles 1 and 2. Evaluate thesis statements a and b based on the criteria in 1 above.
  1 'Evaluate the effects of telecommuting on family life.'
     a Telecommuting is the process of using telecommunications tools to work from home.
     b This essay discusses the effect of telecommuting on family life, exploring the significance of flexible working arrangements.
  2 'Explain why an effective online marketing strategy is essential for modern companies.'
     a Companies now spend more money on online advertising than they do on television advertising.
     b Younger people use the internet more than television and other media – therefore it is essential for a company to have an effective online strategy.

TASK 5 Writing a thesis statement

1 Work in pairs. Read the essay title and discuss your opinion on the effects of telecommuting (working from home using the telephone, email, etc.).

> **TITLE:** *Evaluate the effects of telecommuting on family life.*

2 Decide if the effects of telecommuting (1–5) are advantages or disadvantages. Add at least one advantage and one disadvantage of your own.
  1 The boundary between work and home life is not clear.
  2 There is no clear time for starting and finishing work.
  3 You spend less time travelling.
  4 You spend less money travelling.
  5 You need more space to work in at home.

3 Use your ideas from 2 to write a thesis statement for the essay in 1.

Stating aims and purpose

A statement of purpose can be written in a personal or impersonal style. Although both are possible, it is more usual to use an impersonal style to present your aims. Compare:

Personal	**Impersonal**
In this essay I plan to …	*The aim of this essay is to …*
I intend to look at / focus on / discuss …	*This essay will look at / focus on / discuss …*
I will argue that …	*The effects of … will be examined.*
I plan to examine the effects of …	*It could be said / argued that …*

TASK 6 Stating aims using an impersonal style

1 **Rewrite statements 1–5 so that they are more impersonal in style.**

  1 In my opinion, telecommuting has a negative effect on family life and I want to discuss the effects in this essay.

  2 In this essay I will look at the positive and negative effects of the internet on the developing world.

  3 I intend to show that blogging is an essential marketing tool in any modern marketing communications package.

  4 First I plan to examine the history of blogging followed by my analysis of its effectiveness in business-to-business communication.

  5 I will argue that globalization would not have been possible were it not for the development of the internet.

2 **Select one of the essay questions in this module and write a sentence stating the aims.**

TASK 7 Writing an introduction

1 **You are going to write an introduction of about 120 words. Read the essay title and points 1 and 2 below.**

> **TITLE:** *'The development of the internet has had the biggest single impact on modern life.' Discuss.*

  1 Read the essay outline to help you plan your introduction.
  Paragraph 1 – What factors have had an impact on modern life.
  Paragraph 2 – Why other factors such as international travel, the rise of English, and greater political unity have had less of an impact.
  Paragraph 3 – Why the internet has had the most significant impact – changes to education, working lives, social structures, and health

  2 When you write your introduction, make sure that:
  - you move from a general statement to more specific information
  - you include a thesis statement containing a clear opinion, not just a statement of fact
  - the thesis statement indicates the structure of the essay, OR you include an additional sentence outlining the main points your essay will cover (a statement of purpose).

Sample answer page 190

TASK 8 Evaluating peers' introductions

1 **Work in pairs. Evaluate your partner's introduction using questions 1–4.**

  1 Does it move from general to specific information?

  2 Does it include a thesis statement?

  3 Is the opinion in the thesis statement clear? If not, rewrite it in your own words.

  4 Does it indicate the essay's structure? What order would you expect the points to be in?

Vocabulary Essay verbs

When you first read an essay title, it is important to identify whether the focus is on a descriptive or evaluative approach. You can do this by focussing on the verb used in the title, as it will express what a tutor expects of you. Understanding and interpreting essay verbs also helps to inform your choice of essay structure when planning, and how to express your thesis statement in the introduction.

TASK 1 Identifying essay focus

1 Put the common essay verbs under the correct heading.

analyse   compare   contrast   describe   discuss   evaluate   illustrate   justify

Essays with an element of description	**Essays with an element of evaluation**

2 Match thesis statements 1–6 with an appropriate essay verb.

compare   demonstrate   discuss   examine   evaluate   illustrate

1 This essay will first address the benefits of government funding primary education, and then consider the situation regarding secondary education.

2 This essay will show the function and process of photosynthesis.

3 This essay will look in detail at two of the main theories of economic growth.

4 This essay will argue that the internet has had the greatest impact on the modern world, by giving examples of where and how it has impacted on everyone's life.

5 This essay will explain the four key theories of motivation.

6 This essay will judge the success of the recent government environmental policies.

3 Match the two essay verbs to the plans below.

discuss   contrast

PLAN 1	**PLAN 2**
• **Introduction** Main argument and opinion	• **Introduction** Introduce the differing sides
• **Paragraph 1** Alternative arguments	• **Paragraph 1** One theory of economic growth
• **Paragraph 2** Justification of main argument	• **Paragraph 2** Second theory of economic growth
• **Conclusion** Restatement of main argument	• **Paragraph 3** Key differences
	• **Conclusion** Summary of key distinguishing points

TASK 2 Using essay verbs

1 Rewrite the sentences using an appropriate essay verb.

1 This essay talks about the problems of urbanization. → This essay will discuss the issue of urbanization

2 This essay decides which theory is better.

3 This essay tells you the main points of Macro-economic theory.

4 This essay explains why further research is needed in the field.

2 Look for essay titles in your own area of study and do the following tasks.

1 Decide if the essay is evaluative or descriptive.

2 Create a thesis statement for the essay.

3 Draft a rough plan for the essay.

ACADEMIC FOCUS: REFERENCING

LEARNING OBJECTIVES

This unit covers:

Listening

- Using visuals to assist with note-taking in lectures
- Using notes to write a summary
- Understanding and using references to visual information

Speaking

- Using a text to support an opinion
- Using language for managing a discussion
- Referring to other people's ideas

Reading

- Recognizing objectivity in a text
- Identifying and understanding references in a text
- Using source texts in writing

Writing

- Identifying and analysing types of citation in context
- Paraphrasing ideas from a source
- Planning and writing an accurately-referenced paragraph

Vocabulary

- Selecting and using linking expressions
- Using cohesive language in texts

Discussion

1 **Work in pairs and discuss questions 1 and 2.**

   1 What does the word *innovation* suggest to you?

   2 How important is innovation for human progress?

2 **Which of 1–3 is most important for your personal and academic development?**

   1 innovative systems, e.g. in everyday activities such as banking

   2 innovative solutions to difficult problems, e.g. reducing unemployment

   3 innovative technology, e.g. in a business or educational context

3 **Work in groups. Think of an innovative product or practice in one or more of the following areas 1–4.**

   1 education

   2 the environment

   3 business

   4 technology

   Explain why you think it is innovative. Use the following phrases to help you.

   In terms of innovation I think that …

   A recent business practice that I find interesting is …

Most lecturers use visuals in the form of slides. These may include text, images, or both. They are intended to illustrate or help you understand what the lecturer is saying. You will need to be able to deal with visual information while you listen. Some visuals contain limited information such as key terms and concepts; others are more complex. Recognizing phrases used to refer to visuals will help you understand the key information.

This module covers:

- Using visuals to assist with note-taking in lectures
- Using notes to write a summary
- Understanding and using references to visual information

TASK 1 Predicting content using visual information

1 **You are going to watch extracts from a lecture. Look at slides 1–6 and predict (a) the subject of the lecture, and (b) the purpose of each slide.**

Major construction projects: innovation & risk in airport design

- Introduction and overview
- Two projects: Chek Lap Kok (Hong Kong International airport) and London Heathrow Terminal 5
- Analysis of risk
- Evaluating the projects

Slide 1

Slide 2

Slide 3

Slide 4

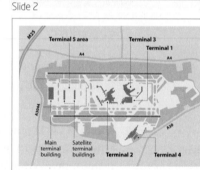

Slide 5

Characteristics of major infrastructure projects

1 Serious risk in most projects
2 Non-standard technology and design
3 Many different groups involved
4 Main idea decided early – "lock-in"
5 Changes during the project
6 Planning for "unplanned" events
7 Poor information about costs, benefits, and risk
8 Increases in costs   (Flyvbjerg, 2009)

Slide 6

TASK 2 Using visuals to assist with note-taking

1 ▷8.1 **Watch Extract 1 and note down one piece of information for each point on slide 1.**

2 ▷8.2 **Read the notes below on slide 2. Watch Extract 2 and add any necessary details.**

Hong Kong

- old airport Kai Tak (NE of city)
  - risky location – planes had to fly low
  - limited space for development

- new airport site Chek Lap Kok (NE of Lantau)
  - engineering challenge – local geography
  - one of largest construction projects of 20th C
  - architects: Foster + Partners
  - completed in 6 years
  - opened in 1998, a year later

Abbreviations
NE = north-east
NW = north-west
SE = south-east
SW = south-west

3 **Evaluate the notes in 2 using questions 1–3.**

1 Are they *complete* (do they include all the main information)?

2 Are they *accurate* (are dates, names, and locations correct)?

3 Are they *clear* and easy to understand?

4 ▷8.3 **Watch Extract 3 and make similar notes on the main points relating to slides 3–5. Evaluate your notes using the questions in 3.**

Referring to visual information Using prepositions and directions

To refer to parts of a slide, or to refer to a geographical location or direction, lecturers often use phrases based on prepositions.

> **On the right-hand side**, you can see the old airport, Kai Tak - it's situated in **the north-east of the city**.
>
> The island known as Chek Lap Kok, **here on the left of the slide**, **off the north coast of Lantau**.
>
> **Near the top of the slide** is the passenger terminal, **on the east side**, **there**. The cargo area is **in the bottom half of the slide**, **to the south**.
>
> The other area **in the centre of the slide** is currently not developed.

You can also use similar phrases when referring to visuals in a presentation.

TASK 3 Using references to visual information

1 ▶8.2 **Watch Extract 2 again and tick the expressions you hear.**

in the top right hand corner   on the left-hand side of the slide
on the left of the slide   on the opposite side   on the east side   to the south
in the centre of the slide   situated to the west of the city   at the top of the slide

2 **Use expressions from 1 to complete the text, based on the information in slide 3.**

As you can see [1]........................., in Hong Kong International Airport, the northern runway is situated [2]......................... of the island of Chek Lap Kok. [3]......................... is the southern runway, while [4]......................... of that is the logistics and cargo area. The train station is located [5]......................... of the island, and if you look here [6]........................., there is a large area designated for expansion.

3 **Work in pairs and practise describing slides 4 and 5 in a similar way.**

INDEPENDENT STUDY

Lecturers vary the amount of detail they include on each slide, from a few key words to many bullet points.

▶ Watch a lecture on an open-source website, e.g. TED.com, and evaluate how the slides support and help you understand the lecture.

TASK 4 Using notes to write a summary

1 **Read the summary of the information in slide 2, based on the notes from Task 2.2.**

Hong Kong's old airport, Kai Tak, was in a risky location as planes had to fly low over the city to land. There was no space to develop the site so it was decided to build a new airport on the island of Chek Lap Kok, off the north coast of Lantau. This presented a major engineering challenge because of the local geography, and it became one of the largest construction projects of the 20th century. The new airport was designed by the architects Foster & Partners, and took six years to complete. It opened in 1998.

2 **Select one of slides 3–5 and write a similar summary based on your notes in Task 2.4.**

TASK 5 Understanding referencing on visuals

1 ▶8.4 **Watch Extract 4 and take notes on the bullet points in slide 6.**

2 **Work in pairs and compare your notes on slide 6. Discuss what information helped you to write your notes, including the language used by the lecturer.**

3 **In Extract 4 the lecturer refers frequently to the work of the Danish academic Professor Bent Flyvbjerg. Watch the extract again or read the transcript on page 215, and note down the phrases the lecturer uses to refer to Flyvbjerg's work.**

TASK 6 Critical thinking – responding to visual information

1 **Look back at slides 1–6 in Task 1. Why do you think the lecturer chose to present the information in this way?**

2 **Do you find it easier to understand slides with visual information or mainly text? Why?**

8B Speaking Seminar discussions (6)

When discussing a text in a seminar, you will often be asked to give your opinion, and to support it using information from the text. You may also need to check that you have understood another speaker, and that they have understood you. It is also useful to refer to what other people say and not just give your opinion in isolation.

This module covers:

- Using a text to support an opinion
- Using language for managing a discussion
- Referring to other people's ideas

TASK 1 Previewing the topic of a seminar

1 Work in pairs and discuss what *technological innovation* means for a company. Think about:

   a why companies need to be aware of innovation in their field

   b the opportunities and threats created by innovation.

2 Compare your answers with another student. Add any other opportunities or threats that you can think of.

TASK 2 Using a text to support an opinion

1 Read opinions 1–3. Then find information in Text 1 on page 199 to support each opinion.

   1 Innovation can help to make a firm more competitive.

   2 Technological innovation means a company can be based anywhere.

   3 Technological improvements mean that not only large companies are global.

2 ◀))8.5 Listen to Extract 1 from a seminar in which two students are discussing the ideas in Text 1. Note down the ideas from the text that each student refers to.

3 ◀))8.5 Listen to Extract 1 again or read the transcript on page 215. Note down the phrases the speakers use to (a) check their understanding, and (b) refer to what the other person has said.

ACADEMIC LANGUAGE

Managing a discussion

In discussions, speakers often use a range of expressions to check understanding and to refer to what other people have said.

Checking that you understand	**Checking that other people understand you**
So what you're saying is ...	*Do you see what I mean?*
If I understand you correctly, you think / mean ...	*Do you follow what I'm saying?*
So do you mean ...?	*Does that make sense?*

Referring to what someone else has said

As you said, ...

And following on from that point, ...

You made an interesting point about ...

TASK 3 Using language for checking understanding

1 **Complete the extract with expressions from Academic Language.**

A But it's common sense that spending money on research and development is an advantage to a firm, isn't it?

B ¹ .... companies are going to be more successful the more they spend? I'm not sure I agree with that. That means that a lot of companies must waste a lot of money never really going anywhere. I mean, if it was that easy everyone would do it. ² .... ?

A Well, yes, I think so ... ³ .... , you think a lot of money is invested and effectively it's wasted. They never get it back.

B Exactly. It's not that simple. If research equals success, equals profit ... everyone would do it. ⁴ .... , a lot of the time there's no return on the investment.

2 ◀)) 8.6 **Listen to Extract 2 and check your answers.**

INDEPENDENT STUDY

There will often be times when you don't understand something in a text or a discussion.

▶ Asking tutors questions to check that you've understood something correctly is an important interaction.

TASK 4 Referring to other people's ideas

1 ◀)) 8.7, 8.8 **Listen to Extracts 3 and 4 from a discussion based on the following statement. Compare the two extracts and answer questions 1 and 2.**

Companies that fail to innovate will be unsuccessful.

1 In which extract do the speakers refer to what other people have said?

2 How does it affect the discussion when the speakers <u>don't</u> refer to each other's ideas?

2 ◀)) 8.7, 8.8 **Listen to Extracts 3 and 4 again or look at the transcript on page 216. Note down the phrases the speakers use to refer to what other people have said.**

TASK 5 Preparing for and taking part in a seminar discussion

1 **You are going to take part in a discussion based on the following statement. Read questions 1–4 and note down your ideas.**

'Companies who do not innovate are putting themselves at risk.'

1 Why do companies innovate?

2 What is the risk of innovating?

3 What are the risks to a company when their competitors innovate with new technology?

4 What type of company would be negatively affected by these innovations?

   music downloads   mobile phones   online holiday booking

2 **Read Text 2 on page 200 and identify any information you could use to support your ideas.**

3 **Identify any information from Text 1 on page 199 that you could use in this seminar.**

4 **Make notes on the points from Texts 1 and 2 that you want to refer to in the discussion.**

5 **Work in groups and discuss the statement in 1. Make sure that you:**

• refer to your notes on any useful points from the texts

• check that you understand other speakers and that they understand you

• refer to any points made by other speakers.

TASK 6 Reflecting on performance in a discussion

1 **In your groups, discuss your own performance and note down areas for improvement. Use questions 1–3 to help you.**

1 Did you manage to make points based on your notes on the texts?

2 Did you check your understanding, and other people's understanding?

3 Did you refer to any points made by other speakers?

2 **Think of at least one way to improve your participation in a future discussion.**

Sources are typically used by writers to strengthen a point that they want to make. Noticing how sources are used in a text can help you to integrate them effectively into your own writing. The use of more than one source can also make writing more effective. Academic texts frequently use the passive voice, which is seen as more impersonal than expressions such as 'I'. Understanding how and why these features are used can improve your own writing.

This module covers:
- Recognizing objectivity in a text
- Identifying and understanding references in a text
- Using source texts in writing

TASK 1 Previewing a topic

1 **Work in pairs and discuss questions 1–3.**

  1 In what ways can competition between companies be both positive and negative?

  2 Pharmaceutical companies make drugs that help sick people. Is it right that these companies make a profit? Should drugs be available to anyone who needs them, not only people that can afford them?

  3 *Nanotechnology* is now used in pharmaceutical innovations. Do you know any other products that contain nanotechnology?

TASK 2 Identifying the main ideas in a longer text

1 **Read the text quickly and identify which paragraphs 1–5 contain main ideas a–e.**

  a The advantages and disadvantages of nanotechnology

  b The positive and negative effects for society of competition between companies

  c The rights and wrongs of making money from drugs

  d A definition of nanotechnology

  e The negative effects of monopolies on competition

2 **Read the two paragraphs on competition in more detail. Note down any further ideas on the positive and negative aspects of competition between companies.**

3 **Read the two paragraphs on nanotechnology in more detail. Note down any information you could use to answer the following essay title.**

> **TITLE:** *Discuss the advantages and disadvantages of nanotechnology.*

TASK 3 Recognizing objectivity in a text

1 **Read sentences 1–5. Which sentences do *not* state whose views are being expressed?**

  1 However, scenarios have been suggested where such technology, once released, may turn all matter into 'grey goo'.

  2 Marx was a fierce critic of the motivation for investment or what he referred to as 'accumulation'.

  3 Joseph Schumpter saw capitalism as being a process of 'creative destruction'.

  4 The pharmaceutical industries are often accused of abusing their monopoly powers.

  5 It is argued that they seek to exploit large monopoly profits by selling drugs which are heavily branded to rich people in the developed world.

2 **What language in sentences 1–5 helped you to answer the question in 1?**

3 **In the sentences you identified in 1, why do the authors *not* refer to the person or organization whose views are being expressed?**

1 The most recent of the new technologies is nanotechnology. This technology enables materials and machines to be created that operate at the nanoscale. A nanometre is approximately the size of a billionth of a metre. To put this into context, each page of this book is about 100,000 nanometres in thickness. The uses of this technology are not yet at an advanced scale. However, <u>it is thought</u> that the new technologies will be able to lead to advances in all of the following areas:

1 providing renewable clean energy
2 supplying clean water globally
3 improving health and helping people live longer
4 healing and preserving the environment
5 making information technology available to all
6 enabling space development.

2 A review of websites such as www.nano.gov, www.nanotech-now.com shows enormous potential. Already carbon 'nanotubes' have been developed to produce light much more efficiently. Their use in solar panels <u>is seen</u> as being able to dramatically cut the cost of solar power. There is the prospect that the technology will also help in a range of energy reducing activities. Nanomachines may well be able to be introduced into the body and perform micro-operations not possible with existing medical technology. However, scenarios have been suggested where such technology, once released, may turn all matter into 'grey goo'. Whilst this appears to be highly unrealistic the reality is that there is not clear evidence of exactly how such small particles might behave when set free into biological systems (see www.worldchanging.com. This website offers a balanced view on the costs and benefits of technology).

3 Indeed there are many people who question the real motivation for developing higher levels of technological developments. We have seen how technology is important for enhancing competition but what happens if this then becomes a weapon for actually replacing competition by establishing and creating market dominance? For many commentators this is an inevitable consequence of capitalism with the primary aim of the development of the technology not being for the good of society but for the ability of one business to make more profit for itself. The German philosopher and economist Karl Marx was a fierce critic of the motivation for investment or what he referred to as 'accumulation'. For Marx it was an essential paradox of capitalism that businesses were forced to try to do better than the competition by constantly having to invest. This meant that all businesses <u>were constantly forced</u> to spend more and more on investment and yet face falling profits. Later Marxists argued that in fact what would happen is that the strongest would survive and capitalism would become dominated by large monopoly enterprises. In the 20th century an influential writer in this area was Joseph Schumpter. He saw capitalism as being a process of 'creative destruction' by which he meant that companies through innovation would be able to create monopoly positions. However, they would face the prospect of other businesses developing alternative technologies which enabled them to provide new products or cut costs. Capitalism would be destructive in the sense that old companies, products and processes would decline to be replaced by newly created and better ones.

4 For believers in free market capitalism all technology reduces costs and improves choice for consumers. Complex technologies involve high sums of money spent on research and development which becomes a barrier to entry into an industry. The pharmaceutical industries are often accused of abusing their monopoly powers. However, developing new medicines can involve very expensive research and development costs which companies are keen to get back. One way of doing this is to protect themselves through intellectual property rights in the form of copyright or patents. If a dominant market position <u>can be established</u> then it can be very difficult for new entrants. Even where such new entrants develop less technologically expensive alternatives the dominant company can seek to protect its position through aggressive marketing.

5 This raises ethical questions. Many people are critical of the power of the 'Big pharma'. It is argued that they seek to exploit large monopoly profits by selling drugs which are heavily branded to rich people in the developed world. This could be justified in this context as health systems in the developed world enable most people who need these drugs to acquire them (although not all people). In the case of global markets though there is a problem. In the developing world low incomes and poorly developed health systems mean people here do not have access to the drugs they need. These drugs could now be produced more cheaply and sold as generic drugs by local companies under licence but <u>are prevented</u> from doing this by the reluctance of the western pharmaceutical companies to 'give away' their intellectual property rights.

SOURCE: Wetherly, P. & Otter, D. 2011. pp.82-3. *The Business Environment: Themes and Issues* 2nd ed. Oxford: Oxford University Press.

GLOSSARY

barrier to entry *(n phr)* something that makes it hard for companies to enter a market

grey goo *(n phr)* a useless material

intellectual property rights *(n phr)* the ownership of an idea

paradox *(n)* a situation that is hard to understand because it contains two opposite characteristics

The passive (1) Understanding the use of active and passive forms

Academic texts often contain a mixture of active and passive verb forms. In sentences using the active form, the subject identifies the agent who carries out the action:

*Later Marxists **argued** that in fact what would happen is that the strongest would survive.*

Using the passive form allows the author to:

(1) keep the focus on an object, action, idea, or event rather than who or what carries it out:

*Already carbon 'nanotubes' **have been developed** to produce light much more efficiently.*

(2) be objective - i.e. to make a statement without expressing their own stance:

***It is argued** that they seek to exploit large monopoly profits …*

Referring to the agent is optional and normally uses *by* + a noun phrase:

*These drugs could now be produced more cheaply and sold as generic drugs **by local companies**.*

TASK 4 Using active and passive forms

1 **Correct the mistake in each sentence. Then decide whether sentences 1–6 are in the active or passive form.**

  1 Most companies have been protected their profits by ensuring they hold intellectual property rights.

  2 Many companies have accused of trying to obtain a monopoly to limit competition.

  3 It expects that nanotechnology will provide many benefits for society.

  4 Millions of dollars have spent on researching thousands of medical procedures and drugs.

  5 Marxists are argued that capitalism is not good for innovation.

  6 This meant that all businesses constantly forced to spend more and more money on R&D.

2 **Look back at the underlined examples of the passive form in the text and say why the authors have chosen to use the form in this context.**

TASK 5 Identifying and understanding references in a text

1 **Scan paragraphs 2 and 3 of the text and identify the five references to external sources.**

2 **Match each reference to function a or b.**

  a Offering further information on a topic. (x3)

  b Presenting a stance on a topic. (x2)

3 **According to the text, which <u>two</u> stances from a–c are supported by Marx?**

  a Investments are made by companies for the good of society.

  b Companies invest to beat other firms.

  c Capitalism will lead to less competition.

4 **Do the authors use Schumpter to support or oppose Marx's stance on monopolies?**

5 **Summarize the stance of Marx and Schumpter in one sentence.**

TASK 6 Using source texts in writing

1 **Read the two paragraphs on page 113. Identify features a–e in paragraph 2, following the model in paragraph 1.**

  a Topic sentence

  b Explanation

  c Reference to a source

  d Paraphrase of the information in the source

  e Evaluation

Paragraph 1

Vast sums of money are spent by companies attempting to gain a competitive advantage over other firms. It is therefore understandable that firms attempt to maximize profit at the point of sale. As Wetherly and Otter (2011) point out, pharmaceutical companies predominantly sell into the developed world where a high price can be charged for a branded drug. Whilst this may be considered unethical by some it is perhaps inevitable considering the risks involved when making such a capital outlay.

Paragraph 2

Some would argue that competition is largely for the good of the consumer. Competition can both drive down prices and increase choices. However, according to Marx and Schumpter (cited in Wetherly and Otter, 2011) competition is actually likely to lead to a decrease in choice as one firm comes to dominate the market. So in the long term competition may neither drive down prices nor increase the product range, but in actual fact have the opposite effect.

2 You are going to write two paragraphs for an essay using the text on page 111 as a main source. Use topic sentences 1 and 2 to start each paragraph. Note down any further information from the text that you can include in each paragraph.

   1 Even a company with a monopoly faces the risk of competition from potential competitors.

   2 Companies aim for a monopoly, or at least a controlling position, in order to protect themselves from competition.

3 Compare the original quotation from the text and the paraphrase used in paragraph 1.

   Original quotation: *Many people are critical of the power of the 'Big pharma'. It is argued that they seek to exploit large monopoly profits by selling drugs which are heavily branded to rich people in the developed world.*

   Paraphrase: *As Wetherly and Otter (2011) point out, pharmaceutical companies mostly sell into the developed world where a high price can be charged for a branded drug.*

4 Rewrite the information you selected in 2 using your own words. Introduce it using the phrases below.

   According to Wetherly and Otter (2011) ...

   As Wetherly and Otter (2011) point out ...

   Wetherly and Otter (2011) state that ...

5 Look at the final sentences in paragraphs 1 and 2 again. Use these as models to write a concluding sentence for each of your own paragraphs. Make sure your concluding sentence says how the information you selected from the text relates to, or supports, the topic sentence.

6 Write your two paragraphs in full. Make sure that each paragraph includes:

   • the topic sentence
   • an explanation or example to support the topic sentence
   • a reference to a source
   • a paraphrase of the information in the source
   • a comment on the importance of the information in the source.

TASK 7 Critical thinking – evaluating your writing

1 Compare your paragraphs with another student. Use questions 1–4 to evaluate (a) your own writing, and (b) your partner's writing.

   1 Is there an explanation or example to support the topic sentence?

   2 Does the selected information from the source support the main point in the topic sentence?

   3 Is the information rewritten in your / their own words?

   4 Does the concluding sentence provide a comment on the information in the source?

When writing a paragraph, it is important to provide a balance of your own ideas and material from other sources. When citing sources, you need to decide whether to **summarize**, **paraphrase**, or directly **quote** the material in the original source. Paraphrasing involves rewriting the vocabulary and grammar of a short piece of text, using your own language. In order to avoid plagiarism, you also need to correctly reference the material.

This module covers:

- Identifying and analysing types of citation in context
- Paraphrasing ideas from a source
- Planning and writing an accurately-referenced paragraph

TASK 1 Gaining an overview of a source text

1 **Read Text 1 and decide which sentence expresses the main point.**

Innovation - Research and development

TEXT 1

Innovation is a key function of any business. [...] R&D is one form of innovation and is directly associated with developing existing products or creating new ones. Many businesses spend vast sums of money on R&D (especially the pharmaceutical industry) as this can extend the **product life cycle** by developing new ways to use existing products (such as increasing the functionality of a mobile phone); or by indicating new directions for the company (such as Apple - branching off from PCs to iPods and iPhones). If successfully applied, R&D can allow the business to find gaps in the existing markets or of course open up new markets entirely.

However, R&D is expensive, time consuming, and, if in the wrong direction, can be quite destructive for a business. The examples of Enron, where the creed was 'innovate or die', or the banking crisis in 2008, serve as examples of innovation that was inappropriate and badly managed.

SOURCE: Clark, P., Golden, P., O'Dea, M., Weiner, J., Woolrich, P., & Olmos, J. (2009). pp.268-9. *IB Business and Management Course Companion.* Oxford: Oxford University Press.

GLOSSARY

R&D *(n)* research and development

2 **Decide which sentence 1–3 is a summary, a paraphrase, or a quotation.**

1 Clark et al. (2009, p.268) state that 'innovation is a key function of any business'.

2 Two key purposes of Research and Development are identifying gaps in existing markets and developing brand new markets (Clark et al., 2009, p.268).

3 In their text 'Innovation – Research and development', Clark et al. (2009, pp.268–9) discuss the role played by R&D in product development, and warn that R&D is both expensive and time-consuming, as well as potentially destructive.

TASK 2 Identifying and analysing types of citation in context

1 **Read the body paragraph, and complete column A of the table with the terms below.**

~~rationale~~   definition plus a quotation   ~~example~~   topic sentence
paraphrase   concluding sentence including evaluation   ~~summary~~

Sentence	A What the sentence is expressing	B Whose ideas	C Whose language
1		*the student*	*the student*
2		*Clark et al.*	
3		*the student + Clark et al.*	*the student + Clark et al.*
4	*rationale*		
5	*summary*		
6	*example*		
7			

2 **Complete columns B and C, noting whose idea is stated in each sentence of the paragraph, and whose language is used to express it.**

[1]There are several different types of innovation in business. [2]One type of innovation is research and development (R&D) into new product areas (Clark, Golden, O'Dea, Weiner, Woolrich, & Olmos, 2009, p.269). [3]Innovation involves creating something new, and is a 'key function of any business' (Clark et al. 2009, p.268). [4]One reason why businesses need innovation is because technology is developing rapidly, and businesses need to keep up with these developments. [5]Clark et al. (2009, p.269) also state that, although it is expensive and possibly risky, R&D can increase the life of an existing product and branch out into new product areas. [6]For instance, British clothing designer Paul Smith has successfully extended his brand into perfumes. [7]These developments show the importance of product innovation through R&D in a business context.

TASK 3 Choosing the most appropriate form of citation

1 Read Text 2 and note down the essential information relating to (a) innovation, and (b) creativity.

Innovation and creativity

TEXT 2

[1]Successful entrepreneurs and owners of small businesses are innovative and creative. [2]**Innovation**, or the production of something new or original, results from the ability to conceive of and create new and unique products, services or processes. [3]Entrepreneurs identify opportunities in the marketplace and visualize creative new ways to take advantage of them. [4]Innovation is usually included in any definition of creativity. [5]Although not all entrepreneurs develop new products or services, or discover new resources, every person who establishes an enterprise, and who adds value and ensures that an enterprise continues to exist (thereby developing job opportunities) is involved in economic creation. [6]'**Creativity**' refers to the creation of something new, for example, the creation of a new business by developing a new product or service, building an organization by financial manipulation, reshaping an existing business, or creating a business that will survive on its own and generate a financial fortune as testimony to the entrepreneur's skill. [7]Basically, creativity involves new ideas, and any application of these new ideas is based on innovation.

[8]However, as well as involving the identification of opportunities and solutions, creativity can also involve the adjustment or refinement of existing procedures or products. [9]Although entrepreneurs understand the importance of innovation, they often view the risk and the high investment that the development of innovative products or services requires as being out of proportion to the potential profit. [10]This explains why entrepreneurs often creatively adapt innovations of competitors by, for example, product adjustments, imaginative marketing and client service. [11]Thus their creativity finds expression on the continuum of innovation and adaptation.

SOURCE: du Toit, G. S., Erasmus B. J., & Syrydom, J. W. (2010). p.49. *Introduction to Business Management* 8th ed. Oxford: Oxford University Press.

GLOSSARY

continuum *(n)* a series of similar items in which each is almost the same as the ones next to it but the last is very different from the first

result from *(v)* to happen because of sth else that happened first

testimony *(n)* a thing that shows that sth else exists or is true

2 Identify the sentence(s) from Text 2 which gives information for items 1–3.

1 a definition of *innovation*

2 an explanation of *creativity* with examples

3 how entrepreneurs use innovation and creativity

3 Decide if you would cite each item 1–3 in 2 above as a quotation, a paraphrase, or a summary. Use the following guidelines to help you.

- Is the original sentence clear, brief, and well-written – would it work well as a *quotation*?

- Does the original sentence contain some useful and relevant points, which you could put into your own words – as a *paraphrase*?

- Is the original material more than two sentences? Can some points (e.g. supporting ideas and examples) be missed out – would it work best as a *summary*?

The passive (2) Using active and passive forms to change the focus of a sentence

When you paraphrase a sentence, you need to decide on your main focus, and whether this needs to change from the focus of the original sentence. This determines whether you use an active or passive verb form.

In the following sentence from Text 2, *innovation* is the main focus. The verb is in the passive form because *innovation* has something 'done' to it, rather than 'doing' something:

> *Innovation **is** usually **included** in any definition of creativity.*

If you change the focus (or subject) of the sentence to *definition of creativity* or *researchers*, you have to change the verb to the active form because the focus has moved to the agent of what is 'done' to *innovation*:

> *Any definition of creativity usually **includes** innovation.*
>
> *Researchers usually **include** innovation in any definition of creativity.*

TASK 4 Using active and passive forms

1 **Read sentences 1–5, adapted from Texts 1 and 2, and:**
   - identify the topic (the main focus of the sentence)
   - find the main verb, and decide whether it is in the active or passive.

   1 Many businesses spend large amounts of money on R&D.
   2 R&D is directly associated with developing existing products or creating new ones.
   3 R&D can extend the product life cycle by finding new ways to use existing products.
   4 Entrepreneurs often creatively adapt innovations by their competitors.
   5 If successfully applied, R&D can allow the business to find gaps in the existing markets.

2 **Rewrite the sentences from 1, so that you change the focus. Use the appropriate form of the verb, active or passive, and the opening phrases below.**

   Example: *Entrepreneurs **identify** opportunities in the marketplace.* (active)
   ↦*Opportunities in the marketplace **are identified** by entrepreneurs.* (passive)

   1 Large amounts of money _____ .
   2 Researchers _____ .
   3 Product life cycles _____ .
   4 Competitors' innovations _____ .
   5 If entrepreneurs _____ .

> **INDEPENDENT STUDY**
>
> The passive form is frequently used in academic texts.
>
> ▸Find two or more texts related to your area of study. Identify the verb forms and decide whether they are in the active or passive, and why.

TASK 5 Paraphrasing a sentence from a source

1 **Look again at sentence 7 from Text 2. Decide which paraphrase 1–2 is the most effective. Use the critical questions below to guide you.**

   Sentence 7: Basically, creativity involves new ideas, and any application of these new ideas is based on innovation.

   Paraphrase 1: Creativity essentially means thinking of new ideas and innovatively applying these ideas to something. (du Toit, Erasmus, & Syrydom, 2010, p.49).

   Paraphrase 2: Essentially, creativity comprises novel thoughts, and any use of these novel thoughts is built on originality. (du Toit, Erasmus, & Syrydom, 2010, p.49).

   Critical questions
   - Is the paraphrase clear and easy to understand?
   - Does the paraphrase contain all the points of the original sentence?
   - Does the paraphrase follow a different sentence pattern to the original, and use some different word forms?
   - Is there a balance of original words from the source, e.g. key terms, and new / different words?
   - Is a reference included, and is it correct?

2 Write a similar paraphrase of sentence 8 from Text 2. Follow guidelines 1–4.

Sentence 8: However, as well as involving the identification of opportunities and solutions, creativity can also involve the adjustment or refinement of existing procedures or products.

   1 Note down all the points in the sentence.

   2 Decide which words to keep, i.e. key concepts and technical terms.

   3 Use a different sentence pattern.

   4 Include a reference to the original source.

3 Write a similar paraphrase of either sentence 5 or sentence 9 from Text 2 using the guidelines in 2.

4 Look at the following example, which is a referenced quotation from Text 1. Write a similar sentence including a quotation for sentence 2 of Text 2. Remember to include a reference.

   Example: *Clark et al. (2009, p.268) state that 'innovation is a key function of any business.'*

   Sentence 2: *Innovation, or the production of something new or original, results from the ability to conceive of and create new and unique products, services or processes.*

5 Compare your sentences in 2, 3, and 4 with another student. Use the critical questions in 1 to evaluate (a) your own sentences, and (b) your partner's sentences.

TASK 6 Writing an accurately-referenced paragraph

1 You are going to write a paragraph on the role of innovation and creativity for entrepreneurs. Plan your paragraph by following stages 1–5. Make notes for each stage.

   1 Decide on the purpose of the paragraph, and the main point that you want to make.

   2 Think of an explanation or example to develop your main point.

   3 Check if there are any key terms that you need to define.

   4 Select at least two items of supporting material from Texts 1 and 2 to incorporate into your paragraph.

   5 Decide what you will say as an evaluation in your concluding sentence.

2 Write a paragraph of approximately 120 words using your notes from 1. You can refer to the sample paragraph in Task 2.1 to help you organize your writing. Make sure your paragraph includes features 1–5.

   1 A topic sentence that clearly states your main point

   2 An explanation or example to give further information about your main point

   3 A definition of key terms, if necessary

   4 Relevant supporting material from Texts 1 and 2, incorporated as summary, paraphrase, or quotation, with a reference to the main source

   5 A concluding sentence, including any further explanation and/or evaluation

Sample answer
page 190

TASK 7 Critical thinking – evaluating your writing

1 Check your paragraph using critical questions 1–5.

   1 Does the paragraph contain one topic and one main point?

   2 Is it clearly organized?

   3 Does it include at least two items of supporting material from the source texts in the form of a summary, paraphrase, or quotation?

   4 Are the citations of source material introduced clearly, correctly referenced, and explained or evaluated as necessary?

   5 Is there a range of sentence patterns, especially where source material is paraphrased?

2 Compare your paragraph with at least two paragraphs written by other students. Use the critical questions in 1 to evaluate each other's paragraphs. Try to identify one thing that could be improved in each paragraph.

It is important to connect your ideas within a paragraph or longer piece of writing. It helps to make your writing clear, logical, and easier for the reader to understand. Cohesive words or phrases help show how the ideas are connected, for example, they show the time order – *while, since*; highlight additional information – *in addition, moreover*; and give examples – *for example, for instance*.

TASK 1 Selecting and using linking expressions

1 Match each linking word or phrase to its use.

also   although   as a result   firstly   furthermore   however   in conclusion
in general   lastly   likewise   specifically   similarly   thus

Time / Sequencing	Comparison	Contrast	Additional information	Examples	Cause and effect	Concluding ideas

2 Select the correct word to complete sentences 1–7.

1 Firms can create new and improved goods and services, revive old products, and consequently enter new markets. *Furthermore / Similarly*, as a result of innovation they can end up with powerful market shares and have valuable products, designs, and brand names.

2 Technology makes it increasingly easy for a company to become global. Technology *has thus / likewise* made the rapid growth of the multinational corporation easier.

3 Companies can have subsidiaries in many countries but with business strategies, production, and distribution still being determined and controlled by head office in a single nation. *So / Firstly* multi-national corporations like Unilever are able to employ around a quarter of a million people in 100 countries and sell its products in 150 countries.

4 The company, through innovation, created a monopoly position. *However / Therefore*, they soon faced the prospect of other businesses developing alternative technologies which enabled them to provide new products or cut costs.

5 Innovation is usually included in any definition of creativity. *Although / In general* not all entrepreneurs develop new products or services, or discover new resources, every person who establishes an enterprise is involved in economic creation.

6 There are a number of reasons companies innovate. *Firstly / Specifically*, it is to maintain a competitive edge in the market. Secondly, it is to enable them to enter new markets.

7 *In conclusion / Similarly*, this essay has argued that innovation is a sign of progress in an economy and that it is inevitable that certain forms will fail.

TASK 2 Using cohesive language in texts

1 Complete sentences 1–4 with words / phrases from the list.

as a result   firstly   for example   furthermore   secondly   thus

1 There are a number of ways new opportunities are presented to firms. .... firms can develop new products; .... they can choose to enter new markets.

2 Innovation can help establish a strong brand. .... consumers are more aware of brand identity. .... the iPad has made Apple the biggest player in tablet technology.

3 Being innovative with technology can ensure long-term success. .... it can open new, diverse markets.

4 Financial stability has a positive effect of mental well-being. .... economic success impacts on the health of a nation.

UNIT 9 Consumption

ACADEMIC FOCUS: COMPARISON AND CONTRAST

LEARNING OBJECTIVES

This unit covers:

Listening
- Using Venn diagrams to take and organize notes
- Analysing descriptions of similarity and difference
- Recognizing and using comparative adjectives

Speaking
- Comparing and contrasting different pieces of research
- Preparing for, participating in, and evaluating a seminar discussion

Reading
- Analysing models and theories in a text
- Understanding comparison in text
- Identifying and evaluating authorial stance

Writing
- Introduction to essay writing
- Writing an effective conclusion
- Planning and organizing comparison essays

Vocabulary
- Identifying comparing and contrasting language
- Using comparative and contrasting structures

Discussion

1 **Work in pairs. Read the statistics and discuss questions 1–3.**

   a The richest 20% of the world's population are responsible for over 75% of the world's consumption, whereas the poorest 20% are responsible for consuming only 1.5% of the world's resources (World Bank, 2008).

   b 12% of the world's population live in North America and Western Europe, and account for 60% of personal spending, while the one-third living in South Asia and sub-Saharan Africa account for only 3.2% (worldwatch, 2011).

   c In 2008 the bottled water industry was worth $60 billion and sold 241 billion litres of water (Assadoumian, 2010). There are estimated to be 1 billion people without access to clean water (worldwatch, 2011).

   1 Which statistic surprises you the most?

   2 Do you live in a country where consumption is high? What do most people spend their money on?

   3 Has consumption changed much in your country in the last 50 years? Think about what people buy.

2 **Work in pairs. Discuss questions 1–3 with reference to consumption of resources like food, water, energy, and consumer goods.**

   1 What, if anything, worries you about your own consumption? What changes could you make?

   2 What are the possible risks of people continuing to consume so much?

   3 Are high levels of consumption always a bad thing?

9A Listening Lectures (7)

The comparison of two ideas, theories, or groups is a common feature of many lectures. When you listen to a lecture that includes comparison, it can be helpful to organize your notes related to each item in diagram form, for example, a Venn diagram. This can help to clarify the similarities or differences between the two items. Lecturers may use a variety of language structures to make comparisons – recognizing these structures will help you understand the comparative relationships being described.

This module covers:

- Using Venn diagrams to take and organize notes
- Analysing descriptions of similarity and difference
- Recognizing and using comparative adjectives

TASK 1 Predicting the content of a lecture

1 You are going to watch part of a lecture on marketing new products. Put the six products in pairs according to their function, and decide which product in each pair was the first to be released.

2 Based on your ideas in 1, what do you think will be the theme of the lecture?

1 How companies market innovative new products.

2 How companies differentiate their products from those of their competitors.

3 ▶9.1 Watch Extract 1 of the lecture and check your answer to 2.

Microsoft Zune   Apple iPod

TASK 2 Using Venn diagrams to take notes

1 Which words / phrases below refer to *similarities* between two items or ideas, and which refer to *differences*?

different   both   more attractive   superior   bigger   better   equally good

2 ▶9.2 Watch Extract 2 of the lecture comparing two competing products. Complete the notes, which are organized into a Venn diagram.

Android phone   iPhone

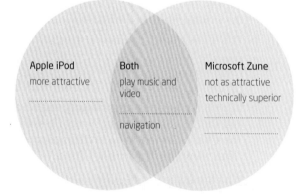

Apple iPod
more attractive
....

Both
play music and video
....
navigation

Microsoft Zune
not as attractive
technically superior
....
....

Nook Tablet   Kindle e-Reader

3 Compare your notes with another student. Discuss the similarities and differences between the two products and decide why one was more successful than the other.

TASK 3 Understanding descriptions of similarity and difference

1 ▶9.3 Watch Extract 3 and label the diagram with terms 1–5.

1 Early adopters
2 Laggards
3 Late majority
4 Innovators
5 Early majority

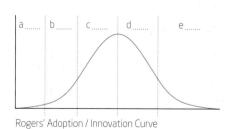

Rogers' Adoption / Innovation Curve

2 Work in pairs and discuss questions 1–2.

1 Why are innovators and laggards not likely to buy the same products?

2 Where would you place yourself / your friends / your family on the diagram in relation to different technologies, e.g. phones, tablets, social media?

TASK 4 Taking detailed notes from a longer extract

1 ▶9.4 Watch Extract 4 of the lecture and make notes on the two types of products, 'revolutionary' and 'me-too' products, under headings 1–4.

1 Communicating benefits to consumers

2 Taking risks

3 Pricing

4 Being successful / Gaining market share

2 Compare your notes with another student. Check whether you identified the same points.

3 Organize your notes on the two types of product using a Venn diagram.

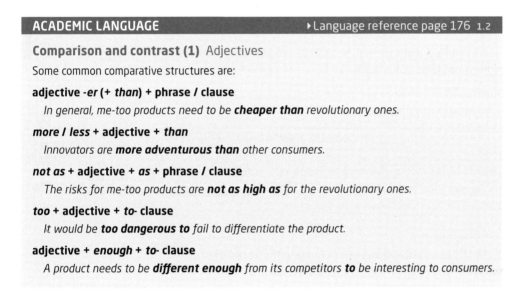

ACADEMIC LANGUAGE ▶Language reference page 176 1.2

Comparison and contrast (1) Adjectives

Some common comparative structures are:

adjective -er (+ *than*) + phrase / clause

*In general, me-too products need to be **cheaper than** revolutionary ones.*

more / less + adjective + *than*

*Innovators are **more adventurous than** other consumers.*

not as + adjective + as + phrase / clause

*The risks for me-too products are **not as high as** for the revolutionary ones.*

too + adjective + to- clause

*It would be **too dangerous to** fail to differentiate the product.*

adjective + enough + to- clause

*A product needs to be **different enough** from its competitors **to** be interesting to consumers.*

TASK 5 Using comparative adjectives

1 Complete sentences 1–5 with the correct form of the adjective in brackets.

1 Innovation is _____ (risky) creating a me-too product.

2 Prices for me-too products are not _____ (high) for revolutionary products.

3 People are often _____ (confident) about buying a new product _____ buying an established product.

4 Revolutionary products are _____ (expensive) for many consumers to buy.

5 Early adopters are usually _____ (rich) to take risks with money.

TASK 6 Critical thinking – responding to the content of a lecture

1 Use your notes from Tasks 3 and 4 to decide which products, revolutionary and me-too, would be successful with the different consumer groups in Rogers' adoption curve.

2 Work in pairs and discuss questions 1 and 2.

1 Rogers' adoption curve model was based on bringing the findings of over 500 studies together. What are the strengths and weaknesses of using such an approach?

2 Businesses often compare consumers using labels like 'innovators'. What are the strengths and weaknesses of using this approach?

INDEPENDENT STUDY

As lectures cover a lot of information, it is important your notes are clear and well-organized.

▶ Find out the title of your lectures in advance so you can best plan your note-taking, e.g. use Venn diagrams for contrast / comparison, or two columns for problem / solution lectures.

Seminars provide an opportunity to discuss your reading or research. As a number of students may do this in one seminar, there are opportunities to compare and contrast material. You may be given time to prepare for a seminar, and be allocated a particular text or question to discuss further. This preparation time should give you the opportunity to evaluate any research on the topic, before you discuss it with other students.

This module covers:

- Comparing and contrasting different pieces of research
- Preparing for, participating in, and evaluating a seminar discussion

TASK 1 Predicting the content of a seminar

1 **You are going to listen to extracts from a seminar discussion about the factors that affect people's happiness. Work in groups and discuss questions 1 and 2.**

 1 How important is each factor a–f in contributing to happiness?

 2 Does each factor contribute to <u>most people's</u> happiness, or the happiness of a small number of people?

a health	c education	e personal relationships
b employment status	d level of income	f possessions

2 **Read the tutor's online posting. Predict which <u>two</u> factors from a–f are most likely to be identified by research as the 'main contributing factors to happiness'.**

> **Aim:** to compare and discuss three pieces of research on happiness, and which factors (e.g. wealth / other?) contribute to happiness
>
> **Research question:** *What seem to be the main contributing factors to happiness?*
>
> **Format:** students present the main findings of the research they have read; seminar participants note down the main conclusions & ask questions, followed by discussion

3 **Match references 1–3 to descriptions a–c.**

 1 Ballas, D. & Dorling, D. (2007). Measuring the impact of major life events upon happiness. *International Journal of Epidemiology*, 36: pp.1244–52.

 2 Choudhary, M. A., Levine, P., McAdam, P. & Welz, P. 2012. *The happiness puzzle: analytical aspects of the Easterlin paradox. Oxford Economics Papers*, 64 (1) pp.27–42.

 3 Rodríguez-Pose, A. & Maslauskaite, K. (2011). Can policy make us happier? Individual characteristics, socio-economic factors and life satisfaction in Central and Eastern Europe. *Cambridge Journal of Regions Economy and Society* 4 (4)

 a research on happiness from a political perspective, with a specific geographical focus

 b an assessment of how different life events affect happiness

 c an analysis of a particular theory about happiness

GLOSSARY

The Easterlin paradox refers to research by Richard Easterlin published in 1974, which suggests that although people are becoming wealthier and consuming more, they are not happier.

TASK 2 Taking notes on key information

1 ◀))9.5 **Listen to Extract 1, the first student presentation. Note down the key information using headings 1–9.**

 1 Main reference: *Ballas & Dorling*

 2 Aim of the research:

 3 Main perspectives:

 4 Context of the research (time period, places):

 5 Key details of the research (type and size of research):

 6 Factors identified as influencing happiness:

 7 Main results:

 8 Conclusions:

 9 Any other interesting details / quotations from the research:

2 ◀))9.6 Listen to Extract 2, the second student presentation. Note down the key information using the same headings as in 1, where possible.

3 Compare your notes on Extracts 1 and 2 with another student. Help each other to complete any missing information. Then look at the transcript on page 217.

4 Compare the information you noted down in 1 and 2 using the following phrases.

Compared with …   … is similar to …   In comparison with …   In contrast, …

TASK 3 Comparing and contrasting types of research

1 Work in groups and discuss questions 1–3.

1 How accurate were your predictions in Task 1 about the main factors affecting happiness?

2 According to the two presentations you listened to in Task 2, which of these factors a–e are most important?

  a health
  b employment status
  c education
  d income
  e personal relationships

3 Identify any key information that supports your ideas in Task 1.2.

2 Use your notes from Task 2 to compare and contrast research in the two presentations, based on the following points:

- the context of the research
- the main perspectives
- the type of research
- the main factors identified in the research
- the results and conclusions.

TASK 4 Preparing for and taking part in a seminar discussion

1 You are going to take part in a seminar discussion on the question below. Individually, prepare at least two points to make, based on the information from the two presentations you listened to.

'What seem to be the main factors contributing to happiness?'

2 Work in groups. As you discuss the question in 1, make sure you follow guidelines 1–4.

1 Keep focused on the central question.

2 Contribute with your own points.
Income seems to be less important than …
Compared to health, …

3 Use your notes from Task 2 to support your points.
According to Ballas and Dorling …
Rodríguez-Pose and Maslauskaite argue that …
The main findings of Easterlin are …
Research has shown that …

4 Try to reach a conclusion based on the points made.
The main factors seem to be …
What seems important is …

INDEPENDENT STUDY

It is important to prepare properly before you participate in a seminar – your tutor will value a contribution based on reading rather than an unsupported opinion.

▶ Look at texts from two opposing stances to give you a balanced overview of topics before seminar discussions.

TASK 5 Evaluating your performance in a seminar discussion

1 Work in groups and evaluate your own performance in the discussion. Use questions 1–4 to help you.

1 Did you stay focused on the question throughout the discussion?

2 Did the other students clearly understand your contribution?

3 Were the points you made supported by research where appropriate?

4 Did you help each other to reach a conclusion?

2 Think of one thing you could do to improve your performance in future discussions.

Reading Textbooks (9)

The information in textbooks often compares two or more theories, models, or ideas. These comparisons usually contain description and definition, examples, and evaluation. When reading this material, you need to identify what is being compared, and the main similarities and differences. You also need to be able to evaluate how important these are. Comparisons may be made across different contexts, times, places, and theories.

This module covers:

- Analysing models and theories in a text
- Understanding comparison in text
- Identifying and evaluating authorial stance

TASK 1 Previewing text and context

1 **Work in groups and discuss questions 1–4.**

1 Put the following reasons for reading and listening to the media in order of importance for you.
   - to get information about current affairs and/or sport
   - to practise your reading, writing, and listening skills
   - to be entertained

2 Do you use any interactive media, e.g. a blog or a discussion forum, where you can post comments?

3 Which media do you trust most for factual content (e.g. television, the internet, magazines)?

4 Do you have any influence over the media in any way?

TASK 2 Analysing models and theories in a text

1 **You are going to read three short texts about news media. Read Texts 1 and 2 and note down two or three key words / phrases which refer to the main idea of each model or theory.**

Example: *Consumerist model – news: profit-driven*

Consumerist model   TEXT 1

Under the consumerist model the manufacture of news is profit driven; news is seen primarily as a business enterprise, with news as a commodity.

SOURCE: Bainbridge, J., Goc, N., & Tynan, L. (2011). p.42. *Media and journalism* 2nd ed. Oxford: Oxford University Press.

GLOSSARY

commodity *(n)* [economics] a product or a raw material that can be bought and sold

Consumption and production   TEXT 2

Both mass-society and Marxist theory assumed that the content of the media is shaped by those who own and control them. An alternative approach argues that the content of the media is determined by market forces. Thus the content of, say, newspapers is shaped not by their owners but by the readers who buy them. Newspapers and broadcasters are ultimately concerned with circulation and audience figures. The market rules and the media will deliver whatever the consumer wants.

SOURCE: Fulcher, J., & Scott, J. (2011). *Sociology* 4th ed. p.353-4. Oxford: Oxford University Press.

GLOSSARY

circulation *(n)* the usual number of copies of a newspaper or magazine that are sold each day, week, etc.

2 **Work in pairs. Discuss whether you agree with the ideas described in Texts 1 and 2. Give reasons.**

TASK 3 Identifying specific ideas in a text

1 Read Text 3 and identify the ideas you noted in Task 2.1.

2 Select the statement a–c that best describes how the text insert *Consumerist model* relates to the rest of Text 3.

  a It summarizes the text.

  b It offers a conclusion and evaluation of the text.

  c It defines and explains the topic of the text.

News audiences as consumers

¹There has been a significant change in recent decades in the way the media proprietors view their audiences. ²Media owners now see readers, listeners and viewers as consumers of their commodities, in much the same way as the owners of retail chains see their customers as the consumers of the products they sell. ³As Hirst and Patching (2005: 104) claim, media industries today 'treat their audiences as "consumers" of news, entertainment, information, sport, and associated product packaging'. ⁴Again, this change might not be as recent as we think. ⁵Fifty years ago, at the height of Senator Joseph McCarthy's anticommunist campaign in the USA, television and radio journalist Ed Murrow criticized the media for entertaining people at a time when they should have been informing the public of the threat to free speech and personal freedom.

Consumerist model

Under the consumerist model the manufacture of news is profit driven; news is seen primarily as a business enterprise, with news as a commodity.

⁶Fifty years later, Ed Murrow's revealing words echo in a world unsettled by threats to global peace, and where hard news and investigative reporting are being increasingly replaced by infotainment. ⁷In the early twenty-first century, celebrity news often dictates the news agenda. ⁸While often quoted, Murrow's criticism of the lack of endeavour by journalists and news corporations at a time when the USA was swept up in a wave of anticommunist sentiment, had little influence on stopping the commercialization of news. ⁹The public are becoming increasingly affluent and consumerist, and they demand to be entertained as well as informed. ¹⁰This means the role and relevance of the investigative journalist is increasingly being challenged.

SOURCE, adapted from: Bainbridge, J., Goc, N., & Tynan, L. (2011). p.42. *Media and journalism* 2nd ed. Oxford: Oxford University Press.

GLOSSARY

affluent *(adj)* having a lot of money and a good standard of living

claim *(v)* to say that sth is true although it has not been proved and other people may not believe it

endeavour *(n)* an attempt to do sth, especially sth new or difficult

infotainment *(n)* television programmes, etc. that present news and serious subjects in an entertaining way [***info**rmation* + *enter**tainment**]

proprietor *(n)* the owner of a business, a hotel, etc.

3 Identify which sentences 1–9 contain material on news audiences as *consumers*. Underline the words / phrases which relate to this.

  Example: ²*Media owners now see readers, listeners and viewers as <u>consumers of their commodities</u>, in much the same way as the owners of retail chains see their customers as the <u>consumers of the products</u> they sell.*

4 Select two of the sentences you identified, and write a citation for each one. Decide whether to use a quotation or paraphrase, and remember to include a reference.

  Example: *Bainbridge, Goc, and Tynan (2011, p.42) explain how readers, listeners, and viewers of media are compared to consumers of products sold in retail chains.*

TASK 4 Understanding comparison in a text

1 Decide whether the main comparisons in Text 3 are between different *times*, *places*, or *theories*.

2 Read paraphrases 1–9 of sentences 1–9 in Text 3, and decide whether each one is *true* or *false* based on the information in the text.

  1 Media owners' views of their audience have remained the same.

  2 Media owners see their readers, etc. as consumers.

  3 Media industries treat audiences as consumers.

  4 The shift (in sentence 1) has happened over the last few years.

  5 The journalist Ed Murrow criticized the media for offering too much information rather than entertainment.

  6 Murrow's criticisms are still significant.

  7 News is led by celebrity news in the 21st century.

  8 Murrow's criticism of journalists has greatly influenced the commercialization of news.

  9 The public wants not only information but entertainment, so investigative journalism is becoming less important.

3 Correct the sentences you identified as false.

                                        changed

  Example: *Media owners' views of their audience have ~~remained the same~~.*

TASK 5 Identifying and evaluating the authors' stance

1 Decide which sentences 1–9 in Text 3 express the authors' stance.

2 Underline the words / phrases in sentences a–d below that indicate the authors' stance.

  Example: *There has been <u>a significant change</u> in recent decades in the way the media proprietors view their audiences. (sentence 1)*

> a Again, this change might not be as recent as we think. (sentence 4)

> b Fifty years later, Ed Murrow's revealing words echo in a world unsettled by threats to global peace, and where hard news and investigative reporting are being increasingly replaced by infotainment. (sentence 6)

> c While often quoted, Murrow's criticism of the lack of endeavour by journalists and news corporations at a time when the USA was swept up in a wave of anticommunist sentiment, had little influence on stopping the commercialization of news. (sentence 8)

> d The public are becoming increasingly affluent and consumerist, and they demand to be entertained as well as informed. This means the role and relevance of the investigative journalist is increasingly being challenged. (sentences 9 and 10)

3 Decide whether the words / phrases you underlined are comparative, evaluative, or both. Look at the language carefully in its context in the original text to see how it is used.

  Example: *The phrase 'significant change' in sentence 1 is evaluative rather than comparative. The authors use the adjective 'significant' to show their opinion on the change – they see it as important.*

INDEPENDENT STUDY

Comparisons in academic texts are typically evaluated – for example, if two systems are shown to have differences, then one system is likely to be shown to be more effective.

▶ Look at a chapter of a textbook from your area of study. Look for comparisons of important ideas, systems, etc. and identify any evaluation made by the authors.

Comparison and contrast (2) Understanding longer phrases and structures

Academic texts often use longer phrases or structures to show **similarities** (comparison). Such phrases 'balance' the two things being compared. For example, in the following sentence, media owners are compared to the owners of retail chains:

> *Media owners now see readers, listeners and viewers as consumers of their commodities, **in much the same way as** the owners of retail chains see their customers as the consumers of the products they sell.*

Other structures that are used in this way include *in the same way as, just as,* and *just like* (less formal).

To show **differences** (contrast), longer phrases or structures include:

> *Again, this change **might not be as recent as** we think.*

> *Thus the content of, say, newspapers is shaped **not** by their owners **but** by the readers who buy them.*

> *In the consumerist model, content of the news is driven by the market **rather than** the producer.*

TASK 6 Using comparison and contrast phrases

1 **Match sentence halves** 1–5 **to** a–e **using the phrases below.**

as complex as   in the same way   in a similar way   rather than   not … (but)

1 In this model, listeners and viewers are seen

2 The consumption of news can be analysed

3 In some contexts, the term *model* can be defined

4 One of the most significant aspects of consumer behaviour in economies

5 Television programmes in public service broadcasts are influenced by legal obligations

a the European Union is consumer loyalty.

b as passive consumers but as active analysts of currently available options.

c by consumer preferences.

d to the term *theory*.

e as the consumption of the latest products and services.

TASK 7 Critical thinking – responding to ideas in a text

1 **Work in groups. Read statements** 1–3 **taken from Texts 1–3 and discuss whether the information in each statement is (a) true, and (b) something positive. Give reasons.**

1 'Under the consumerist model … news is seen primarily as a business enterprise, with news as a commodity.' (Text 1)

2 'The content of newspapers is shaped by the readers who buy them. The media will deliver whatever the consumer wants.' (Text 2)

3 'The public are becoming increasingly affluent and consumerist, and they demand to be entertained as well as informed. This means the role and relevance of the investigative journalist is increasingly being challenged.' (Text 3)

This module is the first of four writing modules that look at writing different types of essay. It is important to understand some of the basic principles common to many different types of essay. Becoming familiar with these principles will help you to apply them to different contexts within your own area of study. In this module, you will learn how to structure a comparison essay and practise some of the language associated with this type of essay.

This module covers:
- Introduction to essay writing
- Writing an effective conclusion
- Planning and organizing comparison essays

TASK 1 Previewing the topic

1 **Work in pairs and discuss questions 1–3.**

  1 What things do you buy that are different from the things your parents' generation bought? How do you buy them?

  2 Do you have a different attitude to saving and debt from your parents' generation?

  3 Why do you think these differences exist?

2 **Work with another pair and compare your ideas.**

TASK 2 Understanding the purpose of an essay

1 **Read extracts 1 and 2 from the introductions to two different student essays related to consumption. For each extract, decide on the purpose of the essay, a or b.**

> 1 Consumers behave very differently from a generational perspective. In particular, older consumers differ greatly from the younger generation, who are less loyal to particular brands and more suspicious of advertising messages.

  a to argue that the older generation are the most important consumers

  b to show the similarities and differences in consumer behaviour

> 2 If the whole world consumed at the same rate as America, four planets would be needed to maintain the world's current population. People need to evaluate their current consumption patterns if the world is to have a sustainable future.

  a to compare American consumption patterns with others in the world

  b to look at the problem of consumption rates and the need for change

2 **Work in pairs and discuss your answers in 1. Do you agree with the ideas expressed?**

> **INDEPENDENT STUDY**
>
> Always read any assessed questions carefully as a slight misinterpretation could result in you losing marks.
>
> ▶ Look at past essay or exam questions in your subject area. Write an outline of how you would answer the question and check with your teacher that you have understood the purpose correctly.

TASK 3 Analysing a conclusion to an essay

1 **Planning the conclusion of an essay will help with the planning and organization of the main body. Read sentences a and b from the conclusions to two different essays related to consumption. Match them to extracts 1 and 2 in Task 2.1.**

> a It's important for us to reassess our use of goods, and resources generally, in order for society to continue effectively.

> b The loyalty to a particular brand, and the way in which advertising is viewed, differs significantly between generations, with less brand loyalty in the younger generation and more negative views of advertising.

2 Read the features of a conclusion 1–6. Select three features that could appear in the conclusion to the essay below.

> **TITLE:** 'Older people have more disposable income than younger people – they are therefore more attractive to companies as potential customers.' Compare and contrast the advantages of targeting these two consumer groups.

1 a reference to the title and introduction, including the thesis statement

2 a summary of the main points of the essay

3 an evaluation of the information in the essay

4 new information not covered in the body of the essay

5 a reference to, or recommendations for, the future

6 a reference to the findings or results of research

3 Read this conclusion to the essay in 2, and the tutor's comments. Use the comments to complete the criteria for writing an effective conclusion.

A good clear restatement of the main argument

The loyalty to a particular brand and the way in which advertising is viewed differ significantly between generations, with loyalty diminishing in younger generations and the negative views of advertising increasing. As a result companies need to revise their approach to advertising to the younger generation, by delivering a product with a less obvious sell and making the consumer feel like an individual. To continue to be successful top brands need to tailor their message and use the technology available to help them achieve this.

Good evaluation – a clear logical deduction and reasoning based on your evidence in the essay

Useful to mention future implications

This is the first time you have mentioned the use of technology

A good concluding paragraph:

1 summarizes the main points of the essay

2 ....

3 ....

4 ....

TASK 4 Identifying ways of organizing a comparison essay

1 Two ways of organizing a comparison essay are the *block* structure, and the *point-by-point* structure. Match the two structures with descriptions a and b below.

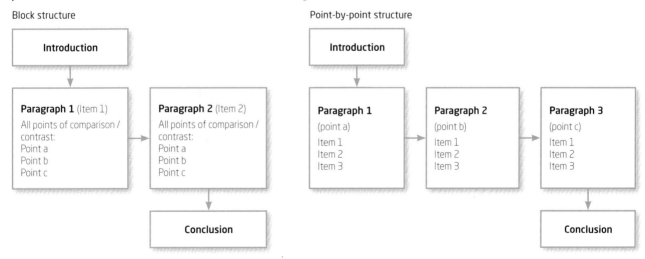

Block structure

Point-by-point structure

a This structure takes each point of comparison related to the main question in turn, and looks at the similarities and differences between the items to be compared.

b This structure takes each item to be compared and groups together all the points of comparison (similarities and differences) related to it.

2 Turn to page 201. Read the essay title and the two essay outlines, A and B. Match each outline to one of the structures in 1.

3 Work in pairs and discuss which structure you think is more effective for answering the essay title on page 201. Give reasons.

TASK 5 Identifying the structure of a comparison paragraph

1 Read the essay title and a body paragraph from the essay. Answer questions 1–3.

1 What is the main topic of the paragraph?

2 What three things does the writer compare to support the main point?

3 Is the writer using a block structure or a point-by-point structure to organize the essay?

> **TITLE:** *'Changes in social attitudes are as important as the economy in determining how we spend our money.' Compare the effects of social attitudes and economic conditions on consumer behaviour in the developed world.*

In the developed world, the attitudes and values that affect social behaviour are changing. This has an effect on consumption generally. One example is the change in gender roles. The traditional view of male and female roles was once common, whereas these roles are now more flexible. Men have taken on more feminine roles such as looking after children, while some women have taken on more masculine roles in the world of business. Society now has a less narrow view of the roles of men and women. In the same way, the rise of globalization has created societies which have a much wider view of the world and their place in it. Many companies operate across national borders, workforces have become more international, and global brands such as Apple, Nike, and Samsung are found everywhere. Attitudes to technology have also changed. In the past, older people were seen as more resistant to change, and especially to new technology. In contrast, older people today are more attractive to marketers – they are more interested in technology, have more disposable income, and are loyal to certain brands. Similarly, younger consumers are also interested in technology and highly aware of brands. All of these changes influence not only what people consume, but also how they consume.

2 Find examples of words / phrases referring to similarities or differences in the paragraph in 1.

ACADEMIC LANGUAGE

Comparison and contrast (3) Referring to similarity and difference

In academic writing, you can use a variety of words or phrases to indicate similarities or differences between two items or ideas.

Referring to similarity

*Many older people are interested in technology, and are loyal to certain brands. **In the same way**, / **Similarly**, younger consumers are also highly aware of brands.*

***Both** older **and** younger consumers are interested in technology, and are loyal to certain brands.*

***Like** older consumers, younger consumers are interested in technology, and are loyal to certain brands.*

Referring to difference

*In the past, older people were seen as resistant to change. **In contrast**, many older people today are attractive to marketers.*

*In the past, older people were seen as resistant to change, **whereas** / **while** today older people are attractive to marketers.*

***In comparison with** previous generations, older people today are more attractive to marketers.*

***Unlike** previous generations, older people today are more attractive to marketers.*

TASK 6 Using language to refer to similarity and difference

1 Complete sentences 1–5 with the most appropriate words / phrases in the list.

in contrast   both … and   while   unlike   in the same way

1 Saudi Arabia is the world's largest producer of oil, ... China is now the world's largest consumer.

2   .... many older consumers, younger consumers are not very brand loyal.

3   The number of people owning cars in the USA more than doubled in the second half of the 20th century. ...., car ownership in China and Brazil has increased by 200% and 120% respectively in the last ten years.

4   .... the Americans .... the Europeans are among the world's largest consumers of resources.

5   The USA consumes 2,500 cubic metres of water per person per year, ... people in Africa consume less than 250 cubic metres.

2 **Look back at the essay outlines A and B on page 201. Use the notes to write at least three similar sentences using phrases from Academic Language.**

    Example: Younger consumers earn less → less disposable income
                   Older consumers earn more → more disposable income
                   *Younger consumers earn less and have less disposable income, **whereas** older consumers earn more and have more disposable income.*

TASK 7 Writing an outline for a comparison essay

1 **You are going to write an outline for a 500-word essay on the following title. Make a list of points to include, using the notes below and your own ideas.**

> TITLE: *'Older people have more disposable income than younger people – they are therefore more attractive to companies as potential customers.' Compare and contrast the advantages of targeting these two consumer groups.*

- Reasons to target older consumers: people are living longer – more older people / prefer older, more familiar brands / have more time and money to spend
- Reasons to target younger consumers: important to build up loyalty to a brand / more interested in new, innovative products / more easily influenced by marketing

2 **Select a suitable structure for your essay: block or point-by-point.**

3 **Organize your notes into an outline for the essay. Your essay should include an introduction, a conclusion, and at least two body paragraphs. Decide what information you will include in each paragraph. Use the Outlines A and B on page 201 to help you.**

TASK 8 Writing a comparison essay

1 **Refer to the essay title and your outline in Task 7, and write your introduction. Include features 1–4 (see Unit 7D for ideas).**

    1 an opening sentence to gain interest   3 a clear thesis statement

    2 relevant background information   4 a statement of purpose

2 **Write a topic sentence for each paragraph, stating the main idea (see Unit 2D for ideas).**

3 **Write the main body paragraphs of your essay using the notes you made in Task 7. Make sure each paragraph:**

- has one clear topic, and that the comparisons made relate to that topic
- includes the language of comparison and contrast as necessary
- has a concluding sentence which restates the main point of the paragraph and gives a brief evaluation (see Unit 2D for ideas).

4 **Write the conclusion to your essay. Make sure that it meets the criteria in Task 3.3.**

Sample answer
page 191

TASK 9 Evaluating peers' essays

1 **Work in pairs. Evaluate your partner's essay using the checklist of questions 1–5 on page 201.**

2 **Give each other feedback on your essays and suggest any points for improvement.**

9E Vocabulary Comparing and contrasting

Recognizing high-frequency phrases that are used to compare and contrast helps you to navigate texts, and understand the development of an author's stance. Using this language in your own work shows your ability to analyse and synthesize ideas from several sources.

TASK 1   Identifying comparing and contrasting language

1   **Put these words / phrases under the correct heading.**

changing   comparable   differ   distinction   difference   distinct from
in common with   in contrast to   resemble   similarity

Comparing	Contrasting

2   **Compare your answers with a partner.**

TASK 2   Using comparative and contrasting structures

1   **Select the correct word to complete sentences 1–8.**

1   The older generation *differs / distinct* from the younger generation in terms of their brand loyalty.

2   There is much that younger generations have in *common / similarity* across cultures.

3   One *similarity / difference* between each new generation and the previous one is the wish to appear different.

4   *Comparable / Changing* trends affect which products consumers prefer to purchase.

5   *In common with / In contrast to* wealthier sectors of society, the working class tend to be more concerned with the here and now than the future.

6   Companies often try to create a product that *resembles / differs from* a successful brand in order to gain from its success.

7   Buying a house is *distinct from / comparable to* starting a family in how it changes your purchasing behaviour.

8   The *distinction / similarity* between cultures is reducing as the world globalizes and becomes 'smaller'.

2   **Complete the paragraph using words / phrases from 1.**

Most countries have a social class system, although these [1]................... between countries. The [2]................... can be in terms of the size of each group or in the way society is organized. One thing that most cultures have [3]................... is that the [4]................... between the working classes from one culture to another are quite striking. The financial limitations that most working people face mean that the purchasing behaviour of the working class in one country is [5]................... that of other countries. In particular, the working classes are more likely to focus on the here and now. This is a [6]................... from other social class groups who often have a longer-term focus on things such as investments and pensions.

3   **Think of two similar and two different views or ideas from your own area of study. Write sentences using the comparing and contrasting language from this module.**

UNIT 10 Crime

ACADEMIC FOCUS: ARGUMENT AND EVIDENCE

LEARNING OBJECTIVES

This unit covers:

Listening
- Examining evidence to prepare for a debate
- Identifying main arguments and supporting evidence
- Identifying and analysing maximizing and minimizing language

Speaking
- Evaluating a case study and identifying options
- Identifying and using hedging language
- Presenting arguments for and against

Reading
- Identifying main arguments
- Understanding and using evaluative language
- Evaluating premise and conclusion in an argument

Writing
- Planning, organizing, and writing an argument essay
- Incorporating evidence in an essay
- Making a text more cohesive by varying vocabulary

Vocabulary
- Presenting and assessing views
- Noticing and interpreting arguments

Discussion

1 **Match statements a–d to the sources of evidence 1–4.**

   a Poverty is the main cause of crime so governments need to address this issue.

   b Many people who commit crimes don't think they will be punished.

   c Crime is less common in modern society than in the past.

   d Violent computer games may actually reduce crime levels.

   1 Deterrents such as prison are mostly irrelevant to people who wish to commit crime. (Wikström, Tseloni, & Karlis, 2012)

   2 Crime in the US is down by over 20 per cent in the last 20 years. (US Bureau of Justice, 2010)

   3 Childhood neglect and childhood family poverty are linked to crime in adult life. (Nikulina, Spatz Widom, & Czaja, 2010)

   4 Studies in laboratories that link violent video games to crime levels fail to take into consideration the fact that such games actually may take individuals away from opportunities to commit crime. (Engelstätter, Cunningham, & Ward, 2011)

2 **Work in pairs and discuss questions 1 and 2.**

   1 Which statement in 1 above do you (a) most agree with, and (b) least agree with? Give reasons.

   2 What reasons might people have for making these statements?

A debate is a formal discussion of a single question or issue (the **motion**). Normally one or more speakers make their points *for* the issue and others speak *against* the issue. As you listen, it is worth taking notes as you may have opportunities to put forward your own points and questions, and possibly vote on the issue at the end of the debate. While listening, you need to work out the speaker's main point, and identify the evidence they use to support this. This will help you evaluate what each speaker says.

This module covers:
- Examining evidence to prepare for a debate
- Identifying main arguments and supporting evidence
- Identifying and analysing maximizing and minimizing language

TASK 1 Preparing to listen to a debate: examining evidence

1 Work in groups. Briefly note down at least two *positive* and *negative* effects of playing computer games, or video games.

2 Read the text on page 202 and check whether it includes any of the effects you noted in 1.

3 Read the text again and note down the evidence provided by each of the sources cited. For each source, decide if the effects are (a) positive, (b) negative, or (c) uncertain.

4 Compare your notes from 3. Based on the evidence in the text, are there any effects of video game playing which can be linked to crime?

TASK 2 Identifying main arguments and supporting evidence

1 You are going to watch extracts from a debate on the possible connection between playing video games and criminal behaviour. What points might the speakers make for or against the main issue?

2 ▶10.1 Watch Extract 1 of the debate and complete the notes.

Main issue (the motion): 'Playing video games leads to increased levels of crime, including violence and antisocial behaviour.'

First speaker: Suzanna Fiorella, ... and social commentator, speaking .... the motion.

Second speaker: Michael Connelly, psychologist and .... expert on .... of technology.

3 ▶10.2 Watch Extract 2, and note down:
- the two questions Suzanna aims to answer
- Suzanna's main arguments in relation to the following points:
  1 video game playing as an activity
  2 players' cognitive skills
  3 the effect on society of playing violent video games
  4 the effect on children of playing video games
  5 any other effects of playing video games.

4 ▶10.2 Watch Extract 2 again, and note down the evidence Suzanna uses to support her arguments.

5 Work in pairs and compare your notes.
  1 Discuss whether you agree with the arguments presented.
  2 Identify any sources in Task 1 that Suzanna refers to.
  3 Think of possible arguments in response to each of Suzanna's points.

TASK 3 Identifying responses to an argument

1 ▶10.3 Watch Extract 3 and note down Michael's responses to the five points made by the first speaker.

2 ▶10.3 Watch Extract 3 again and note down the evidence to support his arguments.

3 Work in pairs and compare your notes.

   1 Decide whether Michael used any of the responses you discussed in Task 2.5.

   2 Identify any further points he made, i.e. points not stated in the text in Task 1.

ACADEMIC LANGUAGE ▸Language reference page 179 22

Maximizing and minimizing language Modal verbs, verbs, and adverbs

Maximizing language
To sound more certain or to **maximize** ('boost') your message, you can use more 'definite' language.
- Modal verbs like *will* and *must*: We **must** be careful about working out causes and effects.
- Adverbs like *absolutely, certainly,* and *definitely*: There's **definitely** plenty of evidence to support this view.
- Expressions like *there's no doubt that*: **There's no doubt that** expert game players perform better in certain areas.

Minimizing language
To avoid sounding too certain when putting forward an argument, you can use specific language to **minimize** or soften what you say. This is sometimes called '**hedging**'.
- Modal verbs like *may* or *can*: Trait aggression **may** increase the negative effects of game play.
- Verbs like *appear, seem,* and *suggest*: There **appears to be** evidence, quite convincing evidence, to **suggest** that many of the effects of playing video games are negative.
- Adverbs like *often* or *probably*: Playing with an aggressive video game was **often** followed by brief aggressive play in 4- to 8-year-olds.
- Phrases like *is likely to* and *I would say*: Any cognitive skill resulting from repeated video game play **is likely to** be limited.

TASK 4 Analysing maximizing and minimizing language

1 Read the text in Task 1 again. Identify the language that shows how certain the writer is.

   Example: *The research on the effects of video game play is <u>even more inconclusive</u> than is the literature on media violence in general.*

2 ▶10.4 Watch eight short clips from Extracts 2 and 3 of the debate. Note down the maximizing and minimizing language the speaker uses in each clip.

3 Divide the expressions you noted into two groups, maximizing and minimizing.

4 Look at the transcript on page 218 and find more examples of maximizing and minimizing language.

5 Select at least three of the expressions you noted and use these to write sentences related to your own area of study.

   Example: *Exposing metal to temperatures above 200°C **can lead to** changes in structure.*

INDEPENDENT STUDY

In lectures and presentations, listening for maximizing and minimizing language will help you understand how certain the speaker is about a point.

▸ Listen to a lecture or presentation online, if possible related to your own area of study. Try to identify any maximizing and minimizing language used by the speaker.

TASK 5 Responding to the arguments in a debate

1 Work in groups. Look back at your notes in Tasks 2 and 3. Evaluate each speaker's argument using questions 1 and 2. If necessary, watch the extracts again or refer to the transcript on page 219.

   1 Is the argument supported by evidence?

   2 Is the supporting evidence relevant, reliable, and convincing?

2 Discuss how far you agree with each speaker's argument. Which speaker do you most agree with, and why?

One common activity in a seminar is to look at the arguments for and against a particular issue. To do this effectively, you need to be able to consider a wide range of perspectives, and to present arguments for and against the issue. It is also usual to express these arguments with caution, to acknowledge the fact that there are often a number of possible arguments that are equally convincing.

This module covers:

- Evaluating a case study and identifying options
- Identifying and using hedging language
- Presenting arguments for and against

TASK 1 Critical thinking – discussing unethical behaviour

1 Work in pairs and discuss which of the actions below are *unethical* (not morally acceptable) and which are *criminal* (against the law). Give reasons.
- Taking stationery (pens, paper, etc.) from your employer for your personal use.
- Using a company credit card for personal expenses and claiming these as work expenses.
- Paying money to an official in order to win a business contract (bribery).

2 Discuss whether it is acceptable for a company to behave unethically if it helps them to stay in business.

TASK 2 Evaluating a situation and identifying options

1 Work in pairs. Read Case Study 1 on page 202 and discuss questions 1 and 2.

1 Which statement a–c best summarizes Bruce's situation?
   a He is being asked to commit a crime.
   b He is being treated unfairly by his employer.
   c He is being asked to behave unethically.

2 Think of at least two options that Bruce has for dealing with his situation. Note down the arguments *for* and *against* each option.

2 ◀))10.5 Listen to Extract 1 from a seminar in which two students are discussing the case study. Note down their suggestions for Bruce's options.

TASK 3 Identifying arguments *for* and *against*

1 ◀))10.6 Listen to Extract 2 of the seminar. Note down the speakers' arguments for and against each option.

2 Compare the speakers' arguments with your ideas from Task 2.1. What similarities and differences are there?

ACADEMIC LANGUAGE

Hedging Forms for expressing caution

In academic situations, arguments are often presented cautiously. You can use a variety of language to **hedge** or express caution.
Modal verbs: *Quitting his job **might** be a good idea.*
Adverbs: *Well, **arguably**, that could put other people at risk.*
Prepositional phrases: ***Generally speaking** companies expect everyone to be a team player.*
Impersonal verb phrases: ***It could be argued that** the last option is preferable.*

TASK 4 Identifying and using hedging language

1 Look at the transcript of Extracts 1 and 2 on page 219 and identify the hedging language.

2 Complete sentences 1–4 about the case study in Task 2 with the words / phrases in the list.

in some respects   could   it might be considered   seemingly

1 _____ acceptable if Bruce left with a few months' notice.

2 _____, his employers had some sort of 'arrangement' with Transition.

3 Talking to his boss _____ be the best option.

4 _____, he doesn't have much choice. He has to carry on working there.

3 Rewrite statements 1–4 so that they are expressed more cautiously.

1 Hard work leads to success.

2 It is wrong to involve other people in your problems.

3 Quitting is one option, but a better one is to consult his line manager.

4 All unethical behaviour is potentially criminal.

TASK 5 Analysing a case study

1 You are going to take part in a discussion about a case study related to corporate crime. Before you read the case study, discuss what you know about the American energy company Enron, and the case known as the 'Enron scandal'.

2 Read Case Study 2 on page 203 and note down the answers to questions 1–3.

1 Why did the SEC make Andersen pay a fine?

2 Why did the shareholders of Sunbeam sue Andersen?

3 Why did Andersen stop trading? What reasons does the text give for their actions?

3 Compare your answers in 2 with another student. Help each other to complete any missing information.

1400 Smith Street

4 Note down any arguments *for* or *against* statements 1–3.

1 Andersen did the right thing by protecting client confidentiality over their obligation to the taxpayers and investors.

2 Andersen should have warned their client about its behaviour.

3 Andersen should not have been so dependent on one client for its income.

TASK 6 Taking part in a seminar discussion

1 Read the statement topic and note down any arguments for and against the statement. Think of reasons to support your argument, and plan what you will say in the discussion.

'White-collar crime is often unethical but is not a serious crime. Business people such as those in the Andersen case should not face prison – they should be made to work for society.'

2 Work in groups and hold the discussion. Use the guidelines to help you.

• Take turns to put forward your argument, with reasons.

• Try to use language to express caution when putting forward your argument.

3 Evaluate your own participation in the discussion. Did you:.

• present your argument clearly?

• provide reasons to support your argument?

• use language to express caution when putting forward your argument?

INDEPENDENT STUDY

When you have to take part in a seminar discussion, it is a good idea to think about the topic in advance, and think of the different possible arguments.

▶ Next time you are in a discussion try to consider as many perspectives as possible and take notes of the different arguments for and against the topic.

You will often read academic texts that contain an argument, or a summary of several arguments, on a particular topic. You need to be able to identify how the arguments and evidence are related, and on what premise the conclusions are based. A **premise** is a statement or idea that an argument is based on. Recognizing the evaluative language the author uses will help you to identify their stance on the strengths and weaknesses of these arguments. Identifying the author's stance makes it possible for you to evaluate the main argument(s) discussed, and draw your own conclusions.

This module covers:
- Identifying main arguments
- Understanding and using evaluative language
- Evaluating premise and conclusion in an argument

TASK 1 Previewing the topic

1 **Work in groups and discuss which items 1–4 are good indicators of intelligence. Try to add other indicators of intelligence to the list.**

1 curiosity
2 accuracy and precision in work
3 flexibility in thinking
4 persistence

2 **Read items 1–6 in the table and decide how a person's intelligence affects each one.**

	no impact ⟶ significant impact				
1 Getting a job	1	2	3	4	5
2 Being creative	1	2	3	4	5
3 Being good at sports	1	2	3	4	5
4 Becoming a criminal	1	2	3	4	5
5 Likelihood of being caught committing a crime	1	2	3	4	5
6 Social status	1	2	3	4	5

3 **Work in pairs and compare your ideas in 2.**

TASK 2 Identifying the main arguments in a longer text

1 **Read paragraph 1 of the text on page 139 and select the best heading for the whole text.**

1 The causes of crime
2 The links between crime and intelligence
3 The impact of low intelligence

2 **Read the whole text and match each main argument a–g to a paragraph 1–7.**

a The level of low intelligence was not well defined. ....
b Researchers were surprised to re-establish the link between intelligence and crime. ....
c Feeble-minded people were thought to be more likely to be criminals. ....
d Intelligence is linked to crime but it is not clear how. ....
e *The Cambridge Study in Delinquent Development* is considered one of the best studies on the causes of crime. ....
f Low verbal ability at a young age is linked to crime. ....
g There was thought to be little connection between intelligence and crime. ....

3 **Decide which sentence, 1 or 2, best describes the purpose of the text.**

1 To present a series of arguments based on different research studies, in order to show that there <u>may</u> be a connection between criminality and intelligence.
2 To present a single coherent argument, in order to persuade the reader that there is a definite connection between criminality and intelligence.

4 Read paragraph 7 and answer questions 1 and 2.

1 Does the author believe there is a clear connection between criminality and intelligence?

2 Identify the language that shows the author's stance on the possible connection between criminality and intelligence.

1 The earliest reputable studies into the link between criminality and intelligence were perhaps those conducted by Goddard (1912), starting with an unscientific study of the Kalikak family. By using a subjective assessment of 'feeble-mindedness' it left more questions than answers. Goddard's later studies were more acceptable 'scientifically', as they used the objective IQ tests to measure for 'feeble-mindedness'. He studied the inmates of 16 prisons, and found that the proportion of feeble-minded inmates ranged from 28 per cent to 89 per cent, the average being about 50 per cent. His results, which were published in 1914, led him to conclude that all 'feeble-minded' individuals were potential criminals.

2 Most research carried out at the time arrived at a similar conclusion until the First World War. During the war the United States army began to test the IQ of their new soldiers. Their aim was to declare all the 'feeble-minded' as unfit for military service. The outcome was that about 50 per cent were 'feeble-minded'. The army could not accept this, and revised the level of 'feeble-mindedness' to recruit more individuals. Following the war, theorists adopted the army's arbitrary revision. Goddard himself admitted that his previous findings were inaccurate. He even accepted that intellect was not purely hereditary but could partially be corrected by careful educational practices.

3 Investigations in the 50 years after 1920 largely failed to discover a connection between criminality and 'feeble-mindedness'. For example, the representative work of Mary Woodward (1955) concluded that 'low intelligence plays little or no role in delinquency'.

4 In Britain, one of the foremost pieces of research in this area is the *Cambridge Study in Delinquent Development* carried out by Cambridge University Institute of Criminology and directed by West. It was a longitudinal study (i.e., followed the subjects over a period of time) on boys from north-east London, who were under scrutiny from the age of 8 until the age of 25. The results of this study have been the material for a number of books dating from 1969. One written by West (1982) draws together all the findings. The survey included a number of factors which are commonly related to criminality, such as parental conflict, separation or instability, unsatisfactory child-rearing (such as neglect, cruelty, incorrect discipline or supervision), pupils who are 'troublesome' at primary school, low income families, large family size (which was found to be a particularly important predictor for those with a number of older siblings), and one or more criminal parents.

5 All those associated with the study were surprised to find that low IQ seemed as closely related to criminality as these other, more widely accepted factors. The average IQ of future juvenile delinquents was 95 and that of future non-delinquents 101. This sounds a very small difference, but its significance is masked because it reflects averages. Close examination showed a lack of delinquent boys in the high IQ group, over 110. It also showed a lot of delinquent boys in the low IQ group, under 90. The far more frequent (almost twice as frequent) appearance of delinquent boys amongst the low scorers was sufficient to allow West to include this as one of the most important predictors of criminality. Even more interestingly, he discovered that low intelligence was particularly closely related to young convictions and repeated crime.

6 Farrington (1992), again working with the Cambridge data, found that a third of those scoring below 90 on a non-verbal intelligence test at ages 8-10 later became convicted young offenders. This is twice as many as those who scored over 90. This may suggest that those with low intelligence are less able to avoid conviction. However, it was also very closely related to high levels of self-reported delinquency. Low non-verbal ability was linked to low verbal ability and to low achievement at school at the age of 11. Both of these were linked to juvenile convictions. They were also connected to students missing classes and leaving school at a young age. However, they were independent of other social links, such as large family size and low income (Lynam et al. (1993)).

7 If there seems to be a relationship between criminality and intelligence the nature of that relationship is both interesting and unclear. Apparently these individuals have difficulty in dealing with abstract concepts and reasoning. This reduces their ability to foresee the consequences of their actions either to themselves or others. They may thus be less likely to be deterred by the possibility of detection, conviction and punishment.

SOURCE: Williams, K. (2008). p.272-4. *Textbook on Criminology* 6th ed. Oxford: Oxford University Press.

GLOSSARY

child-rearing *(n)* looking after a child from a young age to adulthood

delinquent *(n)* a person, especially young, who behaves badly and commits minor crimes

feeble-minded *(adj)* having a low level of intelligence

inmate *(n)* a person in prison

verbal ability *(n)* the ability to speak and express yourself clearly

Evaluative language Adjectives

Authors can express their stance on a subject in different ways. The text contains a number of adjectives that indicate the author's stance on the research and arguments presented. For example:

1 *The earliest **reputable** studies into the link between criminality and intelligence were perhaps those conducted by Goddard (1912), starting with an **unscientific** study of the Kalikak family.*

2 *By using a **subjective** assessment of 'feeble-mindedness', it left more questions than answers.*

3 *Goddard's later studies were **more acceptable** 'scientifically', as they used the **objective** IQ tests to measure for 'feeble-mindedness'.*

In examples 1 and 2 the choice of adjectives indicates that the author thinks these studies were some of the first good studies, but that they had significant weaknesses. In example 3 the author indicates a more positive evaluation.

TASK 3 Understanding and using evaluative adjectives

1 **Find the adjectives in the list in the text on page 139. Decide whether each adjective has a positive or negative meaning in the context in which it is used.**

more acceptable   arbitrary   foremost   objective   reputable   subjective   unscientific

2 **Rewrite sentences 1–6 using an adjective from 1 in place of the words in italics. You may need to change the structure of some sentences.**

Example: IQ studies are considered to be a measure of intelligence *based on fact, not personal opinion.* → IQ studies are considered to be an **objective** measure of intelligence.

1 It is one of the *most important* studies in the field.

2 It was a decision *not based on any particular reason.*

3 It is one of the most *well respected* studies of its kind.

4 The conclusions drawn are *based on personal opinion, not fact.*

5 Many early social experiments were *done without following accepted standards and practices.*

6 Whilst there are weaknesses in the study, the approach is *better for most people* than many previous ones.

TASK 4 Identifying premise and conclusion in an argument

1 **A premise is the statement or idea that an argument is based on. Look at the example and identify the premise and conclusion in sentences 1–3.**

premise   conclusion
↓   ↓

Example: *The majority of inmates in a prison have a low intellect. Therefore intelligence is a major factor in criminal behaviour.*

1 His father is a criminal. He is likely to become one.

2 She committed a crime before. As a result she will probably commit one again.

3 People who live in poor areas commit more crimes. He lives in a poor area, so he will probably go on to a life of crime.

2 **Work in pairs and identify the weaknesses in each argument in 1.**

3 **Read the following premise. According to the text, which conclusion, a or b, does it match?**

An average of 50 per cent of the inmates of 16 prisons were found to be 'feeble-minded'.

a Feeble-minded individuals are potential criminals.

b There is no connection between feeble-mindedness and criminality.

4 Find premises 1–4 in the text on page 139. Identify the conclusion related to each premise.

1 Fifty years of investigations found no link between intelligence and criminality.

2 There were fewer delinquent boys in the high IQ group, over 110, and far more delinquent boys in the low IQ group, under 90.

3 Children with low non-verbal intelligence at ages 8–10 later became convicted juvenile offenders.

4 Low non-verbal ability was linked to low verbal ability and to low school attainment at the age of 11.

5 Work in pairs and discuss which conclusions in 4 follow most logically from their premise.

TASK 5 Evaluating the strength of premises and conclusions

1 Read extracts 1–4 from later in the same text. In each extract, identify the premise and the conclusion.

EXTRACT 1

It is reasonable to accept that those with a lower IQ are less able to avoid detection.

EXTRACT 2

It is also worth noting that criminal activity (such as fraud and white-collar crime), which is likely to mostly be committed by individuals with high intelligence, is generally less likely to be discovered.

EXTRACT 3

IQ theory, far from testing innate intelligence or intellect, assesses the individual's school attainment, i.e. it measures levels of comprehension and vocabulary. The scores would therefore reflect educational attainment or cultural background rather than potential intelligence.

EXTRACT 4

Others allege that IQ tests simply measure class bias. The types of skills which are measured are not objective, but rather represent a cultural skill which is most likely held by, and useful to, a middle-class urban dweller.

2 Which premises and conclusions in 1 do you think most people agree with, and which are the most discussed? Identify the words or phrases in each extract that help you to decide.

TASK 6 Critical thinking – evaluating the arguments in a text

1 Work in groups and discuss questions 1–3. Give reasons to support your answers.

1 The text suggests that intelligence is linked to criminality. Do you agree?

2 Is intelligence innate (something we are born with) or can it be developed through education?

3 Can education reduce the chances of someone becoming a criminal?

2 Find evidence in the main text and the extracts in Task 5 to support your answers.

> **INDEPENDENT STUDY**
>
> Evaluating the strength of an argument is an important academic skill. Conclusions need to be closely linked to the premise to be convincing.
>
> ▶ Find a text from your own area of study. Identify the main arguments presented and evaluate the strength of these arguments.

When writing an argument essay, you need to present a main argument and reach a conclusion. Your argument should be based on logic and evidence, and include supporting arguments to help convince your audience. While presenting your argument, you also need to be aware of counter-arguments, i.e. arguments *against* your argument. You can include some discussion of arguments *against* in order to show that your argument *for* the issue is more convincing.

This module covers:
- Planning, organizing, and writing an argument essay
- Incorporating evidence in an essay
- Making a text more cohesive by varying vocabulary

TASK 1 Identifying types of argument

1 Read the essay title and the two possible introductions. Decide which essay presents:

a a balanced 'for and against' structure, with a similar amount of material for both sides of the argument

b a clear argument for <u>or</u> against the main question, with material that mainly supports the writer's argument.

> **TITLE:** *'Internet-related crime is not as serious as "real-life" crime such as burglary and violent crimes.' Argue for or against this statement.*

Introduction 1

[1]Since the growth of the internet in the 1990s, internet-related crime has become an increasingly worrying problem for society. [2]Internet-related crime refers to any criminal activity carried out mainly over the internet, such as fraud. [3]Other important examples include identity theft, hate crimes, and cyber-bullying. [4]Such crimes are serious, partly because people are often able to carry out crimes over the internet that they would not be able to commit in 'real life'. [5]Using examples and evidence from recent cases in Europe and the USA, this essay argues that all crimes are significant and should be treated seriously, whether or not they are committed in 'real life' or over the internet. [6]This issue is examined from social, legal, and psychological perspectives, which show the seriousness of the challenge facing society today.

Introduction 2

[1]Your internet service provider informs you that your usage is extremely high, even though you do not use the internet very much. What have the other people in your household been doing online? [2]The rise of the internet since the 1990s has created a number of worrying issues: parents' loss of control over what their children are doing, opportunities for misusing the technology, and the growth of serious crimes with serious consequences. [3]Internet-related crime is particularly serious because the victims are often the most vulnerable people in society, for example teenagers and young people. [4]There are many examples of internet-related crime, including piracy, financial scams, and identity theft. [5]In all these types of crime, there is a victim. [6]In this essay, I will firstly present the case for 'real-life' crimes being more serious than internet-related crime. I will then argue that internet-related crime is as serious as any other type of crime, by examining the possibilities for crime provided by the internet, with a particular focus on crimes involving young people.

2 For each introduction, identify the following features.

a an initial statement to gain the reader's attention

b background information to explain the importance of the topic, and provide any definitions and examples

c a supporting citation

d a thesis statement (including a statement of purpose)

3 Match features a–d in 2 to the relevant sentence(s) in each introduction.

4 Work in pairs. Discuss which points in 2 are *necessary* in an essay introduction, and which are *optional*.

TASK 2 Analysing and evaluating essay structures

1 Match essay structures A and B to the two introductions in Task 1.

2 Work in pairs and discuss questions 1 and 2.

STRUCTURE A	STRUCTURE B
• Body paragraph 1 arguments *for* the equal importance of internet-related crime	**• Body paragraph 1** social arguments *for* the equal importance of internet-related crime
• Body paragraph 2 arguments *against* the equal importance of internet-related crime	**• Body paragraph 2** legal arguments *for* the equal importance of internet-related crime
• Body paragraph 3 a counter-argument against the arguments in paragraph 2, leading to evaluation	**• Body paragraph 3** psychological arguments *for* the equal importance of internet-related crime *(In this structure, evaluation is integrated in all three body paragraphs.)*

1 Which essay structure (A or B) offers:
   • a more balanced argument?
   • a point-by-point argument analysed from different perspectives?
   • a structure for a more convincing argument?

2 Which structure would you select to write the essay in Task 1?

TASK 3 Evaluating and ordering supporting arguments

1 Read the essay title and related arguments 1–7, and complete the notes in the table.

> **TITLE:** *'Internet-related crime affects only particular groups and should not lead to a change of focus away from traditional crime fighting.'* Argue for or against this statement.

	Argument	For / against the essay statement	Evaluation
1	The internet can be the 'means to an end', i.e. criminals can use it to commit physical crimes.	*against*	*Anyone can be affected by internet-inspired crime.*
2	The internet can be used to steal intellectual property, such as research into a new product done by somebody else, and use this knowledge for financial gain.		
3	The internet helps anonymity – people can 'disguise' their identity easily.		
4	A large number of people do not regularly use the internet.		
5	The internet covers every area of crime – finance, education, intellectual property, sex – leading to many opportunities to commit different crimes.		
6	Crimes such as robbing a bank or attacking a person cause actual harm and injury.		
7	It is very difficult to 'police' and regulate the internet.		

2 Select the most convincing arguments from 1–7 to include in the essay.

3 Using one of the essay structures in Task 2, work out a logical order for the arguments you have chosen.

TASK 4 Selecting and integrating evidence from a source

1 **Read the text on Cybercrime on page 203 and complete the notes.**

Perspectives: *business,* ....

Definition of 'cybercrime': ....

Examples of threats: ....

Supporting evidence / statistics: ....

2 **Look again at the supporting evidence and statistics you identified in 1. Decide:**

- how this information is relevant to the essay in Task 3
- where you could use it in the essay.

3 **Write one or two sentences incorporating a piece of supporting evidence from the text, including a reference.**

Example: *Clearly internet-related crime is a serious issue. The problem is estimated to cost the UK £10 billion per year (Hamilton and Webster, 2009, p.118).*

ACADEMIC LANGUAGE

Cohesion (4) Using synonyms and other cohesive language in a written text

Cohesive language helps to connect the meaning and ideas in a text. You can make your writing more cohesive by using synonyms, and phrases with similar meanings:

Internet-related crime has become an increasingly worrying problem for society ... Other important examples include identity theft, hate crimes, and cyber-bullying ... Such crimes are serious ...
all crimes are significant and should be treated seriously ... This issue is examined from different perspectives, which show the seriousness of the challenge ...

In this example from the Introduction 1 in Task 1, the writer introduces the **topic**, *internet related crime*, and makes a number of references to the topic, including giving examples: *Other important examples, Such crimes, all crimes.*

The writer also uses **evaluation**. The topic of internet-related crime is given a 'label' (*an increasingly worrying problem*) which is then referred to using different nouns with a similar meaning: *issue, challenge.*

Varying adjectives also helps make the text more cohesive: *worrying → serious*. These in turn can vary their form or word class:

*Such crimes are **serious**.   All crimes should be treated **seriously**.   This demonstrates the **seriousness** of the challenge.*

TASK 5 Making a text more cohesive

1 **Look back at Introduction 1 in Task 1 and identify what the following phrases refer to.**

such crimes   this issue   the challenge

2 **Rewrite Introduction 3 below using the words / phrases in the list to replace the underlined words / phrases.**

these worrying developments   such criminal activity
these crimes   these crimes are   significant   challenge

Introduction 3

Cybercrime and internet-related crime have become some of the most serious problems facing society today. ¹Cybercrime and internet-related crime refer to crimes which take place online rather than in real life. ²These serious problems include fraudulent financial transactions, crimes of a racial nature, and certain sexual crimes. ³Cybercrime and internet-related crime must be taken very seriously because it is often the most vulnerable people in society, such as young people, who are the victims. Young people should be protected, not victimized. This essay examines the serious problems related to cybercrime and internet-related crime, by explaining why the ⁴problem is such a ⁵serious one, and by arguing that ⁶cybercrime and internet-related crime are of equal importance to 'real-life' crime.

TASK 6 Planning and writing an introduction

1 Look again at the three introductions in this module (in Task 1 and Task 5). Identify the sentences from each introduction which relate to features 1–5.

   1 an interesting contextualizing sentence

   2 background information

   3 a definition of key terms

   4 further information, e.g. rationale, explanations, examples

   5 a clear thesis statement (including a statement of purpose)

2 Work in pairs. Compare each of the five features in the three introductions. How are they similar or different?

3 You are going to write an essay of about 500 words in response to the essay title in Task 3. Look back at your notes in Task 3. Write an introduction which includes the features in 1 above (see Unit 7D for ideas).

INDEPENDENT STUDY

It is worth building up a strong resource bank to find evidence to support your arguments.

▸ Use library databases and internet-based resources such as Google Scholar to search for key terms when you are planning your writing.

TASK 7 Writing the main body paragraphs in an argument essay

1 Based on your notes and ideas in Task 3, write three body paragraphs for your essay. Follow guidelines 1–4.

   1 Decide on which structure you will use (see Task 2).
   In a *for* and *against* structure (Essay structure A), include arguments for and against the statement in paragraphs 1 and 2; in paragraph 3, include a counter-argument against <u>one</u> of the arguments in paragraph 1 or paragraph 2.
   In an **argument-driven structure** (Essay structure B), develop your argument in each paragraph by adding new perspectives and supporting evidence.

   2 Write a topic sentence for each paragraph stating your main argument clearly.

   3 For each paragraph, state your main point, add supporting evidence and examples, and evaluate these.

   4 If possible, find further support for your arguments from textbooks or online sources.

TASK 8 Writing a conclusion to an essay

1 Write the conclusion to your essay. Follow guidelines 1–3 (see Unit 9D for ideas).

   1 Refer back to the introduction, and restate the main point or argument – your audience should be very clear about what your conclusion is.

   2 Briefly restate the most important reason(s) for this conclusion, based on the evidence in the essay.

   3 Make recommendations for further discussion, research, or future implications in the area.

Sample answer
page 192

TASK 9 Critical thinking – self- and peer-evaluation

1 Use questions 1–5 to evaluate your essay.

   1 By the end of the introduction, are the aims and organization of the essay clear?

   2 Does the essay follow a logical structure?

   3 Is there enough supporting evidence, and is it relevant to the main argument?

   4 Is any in-text referencing accurate?

   5 Does the essay reach a clear conclusion, based on the arguments you have presented?

2 Compare your essay with at least two other students. Use the questions in 1 to evaluate each other's essays. Try to identify one thing that could be improved in each essay you read.

You can use a range of verbs to present an argument and these verbs demonstrate stance on the point being made. Verbs like *state* show certainty in a stance, whereas a verb like *allege* indicates that the evidence may not be strong. You can further demonstrate your stance with your choice of noun or adjective. Nouns and adjectives show stance through *connotation*, e.g. using a word like *failure* often indicates that the author has negative view of the situation. This is also indicated by the use of adjectives with preffixes that show an opposite, e.g. *un-*, *dis-*, or *mis-*. Understanding vocabulary selection can help you express your stance, and better evaluate arguments.

TASK 1 Presenting and assessing views

1 Match the verb in italics in sentences 1–6 to definitions a–f.

1 It has been *alleged* that the company knew its employees were breaking the law.

2 Early studies *argued* for a biological tendency to commit crime.

3 He controversially *claimed* that physical appearance and crime were linked.

4 Although people *perceive* education to be linked to criminality, the evidence is inconclusive.

5 Johnson *suggests* that social class is linked to crime.

6 Researchers *doubt* that it is both genetic and environmental factors that contribute to criminal behaviour.

a To understand or think of sb / sth in a particular way.

b To state something as a fact but without giving proof.

c To put forward an idea or a plan for other people to think about.

d To give reasons why you think that sth is right / wrong, true / not true, etc.

e To feel uncertain about sth, that sth is not true, or will probably not happen

f To say that sth is true although it has not been proved and other people may not believe it.

2 Read sentences 1–6 and underline the word / words that demonstrates the writer's stance.

1 The main problem in the physical studies was the research method used.

2 It is a mistake to think that genetics is the main determinant of criminal behaviour.

3 The misinterpretation of the data led to a number of people being sent to prison.

4 The narrow sample size makes the study invalid.

5 It is questionable whether the data can be applied to other cultural contexts.

6 The criticism of this book was wholly unjustified.

3 Match each positive stance 1–4 to a negative stance from 2.

1 The study was extensive and thorough.

2 It was a valid approach to take for the type of data required.

3 The accurate interpretation of the data meant there was no possibility of a mistake.

4 The negative interpretation of the data was based on sound evidence.

4 Complete the text using the correct word from each pair.

Early psychologists [1] .... (argued / suggested) for a number of theories that today are widely rejected. Many are not accepted largely due to basic [2] .... (problems / doubts) in the research process such as a control group that ultimately make their conclusions [3] .... (negative / invalid). Although there may have been weaknesses in these theories that made them [4] .... (alleged / questionable), they did make people [5] .... (perceive / criticize) behaviours and ideas in different ways. For example, Goddard's [6] .... (data / claim) that intelligence was linked to criminality has led to a vast growth in the body of research that would otherwise not be possible.

TASK 2 Noticing and interpreting arguments

1 Find an argument text in your own area of study. Underline the reporting verbs and the evaluative language. How would you assess the overall stance presented in the arguments?

UNIT 11 Energy

ACADEMIC FOCUS: PROBLEM AND SOLUTION

LEARNING OBJECTIVES

This unit covers:

Listening
- Identifying and using the language of problems and solutions
- Reviewing notes to identify the need for further research
- Understanding evaluation in a lecture

Speaking
- Selecting and synthesizing information
- Using *wh-* structures to signal and focus key points
- Researching and preparing a group presentation

Reading
- Identifying supporting detail and evidence in a text
- Identifying problems, solutions, and evaluation in a text
- Understanding how meanings are expressed through prepositional phrases

Writing
- Effectively evaluating solutions
- Planning and organizing problem-solution essays
- Evaluating your own work

Vocabulary
- Recognizing problems
- Introducing and responding to problems

Discussion

1   A person's individual energy consumption varies, depending on factors like car use, size of house, flights taken per year, diet, and personal consumption of goods and services. Work in groups and discuss questions 1 and 2.

   1   How do you think your individual consumption might compare to that of other people in your country? Give reasons.

   2   Think of at least three suggestions for reducing your individual energy consumption. For example: cycling instead of travelling by car / bus / train, downloading e-books instead of buying books.

2   Compare and evaluate your suggestions in 1.2 using the following questions.

   1   How easy would it be for you to follow each suggestion?

   2   Which one has the greatest benefit for the environment?

   3   Which one do you think would save you the most money?

11A Listening Lectures (8)

Lectures which include discussion of problems and solutions can focus on either problems or solutions, or both. When a lecture focuses on problems, this may be followed by a seminar or another lecture on solutions. When the lecture focuses on solutions, you may have a seminar or lecture evaluating these solutions. Recognizing language that signals problems and solutions will help your comprehension and note-taking. Recognizing evaluative language will help you to assess the lecturer's stance on possible solutions.

This module covers:

- Identifying and using the language of problems and solutions
- Reviewing notes to identify the need for further research
- Understanding evaluation in a lecture

TASK 1 Using background knowledge to prepare for a lecture

1 **Look at the four main uses of energy. Put them in order from highest to lowest in terms of energy consumption globally.**

  1 Transportation (cars, planes, etc.)   3 Commercial (shops, restaurants, etc.)

  2 Industrial (agriculture, manufacturing, etc.)   4 Residential (houses, apartments, etc.)

2 **Compare your ideas with another student. Give reasons for your selection.**

TASK 2 Understanding the purpose of a lecture

> **Energy in crisis?**
> What is happening to global energy supplies and what we are doing about it
>
> **Dr Stephen Clay**
> Department of Environmental Studies

1 **You are going to watch part of a lecture on global energy supplies. Look at the slide and try to predict at least two things the lecturer will talk about.**

2 ▶11.1 **Watch Extract 1 from the introduction to the lecture and discuss questions 1 and 2.**

  1 What is the key issue facing the world today?

  2 Will the focus of the lecture be mainly on the problem or the solutions?

ACADEMIC LANGUAGE

Problems and solutions

Speakers talking about problems and solutions often use a variety of nouns and verbs. Recognizing key nouns and verbs can help you to identify whether a speaker is discussing a problem or a solution.

> As a country's overall standard of living improves, and its material wealth increases, so too does the **burden** on that country's resources in terms of energy use.

> The development of these newly industrialized economies places increasing **pressure** on the world's energy supplies, particularly oil and gas.

> However, not only are the Chinese authorities looking to **address** these issues within China, they are also **responding** to them in a way that could further enhance their economic growth.

> So, in what ways is China looking to **resolve** these issues? What **solutions** are they currently **implementing**?

TASK 3 Using language to refer to problems and solutions

1 **Categorize the nouns and verbs in the list according to whether they refer to problems or solutions. Check the meaning of any unknown words in a dictionary.**

address   crisis   dispute   improve   issue   option   overcome   resolve   shortage   threat

2 Read the extract from a student presentation on the theme of the lecture. Select a noun or verb from 1 to replace the word(s) in italics.

World energy supply is considered by some analysts to be a ¹*danger* to world peace. It's likely that there will be a shortage of fossil fuels in the future, and any drop in world energy supplies could cause a ²*dangerous situation* on a scale never seen before. One ³*challenge* to ⁴*get through* is that modern life is dependent on high energy consumption. Many countries are looking to ⁵*make better* the energy efficiency of homes and offices. For example, the Chinese government hopes to ⁶*deal with* the issue by introducing a range of solutions. One ⁷*method* is to update and modernize power plants. Additionally, alternative sources such as wind, solar, and biofuels are being explored. However, there has been a recent ⁸*disagreement* about the use of biofuels as an alternative energy source.

3 ◀))11.2 Listen to the extract from the presentation and check your answers to 2.

4 Look at the transcript on page 219, or watch Extract 1 again. Identify any other nouns and verbs related to problems and solutions.

> **Solutions in progress – China**
> - Power plants
> - Energy cap
> - Emerging technologies
> - Local solutions

TASK 4 Taking detailed notes on solutions

1 ▶11.3 Watch Extract 2 and make notes for each solution shown on the slide.

Example: Power plants: *Replacing older inefficient plants*

2 Compare your notes with another student. Check whether you identified the same points.

TASK 5 Reviewing notes to identify further questions

1 Look at the notes on the energy cap solution and questions 1–4. Which questions were written in response to the notes on this solution?

Energy cap:

approx. 8% p.a. (per year) energy consumption

2010 = 3.25 billion tonnes of coal or equivalent p.a.

target growth = below 5% p.a. to 4.1 billion tonnes

Questions:

1 How will this solution work? Has it been done before?

2 How is it going to help the economy?

3 What is the environmental impact of an extra 1 bn tonnes?

4 What measures have been taken? Have they been effective?

2 Review your notes on the other solutions. Write two similar questions for each of the other solutions in Extract 2.

TASK 6 Understanding evaluation in a lecture

1 ▶11.3 Watch Extract 2 of the lecture again and note down the lecturer's evaluation of each solution discussed.

2 Decide if the lecturer's evaluation of each solution is (a) a mainly positive, (b) mainly negative, or (c) neither positive or negative.

3 Identify the language the lecturer uses that helped you decide on your answers in 2.

TASK 7 Critical thinking – responding to the content of a lecture

1 Work in groups and discuss questions 1 and 2.

1 Do you agree with the lecturer's evaluations in Task 6? Give reasons.

2 Give your own evaluation of the solutions. Which one(s) will be most effective?

2 The lecturer says that dealing with the rising demand for energy when traditional sources of energy are running out is 'the key issue facing the world's governments today'. Do you agree? Give reasons and examples.

3 Do you know of any solutions which the government of your country is implementing to help solve this problem? Explain them, and offer your evaluation.

> **INDEPENDENT STUDY**
>
> Adding questions to your notes can help you to remember ideas for further research.
>
> ▶ Each time you are given a seminar topic, note down research questions based on your notes from the lecture.

11B Speaking Presentations (2)

As well as giving presentations in seminars, you may also have to give more formal presentations, on your own or with other students. A group presentation enables you to share the preparation and to give useful feedback on each other's contribution. A key part of preparation is reading and research. You need to select and use relevant information from the sources you have, in order to make your presentation interesting and informative for your audience. Interacting with your audience, for example by asking questions for them to answer, can also help them engage with your ideas.

This module covers:

- Selecting and synthesizing information
- Using *wh-* structures to signal and focus key points
- Researching and preparing a group presentation

TASK 1 Reading to prepare for a presentation

1 **You are going to prepare a group presentation on possible solutions to the future problem of finding additional sources of energy. Work in pairs and discuss questions 1–3.**

  1 Which countries are the biggest consumers of energy used in the world today?

  2 Which countries are likely to be the main consumers in the future?

  3 What does this mean for world energy supplies?

2 **Read the text on page 204 and complete the notes relating to the *situation* and *problems* discussed.**

3 **Work in pairs and compare your notes. Write a summary of the problem in one sentence.**

TASK 2 Analysing the problem and possible solutions

1 **Work in groups and discuss questions 1–4.**

  1 What did you find interesting or surprising in the text?

  2 What is your evaluation of the main problem? (e.g. How serious is it?)

  3 According to the text, what needs to happen in order to provide a solution to the problem?

  4 What is likely to happen if the problem is not dealt with? Consider this question from some of the following perspectives: economics, society, health, the environment, politics.

TASK 3 Analysing structure and content in a group presentation

1 ◀⟩ 11.4 **Listen to Extract 1 from a group presentation about some solutions to the problem discussed in the text in Task 1. As you listen, note down the main points that will be included in the presentation.**

2 **Note down the expressions the speaker uses to:**

  1 introduce the topic of the presentation

  2 preview the key points and explain how the presentation is structured

  3 refer to any limitations (e.g. time available).

3 ◀⟩ 11.5–11.7 **Listen to Extracts 2–4 of the presentation and for each extract note down:**

  1 the solution being presented

  2 the evidence and supporting information for that solution

  3 the speaker's evaluation of the solution.

4 ◀⟩ 11.5–11.7 **Listen to Extracts 2–4 again and note down the expressions the speaker uses to:**

  1 introduce the solution   2 give an evaluation   3 hand over to the next speaker.

Signposting and focusing Using *wh-* clauses

Wh- clauses (structures beginning with *what, why, where, how*, etc.) are often used at the start of a sentence to introduce or draw attention to specific information, including evaluation. This can then be introduced in the second half of the sentence with *is / are*.

What we want to do is to show that there are concerns about …

Where the wind turbines are located is important.

How this can be achieved is still not clear.

As they clearly signal new information for the listener, sentences starting with *wh-* clauses are well suited to spoken presentations.

TASK 4 Using *wh-* clauses

1 **Rewrite sentences 1–4 so that they start with a *wh-* clause.**

Example: *There are two main reasons for this, which I'd like to look at next.*
→ **What I'd like to look at next** *are the two main reasons for this.*

1 I'm saying that environmental and economic considerations need to be balanced.

2 It's now possible, but expensive, to capture and store CO_2.

3 I'd like to emphasize the difficulties involved in dealing with nuclear waste.

4 It's hard to see where 1,200 new wind turbines a week can be situated.

2 ◀))11.8 **Listen to Extract 5 and check your answers. Which words are stressed?**

TASK 5 Researching information to use in a presentation

1 **You are going to work out a solution to the following problem: *We need to produce 6 CMO (Cubic Mile of Oil) to meet the expected growth in global energy needs*. Work in groups and follow steps 1–4.**

1 Look at the table on page 205 and read the information on different energy sources.

2 Select three or four sources of energy from the table which <u>together</u> provide a solution to the problem and would deliver the necessary amount of energy (in CMO).

3 Select from the *key* information in the text on page 204 and the table. Do not try to include everything.

4 Think of questions to help you evaluate your solution. For example: *How effective is this solution? How much energy can it provide? What are the potential problems?*

TASK 6 Planning and preparing a group presentation

1 **In your groups, you are going to give a short presentation of up to five minutes. Plan the content and organization of your presentation using the guidelines on page 205.**

2 **Practise each part individually, then practise as a group. Check the timing.**

TASK 7 Giving and evaluating group presentations

1 **Take turns to give your presentations. As you watch other groups' presentations, note down any points to give as feedback. Use the following questions to help you.**

- Were the solutions presented clearly?
- Was the evidence and supporting information presented effectively?
- Was evaluation included, and clearly presented?
- Overall, was the presentation clear and easy to understand?

2 **Work with one other group, and give feedback based on your notes in 1.**

3 **In your groups, discuss the feedback you have received and think about how you could act on it next time you give a presentation.**

> **INDEPENDENT STUDY**
>
> Feedback from other students - your peers - can be very valuable, as they can offer a different perspective from your teacher.
>
> ▶ When giving presentations, ask one or two other students to prepare feedback for you, and suggest specific areas for them to focus on.

Textbooks frequently present a problem or problems, and it is important that you can identify these problems from different perspectives. You also need to identify and understand any analysis and evaluation of the problem – for example, the main causes, and how serious it is. Analysis and evaluation are often followed by suggested solutions to the problem, and these are also evaluated. The evaluation of the solution answers questions such as: *Will this work? How expensive is it? Is it effective?*

This module covers:

- Identifying supporting detail and evidence in a text
- Identifying problems, solutions, and evaluation in a text
- Understanding how meanings are expressed through prepositional phrases

TASK 1 Discussing problems from a range of perspectives

1 **Match the energy sources in the list with pictures A–F.**

biomass / solid waste incineration .... biofuels .... hydroelectric ....
nuclear power .... solar power .... wind power ....

2 **Work in groups. Discuss what you know about each energy source, using questions 1–3.**

1 What geographical locations is it often found in?

2 Is it a renewable source of energy?

3 Is it used in your own country?

A   B
C   D
E   F

3 **In your groups, identify at least one *problem* for each energy source. Look at the problem from different perspectives, e.g. environmental, financial, political, geographical, technological, ethical.**

Example: *Biofuels use up a large quantity of plants such as maize, which could be eaten by humans or animals. Growing all these plants takes up a lot of space, which again could be used for other purposes.*

TASK 2 Gaining an overview of a text

1 **Quickly read the text on page 153, and identify the energy sources in Task 1.1.**

2 **The heading for the text is missing. Match the possible headings 1 and 2 with the correct description, a or b.**

1 What are the environmentally sustainable options available?

2 Balancing economic and environmental considerations

a a *discussion* of the environmental problems associated with different energy sources

b a *description* of the choices for ways of producing energy that are environmentally sustainable

3 **Read the text and select the most appropriate heading.**

TASK 3 Identifying and reporting essential information

1 **Note down the topic (1–9) for each paragraph 1–9 of the text.**

1 *The main benefits of renewable energy*

2 *The environmental consequences of renewable-energy sources*

3 ....

4 ....

5 ....

6 ....

7 ....

8 ....

9 *Greenhouse gas emissions for coal and gas.*..

2 Note down the main point(s) in each paragraph.

Example: *Paragraph 2: all renewable-energy sources have some environmental consequences*

3 Work in pairs. Use the information from the table and your notes in 2 to give a spoken description of one paragraph from the text. Use an appropriate reporting verb.

contrasts   evaluates   explains   signals   speculates   states   suggests

Example: *Paragraph 1 **explains** the main benefits of using renewable-energy sources compared to conventional energy sources.*

1   There are several benefits of using renewable-energy supplies in preference to conventional sources:
  • they cut carbon dioxide emissions,
  • they decrease a country's reliance on imported fuel and add to diversity of energy supply,
  • they cut emissions of acid rain pollutants, sulphur dioxide and nitrogen oxides.

2   However, all renewable-energy sources have some environmental consequences: their benefits have to be seen in relation to the alternatives. The problems of each individual technology have been discussed in the preceding chapters and a detailed comparison made in the companion text *Energy Systems and Sustainability*.

3   It is unlikely, for example, that there will be much further development of large-scale hydroelectricity within the UK or the EU, apart from re-powering existing schemes. The problems of flooding large areas of land and the possibility of methane emissions from vegetation are sufficient to rule out further expansion. Although this technology is counted as part of total renewable-energy targets, it is omitted from most promotion schemes.

4   Similarly, municipal solid waste (MSW) is widely burned, and contributes to national renewable-energy totals, yet it faces opposition because of fears of dioxin emissions. This, too, is omitted from many promotion schemes, although the gasification and burning of waste, which might have lower emissions, are included.

5   Other forms of biomass also need to be burned cleanly to avoid air pollution. In an extreme case, the Indian government has a policy of promoting LPG and kerosene to *discourage* the use of firewood as a cooking fuel in cities.

6   The intensive cultivation of energy crops is being encouraged although it may require the use of fossil fuel in the production of fertilizers, and the harvesting and transport of the produce.

7   It is difficult to put actual costs to the relative benefits and disadvantages of different technologies. Energy normally has a market-place price in terms of £ per GJ (giga-joule) or pence per kWh (kilowatt hour). What is missing are the 'external costs', which are in effect paid by society. The EU, under its ExternE study, has attempted to evaluate these for various electricity generation technologies (see Table 10.3). It has taken into account a wide range of factors, including health risks and environmental damage, and expressed them in euro cents per kWh. These are, of course, the extra costs in addition to the normal market price of electricity, which as an EU average, is about 4 euro cents per kWh.

8   However, this study specifically excluded global warming costs resulting from the emission of greenhouse gases. For nuclear power and the renewable energy technologies listed above, these costs are small. For coal and gas, it is important to look at the likely carbon dioxide costs under the proposed EU carbon trading arrangements.

9   When coal or gas are used to produce electricity with current technologies, there are significant differences in the total emissions of the greenhouse gases, CO_2, methane and nitrous oxide.

Primary Energy Source	External Costs Euro cents per kWh
Coal	5.7
Gas	1.6
Biomass	1.6
PV Solar	0.6
Hydro	0.4
Nuclear	0.4
Wind	0.1

1 euro cent (2001) = 0.6p
Source: European Commission (2001)

Table 10.3 Estimated external costs of electricity generation from various primary energy sources: European Union average

SOURCE: Boyle, G. (Ed.) *Renewable Energy: Power for a Sustainable Future* 2nd ed. (2004). pp.411-3. Oxford: Oxford University Press.

GLOSSARY

dioxin *(n)* a poisonous chemical used in industry and farming

GJ *(n abbr)* giga-joule , a unit of energy equal to one billion (10^9) joules

LPG *(n abbr)* Liquefied Petroleum Gas

TASK 4 Identifying problems, solutions, and evaluation in a text

1 Complete the table by matching paragraphs 1–9 in the text with descriptions a–i.

	Description	Paragraph
a	Signals a similar problem to the one just discussed, with a different technology (biomass in the form of MSW)	4
b	Signals further problems, leading to evaluation of two types of energy – renewable and fossil fuel – one positive and the other not given	
c	Explains the main benefits of renewable energy sources	1
d	Gives a final evaluation of fossil fuels (coal and gas), and suggests big differences in total emissions	
e	Evaluates the probability of future growth in hydroelectricity, and explains why this is unlikely	
f	Links biomass production to the use of fossil fuels (coal and gas) - this is another problem	
g	Contrasts with the previous paragraph: signals that there are problems with all renewable energy sources, and states that specific problems are discussed in a different part of the text	
h	States another problem with biomass, and gives an example of a situation in a specific country	
i	Explains the difficulty of evaluating different technologies, and gives examples and extra information	7

2 Identify the language in the text which expresses the problems, solutions, evaluation, and contrasts in each paragraph.

Example: 1 There are several _benefits_ of …
            2 _However_ / … have some environmental _consequences_

3 Work in pairs. Compare your answers in 2 and discuss whether each word you identified is *positive*, *negative*, or *neutral*.

Example: Paragraphs 1 and 2 – The word **benefits** is always positive. The word
            consequences seems to be neutral, but in the text it's more negative because it
            follows the word **however**, which signals contrast.

TASK 5 Understanding and summarizing detailed information

1 Study Table 10.3 on page 153 and the related information in the text, and complete the notes.

Geographical / political context: *The European Union*

Year of publication of data: ....

'External costs' relate to: ....

Energy source with highest external cost: ....

Approx. external cost of a typical renewable energy source: ....

Exchange rate: ....

2 Use the information in the text, including the table, to make more detailed notes on each of the following energy sources.

1 hydroelectricity

2 biomass (including municipal solid waste and energy crops)

Example: _Wind energy_
            • _renewable_
            • _small global warming costs_
            • _low external costs = 0.1 euro cents / kWh_

3 Select one of the energy sources from 2 and use your notes to write a summary. Make sure you include:

• a reference to the source (i.e. the original text)

• the main points from the original text.

Example: *According to Boyle (2004), wind energy is one of the fastest-growing renewables*
            and is being developed widely in the UK and Northern Europe. There is
            opposition because of problems with noise, 'visual pollution', and danger to
            birds, but the costs are very low.

Prepositions (2) Expressing meaning using complex prepositions

Academic texts often use complex prepositions (prepositions containing two to four words) to express the relationship between two ideas or objects. One example is *in terms of*, which introduces and specifies the context of something which has just been mentioned:

*The effects of these can be summarized **in terms of** the equivalent amount of CO_2 produced per kWh, as in Table 10.4.*

Examples of other complex prepositions from the text on page 153 include the following:

- *Comparing two items: There are several benefits of using renewable-energy supplies **in preference to** conventional sources.*
- *Connecting two items: Their benefits have to be seen **in relation to** the alternatives.*
- *Making an exception: It is unlikely, for example, that there will be much further development of large-scale hydroelectricity within the UK or the EU, **apart from** re-powering existing schemes.*
- *Including something as part of something else: Although this technology is counted **as part of** total renewable-energy targets, it is omitted from most promotion schemes.*
- *Giving a reason: It faces opposition **because of** fears of dioxin emissions.*

TASK 6 Using complex prepositions

1 **Complete sentences 1–6 with a complex preposition from the list.**

in relation to   as part of   in terms of (x2)   in preference to   because of   apart from

1 Using renewable-energy technologies .... conventional sources can benefit the environment.

2 As with any technology, the benefits of wind power need to be evaluated .... other technologies.

3 There are other factors which must be taken into consideration when planning a new power station, ... simply the financial cost.

4 Renewable energy sources need to be considered .... the wider picture, including fossil fuels like coal and gas.

5 .... concerns about safety, many governments are unwilling to commit to nuclear energy programmes.

6 To be successful, energy policy has to be thought about not only .... a country's geography, but also .... its political structures.

2 **Select at least three complex prepositions from Academic Language and write sentences based on a topic related to your area of study.**

Example: *Law – Legal judgements are normally made **in relation to** the context in which the offence was committed.*

TASK 7 Critical thinking – evaluating content arising from a text

1 **Work in groups and discuss questions 1 and 2, based on evidence from the text. Think about the information in relation to a country or countries you are familiar with.**

1 What are the main advantages and disadvantages of using renewable-energy sources?

2 What are the future prospects for using renewable-energy sources?

2 **Discuss and evaluate possible solutions to some of the problems associated with fossil fuels and renewable energy sources. Think of ways in which your chosen area of study could contribute solutions to the problems.**

11D Writing Problem-solution essays

Problem-solution essays usually follow a fixed structure. Using a fixed structure will help you organize your essay more effectively. A problem-solution essay normally requires evaluation. This is the part of the essay where you will be expected to show your critical thinking skills. There are a number of techniques that you can use to evaluate the solutions, which will ensure that you make the strongest possible case. Using more formal language to present your evaluation will give your essay a more academic feel.

This module covers:
- Effectively evaluating solutions
- Planning and organizing problem-solution essays
- Evaluating your own work

TASK 1 Analysing an essay title

1 **Look at the following essay question and the different features that are highlighted. Work in pairs and discuss questions 1 and 2.**

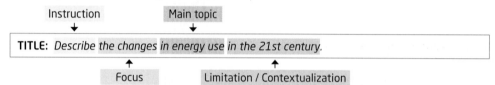

1 Why is it useful to identify the different parts of an essay title?

2 How can analysing the title affect the content and organization of an essay?

2 **Look at essay titles 1–4 and identify similar features. Not all the titles have the same four features.**

1 Describe the main alternative renewable energy sources.

2 Evaluate the alternative renewable energy sources available in the UK as possible long-term solutions to the energy crisis.

3 'Biomass fuel is not an effective solution to the energy crisis as it leads to additional problems such as increased food shortages.' Discuss.

4 Analyse the efficiency of three renewable energy sources.

3 **Which essays in 2 are (a) are problem-solution essays and (b) involve an element of evaluation?**

TASK 2 Identifying and evaluating solutions

1 **Read the essay title, which presents a key problem, and the example solution below. Work in pairs and suggest three more possible solutions.**

> **TITLE:** *'Energy consumption in the developed and developing world is becoming dangerously high.' Suggest and evaluate different solutions for reducing energy consumption.*

Example: *Solution A: Encourage people to change to a vegetarian diet, as the production of meat uses large amounts of energy and water.*

2 **One way to evaluate solutions is to compare them in pairs: A and B, A and C, B and C, etc.**

1 For each pair, decide which is the more effective solution, and write the letter in the correct box in the table. For example, if between A and B you think B is the more effective solution, write B in the box.

	Solution A	Solution B	Solution C	Solution D
Solution A	–			
Solution B	–	–		
Solution C	–	–	–	
Solution D	–	–	–	–

2 Discuss the questions below.
- How many times did you select each solution?
- How do you think using such a technique might help you prepare for a problem-solution essay?

3 Another way to evaluate a solution is to note down the different factors you need to consider. Look again at the essay title and example solution in 1, and add two more factors to the list.

Factors to consider:

How likely people are to follow this suggestion.

How much the suggestion is likely to cost.

4 Write the two additional factors from 3 in the top row of the table.

	1 How likely people are to follow this suggestion	2 How much the suggestion is likely to cost	3	4 ....
Solution A				
Solution B				
Solution C				
Solution D				

5 Look at the notes below on Solution A. Work in pairs and evaluate each of your own solutions in a similar way.

Solution A: Encourage people to change to a vegetarian diet, as the production of meat uses large amounts of energy and water.

Notes (evaluation):

Access to fresh water isn't always available, so how do you ensure that food is hygienic?

A vegetarian diet is expensive in some locations due to the cost of transport, which also increases the amount of energy used.

To produce a kilo of beef costs more per kilo than to produce a vegetable crop, due to the amount of water and energy needed.

6 Use your notes in 5 to give each solution (A–D) a score on a scale of 0 to 4 for each factor (0 = poor; 4 = very good).

TASK 3 Identifying organization in a problem-solution essay

1 Problem-solution essays can be organized in different ways, depending on the number of problems and solutions being discussed. Look at the two structures below and decide which is more suitable.

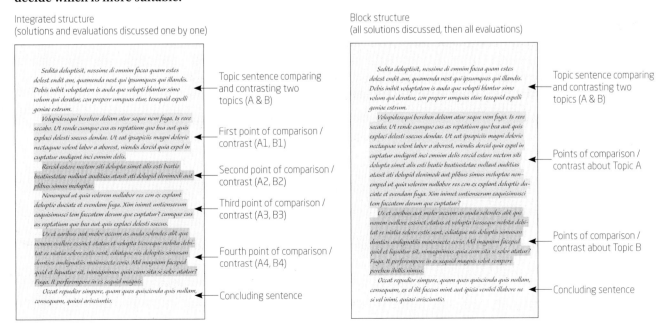

Integrated structure
(solutions and evaluations discussed one by one)

- Topic sentence comparing and contrasting two topics (A & B)
- First point of comparison / contrast (A1, B1)
- Second point of comparison / contrast (A2, B2)
- Third point of comparison / contrast (A3, B3)
- Fourth point of comparison / contrast (A4, B4)
- Concluding sentence

Block structure
(all solutions discussed, then all evaluations)

- Topic sentence comparing and contrasting two topics (A & B)
- Points of comparison / contrast about Topic A
- Points of comparison / contrast about Topic B
- Concluding sentence

2 Read the paragraph below from an essay responding to the essay title in Task 2.1 on page 156. Identify the following features.

- the solution (topic sentence)
- evidence to support the solution
- a positive evaluation of the solution
- a negative evaluation of the solution

Lower consumption of animal products is one of the most effective solutions to reducing energy consumption. America is the second largest energy consumer in the world and currently uses one third of its energy consumption on producing animals for food (UN, 2010). The Food and Agricultural Organization of the UN (2006) also reports that twenty per cent of greenhouse emissions come from the meat industry and that fifty per cent of the world's crops are produced to feed animals. It could be argued that such a change would not only reduce energy consumption but could also increase health throughout the world. There might be a reduction in the intake of calories in the developed world, which would help to reduce the health problems related to obesity. An increase in calorie intake in the developing world would also help combat the issue of malnutrition. While there are clearly a number of benefits to this change it might be challenging to implement. In many cultures meat is seen as a luxury product and its consumption tends to increase in line with the wealth of a nation. Changing dietary habits ingrained within a culture is likely to be a slow process.

3 Find examples of words / phrases that helped you to identify the evaluation in the paragraph.

4 Why does the writer include both positive and negative evaluations?

5 Read the paragraph again and decide if the writer is using an integrated or block structure to organize the essay.

ACADEMIC LANGUAGE ▸Language reference page 179 20

Evaluative language *It* and *There* structures

Using *I* and *we* in academic writing is often seen as too informal and personal. Using *It* and *There* structures helps make your writing more formal and impersonal, and is more appropriate when evaluating ideas, evidence, or arguments.

It could be argued that *such a change would not only reduce energy consumption but could also increase health throughout the world.*

There might be *a reduction in the intake of calories in the developed world …*

While **there are clearly** *a number of benefits to this change,* **it might be** *challenging to implement.*

TASK 4 Using evaluative language with *It* and *There*

1 Complete sentences 1–6 with a phrase from the list. Use the information in brackets to help you.

There is little doubt that   It could be argued that   It must also be recognized that
While it may be true that   ~~There is some debate about~~   There is little to be said for

1 *There is some debate about* the effectiveness of the long-term plans. (this is not agreed on)

2 _____ increased spending on public transport is the most effective solution. (it is a possibility)

3 _____ vegetarianism would be effective in reducing carbon emissions, very few people would be willing to make this switch. (there are limitations to this)

4 _____ changes to consumption patterns need to be made. (this is probably right)

5 _____ the use of one single solution. (this is probably wrong)

6 _____ changing people's behaviour alone would not be sufficient, and that alternative energy sources need to be considered. (acknowledging another point)

TASK 5 Writing a paragraph for a problem-solution essay

1 **Use your notes from Task 2 to write a paragraph similar to the one in Task 3, presenting and evaluating a solution to the essay title in Task 2.1.**

   1 Select one solution (B, C, or D) from Task 2.2, and write a topic sentence clearly stating the solution.

   2 Think of an argument or information to support your solution and write a sentence presenting this.

   3 Look back at your notes evaluating your chosen solution in Task 2.5 and write two sentences, one giving a positive evaluation of the solution, the other giving a negative evaluation. Make sure that you include *It* and *There* structures to give your evaluations.

2 **Organize your sentences into a paragraph of approximately 100 words.**

3 **Work in pairs and evaluate each other's paragraphs. Check that the paragraphs include:**
   - a topic sentence clearly stating the solution
   - evidence to support the solution
   - positive <u>and</u> negative evaluation of the solution using *It* and *There* structures.

TASK 6 Planning and writing a problem-solution essay

1 **You are going to write a problem-solution essay of approximately 500 words in response to the following title from Task 2. Use guidelines 1–6 to help you plan the structure.**

> **TITLE:** *'Energy consumption in the developed and developing world is becoming dangerously high.' Suggest and evaluate different solutions for reducing energy consumption.*

Sample answer
page 193

   1 Analyse the title – how many different elements does it include?

   2 Review your notes on solutions and evaluations in Task 2 and organize them into an outline for the essay. Your essay should include an introduction, a conclusion, and at least two body paragraphs.

   3 Select a structure for the essay, *integrated* or *block*. Decide how many paragraphs to include and what information will go in each paragraph.

   4 Write your introduction, including the features below (see Unit 7D for ideas).
   - an opening sentence to gain the reader's interest
   - relevant background information
   - a clear thesis statement
   - a statement of purpose

   5 Write the main body paragraphs of your essay. Make sure each paragraph includes:
   - a topic sentence clearly stating the solution
   - evidence to support the solution
   - positive and negative evaluation of the solution
   - appropriate phrases to introduce evaluation.

   6 Write a conclusion summarizing the main ideas and restating the main thesis. Remember not to include any new information (see Unit 7D for ideas).

TASK 7 Evaluating your essay

1 **Work in pairs and evaluate each other's essays. Use questions 1–4 to help you.**

   1 Is it clear which solutions are being suggested, and why?

   2 Are the solutions clearly evaluated?

   3 Identify the evaluative language used. Has it been used accurately?

   4 Do the introduction and conclusion include all the relevant features?

2 **Give each other feedback on your essays and suggest points for improvement.**

> **INDEPENDENT STUDY**
>
> Feedback is a key part of the learning process. When you receive feedback on one piece of writing, you should think about how you can use it to improve *all* your essays.
>
> ▶ When you next receive feedback on an essay, make a note of any points that could apply to other essays and check these before you hand in your next assignment.

11E Vocabulary Problems and solutions

Two key vocabulary areas in problem-solution essays focus on the language used to present, and the language used to respond to, problems. Verb + noun collocations and adjective + noun collocations can be used to present or recognize a problem, for example, *a long-term impact* and *address the issue*. Likewise, a variety of verbs and nouns can also be used to highlight ways of resolving problems, for example, *to deal with a response* and *to handle a problem*.

TASK 1 Recognizing problems

1 **Read sentences 1–8 and decide whether they are presenting problems or solutions.**

1 The company faced the dilemma of low short-term growth and high costs, with potential long-term growth.

2 The UN Security Council unanimously adopted a resolution calling for a halt to hostilities.

3 The government responded by banning all future demonstrations.

4 Their habitat is under threat from new road developments.

5 The government needs to address the problem of traffic congestion.

6 The breakdown in talks represents a temporary setback in the peace process.

7 Famine relief provided by developing countries only has a short-term impact and does not deal with the issue in the long term.

8 The government's debt is placing a burden on the whole of society.

2 **Underline the word or phrase in each sentence that you think is key to presenting or responding to each problem.**

TASK 2 Introducing and responding to problems

1 **Complete sentences 1–8 with a word from the list. You may need to change the form of some words.**

address   burden   dilemma   relief   resolution   respond   setback   threat

1 The .... placed on future generations is perhaps too high for society to cope with.

2 In order to .... the problem the government needs to raise significant finances.

3 The peace .... was accepted by all parties.

4 The company suffered a .... in its growth plan.

5 One .... to world security is considered to be food and water shortages around the world.

6 Struggling companies are often faced with the .... of whether to focus on reducing costs, or investing further to achieve better results.

7 The organization .... by cutting 2,000 jobs.

8 The measures brought temporary .... in the aftermath of the earthquake.

2 **Look at the ideas 1–5 and write two sentences for each, presenting a possible problem and a way of responding to it.**

1 Fossil fuels

2 High levels of national debt

3 Crime levels

4 Obesity

5 Aging population

3 **Think about key problems that feature in your own area of study. How could they be presented and responded to?**

UNIT 12 Progress

ACADEMIC FOCUS: CAUSE AND EFFECT

LEARNING OBJECTIVES

Listening
- Recognizing and noting down cause and effect relations in a lecture
- Understanding key cause and effect language
- Categorizing causes, effects, and evaluation

Speaking
- Identifying related ideas
- Evaluating cause and effect relationships
- Using cautious language

Reading
- Identifying cause and effect relationships in a text
- Identifying stance in cause and effect relationships
- Noticing and using prepositional verbs

Writing
- Planning and structuring a cause and effect essay
- Stating cause and effect connections through appropriate language
- Writing and evaluating a cause and effect essay

Vocabulary
- Identifying cause and effect language
- Identifying causes in a text and revising

Discussion

1 Work in groups and discuss which two of the following areas of human progress are the most important. Give reasons.
   - Medical advances (e.g. the development of new drugs and procedures)
   - Technological innovation (e.g. the development of smart phones)
   - Educational progress (e.g. more students going to university)
   - Agricultural advances (e.g. genetically modified plants)
   - Population growth, indicating the successful survival of humans on the planet

2 Select two or three items from 1, and suggest examples of related causes and effects.

   Examples: *Two major effects of educational progress are a better-educated workforce, and ...*
   Agricultural advances have led to increased productivity per hectare of land. Another result of advances in agriculture is ...

3 Present your ideas to the whole class.

Cause and effect relationships are often considered in academic lectures, so it is important to be able to identify whether a particular item is a cause or an effect. The lecturer may focus mainly on the causes of something, or the effects, or a combination of both. Lecturers may use a variety of language to describe causes and effects, and understanding this language is essential to understanding the relationships being discussed. It is also important that you identify a lecturer's evaluation of the causes and effects they discuss.

This module covers:
- Recognizing and noting down cause and effect relations in a lecture
- Understanding key cause and effect language
- Categorizing causes, effects, and evaluation

TASK 1 Previewing the topic of a lecture

1 Work in pairs. Note down some possible effects on human health of living in a city or large urban area. Evaluate each effect, and decide if it is positive or negative.

2 Compare your ideas with another pair. Decide which two effects are the most significant.

TASK 2 Gaining an overview of a lecture

1 ▶12.1 You are going to watch part of a lecture on some specific effects of human progress. Watch Extract 1 from the introduction to the lecture and complete the notes.

Progress – associated with: ....

Focus of lecture: ....

The two main effects / impacts: ....

'Urban heat island' – cause / effects: ....

> **The effects of urbanization on human health**
>
> **Dr Mark Leighton**
> Senior Lecturer,
> Department of
> Environmental Science

ACADEMIC LANGUAGE   ▶ Language reference page 177

Recognizing key cause and effect language

Cause and effect relationships can be expressed in a number of different ways. It can be useful to group together words with similar meanings and grammatical forms, for example, nouns (*effect, consequence, result*) and verbs (*result in, lead to*).

Cause → Effect

 *Rapid growth such as we see around us today … can have serious **consequences**.* (noun)
 *… There are two main issues which **influence** people's health in cities.* (verb)

Effect → Cause

 *Heat stress is a major factor mainly **due to** the 'urban heat island' effect.* (preposition)
 *Urban areas are hotter **because** firstly they're built up, rather than natural.* (subordinator)

Cause → Effect / Cause ← Effect

 *… Heat is also created by people and by traffic. **For these reasons** urban areas are hotter, causing what is known as the urban heat island effect.* (adverbial)

In all cases, it is important to show which is the cause and which is the effect.

TASK 3 Using cause and effect language

1 ▶12.1 Watch Extract 1 again or look at the transcript on page 221. Identify the words / phrases from the list that you hear.

consequences   impacts   effects   influence   lead to   due to   outcome
since   therefore   because   for these reasons   result(ed) in   affect   origin

2 For each sentence 1–5, decide:

a which part of the sentence refers to a cause and which refers to an effect

b which words / phrases from 1 can be used to complete the sentence.

1 High temperatures in cities can have serious _____ for human health.

2 Cities tend to be hotter than the surrounding countryside. _____, heat in urban areas is a serious problem for human health, especially among older people.

3 Traffic emissions can also _____ health problems.

4 Urban areas are hotter _____ they contain few green spaces and mostly consist of buildings and roads.

5 This _____ on human body temperature is _____ unusually high air temperatures.

3 Select three of the words / phrases in 1 and write sentences expressing cause and effect relationships connected to your area of study.

TASK 4 Understanding causes and effects in a lecture

1 ▶12.2 Watch Extract 2 and complete the notes.

Bio-climate → important factor for human health

   ↓

Meteorological variables → _____

   ↓

• air temperature

• _____

• _____

• shortwave _____

• longwave terrestrial emission from the earth

Thermal stress (too much heat) → _____

Global warming → _____

_____ & _____ → Humans produce energy

Cool air → humans use more energy to keep warm →

Warm air → Humans _____

Sweating, breathing deeply → _____ →

Increased air humidity → _____

Two local environmental factors → body temperature

   ↓

_____ & _____

2 Compare your notes with another student and help each other to complete any missing information.

3 Expand your notes into sentences. Use words / phrases from Academic Language and Task 3 to express the cause and effect relationships clearly and accurately.

Example: *Thermal stress (too much heat) → ... possible negative effects for human health*
*Thermal stress **can result in** negative effects for human health.*

4 Connect your sentences in 3 to complete a paragraph about the effects of the bio-climate on human health. The first sentence of the paragraph is provided.

Bio-climate involves meteorological variables such as air temperature, and affects human health in various ways. ...

Symbols:
↓ includes or involves
→ affects / influences

TASK 5 Critical thinking – evaluating the content of a lecture

1 Work in groups and discuss questions 1–3. Give reasons for your views, and use examples from the lecture where possible.

1 Can we have too much progress?

2 Should we be promoting policies to limit progress and growth?

3 Do we need to reduce the size of our cities rather than allowing and encouraging more people to move into them?

2 Look back at the effects you suggested in Task 1. How relevant are they to questions 1–3 above?

INDEPENDENT STUDY

Working out whether something is presented as a cause or an effect is a key listening skill. Identifying any evaluation is also important.

▶ Watch an online lecture related to your area of study, and note down any causes, effects, and evaluation.

Speaking Seminar discussions (9)

In any seminar discussion about cause and effect relationships, you will need to make connections between different issues or ideas. However, rather than simply *describe* cause and effect relationships, you may be asked to *evaluate* the strength of relationship between the cause and the effect. For example, you may be asked to respond to, and evaluate, the points made by other speakers in the discussion.

This module covers:
- Identifying related ideas
- Evaluating cause and effect relationships
- Using cautious language

TASK 1 Previewing the task

1 Work in pairs. Read statements 1–3 and discuss which one you most agree with. Give reasons for your selection.

1 'Economic growth is a key objective for any economy or society.' (Drudy, 2010)

2 'GDP does not consider inequality, pollution, or damage to people's health, and is ultimately making society worse off.' (Friends of the Earth, n.d.)

3 'The way we measure progress should be related to society's ability to provide basic human needs for food, shelter, freedom, etc.' (Costanza et al. 2009)

GLOSSARY

GDP *(n abbr)* Gross Domestic Product - the total value of the goods and services produced by a country in one year

n.d. *(n abbr)* no date - the reference is undated

2 Discuss questions 1 and 2.

1 Why do most governments use economic growth as the main indicator of progress?

2 Do you think economic growth is a good measure of progress?

TASK 2 Identifying related ideas

1 You are going to watch an extract from a student presentation on ways of measuring progress. Before you watch, match situations a–d with reasons 1–4 below.

Situations

a Many people consider that economic growth is not an accurate measurement of progress.

b Economic growth does not automatically mean high employment growth.

c It is not possible to measure the distribution of income using GDP.

d GDP is not reliable as a measure of future progress.

Reasons

1 A society may have high unemployment but still be economically successful.

2 GDP is used to measure overall economic growth.

3 GDP is used as a short-term measure of economic growth.

4 No value is given to goods and services that are not sold.

2 Which reasons in 1 are (a) a direct cause of a situation, and (b) just connected to the situation?

3 ▶12.3 Watch Extract 1 of the presentation and check your predictions.

TASK 3 Evaluating cause and effect relationships

1 ◀))12.4 Listen to two students discussing the question below and note down each student's opinion.

How effective is economic growth as an indicator of progress?

2 ◀))12.4 Listen again and note down the reasons each student gives.

3 Work in pairs and discuss which student's evaluation you agree with, and why.

Expressing caution Giving and responding to opinions

You can use a variety of language to **hedge**, or express yourself with caution. This is especially important when responding to other people's opinions or arguments, and putting forward a different opinion.

Giving an opinion

I would argue that it still gives us a good indication of …

There's also the argument that unemployment can be higher …

Responding to an opinion or argument, and putting forward a counter-opinion

From what he was saying, it seems that economic growth isn't a good indicator of progress, *but I'm not sure I agree*.

Perhaps, but then as we heard, it also doesn't mean we know who's benefiting.

TASK 4 Using cautious language

1 ◀))12.4 **Listen again to the discussion or look at the transcript on page 222. Identify any other language for:**

1 giving an opinion   2 responding to an opinion and putting forward a counter-opinion.

2 **Underline the language expressing caution in sentences 1–4.**

1 I think that, arguably, wealth contributes towards happiness.

2 It's perhaps understandable that countries measure progress in terms of economic growth.

3 Admittedly, there might be other measures of progress, but economic growth is key.

4 The argument for better health and education is true to a certain extent, but neither are possible without economic growth.

3 **Work in pairs and take turns to respond to the opinions in 1. Use the phrases you noted in 1 and 2, and phrases from Academic Language.**

TASK 5 Identifying cause and effect relationships

1 ▷12.5 **Watch Extract 2 of the presentation and identify the main cause and effect relationships between:**

1 Education and economic progress

2 Health and economic progress

3 Education and health

2 ▷12.5 **Watch Extract 2 again and identify any further information that the speaker uses to suppport his arguments in 1. What conclusion does he come to at the end of the presentation?**

TASK 6 Preparing for and taking part in a seminar discussion

1 **Read questions 1–4 and note down some ideas in response.**

1 Does poor health lead to poor economic circumstances?

2 Do poor economic circumstances lead to poor health?

3 Does a better education lead to a better economic situation?

4 Does a better economic situation lead to better education?

2 **Work in groups and discuss the questions in 1. Aim to agree on the cause and effect relationship in each case.**

3 **Evaluate your performance in the discussion, using questions 1 and 2 to help you. Think of one thing you could do to improve your performance in future discussion.**

1 Did you refer to the content of the presentation?

2 Did you use appropriate phrases for giving and responding to opinions cautiously?

Academic texts frequently contain some discussion of a cause and effect relationship. You need to be able to identify the causes and the effects they are related to, and the author's stance on each one. Language such as prepositional verbs (e.g. *lead to, result in*) are frequently used to show cause and effect relationships, and recognizing such language will help you understand these relationships. It is also important to evaluate the strength of these ideas for use in your own writing.

This module covers:

- Identifying cause and effect relationships in a text
- Identifying stance in cause and effect relationships
- Noticing and using prepositional verbs

TASK 1 Previewing the topic of a text

1 **Work in pairs and discuss questions 1–4.**

1 How do factors a–d influence the number of children people decide to have?
   a occupation   b education   c income   d the roles of men and women

2 Why do you think family size varies between different countries?

3 What is the effect of a falling birth rate on a country's population?

4 Why are people in developed countries living longer than in the past?

TASK 2 Gaining an overview of a longer text

1 **You are going to read a textbook extract on changes in age structure during the 20th century. Work in pairs and note down three predictions about the content of the text. Think about:**

- changes in the birth rate (the number of children born per woman)
- the number of older people in society
- differences between *developed* countries (e.g. North America, Europe) and *developing* countries (e.g. parts of Africa, Asia, and Latin America)

2 **Read the text quickly and check which of your predictions are included.**

3 **Based on your first reading, what is the authors' purpose in the text?**

a to explain why the world's population continues to grow

b to describe the effects of an aging population and falling birth rates

c to predict future changes in society

TASK 3 Identifying the main ideas in a longer text

1 **Read the text again and match each summary a–e to a paragraph 1–5.**

a Less developed countries need to continue to develop while they undergo demographic change, in order to control population growth.

b An aging population is causing changes in some parts of the world.

c Demographic changes affect all societies in different ways, but overall populations are getting older.

d A larger aging population means that there will be more interest in improving the quality of people's lives in old age.

e In some countries economic success is preferable to having a large family.

2 **Decide which of the issues a–c has the most significant effect on society. Give reasons, using examples from the text to support your ideas.**

a World population growth

b An aging population

c The pursuit of economic success

Changes in age structure during the 20th century

1 The extraordinary demographic changes that have already taken place in our society did not result from any change in basic aging processes. They are due almost entirely to changes in cultural habits and biomedical practices. These transformations are not limited to the developed societies found in North America, northern Europe and Japan, but are global in their impact. Different societies are simply in different phases of this demographic transition. The relative ratio of birth rates, death rates and net migration determines the age structure of a population. Advances in health and biomedical interventions have greatly reduced early death. The enhanced survival of such groups leads to a large increase in the number of people who reach reproductive age. When this large cohort reaches adulthood but undergoes a decline in fertility rates like those seen in many developed countries, the proportion of older adults in the population increases relative to young ones. Italy and several other developed countries in Europe now have lifetime birth rates of 1.5 or fewer children per woman. This is substantially below the replacement rate (2.1) and maintains a stable age structure in the population when the death rate is low. This means that these low birth rate countries are dominated by one-child families. The United States currently has a higher lifetime birth rate (2.3), but this includes the substantial contributions of new immigrants; if they are excluded, then the US rate falls to about 1.9. Although relatively high, this is still below the replacement level.

2 There are three implications of these numbers. The first is that the projected increase in the world's population must be the result of population growth in less developed societies that have not undergone the same demographic transitions. Thus the most effective way to deal with the human overpopulation problem is not to deny healthcare to elderly people in developed societies (e.g., see Callahan 1987, 199), but to assist these underdeveloped societies to grow to the point where they can undergo the demographic transition. However, these less developed regions are changing, for half of the world's people now live in regions in which fertility is less than the replacement rate of 2.1 (Wilson, 2004). The high population growth areas of the future are in sub-Saharan Africa and much of the Middle East; as well as in India and China. It is a race to see whether they can begin or complete their modern development before their population pressures stop the process and bring grief to the entire world.

3 The second implication is that societies with very low lifetime birth rates are undergoing a change in their age structure, meaning that the ratio of older to younger people is increasing. Because all societies have age-structured societal roles and obligations, this change can force other changes in the way that society distributes opportunities and obligations. For example, people may be asked to work longer and retire later. They may also choose to start a family later as they pursue a career and education.

4 The third implication has to do with the drive to reproduce. Not one country that has undergone the economic and social changes inherent in becoming a developed country has maintained a higher-than-replacement birth rate. The finding that people from different cultures and religious backgrounds are apparently happy to have fewer children for economic success is quite extraordinary. An individual's decision to have children seems to be flexible. However, it is not logical to assume that this low birth rate is the future of all developed societies.

5 The decreases in fertility, driven by socioeconomic considerations, and the decreases in adult death, caused by cultural and biomedical considerations, mean that the proportion of old people may well continue to increase for some time. The significant growth of this segment of the population has important implications for both individuals and families, as well as for public-policy makers and planners. One of these implications will almost certainly be the desire to better understand the biological basis of aging so as to develop interventions. Such interventions will be needed not only to enhance the quality of life of the elderly but also to limit the future economic costs to societies that often only deal with problems as they occur.

SOURCE: Arking, A. (2006). pp.507–10. *The Biology of Aging: Observations and Principles.* Oxford: Oxford University Press.

GLOSSARY

cohort *(n)* a group of people who share a common feature, such as age-group

demographic *(adj)* relating to the population, or groups within a population

replacement rate *(n)* the number of people that need to be born to keep the population at the same level

reproductive age *(n)* the age at which people can have children

TASK 4 Understanding cause and effect relationships in a text

1 Read paragraphs 1 and 2 again, and find information to complete the table.

Paragraph	Cause	Effect
1	Changes in cultural habits and biomedical practices	1
1	2	The age structure of the population
1	3	Reductions in early death
1	People living longer and fewer children being born	4
1	Several European countries have a stable age structure and a low death rate	5
2	6	Projected population growth
2	Half the world's population lives in regions with a fertility rate of less than 2.1	7

2 Underline the language in paragraphs 1 and 2 that expresses the cause and effect relationships in 1.

3 Read paragraph 3 again and the pairs of sentences a–d. For each pair, decide which sentence is the *cause* and which is the *effect*.

a Societies with low birth rates are changing. The ratio of older to younger people is increasing.

b Changes in a society's age structure can create other changes to people's opportunities and obligations. All societies have age-structured roles and opportunities.

c The ratio of older to younger people is increasing. Other changes to people's opportunities and obligations can happen.

d Other changes to people's opportunities and obligations can happen. People may work longer and start a family later.

4 Rewrite the pairs of sentences in 3 using the following words / phrases.

as a result   because   consequently   this means that

5 Read paragraph 4 again and complete the notes.

No developed countries have [1] .... Families [2] ....
as people work to achieve economic success. In the future, birth rates might
[3] ....

6 Read the first sentence of paragraph 5 and complete the diagram.

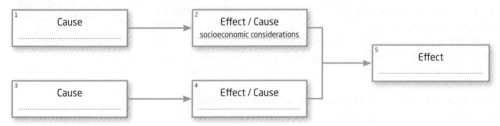

TASK 5 Identifying stance in cause and effect relationships

1 Read paragraphs 4 and 5 of the text again and identify the author's stance on points a–c. For each point, identify the specific words that indicate the author's stance.

Example: The potential effects of population growth in sub-Saharan Africa, the Middle East, India, and China. (paragraph 2)
Stance: *This could have serious negative implications for the entire world.*
Words: *It is a race to see ... bring grief to the entire world.*

a Society's attitude to economic success and having children. (para. 4)

b The likelihood that birth rates will remain low in developed societies. (para. 4)

c The implications of the changes for families, individuals, and policy-makers. (para. 5)

2 What action does the author think will be necessary as a result of the rising numbers of older people?

Prepositional verbs

Prepositional verbs (a verb combined with a preposition) are a typical feature of academic texts.

The extraordinary demographic changes that have already taken place in our society did not **result from** *any change in basic aging processes.*

The enhanced survival of such groups **leads to** *a large increase in the number of people who reach reproductive age.*

The most effective way to **deal with** *the human overpopulation problem is not to deny healthcare to elderly people in developed societies ...*

The verb is not usually separated from the preposition. For example, we say:

The most effective way to **deal with** *the problem,* NOT ~~The most effective way to~~ **deal** ~~the problem~~ **with**.

Other prepositional verbs include: *account for, consist of, depend on, focus on, look at.*

Prepositional verbs with two objects are separated in the active form.

It's a common mistake to **associate** *progress* **with** *economic growth.*

We **based** *our conclusion* **on** *the results of an extensive research project.*

Similar verbs include: *contribute to, relate to.*

Some prepositional verbs are more common in the passive form, for example: *is associated with, is based on, is related to.*

Progress is sometimes **associated with** *economic growth.*

TASK 6 Using prepositional verbs

1 **Complete the text with the prepositional verbs in the list. You may need to change the grammatical form of some verbs. Note that some verbs are separated.**

contribute to   account for   base on   result in   focus on   associate with   lead to

It is likely that developing countries will [1]........................ much of the population growth in the world and will [2]........................ another two billion people .... the world's population over the next 50 years. Much of the population growth is [3]........................ the fact that standards of living are improving in these countries. Many developing countries are attracted by living standards in the developed world and their policy is to [4]........................ achieving the same success. It is partly this drive that has [5]........................ recent population increases. This overall improvement in the standard of living in developed countries has [6]........................ a rise in life expectancy, with people living to an average age of 78, compared with an average of 68 in developing countries. Therefore, [7]........................ past and current trends, countries such as China and India will have very large elderly populations to deal with in the future.

2 **Select three of the prepositional verbs from 1 to write sentences about the ideas expressed in the text.**

TASK 7 Critical thinking – evaluating a text as a source

1 **Work in pairs and look at essay titles 1–3. Discuss which title the text on page 167 would be most useful as a source for. Give reasons.**

1 'Describe and evaluate the main changes in world demographics in the twentieth century.'

2 'The varying demographic patterns around the world are likely to cause a range of problems for different societies. Describe and evaluate the effects of these changes.'

3 'All progress brings with it negative consequences.' Discuss.

2 **Highlight the information in the text that you would include in your chosen essay title. Give reasons for your selection.**

INDEPENDENT STUDY

In Units 9–12 we have looked at some of the most common purposes of academic texts: comparison and contrast; discussion; assessment of problems and solutions; and description of cause and effect. Identifying key features, language, and organizational patterns can help you quickly identify the purpose of a text.

▸ **Next time you read an academic text, read it quickly to identify the author's purpose.**

Writing Cause and effect essays

As with spoken texts such as lectures, written texts can focus mainly on causes, on effects, or on both. It is important to state the connection between the causes and effects and make it clear to readers which is the cause and which is the effect. You can make this connection through language, and through sequence. You need to plan and structure your essay in a logical way, by deciding what is more important to focus on first, a cause or an effect. Throughout your text, you need to use cause and effect language clearly.

This module covers:
- Planning and structuring a cause and effect essay
- Stating cause and effect connections through appropriate language
- Writing and evaluating a cause and effect essay

TASK 1 Analysing a cause and effect paragraph

1 **Read paragraph 1 from an essay and decide whether it is:**

a the introduction   b a main body paragraph   c the conclusion.

> **Paragraph 1**
>
> Technological progress can have many negative consequences for wildlife, especially damage to animal habitats. Urbanization can result in the loss of agricultural land, forest, or both. Depending on the local environment, such land is often the natural habitat of many animal species, including birds and bats, and larger animals such as deer and foxes. The numbers of animals like these quantifiably decline as a result of the construction of buildings and roads on their former habitats. Forest destruction is particularly serious in the Amazon region, sub-Saharan Africa, India, and the Himalayas (Beeby and Brennan, 2008, p.347). Other examples of technological progress include an increase in air travel, resulting in dangers for birds when they encounter aeroplanes, as well as further loss of habitat on the ground due to the building and expansion of airports. Clearly these problems are becoming more serious because of the rapid growth of urban areas in many developing countries, and the increase in air travel.
>
> REFERENCE: Beeby, A., & Brennan, A. (2008). *First Ecology: Ecological Principles and Environmental Issues* 3rd ed. Oxford: Oxford University Press.

2 **Select the most suitable title 1–3 for the essay in 1.**

1 Destruction of the environment is the price we pay for progress. Discuss.

2 Describe the main effects of human progress on the natural environment.

3 To what extent is human progress desirable? Discuss with reference to either environmental or social perspectives.

3 **Decide whether each item in the list from Paragraph 1 is a cause or an effect.**

technological progress   damage to animal habitats   urbanization
loss of agricultural land   numbers of animal species such as birds and bats
forest destruction   construction of buildings, roads, and airports

4 **Connect the items in 3 using arrows (→) to show the causes and effects.**

Example: *technological progress → damage to animal habitats*

5 **Note down all the cause and effect language used in Paragraph 1, including the surrounding words.**

Example: *can have many negative **consequences** for*

6 **Identify any examples of evaluation in Paragraph 1. Make a note of any hedging language used in these evaluations.**

Cause and effect language

When writing a cause and effect essay, it is important to vary the language you use, rather than always relying on the same words and structures. You can do this by using words with a similar meaning, for example:

Nouns: *Technological progress can have many negative **consequences** / **effects** / **results** for animal habitats.*

Verbs: *Urbanization tends to **result in** / **lead to** / **cause** the loss of agricultural land, forest, or both.*

Prepositions: *The numbers of animals like these quantifiably declines **as a result of** / **because of** / **due to** the construction of buildings and roads on their former habitats.*

TASK 2 Varying cause and effect language

1 Read Paragraph 2 from a different essay and identify the cause and effect language.

Paragraph 2

Human beings are naturally driven to make progress in many areas, such as technology and medicine. There are many possible effects of this progress. One effect is an increasing gap between rich and poor, because keeping up with progress and development is expensive. Another effect is a negative effect on the environment such as destruction of the rainforests, because human progress tends to involve constructing new cities and infrastructure. Also, because populations in most countries are rising, there is increasing pressure on limited land resources to provide food to meet this demand. One further important effect of human progress is the increasing expectation to use the latest medical treatments and drugs. There is also a serious effect in terms of pressure on government budgets because of this. Therefore, there are many serious effects of human progress in many different contexts.

2 Rewrite the paragraph using a greater variety of cause and effect language. Refer to Task 1 and Academic Language for ideas.

3 Compare your rewritten paragraph with the original. Which one is more effective? Why?

TASK 3 Evaluating the structure of a cause and effect essay

1 Read the essay title and plan below. Evaluate the essay plan using questions 1–4.

1 Does the plan seem logical and clearly developed?

2 How effectively does each part of the essay lead into the following part?

3 Is all the material in the plan relevant to the essay title?

4 Are the essay title, thesis statement, and conclusion clearly linked?

> **TITLE:** *Identify and discuss the key causes and effects of individual success in education.*

Plan

Introduction:
- Context: the growing importance of education
- Main points: the causes of success are motivation, intelligence, and good teaching
- Thesis statement: each cause of success is examined in a different paragraph; the effects related to each clause are integrated in each paragraph.

Paragraph 1: Motivation drives students to work hard and make progress.

Paragraph 2: Intelligence is a key influence on educational success.

Paragraph 3: Good teaching leads to effective learning and individual achievement.

Conclusion: Each of the three causes discussed is influential, and all three together should have a powerful impact on individual educational success.

2 Work in pairs and compare your responses to the questions in 1.

TASK 4 Writing a paragraph for a cause and effect essay

1 **Plan a body paragraph based on the following essay title. Follow steps 1–6.**

> **TITLE:** *What are the main effects of recent developments in technology on education and learning?*

1 Note down some ideas related to the question.

2 Decide which effect(s) to focus on, and prepare some supporting examples and evidence.

3 Work out the topic and main point of your paragraph. Write the topic sentence.

4 Decide how you will express the causes and effects, and what language you will use.

5 Decide whether to include any evaluation of the effects.

6 Refer to Paragraph 1 in Task 1 as a possible model for organizing your paragraph, or look at Unit 4D, Task 1 on page 058.

2 **Write a first draft of your paragraph, starting with your topic sentence. As you write, think about the following points. Use the questions to guide you.**

- **Coherence** – Does the paragraph contain one main point?
- **Relevance** – Are all the points relevant to the essay title and the topic of the paragraph?
- **Clarity** – Are the cause and effect relationships clearly expressed?
- **Comprehensiveness** – Is there enough supporting evidence and exemplification?
- **Evaluation** – Have you included evaluation where appropriate?

3 **Make any necessary revisions to your paragraph.**

4 **Work in pairs. Read and evaluate each other's paragraphs using the points in 2.**

INDEPENDENT STUDY

Planning an essay is a vital stage, and allows you to find relevant sources to incorporate into your writing.

▶ Extend your range of sources by looking again at texts you have read, and searching for new texts in the library and online. Always note down the source so that you can correctly reference it in your writing.

TASK 5 Planning and researching a cause and effect essay

1 **You are going to write a cause and effect essay on the theme of progress. Start by choosing one of the essay titles 1–5.**

1 Progress tends to be viewed positively. What negative effects of progress can you identify? Refer to one academic discipline such as economics, medicine, or technology.

2 What motivates humans to focus so strongly on progress, and what are the main effects of such motivation?

3 What are the main effects of progress in free trade, industrialization, *or* wireless communications?

4 Identify and discuss the key causes and effects of individual success in education.

5 How has progress in digital technology affected people's access to knowledge and the consumption of news?

2 **Note down your initial ideas for your chosen essay title, and arrange these in a logical order. Use questions 1–3 to guide you.**

1 What is your main focus – the cause(s), the effect(s), or both?

2 How are the ideas connected, e.g. a possible connection, or a very strong cause and effect?

3 What does your audience need to know first, before moving on to the next item?

3 **Work out what further information you need in order to write your essay, for example specific evidence and examples to support your main points.**

4 **As a first step, review some of the reading texts in this book. Identify material in these texts that you could use in your essay. Think about questions 1–3.**

1 Is the material useful and relevant to your essay? How?

2 Does the material support, or give an example of, one of your main points?

3 How much of the material do you need to use, e.g. a short quotation or paraphrase, or a summary of a longer piece of text?

5 **Now think about questions 1–3 above in relation to any other source material that you have found online or in the library.**

TASK 6 Organizing your material and structuring your essay

1 **Use the guidelines below to help you organize your notes from Task 5, and to structure your essay.**

   Body paragraphs and main points
   - Narrow your focus to two or three main points. Give each point one main body paragraph.
   - For each paragraph, decide what to include, like you did in Task 4. Write a topic sentence for each paragraph.
   - Write one or two sentences to summarize your main points. This can form the basis of your conclusion.

   Essay structure and cohesion
   - Include two or three body paragraphs and note down how they are connected.
   - Look at the structure of the whole essay. Work out how to present your causes and effects, starting with what to introduce first.

   Evaluation
   - Come up with an evaluative response for each main point / paragraph. Integrate this in each paragraph, *or* add an evaluative paragraph at the end of the main body.

   Conclusion
   - Read your essay title again carefully, and decide on your main conclusion. Write this down.

2 **Put all this information together in an essay plan. Use the plan in Task 3 as a guide.**

3 **Work in pairs. Take turns to present your plan, and offer critical feedback using the guidelines in Task 3.1 to help you.**

TASK 7 Writing a cause and effect essay

1 **Write a cause and effect essay of approximately 500 words using your notes from Task 5 and following the structure you developed in Task 6. While you are writing, think about points 1–6.**

   1 Are the cause and effect relations clearly expressed?

   2 Is the language accurate, particularly the cause and effect language?

   3 Does the introduction include contextualization and a clear focus? Does it help the reader navigate the essay?

   4 Does each main body paragraph express one main topic / point, and move logically on to the next one?

   5 Is source material included where appropriate, and is it accurately referenced?

   6 Does the conclusion summarize the main points in the text, without adding any new points?

Sample answer
page 194

TASK 8 Critical thinking – self- and peer evaluation

1 **Critically evaluate your essay using the questions in Task 7.**

2 **Work in groups. Read and evaluate one or more essays by other students, and give feedback using the questions in Task 7.**

3 **Using the feedback you have received, make any necessary changes or improvements to your essay.**

The language of cause and effect can be complex, and can be built round nouns, e.g. *cause*; verbs, e.g. *lead to*; adverbials, e.g. *as a result*; prepositions, e.g. *due to*; and subordinators, e.g. *because*. A cause may be given before an effect, or vice-versa, so you need to be able to accurately work out the meaning of cause and effect language to avoid confusion.

TASK 1 Identifying cause and effect language

1 **Complete sentences 1–6 with the cause and effect words / phrases from the list.**

for these reasons   due to   result in   impact   consequence   since   cause

1 One _____ of higher global standards of living is that people's expectations are also higher.

2 Better access to a wider range of foods and the availability of high-calorie snacks can _____ increases in people's weight; _____, care should be taken not to consume too many calories.

3 In most contexts, increased trade is mainly _____ more open markets.

4 Limited exposure to sunlight in northern countries is an important _____ of vitamin D deficiency and associated illnesses.

5 Arguably, education has had the greatest _____ on public health in developing countries.

6 It is unwise to assume that flooding is always the result of natural causes, _____ there might be other causes.

2 **Match the sentence halves.**

1 Environmental air pollution

2 One important source of rapid urban development

3 There can be a lack of community facilities in newly-built suburbs

4 Progress does not always have

a positive effects.

b can result from a number of causes, particularly factories and road traffic.

c as a result of poor planning.

d is a high birth rate.

TASK 2 Identifying causes in a text and revising

1 **Underline the cause and effect language in the following text.**

Air pollution in cities is the result of complex interactions between natural and man-made environmental conditions. Poor air quality in cities is a serious environmental problem and a growing one in developing countries. Emissions from motor vehicles are a very important source of air pollution throughout the world. [...] Urban population growth is caused by migration into cities and a surplus of births in the cities themselves, particularly the high birth rates in the developing countries. A deep structural change is mainly responsible for the migration into cities, especially in the non-industrialized countries. [...] Urban population growth has many consequences. One of them is higher emission of air pollutants. [...] A study of air pollution in 20 of the 24 mega-cities of the world shows that ambient air pollution concentrations are at levels where serious health effects are reported.

SOURCE: Niemela, J. (2011). p.42. *Urban Ecology: patterns, processes, and applications.* Oxford: Oxford University Press.

2 **Now circle the *causes* in the text.**

3 **Select two or three sentences from the text and rewrite these using the opposite structure, i.e. reversing cause and effect. Use a range of cause and effect language.**

Example: *Air pollution in cities is the result of complex interactions between natural and man-made environmental conditions. → Complex interactions between natural and man-made environmental conditions are a cause of air pollution in cities.*

Glossary

Words and phrases used to refer to grammar and other aspects of language in this book.

Active voice the form of the verb which indicates something being done to the **object**, e.g. *Technology has made the growth of companies easier.*

Adjective a word which **modifies** a noun, e.g. *a political issue*, or functions as a **complement**, e.g. *This issue appears political*.

Adverb a word which **modifies** usually an adjective or adverb, e.g. *extremely interesting*, or functions as an adverbial in a sentence, e.g. *However*

Adverbial a word / phrase that adds extra information such as circumstance (how, where, when, why), e.g. *during the 20th century*; stance and perspective, e.g. *in terms of finance*; or linking, e.g. *however, in conclusion*

Affix the term used to cover both **prefix** and **suffix**

Argument a written or spoken discussion based on reason, logic, and evidence; an argument can be the main argument or a supporting argument

Article (1) the most frequent determiners: definite article *the*; indefinite article *a / an*.

Article (2) a type of text which presents facts and argument

Aspect the form of the verb which expresses how an action or state is viewed: in progress (progressive), e.g. *is changing*, and / or completed (perfect), e.g. *has changed*

Auxiliary verb a verb which combines with another verb to indicate tense, e.g. *is / was changing*; voice, e.g. *is cleaned*; aspect, e.g. *has influenced*; or a modal verb, e.g. *can become*

Citation a **summary**, **paraphrase**, or **quotation** which is from a source text

Clause a grammatical unit which normally contains a **subject**, **verb**, and other parts of a sentence; a sentence may contain one clause, or two or more joined together using a **coordinator** or **subordinator**

Coherence how a text is connected in terms of meaning and ideas

Cohesion how a text is connected in terms of meaning and language

Collocation two words which frequently go together, e.g. *significant difference, influential decisions*

Complement the part of the sentence following verbs like *be* and *seem*, e.g. *It seems unlikely*

Compound noun two nouns put together to create one meaning, e.g. *radio journalist*; unlike adjective + noun combinations, the first noun is normally stressed in spoken language

Conclusion the part of a written or spoken text which sums up the main argument of the whole text, usually the end of the text

Conjunction the term used to cover both **coordinator** and **subordinator**

Content word a word which has real meaning rather than just grammatical meaning; nouns, verbs, adjectives, and adverbs are content words

Coordinator a word which joins two units of language: clauses, phrases, or words; the most frequent conjunctions in English are *and, but, or*

Definite article the determiner *the*, which specifies definite meaning

Determiner a word which specifies something about the **head noun**, e.g. *the, some, this*

Evaluation the writer's subjective, evidence-based response to an idea in the text, e.g. *This argument is highly convincing*.

Head noun the main noun in a noun phrase, e.g. *their social, emotional, and personal development*

Hedge / hedging the language and academic practice of 'softening' statements, e.g. *This may result in failure*.

Indefinite article the determiner *a* (*an* before vowels), which specifies indefinite meaning

Infinitive the base form of the verb, with or without *to*, e.g. *consider, to consider*

Intransitive not taking an object, e.g. *They cope well in lessons*.

Introduction the part of a written or spoken text which introduces the topic, focus, aims, and limitations of the whole text

Modal verb an **auxiliary verb** such as *may* and *should*, which expresses objective meanings, e.g. *airborne pollution may result in lung damage*; or subjective meanings, e.g. *you should speak more slowly*

Modifier / modify a word such as *extremely* which adds to or limits the meaning of another word, e.g. *extremely significant*

Noun a word which can refer to anything concrete, e.g. *university*, or abstract, e.g. *success*

Object the part of a sentence, usually a noun phase, which is affected by the action of the verb and which normally comes after the main verb; an object can become the **subject** in the **passive** form of the sentence, e.g. *The internet transformed consumption habits*; *Consumption habits were transformed by the internet.*

Paraphrase a piece of text which expresses similar ideas to another text of similar length but using different language

Participle the form of the verb which ends in *-ing* or *-ed*; used to form the progressive aspect (*-ing*), perfect aspect (*-ed*), and passive voice (*-ed*)

Particle a word, usually an **adverb** or **preposition** of one syllable, which is attached to another word, e.g. *look at*

Passive voice the form of the verb which is used to indicate something being done to the subject, e.g. *salt is then added to the mixture*

Perspective an essentially objective way of viewing something, e.g. *from a medical perspective*

Phrasal verb a verb which contains the base verb + an adverb particle, e.g. *put away*

Phrasal-prepositional verb a verb which contains the base verb + both an adverb and a preposition particle, e.g. *look up to* (admire)

Phrase a structure built round a **noun**, **verb**, **adjective**, **adverb**, or **preposition**, e.g. *a similar problem*

Prefix the first part of some words, which expresses a particular meaning or grammatical property, e.g. *un-, dis-, mega-*

Preposition / prepositional phrase a structure built round a preposition, e.g. *despite this difficulty*

Prepositional verb a verb which contains a base verb + a preposition, e.g. *look into*

Pronoun a word which takes the place of another noun or noun phrase, e.g. *he, it*

Quantifier a **determiner** which specifies the quantity or amount of the following noun, e.g. *many issues*

Quotation a **citation** which uses the exact words of the original source

Relative clause a structure in a longer **noun phrase** which follows the **head noun** and adds extra information, e.g. *the choices that are being voted upon*

Relative pronoun a word that links a **relative clause** to the **head noun**, i.e. *that, which, who, whom, whose*; the relative adverbs *when, where*, and *why* can also be used in a similar way, e.g. *the reason why flooding occurred*

Reporting the practice of informing and presenting information from another **source**

Source the original text from which a **citation** or reference is taken

Stance a way of viewing something which is essentially subjective but based on evidence, and connected to an **argument**

Subject the part of a sentence that normally comes first in a sentence, and which performs the action of the main verb, e.g. *Capital cities in developed countries often have a complex transport infrastructure.*

Subordinator a word which joins two clauses, e.g. *if, while, because*

Suffix the last part in some words, which expresses a particular meaning or grammatical property, e.g. *-tion, -ize, -ship*

Summary a short text which expresses the main argument(s) of a longer text

Tense the form of the verb which relates to time; English has two tenses: present, e.g. *this occurs* and past, e.g. *this occurred*; future time is referred to by using **modal verbs**, e.g. *will, may*, and other expressions, e.g. *The price of oil is likely to rise dramatically over the next decade.*

Thesis statement the part of a text which briefly expresses some or all of the following: purpose, aims, rationale, limitations, organization

Topic sentence a sentence in a paragraph, often one of the first sentences, which expresses the topic of that paragraph

Transitive taking an **object**, e.g. *make a decision*

Verb the part of a sentence which typically comes between the **subject** and the **object**, and can be in the present or past tense, e.g. *Cultural differences influence the way firms in the East and West do business.*

Word class also known as 'part of speech'; the way a word is used in a particular context, e.g. the word *like* can function as different parts of speech: *situations like this* (prep); *she likes economics* (v); *like cases* (adj)

Language reference

In sentences, the main clause elements are subject, verb, object, complement, and adverbial. These are colour-coded throughout the Language reference section.

1 Adjectives

Adjectives are words which go with **noun phrases**, and add information:

- giving qualities or describing something (e.g. *large, modern*)
- classifying (e.g. *political, atmospheric*)
- evaluating (e.g. *important, effective*).

1.1 Meaning

Descriptive adjectives are very frequent in academic writing and can express a wide range of meanings such as colour, size, time, and emotion.

Classifying adjectives are also frequent in academic writing. They often end in -*al*, e.g. *national, social*, but can also have other endings, e.g. *economic*. Classifying adjectives are not usually gradable, e.g. ~~*very economic*~~, and they usually come before nouns rather than after.

Evaluative adjectives are used to express a person's stance, e.g.
*an **effective** and **achievable** goal; These discussions have, however, been enormously **influential**.*

1.2 Form

a Adjectives which are gradable can be used for comparison, e.g. *a **faster** finishing time, the **more developed** countries.*

b Comparison is very common in academic texts. To form the comparative:
- one-syllable adjectives usually add -*er*, e.g.
  *large → larger   the **larger** developing countries*
- some two-syllable adjectives (mainly those with the stress pattern ●•) usually add -*er*, e.g.
  *happy → happier   Can policy make us **happier**?*
- other two-syllable adjectives (including adjectives ending in -*ed* / -*ing* and those with the stress pattern •●), plus adjectives with three or more syllables normally take *more*, e.g.
  *developed → more developed   The **more developed** countries promote liberal trade.*

As noted in Academic Language the main comparative structures are:

adjective -*er* (+ *than*) + word / phrase / clause
*Solar power is now **cheaper than** nuclear energy.*
more / less + adjective + than
*Natural gas is **more expensive than** coal.*

not as + adjective + as + word / phrase / clause
*The costs for consumers are **not as high as** predicted.*

too + adjective + to- clause
*It would be **too difficult to** predict the results.*

adjective + enough + to- clause
*A product needs to be **interesting enough to** attract consumers.*

c Adjectives in the superlative form are less frequent in academic writing.
- one-syllable adjectives form the superlative by adding -*est*, e.g.
  *low → lowest   the **lowest** amount*
- many two-syllable adjectives and nearly all adjectives with three or more syllables have superlative forms using *(the) most*, e.g. **the most vulnerable** areas; one of **the most important** predictors

1.3 Use

When there are two or more adjectives together, the normal order is as follows:
evaluation → description → classification
***serious international** concern, **key social** indicators*
(evaluation → classification)
***existing medical** technology* (description → classification).

Adjectives usually come before nouns, e.g. ***major** cities, **underdeveloped** societies, the **main natural** cause*, but sometimes come after the noun phrase following a verb such as *is / are, seem(s), appear, become*, e.g. *technology is **important**; that seems **likely**.*

Some adjectives can only go before a noun phrase, e.g. *main*.

Others, especially those beginning with *a-*, go after, e.g. *they are **aware** of it.*

2 Adverbs

Adverbs have a very wide range of meanings, and are used to add information either to other words, or sentences / parts of sentences.

Adverbs can add information to or modify, several different **word classes**, including adjectives, e.g. ***publicly** accessible, **enormously** influential*; and other adverbs, e.g. ***relatively** efficiently.*

Sometimes these phrases can be built up into longer structures, e.g. ***publicly** accessible → a **publicly** accessible personal journal.*

Adverbs can also add information to other words and phrases such as **prepositional phrases**, e.g. ***especially** in product markets that needed help and protection*, and **noun phrases**, e.g. ***Only** time will tell.*

Most adverbs are used as **adverbials**, which means they add information to sentences / parts of sentences rather than individual words, e.g. *Social class has **traditionally** been divided into three broad categories.*

Some adverbs can be gradable, like adjectives, e.g. ***more or less automatically**, **most commonly**.*

3 Adverbials

Adverbials are **clause elements**, i.e. parts of **sentences**. Adverbials can normally be added to or taken out of a sentence, and may appear in different positions in the sentence. Adverbials make up about 10% of academic texts and add information such as contextualizing detail, **stance and perspective**, and **linking**.

Adverbials are frequently formed of:
- **prepositional phrases**, e.g. *in the recent past*
- **adverbs / adverb phrases**, e.g. *often, very quickly*
- **adverbial clauses**, e.g. *when it is needed.*

They can also be **noun phrases**, e.g. *every year.*

Contextualizing detail can be added a number of times in one sentence using a number of **circumstance adverbials**:

| when? | | how? |

These drugs could now be produced more cheaply and sold as generic drugs by local companies under licence.

| how / for what? | by whom? | how / in what context? |

Adverbial clauses are clauses which are joined with main clauses to make a **complex sentence**, e.g.

It is clear that the runners must have different goals for the same event, although this does not seem to influence their motivation to participate.

For a change of focus, the order of clauses can be reversed, i.e. *Although this does not seem to influence their motivation to participate, it is clear that the runners must have different goals for the same event.*

Grammatically, adverbials can normally be left out and the rest of the sentence still works, e.g.

Typically updated daily, blogs often reflect the personality of the author. → Blogs reflect the personality of the author.

See **21 Linking adverbials** and **36 Stance and perspective adverbials**

4 Affixes

The term affix covers prefixes and suffixes. Affixes are useful in recognizing word class, which in turn can help with understanding sentence structure.
- Most words ending in the suffix *-ly* are adverbs: an adjective + *-ly* can form an adverb.
- The most frequent noun suffixes include: *-tion, -ity, -er, -ness, -ism, -ment, -ant, -ship, -age, -ery.*
- *-al* is very common for classifying adjectives.
- Other common adjective suffixes include *-ent, -ive, -ous,-ate, -ful, -less, -like, -type.*
- Common verb suffixes include *-ize, -ify*, and *-ate.*

Many words in academic texts can have a number of affixes to build up more complex meanings, e.g. *commerce* (n) → *commercial* (adj) → *commercialize* (v) → *commercialization* (n).

In its original context, *the commercialization of news*, the meaning can be rephrased as 'news has become more commercial'.

5 Articles
See **15 Determiners**

6 Auxiliary verbs

Auxiliary verbs need to be joined with a main verb. There are three auxiliary verbs which are used to form **tense**, **aspect**, and **voice**: *be, have, do.*

There are also about ten **modal auxiliary** verbs, which do not show tense but concepts such as possibility and obligation.

See **23 Modal verbs** and **43 Verbs**

7 Cause and effect language

The language used to express cause and effect is complex, including:
- **nouns** (e.g. *effect, consequence*)
- **verbs** (e.g. *lead to, cause, result from*)
- **subordinators** (e.g. *because, since*)
- **adverbials** (e.g. *as a result, for these reasons*)
- **prepositions** (e.g. *due to, because of*)

and other expressions (e.g. *This is why ...*).

8 Clauses and clause elements

Clause elements are used to build up **sentences**, and they can take many different forms. A **clause** is normally built around a **verb**, and usually contains other clause elements. A **sentence** contains one or more clauses.

subject, **verb**, **object** pattern, with one clause, and optionally one or more **adverbials**: *Bloggers have attitude; Typically updated daily, blogs often reflect the personality of the author.*

More complex pattern with main clause, followed by an **adverbial clause** (a clause which begins with a **subordinator**):

| subordinator |

The boom year for blogging was 2002 as it moved from minority interest into the mainstream.

9 Complements

A **complement** is a clause element which follows certain verbs such as *be* and *seem*, e.g. *An individual's decision to have children seems to be flexible; Goals should be specific, measurable, and behavioural in terms.*

It is called 'complement' because it adds complementary information about the **subject**. The **subject** and the **complement** refer to the same thing, e.g. *An ineffective goal is 'to improve my golf game.'*

In this example, the **complement** provides further information for the **subject** of the sentence: the *goal* is *to improve* the game.

A **complement** is usually:
- an **adjective / adjective phrase**, e.g. *it is **competitive***
- **noun phrase**, e.g. *This could be **the fun of being with the team**.*
- or **prepositional phrase**, e.g. *Many countries are not **in a position to attract foreign investment**.*

A **complement** can also be a *to-* infinitive: *One way of looking at motivation is **to discuss intrinsic versus extrinsic motives**.*

10 Complex sentences

A complex sentence is made up of one main clause, which can stand alone, plus one (or more) **adverbial clauses**. Adverbial clauses are a type of **adverbial**. They start with a **subordinator** (e.g. *if, because, when*) and normally contain a **subject**, **verb**, and sometimes other clause elements. These clauses are also known as 'subordinate clauses', which need to go with a 'main clause'.

As with other clause elements, adverbial clauses can be quite long: *Although a more free market approach may lead to economic growth, there are without doubt costs to the poorest people.*

In some sentences the main verb does not appear for a long time, making the meaning difficult to process. However, adverbial clauses typically come second, after the main clause, e.g. *Class divisions have an economic basis because they result from the distribution of property.*

The above examples of adverbial clauses contain verbs in a **tense** (e.g. *are thinking, result from*) or a modal (*may lead to*). Adverbial clauses can also be based around a verb in the *-**ing*** form, *-**ed*** form, or ***to**-* form:

Starting with an unscientific study of the Kalikak family, it left more questions than answers.

Typically updated daily, blogs often reflect the personality of the author.

To put this into context, each page of this book is about 100,000 nanometres in thickness.

11 Compound sentences

A compound sentence is made up of two (or more) clauses, joined by a **coordinator** (such as *and* for addition, *but* for contrast, *or* for alternatives), e.g. *People have different experiences **and** therefore they have different mental representations.*

Each clause in a compound sentence can stand alone, so a compound sentence can be split into two shorter sentences: *People have different experiences. Therefore they have different mental representations.*

Writers may choose a single compound sentence because the ideas in the two clauses are closely related.

12 Conjunctions

Conjunctions include the two **word classes** of **coordinators** and **subordinators**. See **13 Coordinators** and **38 Subordinators**.

13 Coordinators

The most frequent coordinators in English are:
- *and* (addition)
- *but* (contrast)
- *or* (alternative)

Others include *neither ... nor / either ... or.*

Coordinators can join:

words, e.g. *the structure **and** functions of the mind* [noun + *and* + noun]

phrases, e.g. *It's a useful management style **and** way of organizing a workforce.*

clauses, e.g. *Weber saw the concept as a central feature of social life, **and** it figured in all his sociological studies.*

or **sentences**.

When two or more clauses or sentences are joined using a coordinator, the result is a **compound sentence**, e.g.

*Cars have transformed modern life **and** are one of the great industrial success stories of the twentieth century.*

When the coordinator *and* joins two **verbs**, the verbs can 'share' the subject, so it does not need to be repeated.

14 Definitions and explanations

Various structures can be used to define and explain concepts. Often the **verb** is in the **passive** because the concepts are being focused on first: *Cognition **is based on** one's mental representations of the world.*

Alternatively, the verb may be in the active voice, e.g. *Cognitive psychology **concerns itself with** the structure and functions of the mind.*

Other structures for defining and explaining include **relative clauses**.

15 Determiners

Determiners are words which specify something about a **noun**, such as whether it is definite, or 'known' (e.g. *the, this, our*), or indefinite, or 'not known' (e.g. *a, any, a lot of*). Determiners include:
- **articles** (*a / an, the*)
- **demonstratives** (*this, that, these, those*)
- **possessives** (e.g. *my, our, their, your, its, 's*)
- **quantifiers** (e.g. *some, any, many, few, a lot of, each, several, both, no, a number of, a little*)
- **numerals** (e.g. *one, 2, ½, 20%, two-thirds, first*)
- and some ***wh-* words** (e.g. *whichever, what, which, whose*)

Determiners are often the first word in a **noun phrase**, and therefore a **sentence**. Nearly 10% of all words in academic texts are determiners.

16 The future

As there is no future tense in English, a number of other forms are used. These include:
- the **present tense**, e.g. *Vehicles **need to change**.*
- the **present progressive**. The **present progressive** for referring to the future is particularly used in spoken language, and there are no examples in the written texts in this book.

The **modal auxiliary verbs** are also frequently used to refer to the future:
- will   *It is unlikely that there **will be** much further development of large-scale hydroelectricity within the UK.*
- may / might   *A more free market approach **may lead to** economic growth in the long run.*
- can / could   *Now the question is, **can** the world's farmers **bounce back**?*

Conditional forms are used to express likelihood about something happening in the future:

```
[subordinator] [present tense]
     ↓              ↓
```
*If we **wish to reduce** the role of coal and natural gas, then the alternative sources **will need to provide** a total of between 4 and 5 CMO by 2050.* (more likely)

```
[modal verb will]
```

```
[subordinator] [past tense]
      ↓            ↓
```
*Even if we **were to follow** a more modest growth scenario, the annual global energy demand **could** still increase to 6 CMO by then.* (less likely)

```
[modal verb could in main clause]
```

Mixed conditional forms can be used to express different degrees of likelihood:

*If this number **is exceeded**, the system **becomes** unsustainable and the vegetation and soil **deteriorate**.* (something that is universally accepted or true)

*If it **continues**, desertification **can result**.* (something that is less likely to occur)

Other expressions used to refer to the future are made up of two or more words, e.g.

*More than three billion people **are poised to** sharply increase their standard of living.*

*Infrastructure **is unlikely to be created** through a market-based approach.*

*Yet cars **aren't going to go away**.*

*The sector of the economy that **seems likely to unravel** first is food.*

17 Hedging

See **22 Maximizing and minimizing language**

18 Imperatives

The imperative form of the verb is used to direct the reader / listener to something, e.g. ***See** Table 10.3.*

In imperative sentences, there is normally no **subject**. The imperative form is the base form of the verb, i.e. the infinitive without *to*.

19 -*ing* clauses

An -*ing* clause begins with the -*ing* form of a verb, and can be used as the **subject** of a sentence, e.g. *Adopting a 'one size fits all' policy* will not be effective, as the IMF discovered in the 1980s.

An -*ing* clause can also be used as the **object** of a sentence, e.g. *This requires planning for the future*.

20 *It* and *there* structures

A sentence in English normally needs a **subject**. Sometimes the subject is 'grammatical' but has little meaning:

1   *It is clear that the runners must have different goals for the same event.*

2   *There is the prospect that the technology will also help in a range of energy reducing activities.*

In example 1 the pronoun *it* does not refer to anything. It introduces a **clause**.

In example 2 the word *there* has no real meaning, and is followed by *be* (e.g. *is / are / has been*) and a **noun phrase**.

An alternative to this structure is *The prospect exists that ...*; however, this is less frequently used in academic writing.

21 Linking adverbials

Linking adverbials are used to link or connect parts of text (a new sentence to previous sentence or longer text), e.g. *When expert football players kick the ball directly into the goal during a penalty, it may look like any other goal to some of us. However, this particular kick is the result of many hours of practice.*

This example links the idea in the new (second) sentence back to the idea in the previous (first) sentence. The adverbial *however* shows contrast; in other words the ideas in the two sentences are different.

Linking adverbials tend to come first in a sentence, but can also come later, for example before the main verb, e.g. *They may thus be less likely to be deterred by the possibility of detection.*

Like other **adverbials**, linking adverbials can be in the form of **adverbs** like *however*, or prepositional phrases such as:

in addition   *Governments have increased spending on healthcare. **In addition**, they are funding research.*

for example   *Human actions are affecting climate change. **For example**, demands on water can cause drought.*

by comparison   *Interest in online media has grown. **By comparison**, print distribution figures are falling.*

22 Maximizing and minimizing language

Writers and speakers can express different degrees of certainty and confidence through the use of maximizing and minimizing language.

a   Stating something with a high degree of certainty: using *is / are*, or another verb without an **auxiliary**, e.g. *this particular kick **is** the result of many hours of practice.* An example in the negative form is *The extraordinary changes **did not result from** any alteration of basic aging processes.*

b   When speculating on something, i.e. trying to work out how something happened or how likely it is, the most confident expression is the **modal auxiliary** verb *must*, e.g. *The projected increase in the world's population **must be** the result of population growth in less developed societies.*

c Other modal auxiliary verbs can be used to express lesser degrees of certainty or confidence, e.g. *If it continues, desertification **can result**; A more free market approach **may lead to** economic growth.* These examples show that the writer is not making a very confident statement; the idea being expressed is possible, not certain.

d Choice of **adverbs** indicate an authors' confidence:
Maximizing: *absolutely, definitely, certainly*
Minimizing: *often, probably, possibly*

e Choice of verbs that express 'hedged' opinions are also used in minimizing, e.g. *It **appears** that the research is inconclusive; There **seems** to be a correlation between education and crime.*

23 Modal verbs

Modal verbs are frequently used in academic texts. They show degrees of certainty and confidence (see 22 *Maximizing and minimizing language*), and other meanings such as necessity, obligation, and ability. All modal verbs have at least two different meanings, and each meaning has at least two modal verbs to express it. In order of frequency, these are:

- *will* (predictions, future certainty, conditionals, etc.)
- *would* (conditions, past habits, future in the past, etc.)
- *can* (possibility, ability, general truths, predictions, etc.)
- *could* (possibility, permission, predictions, etc.)
- *may* (possibility, predictions, permission, general truths, etc.)
- *should* (likelihood, desirability, suggestions, predictions, etc.)
- *must* (obligation, necessity, deductions, conclusions, regulations, etc.)
- *might* (prediction, possibility, permission, etc.).

In addition, *ought to* can be classed as a modal (or semi-modal). The modal verb *shall* is the least frequently used; neither *ought to* nor *shall* occurs in the texts in this book.

The following examples show various frequent meanings and the modal verbs used:

*This set of experiences **will** influence the way they think about the world.* (prediction)

*When bloggers added their comments, other web users **would** access those opinions.* (habit in the past)

*For the commercial organization, a blog **would** be a full-time job for a member of staff.* (condition)

*Technology **can** make it easier for small firms to compete with large.* (possibility)

*There is much speculation on what boys and girls **can** or cannot do well.* (ability)

*Global energy demand **could** still increase to 6 CMO by then.* (prediction)

*Although a more free market approach **may** lead to economic growth in the long run, there are without doubt short-run costs to the poorest people.* (likelihood)

*This year we **must** report that progress has virtually ground to a halt.* (necessity / obligation)

*It is clear that the runners **must** have different goals for the same event.* (deduction)

*In some organizations, outsourcing the blog to a professional **might** be the best option.* (speculation)

Modal verbs can be used with **passives**. In this case they are followed by *be* plus the main verb, e.g. *People **may** be asked to work longer and retire later* = 'someone (but we do not know who) may ask people to work longer and retire later'.

In academic texts, some **verbs** usually occur with a modal verb, e.g. *interact, guarantee, survive.*

24 Nouns and noun phrases

Noun phrases are the most important structures in academic texts because they make up most of the text. A lot of information can be packaged into noun phrases, and as a result they can be very long and complicated.

Noun phrases typically account for about two-thirds of the words in academic texts. A noun phrase can be one word or more. A **pronoun**, e.g. *it*, is also a noun phrase. There is no limit to the length of a noun phrase.

Noun phrases are built round one noun, the head noun. This is the noun which can be replaced by a pronoun. The pronoun then takes the place of the whole noun phrase. The head nouns are given in **bold** in all the examples in this section:

*the **planet** → it; Billions of **hours** → They / These; the **content** of the media → it.*

The noun phrase must agree with the **verb**, e.g. *The boom **year** for blogging was ...* (not *were*).

Sometimes identifying the head noun can be difficult, e.g. ***One** of the latest developments suitable for use by the online marketers is ... → It is ... / This is ... .* The verb 'is' in this example shows that the head is *One*, and not *developments*.

Noun phrases are frequently used as the **subject** and/or **object** in a sentence. They are also found as part of larger structures, for example when a long noun phrase is made up of a number of shorter noun phrases. Noun phrases also frequently follow **prepositions**, to make up a **prepositional phrase**. Headings and titles are often noun phrases, e.g. ***Principles** that define the cognitive level of analysis.*

The main noun phrase structures can be represented in the following five broad patterns and combinations:

24.1 Pronoun as head noun

Many noun phrases are made up of a pronoun, sometimes with other words, but usually without.

The pronouns often refer back to information in previous sentences, e.g.

*The study was conducted in London. **It** looked at boys from different social classes.*

*Bloggers have attitude. **They** have opinions on everything.*

Sometimes noun phrases are complements, with the pronoun as the head noun, e.g.

Intrinsic motives are **those** *that come from within the individual.*

24.2 (Determiner) + adjective(s) and/or noun(s) + head noun

Noun phrases frequently have a mixture of any combination of determiner / adjective / noun before the head noun, for example:

an alternative **approach** (determiner + adjective + head noun)

audience **figures** (noun + head noun)

fossil plant **remains** (noun + noun + head noun)

these less developed **regions** (determiner [the demonstrative *these*] + *less* + adjective + head noun)

a similar class **situation** (determiner + adjective + noun + head noun)

global temperature and rainfall **patterns** (adjective + two nouns joined by the coordinator *and* + head noun]

24.3 Head noun + prepositional phrase

A very frequent noun phrase pattern is a **prepositional phrase** following the head noun. Usually, the prepositional phrase begins with frequent prepositions such as *of, for,* and *on,* for example: *the* **process** *of desertification; the* **desire** *for personal vehicles; Humanity's* **demands** *on the earth; archaeological* **evidence** *such as ancient rock art.*

24.4 Head noun + relative clause

Relative clauses directly follow their head noun, and normally begin with a **pronoun**, known as a relative pronoun, which functions as the 'subject' or 'object' of the clause. The pronoun is followed by a **verb**, which may be in a **tense**, **modal verb**, or *-ing / -ed* form, plus normally the **object** of the clause: *a set of mental* **processes** *that are carried out by the brain.*

The pronoun can be missed out if it is the **object** of the clause, e.g. *The* **distinctions** ~~that~~ *he made between class, status, and party.*

In some relative clauses the verb is in an *-ing / -ed* form, e.g. *Most* **research** *carried out at the time.* This example can be rephrased as *Most research which was carried out at the time.*

All the examples above are of defining relative clauses. These follow on directly from the head noun (without any punctuation) and are necessary to complete the meaning of the noun phrase. Non-defining relative clauses normally begin with *which*, add extra meaning, and are optional: *The main natural cause is connected to climate, which has changed throughout geological time.*

24.5 Combinations and variations

Many variations of the above patterns are used in academic texts, e.g.

The earliest reputable **studies** *into the link between criminality and intelligence*
(determiner + adjective + adjective + head noun + prepositional phrase)

The extraordinary demographic **changes** *that have already taken place in our society*
(determiner + adjective + adjective + head noun + relative clause)

the **inequalities** *in life chances that we examine in Chapter 18*
(determiner + head noun + prepositional phrase + relative clause)

Some noun phrases have two nouns as head, joined by a **coordinator** such as *and*: *the* **structure and functions** *of the mind.*

Similarly, a number of noun phrases can be joined by commas and a coordinator (usually *and*) to form the **subject** of a sentence, e.g. *Eroding* **soils**, *deteriorating* **rangelands**, *collapsing* **fisheries**, *falling water* **tables**, *and rising temperatures are converging to make it more difficult to expand food production fast enough to keep up with demand.*

Occasionally there can be an **adverb**, e.g. *worldwide,* after the head noun: *Temperature and rainfall* **patterns** *worldwide.*

Another frequent pattern is for a phrase expressing a similar idea in different words, or a phrase giving an example, to follow a head noun, e.g. *This* **shortfall**, *the largest on record; The U.N. Food and Agriculture* **Organization** *(FAO).*

Some noun + noun combinations have become fixed, e.g. *greenhouse* **gases**, *water* **table**. These are sometimes known as 'compound nouns'. The first noun is related closely to the head noun in some way, such as a part or type.

See **1 Adjectives** and **15 Determiners**

25 Numbers

Numbers are mostly written using figures, e.g. *1, 110.* Numbers below 10 are often written in full, especially when they are followed by a noun, e.g. *these* **three** *types of goals.*

Numbers are pronounced in different ways depending on what they represent. The following examples from the texts in this book are presented with the way of pronouncing them in brackets. Sometimes, there are minor differences between North American (NAmE) and British English (BrE).

Sequencing

Unit 1 [unit one]

Table 10.3 [table ten point three]

figure 4.31 [figure four point three one, NOT figure four point thirty-one]

Dates

1902 [nineteen oh two]

1912 [nineteen twelve]

2002 [two thousand and two / two thousand two *NAmE* / twenty oh two *NAmE*]

2012 [twenty twelve / two thousand and twelve / two thousand twelve *NAmE*] *the 1980s* [the nineteen-eighties];

Hirst and Patching (2005: 104) [Hirst and Patching two thousand and five, page a hundred and four / one oh four]

Quantities, amounts, fractions, percentages, distances, volume

over 110 [over a hundred and ten / over one hundred and ten / over one hundred ten *NAmE*]

a 10km run [a ten kilometre run / a ten k run]

2.5 billion in 1950 to 6.1 billion in 2000 [two point five billion in nineteen fifty to six point one billion in two thousand]

640 million [six hundred and forty million / six hundred forty million *NAmE*]

316 parts per million [three hundred and sixteen parts per million / three hundred sixteen parts per million *NAmE*]

1,855 million tons [one thousand eight hundred and fifty five million tons / one thousand eight hundred fifty five million tons *NAmE*]

CO_2 [C O two]

0.8 CMO [nought point eight C M O / point eight C M O / zero point eight C M O]

4 percent [four percent]

only 1/20th of the world population [only one-twentieth of the world population]

Ages

ages 8–10 [ages eight to ten / eight through ten *NAmE*]

26 Objects

Objects follow the main verb in many sentences in the **active** voice. When a sentence is in the **passive**, the object becomes the **subject**. Like the **subject**, the **object** in a sentence is most likely to be a noun phrase:

Cars offer unprecedented freedom, flexibility, convenience, and comfort.

However, all renewable-energy sources have some environmental consequences.

As with subjects, an object can also be other structures, including ***wh*- clause**, ***that* clause**, ***to*- clause**, or *-ing* **clause**.

The article contradicted ***what I had written***.
I would like to recommend ***that you rewrite your essay***.
I have decided ***to change course***.
Many students prefer ***learning individually***.

27 Passive voice

The passive voice is very frequent in academic texts. It is used for a number of reasons:

- when the focus is on something abstract:
  *A cognitive schema **can be defined as** networks of knowledge, beliefs, and expectations.*
- to avoid mentioning who or what does something, because it is not important:
  *The report **was published** in early 2009.*
- to avoid mentioning who or what does something to create a sense of 'objective distance': *It **is understood** that these changes to policy have caused concerns.*

When the passive is used, the **tense** and **aspect** combinations remain the same as if the verb was in the active. For example the sentence *The intensive cultivation of energy crops **is being encouraged*** contains the passive form of the **present progressive**. The present progressive would also be used if the sentence was written in the active, e.g. *People **are encouraging** the intensive cultivation of energy crops.*

See **41 Tense and aspect** and **43 Verbs**

28 Prepositions and prepositional phrases / directions

Prepositions are the most frequent grammatical words in academic texts, occurring on average every seventh word. The following sentence shows typical uses of prepositions in a written academic text: *The boom year **for** blogging was 2002 as it moved **from** minority interest **into** the mainstream **of** the Internet.*

Prepositions are used so frequently because they express a wide range of meanings connected with:

- time (e.g. ***in** 1996*)
- place (e.g. ***at** the World Food Summit in Rome*)
- process (e.g. ***by** the brain*)
- cause (e.g. ***because of** fears of dioxin emissions*)
- purpose (e.g. ***for** various electricity generation technologies*)
- concession (e.g. ***despite** careful planning*)
- degree / quantity (e.g. ***from** 14 **over** par **to** 11*)
- receiver (e.g. ***to** the poorest people*).

Prepositional phrases are used as **adverbials**, e.g. *for coal and gas*, and following **noun phrases**, e.g. *disadvantages **of different technologies***.

There are also many fixed phrases which begin with prepositions, e.g. *in the end, in addition, by then*.

Prepositional verbs are made up of a verb, e.g. *look*, plus a preposition, e.g. *into, after, for*.

29 Prefixes

See **4 Affixes**

30 Prepositional and phrasal verbs

Prepositional verbs are used frequently in academic texts because they refer to a wide range of cognitive processes, e.g. *Outcome goals **focus on** the competitive results of the game; We will **look at** each of these.*

Prepositional verbs are made up of a verb plus a preposition. These two parts are not normally separated, but sometimes they can be separated with an **adverbial**, e.g. ***focus** mainly **on***.

Phrasal verbs are not very frequent in academic texts because they refer mainly to everyday physical activities rather than cognitive ones, e.g. *However, developing new medicines can involve very expensive research and development costs which companies are keen to **get back**.* (= recover)

The most frequent phrasal verb in academic texts is *go on*, i.e. 'continue'.

31 Progressive forms

The progressive aspect shows that something is not complete but in progress, e.g. *The public **are becoming** increasingly affluent and consumerist.*

It is formed using the verb *be* plus the *-ing* form of the main verb.

Progressive forms can also be used with the other aspect, i.e. the perfect aspect, as well as **modal verbs**, e.g. *The media **should have been informing** the public of the threat to free speech.*

In the **passive**, the progressive form is marked by the **auxiliary verb** *be*, e.g. *The role and relevance of the investigative journalist increasingly **is being challenged**.*

32 Pronouns

There are three main types of pronouns:

personal, e.g. *it, she, I* (subject)
him, us, them (object)   *his, hers, theirs* (possessive)

relative, e.g. *which, that, who*

and interrogative, e.g. *who, which, what*

Pronouns are words which take the place of a **noun phrase**, e.g. <u>People</u> *are not likely to deliberately damage the land which **they** depend on for their survival;* the pronoun *they* takes the place of the noun *people* after it has been mentioned.

Pronouns are the only words in English which change their form depending on whether they are in the **subject** or **object** position, e.g. *He* (subject), *him* (object).

33 Relative clauses

See **24 Nouns and noun phrases**

34 Reporting verbs and reporting structures

There are a large number of reporting verbs in English, but a smaller number are frequently used, e.g.

*Giles (2003) **reports** that the research on the effects of video game play is inconclusive.*

*Gentile et al. (2004) **found** increased levels of anti-social effects in children.*

*Most research carried out at the time **arrived at** a similar conclusion.*

These examples use the reporting verb in the **present tense**. Other reporting structures include *It* and *There*.

35 Simple sentences

There are a small number of frequent sentence patterns in English. Sentences in English usually follow a pattern based around **Subject (S)** – **Verb (V)** – **Object (O)** or **Complement (C)**. The 'SVO' pattern is very frequent.

Clause elements of Subject, Verb , and Object can vary in length and form.

The subject can be very short, often a **pronoun**, e.g. *This raises ethical questions*.

Often when the subject is short, the **object** can be long, e.g. *Schema theory suggests that what we already know will influence the outcome of information processing*.

Less frequently, the subject is very long, e.g. *Murrow's criticism of the lack of endeavour by journalists and news corporations had little influence on the commercialization of news*.

The longer the subject, the more difficult it is to process the meaning of a sentence.

Simple sentences often contain one or more Adverbials (A).

See **3 Adverbials**, **10 Complex sentences**, and **11 Compound sentences**

36 Stance and perspective adverbials

Stance is often expressed through **adverbials**:

These are, of course, the extra costs in addition to the normal market price of electricity.

Obviously this can result in mistakes.

Further examples of stance adverbials include:

- Arguably   *Cars are arguably one of the greatest man-made threats to human society.*
- Without doubt   *There are without doubt short-run costs to the poorest people.*
- (Even more) interestingly   *Even more interestingly, he discovered that low intelligence was related to repeated crime.*

All the adverbials in these examples express the stance of the writer or speaker.

Perspective can also be expressed through adverbials, e.g. *economically, technologically, in financial terms*.

37 Subjects

The **subject** of a sentence typically comes early in a **sentence** and performs the action of the **verb**, e.g. ***Population growth** has tripled world grain demand over the last half-century.*

The subject of a sentence is usually a **noun phrase**, e.g. *Yet **cars** aren't going to go away.*

The subject can also be other structures, such as a ***wh*- clause**, or *-ing* **clause**, e.g. ***What is missing** are the 'external costs', which are in effect paid by society.*

38 Subordinators

Subordinators are grammatical words which introduce a subordinate clause, e.g. *Its significance is masked because it reflects averages.*

A subordinate clause is joined to a main clause. Only a main clause can stand alone; a subordinate clause cannot. Typically, subordinate clauses are the second clause in a sentence because they tend to add new information. One or two subordinators, e.g. *if*, usually come first.

There are a large number of subordinators in English which express a wide range of meanings, for example:

- time (*when, while*)
- place (*where, wherever*)
- manner (*as, like*)
- cause (*because, since*)
- purpose (*so that, in order to*)
- condition (*if, unless*)
- concession (*although, even though*)
- contrast (*while, whereas*)

Some subordinators can have two or more meanings, e.g. *while* can show contrast, concession, or time.

See **10 Complex sentences**

39 Suffixes

See **4 Affixes**

40 *That* clauses

The grammatical word *that* is used frequently in a number of different ways:

- As a relative clause: *It is vital that news agencies continue to report rather than entertain.*
- As the complement clause in a sentence: *There is a possibility that the relationship between consumer and producer may evolve.*
- As the **object** of a sentence following certain verbs (*hope, believe, argue, suggest*): *They argue that performance is regulated by the conscious goals.*

The following nouns often occur in academic texts, followed by *that* clauses: *belief, claim, conclusion, doubt, fact, hope, idea, observation, possibility, report, suggestion, view.*

41 Tense and aspect

In English there are:

- two **tenses**   present and past
- two **aspects**   perfect and progressive

A verb can be either in a tense (present or past), or combined with a **modal**, or in the *-ing* / *-ed* / *to-* infinitive form.

Tenses can be combined with aspects, giving eight tense / aspect combinations. Most verbs in academic texts are in the present or past simple (i.e. without an aspect.) The present perfect is also used, often for reporting research.

Other past tense forms, e.g. past progressive, are rarely used in academic texts.

The **present** tense (sometimes known as the 'present simple') is used for universal truths, reporting the ideas of others, and habits, etc.: *All renewable-energy sources **have** some environmental consequences; An individual's decision to have children **seems to be** flexible.*

The **present progressive** is used for something which is still in progress and has not yet been completed, e.g. *Life expectancy **is plummeting** in sub-Saharan Africa.* It is formed using the verb *be* in the present tense, i.e. *am / is / are*, and the main verb ending in *-ing*.

Sometimes more than one main verb can be used in one sentence, and these verbs can share the same **auxiliary verb**, e.g. *When people **are thinking about** how best to solve a mathematical problem, **trying** to remember the title of a book, **observing** a beautiful sunset, or **thinking about** what to do tomorrow, they are involved in cognitive processing.* The action in progress can be very short, i.e. just a few moments, or very long, i.e. many years: *The land in the photo **is turning into** a desert.*

The **present perfect** is used to connect events in the past to the present, particularly for experiences and events which still have some significance in the present. It is also used for reporting, and for recently completed events: *Technology **has** thus **made** the rapid growth of the multinational corporation easier; There **has been** a significant change in recent decades.* The present perfect is formed using the present tense of *have*, i.e. *has, have*, plus the third form of the verb (past participle), e.g. *taken*.

The **present perfect progressive** combines the meanings of perfect and progressive to express both completion and progression, e.g. *Temperature and rainfall patterns worldwide **have** certainly **been changing**.* This example shows that the results of temperature and rainfall patterns can be seen today, but also that the process has not finished yet, i.e. it is still going on / in progress.

The **past** tense (sometimes known as the 'past simple') is used to report events that happened in the past. It is used frequently in narratives, sequences of events, and specifying when something happened: *8,000 years ago the climate in North Africa and the Middle East **was** much wetter than it is today; The success of the export-led Asian Tigers **did not happen** without government intervention.*

The **past progressive**, **past perfect**, and **past perfect progressive** are not very frequent in academic texts, and are not used in any of the texts in this book.

See **16 The future** and **43 Verbs**

42 *To-* clause

To- clauses are sometimes known as 'infinitive clauses', and can be used as **objects** in a sentence, e.g. *The dominant company can seek to protect its position through aggressive marketing.* They often express purpose.

43 Verbs

There are five possible different patterns following verbs. Many verbs have only one pattern, but some verbs can have more than one, e.g.

He's reading. (the verb *read* is used without an object).

She's reading a report. (the verb *read* is used with an object).

She read her student a story. (the verb *read* is used with two objects)

1 Verbs used without an object, e.g. *Humanity's demands on the earth **have multiplied** over the last half-century as our numbers **have increased** and our incomes **risen**.* The three verbs in this sentence are used without an object. However, these verbs may

be followed by an **adverbial**, e.g. *Incomes* ***have risen*** *even faster than population.*

2 Verbs used with a complement, e.g. *Serious droughts* ***have become*** *more common; Humans* ***are*** *active processors of information.* These verbs need a complement to complete the meaning, so the complement is necessary and cannot be missed out.

3 Verbs used with one object, e.g. *Government bodies* **arrange** *all production; Psychologists* **identify** *three types of goals.* These verbs need an object and this cannot be missed out.

4 Verbs used with two objects, e.g. *Possession of economic resources* ***gives*** *people their power to acquire income and assets.* In this example, the direct object of the verb *gives* is *their power …*, and the indirect object is *people* = 'the power is given to the people.' There are a limited number of verbs with this pattern.

5 Verbs used with one object plus one necessary adverbial / complement, e.g. *Technology* ***has*** *thus* ***made*** *the rapid growth of the multinational corporation easier.* In this example, the object of the verb has *made* is *the rapid growth of the multinational corporation*, but the complement *easier* is also a necessary part of the pattern and cannot be missed out.

Some verbs, such as *put*, require an object and an adverbial, e.g. *They* ***are putting*** *pressure on the roads of today's cities.* This example shows that both the object *pressure* and the adverbial *on the roads of today's cities* are necessary to complete the meaning.

44 *Wh-* clauses

Clauses which begin with a *wh-* word, e.g. *what, where*, can be used as the subject in a sentence, e.g. *What he means by this is that the inequalities in life chances are determined by market position.*

A *wh-* clause can also be the **object** of a sentence.

45 Word class and word families

About half the words in academic texts are from the four meaning-carrying word classes:

nouns, verbs, adjectives, and **adverbs**.

The remaining half are grammatical words:
prepositions, determiners, primary auxiliaries, pronouns, coordinators, modal auxiliaries, subordinators, and other categories.

Most grammatical words have only one form, and some other words have only one **word class**, e.g. the adjective *widespread*.

It is very common for **nouns, verbs, adjectives**, and **adverbs** to have more than one form: *concept* (noun), *conceptual* (adjective), *conceptualize* (verb), *conceptually* (adverb). Identifying and understanding word class can make it easier to understand sentence structure and meaning.

Additional reference material

Plagiarism

What is plagiarism?

Plagiarism is when you hand in work for an assessment and part or all of the work is not your own. It is considered to be a serious matter in academic institutions. If a student plagiarizes someone else's work they may lose grades, or fail part or all of their course.

Typical examples of plagiarism include:

- copying material from another source (e.g. textbook, internet text) without properly referencing it
- handing in work that is not entirely your own
- presenting any material, idea, research, argument, etc. as your own when it is actually from another source
- handing in work for assessment that has already been assessed somewhere else.

Remember that using material without acknowledgment from <u>any</u> source is plagiarism – even if the source is unpublished, or is a lecture. There are other examples of plagiarism that also mean it is very important to clearly understand academic referencing. For example, it could be considered plagiarism if you copy an extract word for word and reference it, but then forget to use quotation marks so the text looks like a paraphrase rather than a direct quotation. It is important to remember that anything 'borrowed' from another author must be 'given back' by acknowledging it properly and accurately. It is also important to realize that this process also applies to other forms of media, e.g. visuals such as graphs, illustrations, or photos; or machine code; or mathematical proofs.

Most institutions have their own policy on plagiarism which is explained on their website. For example, the University of Oxford offers a clear definition, description, and advice on plagiarism at:
http:/www.admin.ox.ac.uk/edc/goodpractice/about/

Why is plagiarism wrong?

As in the wider world, basic honesty in the academic world is expected. Most people don't steal, and also don't plagiarize. Plagiarism is easy to do, and easy to detect. At university, you are there to learn. Trying your best to complete an assignment independently, no matter how difficult it might seem, is a learning experience. By plagiarizing, you won't learn very much, you won't develop your academic 'voice', and you won't be making progress. Most students work hard to produce their own work, and it is seen as unfair if a student plagiarizes, but receives the same qualification as someone who does not. A qualification is an indication of someone's knowledge and skills. If plagiarism is involved, the student won't necessarily have such knowledge and skills. This could have serious consequences – for example, no one wants to be treated by a pharmacist who isn't competent because they cheated in their coursework.

What do tutors and professors think about plagiarism?

Plagiarism wastes a lot of time. As experts in their field, tutors are skilled at detecting plagiarism, but this takes away time when they could be assessing student's own work. The signs tutors look for when reading assignments are:

- written work that is not properly referenced
- texts which have obvious differences in accuracy and style between paragraphs
- written work which is obviously above the level of the student.

It is not acceptable to get a large amount of help in writing assignments from a friend or family member. It is also unacceptable to use a professional agency to help in writing assignments.

How can you avoid plagiarism?

The best way to avoid plagiarism is to follow these six guidelines.

1. Be informed – read the information on plagiarism on your university or college website. Make sure you understand it, and keep up to date with any changes in policy.
2. Be honest – don't try to deceive your tutor by handing in work which is not your own.
3. Be professional – follow academic convention by referencing all the material you have taken from other sources.
4. Be cautious – if you are unsure about whether to include a reference, check with your tutor. If this isn't possible, include the reference anyway.
5. Be individual – discuss ideas and assignments with other students, but write on your own.
6. Be smart – don't avoid plagiarism because you'll be punished, avoid it because you'll learn more.

Citation: summary, paraphrase, and quotation

What is citation?

Citation refers to the use of material from another source in your writing in order to add support and examples. The main forms of citation are summary, paraphrase, and quotation. With all of these, you need to reference the material correctly. If not, it will be seen as plagiarized.

What is a summary?

A summary of a text is an efficient and concise way of presenting ideas and information from other sources. It allows you to include a large amount of information in a small number of words. A summary is shorter than the original text, but there is no special length for a summary. You can summarize many types and lengths of text, including: a few sentences or a paragraph; a section or chapter in a book; part of an article; the work of a particular researcher. A summary should:

- be as brief as possible
- be easy to understand – perhaps written in simpler language than the source text
- include the main points of the source text, but not the details such as examples
- use different language, i.e. not closely based on the language of the source text
- only include information in the source text, and not include extra information, such as evaluation, which is not in the source text.

What is a paraphrase?

In order to use the same ideas as the source text, including the main idea and any examples, you can paraphrase part of the text. A paraphrase focuses on the idea or information in the original text, rather than on particular language. A paraphrase is normally quite short: a phrase, part of a sentence, a whole sentence, or perhaps more than one sentence. It is usually a similar length to the source text. It is unusual to paraphrase a longer text – write a summary of it instead.

To paraphrase successfully you have to do all the following:

- Incorporate all the ideas and information in the source text.
- Keep the same meaning as the source text.
- Use mostly your own language, which may mean a different sentence structure, different phrasing, different general and academic words (using synonyms and rephrasing) but the same technical and conceptual words, e.g. *cell*, *globalization*.
- Make sure your paraphrase doesn't use language that is too similar to the source text, but is of a similar length.
- Make sure that the paraphrase is clear, and is accurate in terms of language and content.

The best way of paraphrasing a short piece of text is to read it carefully, note down the information it contains, and then write your paraphrase based on your own notes. You can then check your paraphrase against the original text using the points above as guidelines. Changing a short text word by word, phrase by phrase, and sentence by sentence does not make an effective paraphrase. For example, compare paraphrases 1 and 2 of the following extract from *The Globalization of World Politics* (5th edition) by Baylis, Smith, & Owens (2011, p.348):

Original text

Economists claim that globalization's opening up of markets can increase efficiency and reduce pollution, provided that the environmental and social damage associated with the production of a good is properly factored into its market price.

Paraphrase 1

Economists argue that globalization's development of markets may enhance efficiency and lessen pollution, on condition that the environmental and social harm caused by production of a good is correctly reflected in its real cost (Baylis, Smith, & Owens, 2008, p.348).

Paraphrase 2

Positive effects of globalization identified by economists can include efficiency gains and pollution reduction, although the price of a good should reflect the full costs of producing it, including environmental and social costs. (Baylis, Smith, & Owens, 2008, p.348).

Both paraphrases 1 and 2 are correctly referenced, of a similar length to the original text, and contain all the points of the original text. Also, they keep the same technical terms such as *globalization*, *good* (i.e. *product*), and *environmental*. However, paraphrase 1 is not a good example because it follows the structure of the original text too closely – it is not enough to simply change a few words using synonyms and rephrasing. Paraphrase 2 is a good example because it expresses the ideas of the original text using a different structure, with appropriate use of synonyms and rephrasing, e.g. changing word forms and phrases: *can increase efficiency and reduce pollution → can include efficiency gains and pollution reduction*.

What is a quotation?

A quotation from an original source uses the same language, and you can use part of a sentence such as a word or phrase, a whole sentence, or occasionally several lines. The main reason to use a quotation rather than a paraphrase is that the language (words / phrasing) of the original source is particularly clear and significant. Quotations are often used for definitions, such as in the following extract from *The Globalization of World Politics* (5th edition) by Baylis, Smith, & Owens (2011, p.217–8):

Because war is a fluid concept, it has generated a large number of contradictory definitions ... A more useful definition in this sense is Hedley Bull's. It is 'organised violence carried on by political units against each other' (Bull 1977: 184). Bull goes on to insist that violence is not war unless it is both carried out by a political unit, and directed against another political unit.

This extract forms part of a longer paragraph which presents and discusses different definitions of war. It is appropriate to use quotation because the language of the original source has been carefully written and it is useful to present this original language without changing it, i.e. by using a quotation. Notice that in the last sentence of the above extract, the writers of the textbook (Baylis, Smith, & Owens) add further clarification to the definition by using a paraphrase or summary.

Proofreading and self-editing

What are proofreading and self-editing?

Proofreading involves checking for mistakes in certain language areas, such as the following:

- spelling
- punctuation
- subject-verb agreement in the present simple
- tenses in general
- extra words such as determiners (*a, an, the, this*)
- missing words such as determiners (*a, an, the, this*)
- connections between sentences
- prepositions (*from, in, on, to*)
- word class (adjective, adverb, noun, verb)
- word order in noun phrases
- voice (active / passive)
- style (formal / informal)

Self-editing is where you change the text in one way or another – such as changing the word order, expanding information, or redrafting (writing the text again).

Proofreading and self-editing do not just happen at the end of the writing process – they both take place while the writing is in progress. The process of writing involves looking back at the text you have already written, and planning what you are about to write. To help these processes to work effectively, it is useful to stop writing after short periods in order to review your text.

After you have finished writing a text, it can be difficult to do both the proofreading and self-editing simultaneously, so focus on them separately. Also, each time you self-edit a text, proofread it afterwards because you may have 'edited in' mistakes.

Why are proofreading and self-editing important?

Learning to take responsibility for your written work is part of the academic process. The student who hands in work in the hope that their tutor will 'sort it out' is being unrealistic and lazy. Having to proofread and self-edit your work puts you in the position of the people who will ultimately read your writing. It helps you think about the effect of your writing on the reader. If your work contains too many mistakes in grammar, spelling, or punctuation, these might affect the reader's understanding of the main points you want to make. If the number of such mistakes is high, the reader might become frustrated, and may even stop reading your assignment.

What strategies can you use for proofreading?

There are a number of things you can do to proofread your work effectively. Try some of the following:

1 Make a list of mistakes you know that you make repeatedly and check for these in your written work.

2 Make a checklist of common mistakes made by most people to check for in your written work.

3 Categorize both types of mistakes in 1 and 2 to help you recognize them (e.g. spelling, punctuation).

4 Check for one type of mistake at a time as you proofread, e.g. spelling. If you find other mistakes at the same time, correct them, but don't lose your focus.

5 Put your work aside for a period of time, at least twenty-four hours if possible, and then proofread it again.

6 If your work has been typed, print it out and then look for mistakes that you often make when typing.

7 Read your work aloud – you may notice mistakes more quickly.

8 Practise proofreading using your own work. When you give it to your teacher for correction, keep a copy. Once the original has been corrected and returned to you, try correcting the clean copy of the original yourself. Finally, compare it with the teacher's corrected version.

9 Practise correcting mistakes with other students as part of your independent study. For example, choose a paragraph of approximately 120 words from the internet. Then introduce ten different mistakes. Next, print out a copy for your partner to find the mistakes. Finally, let them compare their corrections with the original text.

10 Discuss your mistakes with other students, check if you make the same kind of mistakes, and discuss the reasons why.

11 Make a list of mistakes that you typically make because of your first language.

12 Number and date all the work you hand in for correction to monitor your progress over the course of your academic studies.

What strategies can you use for self-editing?

As with proofreading, there are a variety of strategies you can adopt. Try some of the following:

1 Keep copies of drafts of your writing before you edit the final text. Referring back to previous versions can show you where changes were made.

2 Edit by hand on a print out, and then type the edits on computer.

3 Print your text. Then cut it into sections and reassemble them, making any changes and inserting any additions. Number the changes and additions so you can check you have made them all. It is also a useful way of seeing a part of a text you are editing in relation to the whole text.

4 Check that you use vocabulary consistently.

5 Check that you include only information that is relevant.

6 Check that the connections between the paragraphs and different stages in the text fit together.

7 Check that there is coherence between the text title, and the text throughout. As an initial check, read the introduction, the thesis statement, the topic sentences, and finally the conclusion.

8 Read the text aloud, or record yourself reading it, and listen to check that you understand it.

9 Write a brief summary of your text in bullet points and then compare your summary with the text. Redraft and repeat the process.

10 At the end of the self-editing process, proofread your text again to check you haven't introduced any further mistakes.

Writing Sample answers

Unit 3D TASK 7 (page 047)

'Describe a theory of motivation that you know about, and show how the theory can be applied to work, or a sport.'

Visualization is the process of picturing yourself achieving your goals or fulfilling your ambitions.[1] It is based on the idea that people who visualize their performance, and imagine themselves achieving their goals, can be more successful in reaching these targets.[2] For example, someone who pictures themself taking perfect shots in a game often feels more confident, and their performance can be improved in real-life sporting situations (where there is greater pressure).[3] Today this technique is used by many top sports stars as an approach to enhancing their performance, and can be applied in many ways.[4]

▶ Key features in Academic writing

[1] A clear definition of term 'visualization'.
[2] An explanation which adds more detail.
[3] An example that further clarifies the definition.
[4] A clear lead in to the next paragraph.

Unit 4D TASK 6 (page 061)

Much of the world's modern economy would not be able to function without natural resources extracted from the earth.[1] The discovery and use of fossil fuels was in part responsible for the early industrialization and economic development of Europe and North America.[2] Similarly[3], it[4] continues to play a key role in the growth of some of the world's leading economies today. For example, most manufacturing, transportation, and use of goods is dependent on the availability of fossil fuels. The global economy has become even more reliant[5] on natural resources in many other aspects of life. For instance, many electronic and telecommunication devices are dependent on rare metals such as coltan and cadmium that need to be extracted from mines. Consequently, it is likely that mankind will continue to be economically dependent on nature for quite some time.[6]

▶ Key features in Academic writing

[1] A clear paragraph topic.
[2] An example which helps to extend main idea.
[3] An adverbial used to link ideas.
[4] A referent used to vary vocabulary, and reduce repetition.
[5] A synonym used to give greater lexical range.
[6] A clear concluding sentence with linking expressions used for greater cohesion.

Unit 5D TASK 6 (page 075)

Summary of trait theory paragraph

In their text on Leadership theory, Clarke et al state that innate personality features underpin the concept of trait theory – that certain individuals are born to lead. However, others argue experience also impacts on leadership skills and qualities.[1]

▶ Key features in Academic writing

[1] Own language used to capture main ideas of paragraph.

Unit 6D TASK 8 (page 089)

'Equality and quality of life are more important than economic and technological growth.' Discuss.

Quality of life is arguably linked to increases in wealth both individually and as a nation as a whole. Without a high GDP it is debatable whether a country could provide services, such as education and healthcare, which are linked to a higher standard of living.[1] Bowles, Edwards, and Roosevelt (2005, p.8), argue that there is a clear link between capitalism and growth.[2] They argue that 'wherever and whenever capitalism took hold, people's incomes and consumption levels began to rise in a sustained way.'[3] These increases in income provide people with the financial means to improve their quality of life. However, capitalism does not focus on equality between individuals and such a system often results in a widening gap between the rich and poor. Therefore equality and quality of life are unlikely to go hand in hand as the latter is too intrinsically linked to economic growth.[4]

▶ Key features in Academic writing
[1] A clear link to the essay title.
[2] Use of a source to support a main idea.
[3] A relevant quotation that shows understanding of source, and directly relates to essay topic.
[4] A clear concluding sentence that sums up writer's stance, while referring to essay title.

Unit 7D TASK 7 (page 103)

'The development of the internet has had the biggest single impact on modern life.' Discuss.

Between 2000 and 2011 there was over a 500% growth in the numbers of people using the internet worldwide. By 2011 internet usage and access stood at nearly 2.3 billion people, or one-third of the world's population (Internet world stats, 2012).[1] Such growth, not only in terms of numbers, but also in the variety of tasks that can now be performed over the web, has clearly had a profound impact on modern life.[2] However, this essay will argue that the discovery and use of fossil fuels has had a much wider impact.[3] This essay will firstly evaluate the impact of the internet on modern life, followed by an evaluation of the impact of fossil fuels on the world today.[4]

▶ Key features in Academic writing
[1] Statistics used to provide background information, and get reader's interest.
[2] A clear transition from broader background content to topic specific material.
[3] A clear thesis statement with a rationale for arguing against the question statement.
[4] A statement of aims that outlines the essay structure.

Unit 8D TASK 6 (page 117)

The role of innovation and creativity for entrepreneurs.

Innovation is the process of developing unique and creative new ideas or ways of approaching something and is key to successful entrepreneurship.[1] However, it is not simply just the idea or approach that is enough to bring a product to market. Du Toit, Erasmus, & Strydom, (2010) argue that what makes an entrepreneur stand out from other business people is their ability to spot market opportunities and see unique and creative methods that exploit these.[2] Innovation is therefore so interconnected with entrepreneurship that it could be argued it is actually what distinguishes the concept from other business people and business activities. Without innovation and creativity, a business person, no matter how enterprising, is not an entrepreneur.

▶ Key features in Academic writing
[1] A clear topic sentence.
[2] An effectively chosen quote to support main ideas.

'Older people have more disposable income than younger people – they are therefore more attractive to companies as potential customers.' Compare and contrast the advantages of targeting these two consumer groups.

In developed countries, younger generations are facing growing financial pressures, with costs for education and housing increasing, and recent economic crises impacting negatively on their prospects for employment. In contrast, older people tend to be better off with fewer debts and greater financial security. Whether companies should aim for the wealthier older generation as their target consumers, or look to the future and try to attract the less affluent younger generation depends on their products and strategy. This essay will compare and contrast the advantages of targeting these two groups.

Older people are living longer than ever before, so the number of years they spend consuming products and services is extended, making them a more attractive prospect for companies. They also tend to display more brand loyalty – especially to older and familiar brands – so once they become a consumer of a product they continue to consume on a regular basis (Hoyer and MacInnis, 2010, p.306). In addition, having benefited from lower housing and education costs, they are in a better financial position than younger generations, and so have more money to spend. As a result of these factors, there are clear advantages for companies who decide to target the older generation. However, it is also worth considering the potential benefits of targeting the younger generation.

In contrast to their parents, young people have less money to spend and more pressures on their time. They are also more heavily influenced by marketing and therefore often switch brands on a regular basis, making it harder for companies to secure their loyalty (John et al. 2006, pp.549–63). However, they also represent the future and are far more willing to embrace new innovative products. Companies who can exploit the younger generation's enthusiasm for innovation can design their marketing campaigns accordingly, for example making use of social media and other online marketing avenues as a way to generate interest.

In conclusion, it is clear that companies who succeed in targeting the older generation as their consumers will benefit from having a loyal and relatively affluent customer base. However, the benefits of this strategy to the company are highly dependent on the type of product they are offering, and how they intend to develop their products in the future. Companies who value innovation would do better to target the younger generation since these consumers are keen to embrace new technology. They also represent the future, and if companies are able to exploit marketing methods in a clever way they could secure the loyalty of the younger generation for decades to come. Essentially it is the responsibility of every company to assess their products and their future strategy carefully before deciding on which generation to target as their consumers. They must also carefully consider both the short- and long-term implications of their decisions.

References

Hoyer, W. D. & MacInnis, D. J. (2010). *Consumer Behavior.* United States: South-Western Cengage Learning.

John, D. R., Loken, B., Kim, K., & Monga, A. B. (2006). *Brand Concept Maps: A Methodology for Identifying Brand Association Networks.* Journal of Marketing Research.

Unit 10D TASK 8 (page 145)

'Internet-related crime affects only particular groups and should not lead to a change of focus away from traditional crime fighting.' Argue for or against this statement.

The internet has been a tool that has transformed many aspects of our daily life, from how we interact socially, to the structure and methods for doing business. Whilst the general perception is perhaps a positive one, there have inevitably been a number of negative developments with the growth of the internet. One such example is the rise in the use of the internet to commit criminal acts. It has been estimated that cybercrime costs UK businesses £10 billion annually – a figure rising to £33 billion per year in the US (*Financial Times*, 5 May 2006). One view is that since not everyone engages with the internet, the potential impact of cybercrime on society as a whole is more limited than other traditional forms of crime. However, this essay will argue that either directly or indirectly everyone feels the consequences of internet crime, therefore a change in the way we deal with this is needed.

Virtually every aspect of life that people engage with in the real world can now be encountered in the virtual world – finance, education, intellectual property, sex. Consequently, this leads to many possibilities to commit different crimes from the theft of knowledge and ideas, to that of stealing someone's identity. Hamilton and Webster (2009, p.118) argue that the internet is an appealing medium through which to commit crime as there is increased anonymity due to the distance from which crimes can be committed. Thus if something so prevalent is allowing crime to be committed in a new manner then arguably a new approach to dealing with it is required.

One common argument against changing crime fighting methods is that a significant proportion of the world does not have access to, or use of, the internet. In 2012 approximately only one third of the world had access to the internet (Internet World Stats, 2011). In contrast, all people are at risk from traditional crimes such as burglary or physical attacks, and as a result some believe that we should persist with traditional approaches for countering crime.

The crimes perhaps most commonly associated with the internet are identity theft or financial crimes. However, the internet can be used to commit a much wider range of crimes and can be used as a means to an end to commit physical crimes. Knowledge that can be gained through the internet has enabled people to have access to information that would have been limited to just a few individuals previously. For example, the internet allows people greater access to instructions on how to make and use weapons. This information has been used by individuals committing terrorist acts. The internet also gives the criminally-minded the ability to communicate their beliefs, and share these with others in a negative manner, for example, by inciting racial hatred.

In conclusion, while the internet may not be used by all people in all societies, in certain countries its use impacts on many people's daily lives. Many of these functions are positive, but there are definite risks. The internet is not only a tool to directly commit crime but one also to garner knowledge that enables people to commit many more crimes not traditionally associated with the internet. These criminal activities could have effects which impact far beyond the online world. Structural changes in the organization of society inevitably lead to a need to deal with crime in a new way. As the internet allows for crime to be committed using different approaches, our methods of policing crimes need to change too.

References

Hamilton, L. & Webster, P. (2009). *The International Business Environment*. Oxford: Oxford University Press.

Internet World Stats. (2011). *World Internet Users and Population Stats*. available from: http://www.internetworldstats.com/stats.htm. Retrieved: 28/05/2012.

'Energy consumption in the developed and developing world is becoming dangerously high.' Suggest and evaluate different solutions for reducing energy consumption.

According to McKinney, Schoch, and Yonavjak (2007) world energy consumption nearly doubled between 1970 and 2000, and is set to double again between 2000 and 2030. With the vast majority of energy being provided by limited stocks of fossil fuels, and their known impact on the environment, it is perhaps not surprising that many people consider these levels to be dangerously high. While this growth has gone hand in hand with population growth, it has been worsened by the fact that people's consumption patterns are increasing – rising standards of living have further impacted on the levels of consumption. This essay will suggest two main solutions that focus on lifestyle changes that will help tackle the problem.

Lower consumption of animal products is one of the most effective solutions to reducing energy consumption. America is the second largest energy consumer in the world and currently uses one-third of its energy consumption on producing animals for food (UN, 2010). The Food and Agricultural Organization of the UN (2006) also reports that twenty per cent of greenhouse emissions come from the meat industry, and that fifty per cent of the world's crops are produced to feed animals. It could be argued that changing consumption patterns would not only reduce energy consumption but could also increase health throughout the world. There might be a reduction in the intake of calories in the developed world, which would help to ease the health problems related to obesity. While there are clearly a number of benefits to this change, it might be challenging to implement. In many cultures meat is seen as a luxury product and its consumption tends to increase in line with the wealth of a nation. Changing dietary habits ingrained within the history of a culture is likely to be a slow process.

The second solution would be for people in certain countries to reduce the amount of time spent at work as a solution to increased sustainability. De Graaf (2010, pp.173–7) argues that shorter working hours not only have a positive impact on areas such as family life, health, and the wider community, but also on the levels of consumption – many of which are primary or secondary uses of energy. For example, people tend to consume fewer convenience products that are highly processed and packaged, and have time to use slower, more environmentally friendly forms of transport. A positive impact on energy consumption would be amongst the areas of life that would improve.

In conclusion, ultimately green energies are likely to be needed to sustain our levels of energy consumption, yet at the moment their availability and efficiency is not particularly widespread. A meat-based diet is high in energy use and a change to a vegetarian or vegan diet could help reduce consumption levels, though it may be hard to convince people to change their diet. Alternatively, people could be encouraged to work less in order to consume less energy. Unfortunately, while these solutions have great potential, they do require people to change at an individual level, which can be challenging to implement without accompanying changes in government policy.

References

McKinney, M. L., Schoch, R. M., & Yonavjak, L. (2007). *Environmental Science: Systems and Solutions. 4th Edition.* Sudbury: Jones and Bartlett Publishers Inc.

De Graaf, J. (2010). 'Reducing work time as a path to sustainability' In Maniates, M. (2010). *State of the World 2010: Transforming Cultures From Consumerism to Sustainability.* Worldwatch Institute.

Identify and discuss the key causes and effects of individual success in education.

As a country's economy grows and develops so too does the demand for education. There is a perception that a high level of education can lead to a successful career, and as a result greater and greater numbers are seeking to be educated at a higher level. In such a market being successful in education is likely to play a role in success throughout people's lives. This essay will look at the main factors affecting educational success and argue that motivation, intelligence, and teacher attitudes are key.

Motivation plays a key role in the success of many students as performance is driven by the desire to achieve a goal. However, simply setting a goal is not sufficient in motivating a student and in some cases may in fact lead to demotivation. Crane and Hannibal (2009, p.303) believe that in order to work well people need to set an exact goal that can be both measured and linked to a particular behaviour, for example, a certain approach and method of working in order to achieve a realistic goal. Therefore, those that are the most goal-driven in an academic environment are perhaps the most likely to stand out as successful.

Another factor influencing educational success is the attribute of intelligence. Educational attainment and life achievement are strongly dependent upon intelligence. According to Delius and Delius (2012, p.693) intelligence is the best predictor of educational success and life-long income. When intelligence and motivation occur together, there is potential for students to achieve the educational success that would lead to greater long-term financial gain. In fact, these two factors could be key causes in establishing differences in individual rates of success.

A final point that plays a role in educational success is teacher attitude. Numerous studies have found that lower teacher expectations impact negatively on students. Furthermore, in environments where students perceive the teaching as supportive there is a correlation with positive academic performance (Klem and Connell, 2009, pp.262–73). Thus students who perceive themselves to be in a supportive academic environment are perhaps more likely to be academically successful.

In conclusion, perhaps unsurprisingly, one of the key factors in individual academic success is that of intelligence. However, no single factor is the sole key to academic success; factors such as the educational environment and the motivation of the student are powerful in shaping the difference in individual success.

References

Crane, J. & Hannibal, J. (2009). *IB Psychology: Course Companion*. Oxford: Oxford University Press.

Delius, J. D. & Delius, J. A. M. (2012). 'Intelligence and Brains: An Evolutionary Bird's-Eye View'. In Zentall, T. R. & Wasserman, E. A. (2012). *The Oxford Handbook of Comparative Cognition*. Oxford: Oxford University Press.

Klem, A. M. & Connell, J. P. (2009). *Relationships Matter: Linking Teacher Support to Student Engagement and Achievement*. Journal of School Health. Vol 74:7.

Additional material from units

Unit 1B Speaking TASK 4 (page 011)

Checklist for evaluating a short presentation

		Yes	No
1	Is the aim of the presentation clear?		
2	Is the aim achieved by the end of the presentation?		
3	Is the presentation well organized and easy to understand?		
4	Is it clear when the speaker moves from one part of the presentation to the next part?		
5	Think about the order in which the information is presented. Is it logical and clear?		
6	Does the presenter speak clearly, and give clear explanations?		
7	Is there anything that could be improved?		

Unit 2A Listening TASK 8 (page 023)

1 Evaluate the following strategies for listening to a lecture.

		Useful	Not useful	Don't know
1	Listening to longer lecture extracts without taking notes or understanding everything, to become more familiar with lecture style, structure, and language			
2	Listening to short lecture extracts several times, in order to understand a part of the lecture very well			
3	Listening to a lecture extract while reading the transcript			
4	Listening to lecture extracts, making notes on the main points, then checking with the transcript			
5	Attending live lectures and recording them to listen to again afterwards			
6	Preparing in advance by reading key texts, then following up the lecture with more reading			

Unit 4B Speaking TASK 6 (page 053)

Guidelines for preparing a short presentation

Preparing your ideas

1 Select two perspectives to focus on (e.g. economic, environmental, social)

2 Decide what main points you want to include

3 Decide what background information you need

4 Think about your own stance – what do you want your audience to understand?

Researching

1 Decide what numerical information or other data you need

2 Search online to find out key facts and figures, and examples to support your main points

3 Use multiple sources to make sure your information is accurate

Preparing to speak

1 Introduce the structure and the main points clearly

2 Use signposting language to introduce new points

3 Use examples to support your main points

4 Include numerical information and check your pronunciation of numbers

5 Practise what you are going to say – aim to speak for about 3 minutes

Unit 4B Speaking TASK 7 (page 053)

Checklist for evaluating a short presentation

		Yes	No
1	Was the structure of the presentation introduced at the start?		
2	Were the main points introduced clearly?		
3	Was it clear when the speaker moved from one point to the next point?		
4	Did the speaker discuss different perspectives and give examples to support these?		
5	Were all numbers spoken clearly and correctly?		
6	Is there anything that could be improved?		

Unit 6A Listening TASK 1 (page 078)

Brief contents

01   Introduction: 'business' and its 'environment'
02   The economic environment
03   The technological environment
04   The political-legal environment
05   The social and cultural environment
06   Keeping the country stable
07   Can the marketplace be ethical? Corporate social responsibility
08   Achieving a better work-life balance
09   Europe: an ever-closer union of member states?
10   Business and the changing public sector
11   Business in the political arena
12   Globalization of business
13   Balancing business freedom and the authority of the law
14   Entrepreneurship and enterprise
15   Business and sustainable development
16   Conclusion: themes and issues – looking ahead

SOURCE: Wetherly, P. & Otter, D. (2011). pp.vii-viii. *The Business Environment: Themes and Issues (2nd ed.).* Oxford: Oxford University Press.

Pre-seminar reading

Transportation trends: headed in the wrong direction

We need to admit that current global transportation trends aren't sustainable and that today's transportation system, particularly in America, is highly inefficient and expensive. Vehicle sales, oil consumption, and carbon dioxide (CO_2) emissions are continuing to increase globally. One-fourth of all the oil consumed by humans in our entire history was consumed from 2000 to 2010. If this trend continues the world will consume as much oil in the next several decades as it has throughout its entire history to date. The increasing consumption of oil, and the carbon dioxide emissions resulting from it, are the direct result of dramatic growth in oil-burning motor vehicles worldwide. Unless there are dramatic events such as war, economic depression, or newfound political leadership, these trends will continue.

America leads the world in car ownership today, with more than one car for every driver. Other nations are following its lead. Car ownership and use are increasing everywhere. The desire for cars is growing, and while it can be slowed it probably can't be stopped. The estimated 85 per cent of the world's population still without cars wants the same lifestyle that Americans have. A survey conducted in 2004 found that more than 60 per cent of residents in the seven fastest growing nations, including China and India, want to own a car.

As global wealth grows, especially among the 2.4 billion citizens of China and India, so too will personal car use. Carmakers are increasingly focusing their efforts on emerging markets, with their high growth. Our projection, with input from a number of other experts, is that the number of motorized vehicles around the globe - cars, trucks, buses, scooters, motorcycles, and electric bikes - will increase by three per cent annually. By 2020, there will be more than two billion vehicles, at least half of them cars. The slowest car growth is expected in America (less than 1 per cent a year) and Western Europe (1 to 2 per cent), while the number of cars in China and India is expected to grow more rapidly, at around seven to eight per cent per year. Growth in vehicle use continues despite the fact that China, India, and many other countries don't have oil supplies to fuel their expanding vehicle numbers. Can countries peacefully coexist as they compete for increasingly limited petroleum resources?

SOURCE: Sperling, D. & Gordon, D. (2009). pp.3-4. *Two Billion Cars: Driving Towards Sustainability.* Oxford: Oxford University Press.

2 **Note down the main points for each paragraph.**

Paragraph 1: ....

Paragraph 2: ....

Paragraph 3: ....

3 **Make brief notes on any points in the text you would like to include in the discussion, and think about the phrases you could use to refer to them.**

The Enrichment of Material Life

TEXT 1

The technological changes of the past five centuries have been accompanied by significant increases in people's living standards. Before the capitalist period, living conditions improved or deteriorated with changes in the weather, epidemics, and other natural phenomena, because most people made their livings by farming, herding, or hunting and gathering. But wherever and whenever capitalism took hold, people's incomes and consumption levels began to rise in a sustained way. Although the rises were sometimes followed by declines, over a long period there have been – and continue to be – substantial improvements in living standards.

SOURCE: Bowles, S., Edwards, R., & Roosevelt, F. (2005). pp.8-9. *Understanding Capitalism: Competition, Command, and Change.* Oxford: Oxford University Press.

Radical / Marxist views: globalization is bad – the dependency tradition

TEXT 2

The person most associated with radical views of capitalism was Karl Marx. For Marx, 19th-century capitalism posed what he saw as a central 'contradiction'. He agreed that capitalism led to unprecedented growth but he argued that there was a problem. The social system of capitalism is very unequal and access to resources and political power is concentrated in the hands of a few people, the owners of capital or capitalists. The source of this growth was the ability of capitalists to exploit their workers and as growth and wealth increased the conditions of workers would deteriorate. This is a central Marxist idea: that growth, rather than benefiting everyone, can lead to inequality, providing the conditions for a socialist revolution where the workers would take control of the economy and run things in the interests of the whole of society, and not for the rich elites. However, such a revolution would only occur after a long period of capitalist expansion which would succeed in industrializing the economy.

SOURCE: Wetherly, P. & Otter, D. (2011). p.341. *The Business Environment: Themes and Issues (2nd ed.).* Oxford: Oxford University Press.

Roaring tigers and flaming dragons?

TEXT 3

In the 1970s, the Southeast Asian economies of South Korea, Thailand, Malaysia, the Philippines, Hong Kong, and others experienced dramatic economic growth. These countries are referred to as the **newly industrialized countries**, (NICs), and their success has caused intense debates as to why they have grown so fast.

For pro-capitalist economists, the NICs have shown the success of the free-market approach. Far from turning their backs on the global economy, these countries have embraced the opening up of world trade. In these countries trade truly has been the engine of growth.

However, other economists argue that, while the NICs have used trade, this was not the only thing that they did, and we need to consider the social and economic changes that they made *before* they felt able to benefit from trade openness. For the Indian economist Amartya Sen, it was important for these countries to get the social infrastructure in place before opening up to international trade. For the American economist Joseph Stiglitz, the road to the market has to be a gradual one, and cannot begin until the state has taken action to reduce poverty.

SOURCE: Wetherly, P. & Otter, D. (2011). p.346. *The Business Environment: Themes and Issues (2nd ed.).* Oxford: Oxford University Press.

Unit 6D Writing TASK 8 (page 089)

Checklist for evaluating paragraphs

- Have you included material from at least two sources?
- Does the paragraph develop the topic clearly and logically?
- Do the citations support your main argument?
- Have you used a range of reporting verbs / structures?
- Are the references correctly presented in terms of names, dates, spelling, and punctuation?

Unit 8B Speaking TASK 2 (page 108)

TEXT 1

Technology opens up many domestic and foreign opportunities for businesses who are ready to take advantage of them.

Opportunities

New goods and services - Companies can create new and improved goods and services, revive old products, and consequently enter new markets. Furthermore, as a result of innovation, they can also end up with large market shares and have more valuable products, designs, and brand names. The Danish firm Lego is a good example of a firm using technology to renew a declining product, the toy building brick. The Lego brick is now sold with electronic technology, allowing customers to build a range of moving robots.

Global organization - Technology makes it easier for a company to become global. It can also be economically active in many different locations. Technology has therefore made the rapid growth of the multinational corporation easier. Companies can now have subsidiaries in many countries, but their business strategies, production, and distribution can still be controlled by their head office in one country. So, for example, multinational corporations like Unilever are able to employ around a quarter of a million people in 100 countries and sell their products in 150 countries.

Small firms - Technology can make it easier for small firms to compete with large ones. For example, the internet enables all firms to communicate with customers both at a national and at international level, and to sell their goods and services at relatively low cost. Small companies can design their own websites for as little as a few thousand pounds. Firms producing for niche markets, can use the web to reach customers who are of little interest to larger distributors such as the American firm Wal-Mart.

SOURCE: Hamilton, L. & Webster, P. 2009. p.199. *The International Business Environment.* Oxford: Oxford University Press.

GLOSSARY

niche market *(n)*   a small and specialized market

subsidiaries *(n pl)*   smaller companies partly or wholly owned by another company

Technology and Business

While technology offers many opportunities for businesses, it can also pose many threats and challenges.

Businesses have to prepare for new technology and to take advantage of the opportunities offered by technology to develop new products and new methods of production and distribution, to create new markets, and to take advantage of new ways of organizing their business. Innovation involves changes in products or processes and it can be risky, especially for firms who are not good at managing change effectively, because new products may not succeed and new production processes may not deliver the expected benefits. Most innovations fail. In IT projects, the failure rate in the UK has been estimated by analysts at more than 80% and that rate has not changed much since the mid-1990s.

If firms are not prepared, new technology can result in them going out of business. The economist Joseph Schumpeter called this the process of 'creative destruction'. He argued that innovation over a period of time, by bringing in new products, new sources of supply, and new types of organisation could create a form of competition that threatens a company's very existence. For example, the chief executive of Proctor and Gamble said, 'People ask me what I lose sleep over. If someone announced an alternative to washing powder for laundry, suddenly I've got an US$11billion business that's at risk' (*Financial Times*, 22 December 2005). HMV, the UK music retailer, underestimated the threat from online competition both in terms of physical CDs and in music downloading. Its share price fell sharply.

Even firms with monopoly positions can find themselves threatened by new technology. In the telecommunications industry, national monopolists such as BT, Deutsche Telekom and France Telecom who owned networks of telephone lines, found themselves under threat from mobile phone companies and from firms using satellite systems.

Such competition may come from outside existing boundaries of an industry. Companies like Amazon, using the web as a new business model, have made a significant impact on traditional booksellers. Not only does Amazon provide a greater choice of books, it also uses digital technology that allows customers to read extracts from millions of pages. In the travel business, the internet has created competition between travel agents and established airlines, and the new online providers in a battle to win customers. Online agents such as Expedia and Travelocity have shaken up the travel booking business, while low-cost airlines like Ryanair and easyJet have used the internet to cut the costs of their reservation systems. This has made them even more price competitive, and has forced their established rivals, such as BA, Air France and KLM, to extend their online reservation service. As a consequence, more and more flights and trips are being booked over the internet rather than through call centres or high-street travel agents. Some commentators estimated that online booking accounted for a third of the USA's US$200 billion travel market in 2005. US railway and airline customers book almost half of their trips online (*The Economist*, 29 September 2005).

SOURCE: Hamilton, L. & Webster, P. (2009). pp.204-6. *The International Business Environment.* Oxford: Oxford University Press.

2 **Read the essay title and the two essay outlines, A and B. Match each outline to the most appropriate structure: block, or point-by-point.**

'Compare and contrast the spending habits of consumers aged 20–30 and those of consumers aged over 45. What are the implications for companies targeting these groups?'

OUTLINE A

- **Introduction (including thesis statement)**
- **Body paragraph 1: Younger consumers**
  - Earn lower salaries (just starting career)
  - Spend more of their income on basic needs (e.g. food, accommodation)
  - Spend money on leisure activities (e.g. sport, socializing, travel)
  - More relaxed about debt and less likely to save
- **Body paragraph 2: Older consumers**
  - Earn higher salaries
  - Spend less of their income on basic needs
  - Spend money on leisure activities
  - More likely to save (children's education, retirement)
- **Conclusion**

OUTLINE B

- **Introduction (including thesis statement)**
- **Body paragraph 1: Salaries**
  - Younger consumers earn less → less disposable income
  - Older consumers earn more → more disposable income
- **Body paragraph 2: Spending**
  - Younger consumers spend more on basic needs
  - Older consumers spend less on basic needs
  - Older and younger consumers spend on leisure activities
- **Body paragraph 3: Saving**
  - Younger consumers less likely to save - have less money to spare
  - Older consumers more likely to save (children's education, retirement)
- **Conclusion**

Checklist for evaluating your partner's essay.

1 Is it clear which consumer group they think should be targeted, and why?

2 Do the introduction and conclusion include all the relevant features?

3 Identify the comparative language used. Has it been used accurately?

4 Do any citations used include the correct information such as the page number, date, author's name?

5 Does each paragraph have one clear topic and does everything in it relate to that topic?

Research on the effects of video games

Giles (2003) reports that the research on the effects of video game play:
- Is even more inconclusive than the literature on media violence in general (Griffiths, 1997).
- Has found evidence that trait aggression in adults may increase the negative effects of game play (Anderson and Dill 2000), although this finding was not repeated with teenagers (Warm, 2000).
- Found general increases in short-term hostility as a result of video game play in general, regardless of violent content (Anderson and Dill, 2000).
- Suggests any cognitive skill resulting from repeated video game play is likely to be very localized. Sims and Mayer (2002) found Tetris players showed increased performance in mental rotation tasks involving shapes similar to the ones used in the game, but performed no differently from the control group on tasks involving other kinds of shapes.

Pakes and Winstone (2007) cite Bensley and Van Eenwynk's (2001) analysis of 28 research studies which found playing with an aggressive video game was often followed by brief aggressive play straight afterwards in 4- to 8-year-olds. However, this was not consistently found for other age groups (due to the design of the studies), leading the authors to conclude that, although video game realism may change in the future, the 'current research evidence is not supportive of a major concern that violent video games lead to real-life violence'.

Gentile et al. (2004) found increased levels of video game playing and anti-social effects in children, even for non-aggressive children, which could be reduced by parental control and limits.

SOURCE: Hill, G. (2009). p.252. *AS & A level Psychology Through Diagrams.* Oxford: Oxford University Press.

GLOSSARY

tetris *(n)* a video game where players have to arrange coloured shapes into patterns

trait aggression *(n)* a personality tendency to respond aggressively to certain situations

Case study 1

Bruce was twenty-six years old when he joined a large accounting firm after graduating with a good degree in commerce. He was assigned to a team of auditors at Transition Technologies, which had just been taken over by Paradox Corp. Bruce's firm had been the auditors at Transition before the takeover and had offered to continue at around half the usual price. Short cuts in auditing resulted. Proper auditing procedures were not followed, and Bruce was frequently left to make important decisions by himself, although he was not experienced. Bruce knew that he was in a competitive environment and that he was, in a sense, on trial. He did not agree with the short cuts and felt that it was unfair to Transition and himself that he was sometimes left to deal with matters beyond his experience. But he also remembered being asked at his job interview if he was a team player who could carry other members of the team when the situation required.

SOURCE: Grace, D. & Cohen, S. (2009). p.163. *Business Ethics (4th ed.).* Oxford: Oxford University Press.

GLOSSARY

auditor *(n)* sb whose job is to examine the financial records of a company to ensure they are accurate

short cut *(n)* a way of doing sth that is quicker than the usual way

Case study 2

In June 2002, after ten days of discussion of the evidence, a jury in Houston, Texas, in the USA, convicted the accountancy firm Arthur Andersen of 'obstruction of justice' in the Enron case. Andersen then announced that it would stop auditing publicly-listed companies. This was the fall of one of the world's largest accounting firms. The company had revenues of over US$9 billion, and 85,000 employees in 84 countries, and its fall caused shock around the world.

The company was founded in 1913 by Arthur Andersen, and was always known for its honesty and integrity. However, its pursuit of profit led to its involvement with some dubious corporate clients including Enron, WorldCom, and Sunbeam.

The effect of dealing with such clients cost Andersen its reputation and a lot of money. The American financial regulator, the SEC (Securities and Exchange Commission), fined Andersen $7 million for overestimating the earnings of Waste Management Corporation by $1.4 billion. When the electrical products company Sunbeam admitted overestimating its earnings, the shareholders sued Andersen, and the firm had to pay $110 million.

So why did a firm based on integrity abandon its values? The American politician Barbara Toffler describes Andersen as 'rotting from within', and being a victim of its own decision to put the protection of client confidentiality above its responsibility to shareholders and taxpayers. According to Toffler, Andersen lost its independence when it put its profitable consulting services above its role as auditor, and became less willing to risk the anger of its clients. This may be the reason it failed to warn Enron, WorldCom and other clients about their revenue statements.

Andersen's independence had been compromised, and the firm was unable to continue. The company was Enron's auditor for 16 years. In 2002 alone, Enron paid Andersen $25 million in auditing fees, and $27 million for consulting services.

SOURCE: Grace, D. & Cohen, S. (2009). *p.165. Business Ethics (4th ed.).* Oxford: Oxford University Press..

GLOSSARY

dubious *(adj)* probably not honest

fine *(v)* to make sb pay money as a punishment

integrity *(n)* the quality of being honest and having strong moral principles

sue *(v)* make a claim for money in a court of law

Global Threats – Cybercrime

Increasing global interconnectedness has been accompanied by the development of new threats which can have a major impact on business. Advances in communications technology have made it easier to commit crimes using computers and the internet. This fast-growing threat is called cybercrime. It is easier because it can be done at a distance and with anonymity. It includes identity theft where personal information, for example, from customers is stolen. Users are lured to fake web sites where they are asked to enter personal information such as usernames and passwords, phone numbers, addresses, credit card numbers, and bank account numbers. The information can be used to empty bank accounts or to buy goods and services using fraudulently obtained credit card details. It also includes hacking into computers to get access to confidential business information, and the creation and distribution of viruses and worms on business computers. Cybercriminals may threaten to use the information they have stolen to attack companies' systems. [...]

It is estimated that, in Britain alone, six million people illegally download films and music every year, costing film and music companies billions of pounds in lost revenues. In the UK, cyber-attacks are estimated to be costing businesses £10 billion a year. In the USA, the FBI estimated that cybercrime costs US businesses £33 billion a year (Financial Times, 5 May 2006).

SOURCE: Hamilton, L., & Webster, P. (2009). p.118. *The International Business Environment.* Oxford: Oxford University Press.

GLOSSARY

fraud *(n)* the crime of cheating sb in order to get money or goods illegally

fraudulently *(adj)* doing sth by fraud

lure *(v)* to persuade or trick sb to go somewhere or to do sth by promising them a reward

threat *(n)* the possibility of trouble, danger, or disaster

2 Read the text and complete the notes relating to the situation and problems discussed in the text.

The world currently consumes energy equal to 3 CMO (cubic miles of oil) each year. It uses 1.0 CMO from oil, 0.8 CMO from coal, 0.6 CMO from natural gas, and approximately 0.2 CMO each from hydro-electric power, nuclear, and wood. Although its population is only 1/20th of the world population, the United States uses about one-fifth of the world's energy. There will soon be substantial increases in global energy demand: more than three billion people are poised to sharply increase their standard of living, and in India and China there are already large groups of people whose wealth equals that of the average citizen of richer countries such as Sweden and Switzerland. Business as usual for the world – which includes a steady improvement in energy efficiency – would place the annual global demand for energy in 2050 at around 9 CMO. Even if we were to follow a more modest growth scenario, the annual global energy demand could still increase to 6 CMO by then. We therefore predict a need for additional energy sources capable of delivering a minimum of an additional 3 CMO annually. Fifty years from now, the 1 CMO a year we now obtain from oil will also have to be replaced, adding another CMO to the demand for alternative sources. And if we wish to reduce the role of coal and natural gas, then the alternative sources will need to provide a total of between 4 and 5 CMO by 2050.

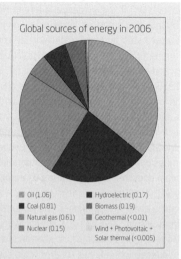

Global sources of energy in 2006

- Oil (1.06)
- Coal (0.81)
- Natural gas (0.61)
- Nuclear (0.15)
- Hydroelectric (0.17)
- Biomass (0.19)
- Geothermal (<0.01)
- Wind + Photovoltaic + Solar thermal (<0.005)

SOURCE: Crane, H. D., Kinderman, E. M., & Malhotra, R. (2010). *pp.264–5. A Cubic Mile of Oil.* New York: Oxford University Press.

GLOSSARY

CMO *(n abbr)* cubic mile of oil, equivalent to 2.62 x 1010 barrels of oil (i.e. 2.62 billion)

geothermal *(adj)* connected with the natural heat of rock deep in the ground

thermal *(adj)* connected with heat

Situation

- Current global energy consumption: 3 CMO per year, of which:
  - 1.0 CMO from oil
  - 0.8 from ....
  - – ....
- USA has 1/20th of world's population, but uses ....
- Global energy demand ....

Problems

- Expected annual global demand for energy in 2050 is ....
- ....

Energy source	Problems / challenges / issues
Petroleum Current reserves (CMO): 46+ Estimated reserves (years): 50	• difficult to maintain / increase production • rising costs, especially technology costs • difficult to find and access new oil fields
Natural gas Current reserves (CMO): 42 Estimated reserves (years): 100	• located mainly in Russia and Middle East • consuming nations globally have to rely on producing nations (risk to supply) • further natural gas resources have been located in sands, but suitable technology is not yet developed to access these
Coal Current reserves (CMO): 120 Estimated reserves (years): 80	• distributed widely in the world, except Middle East • the cheapest energy source, but also the dirtiest, especially CO_2 emissions • to meet rising demand, coal consumption needs to increase from 0.8 CMO/year to over 2 CMO/year by 2060, meaning that 5,000 new coal-fired plants need to be built, about two new plants each week for 50 years
Nuclear Current reserves (CMO): 28 (of uranium) Estimated reserves (years): 50+	• global uranium reserves are equivalent to 28 CMO • there is widespread opposition to nuclear power • to meet demand one new nuclear plant needs to be built per week for the next 50 years
Geothermal	• current production is only 0.05 CMO, but is expected to double in next 10 years • global potential is up to 4 CMO, of which 0.8 CMO suitable for electricity production • new technologies needed to extract energy from deep, hot, dry rocks
Hydroelectric	• limited potential for expansion: most large rivers of the world already have power plants • large populations may have to be relocated when new dams are built • the world's largest hydroelectric project, Three Gorges Dam, was built over 15 years and cost $30 billion. To produce 1 CMO annually means building equivalent of 153 Three Gorges Dams, i.e. one every four months for the next 50 years
Wind	• annual global potential for wind energy production is over 40 CMO, but it requires a large amount of land • to produce 1 CMO means 1,200 new turbines each week for 50 years • turbines can affect wildlife, especially birds
Concentrated Solar Power	• the earth receives 23,000 CMO of energy per year from the sun • limited number of suitable locations, with currently few large projects • to produce 1 CMO from solar power, 70,000 large-scale projects would need to be built, i.e. 27 per week for 50 years
Photovoltaics (PV)	• located on people's rooftops, where the energy is used • currently the most expensive alternative energy source • to produce 1 CMO from rooftop PV systems would mean installing 250,000 systems every day for 50 years
Biomass	• total global potential of 20 CMO/year • plants grown for fuel mean less available for food • biofuels from other plant sources (e.g. algae) are possible: 1 CMO would require 390,000 square km of land, i.e. 1/30th that of conventional biomass

SOURCE: Adapted from information in: Crane, H. D., Kinderman, E. M., & Malhotra, R. (2010). pp.266-72. *A Cubic Mile of Oil.* New York: Oxford University Press.

Planning a presentation

1 Decide on the main points to include – these are essentially the solutions (the individual energy sources) you selected in Task 5.

2 Decide on an order for the points, and how much detail to include.

3 If possible, prepare some visuals: a small number of slides with images and/or text. Include only a few key words or phrases on each slide.

4 Think about the language you will use. Refer to your notes from Task 3 for ideas.

Organizing a presentation

Stage 1 Introduction: open the presentation, introduce the group, state the title, give an overview of the aims of the presentation

Stage 2 Main body: present each main point (solution), with evidence and/or supporting information, and evaluation.

Stage 3 Conclusion: give a brief evaluation of the overall solution, conclude the presentation

Transcripts

Unit 1

Listening

▶ **1.1 Extract 1**

Mohammed OK. My name's Mohammed. I'm going to tell you about my experience of the pre-sessional course I took here at the university. I studied a three-month course in Academic Reading and Writing. So, firstly, I'm going to talk about my experience of the course itself … and then tell you something about how the course was helpful for me in my degree.

Julia So I'm here today to tell you about my time on the Bachelor's degree in Business Studies, the BSc. in Business Studies. I started my degree two years ago, and I'm now starting my final year, so I think I have quite a lot of experience that could be helpful to you. I've divided my presentation into three main parts: getting good marks, work experience, and the dissertation.

Luke Hello. Good afternoon. My name's Luke. I have to say it's a bit strange being back here, but it's nice to be back too. I actually completed my Master's in Food Science two years ago, but I was really pleased when I was asked to come back and share my experience with you. Just to give you a brief overview: first, I'll talk about the academic and professional skills you get on the programme, and then I'll talk about how to get the best support while you're here.

▶ **1.2 Extract 2**

At the beginning I wasn't too happy about having to take an English course. I studied English at school for ten years, and I just wanted to get on with studying my degree. You know, I felt I knew all that was needed to know and that I'll be fine. But now, looking back, I'm really pleased that I took the course. There are big differences between the English classes I had at school and the classes I took here.

Firstly, academic reading. In school reading was mainly to start a discussion or to learn vocabulary or grammar. We didn't have to do much with the actual text. To give you an idea of what I mean, in academic situations you're always reading for a reason – for example, to write an essay, to give a presentation, to prepare for a test. So you need to learn how to use the information in the texts in these kinds of assessments. You also need to understand the writer's opinion, so you can use it to support your argument. Then, also, you have so much more reading to do, and it can be difficult to decide what you need to read and what makes a good source.

You know, this course really helps you to deal with these challenges. So to go back to what I was saying earlier, the reading needs to be used in the writing, and this is the other big area the course helped me with. I learnt useful things like how to summarize, how to paraphrase, how to reference work correctly in my writing … all really useful stuff. At the time I didn't think it was that important, but then one time I lost 10 per cent of my mark because of poor referencing, so … well, yeah, then I realized how important it was.

▶ **1.3 Extract 3**

Probably the main thing you'll all want to know is, how can I get really good marks? As you know, the university gives degrees in four classifications. And really, to get the top classifications, you have to be able to demonstrate your critical thinking skills. So you have to learn to challenge ideas and not just accept everything that you read, or that you're told. It's almost impossible to get a good mark unless you do this – and for me that was the biggest difference from school. And also, you need to pay attention to your feedback you get from your tutor. Don't just look at the mark – look at the comments and see the areas your teachers want you to improve.

OK, let's move on and talk about work experience. It may seem a bit early to be talking about this now, at the start of your degree, but actually you do need to start thinking about it. As you all know, there are lots of people graduating from university every year, so you need to make yourself look different from everybody else. One way to do this is to get work experience – it shows that you not only know the theory, but that you can also … you know, function in the real world.

OK. Lastly, it's important to start thinking about your dissertation, as early as possible. The dissertation counts for 30 per cent of your mark on this course, and you have to research it for a whole academic year. So it needs to be something that you're really interested in. It also needs to be an area that's not too broad – nine months isn't that long, so you know, … keep it focused. Your dissertation is a real test of your academic abilities and it will probably decide the degree classification you get. So it's never too early to start thinking about it.

▶ **1.4 Extract 4**

The main reason I chose to study Food Science here is because of the support you get as a student … and the skills development. Obviously it's important to know your subject well, but once you leave you may have to work in a lot of different professional contexts.

So two things that are really important to learn and improve are your writing and your presenting skills. These will help you get better marks in your course modules, but also they're really important when you start working. In a lot of jobs, you'll have to report things like research findings, or results of tests and experiments … er, that can be in writing or in a presentation.

There are important rules about what's expected of you as a student, as a professional, in terms of skill. And this course can really help you develop those skills. I know that for many of you, this course is probably a career change. It is for nearly 30 per cent of students every year. It can be difficult, because you may have been an expert in another field in the past, I don't know, accounting or something. But now you're not an expert and you aren't used to being a student any more. Another 30 per cent of you probably come from different educational systems. This course is very international, and the tutors all know that it can be difficult to understand the expectations of a new system. But for both of these groups, I think this course provides really excellent support so, you know, make use of it if you need it.

So, to sum up, I would say don't just learn your subjects – develop other skills and don't worry if you're finding it hard. There's lots of help and support available.

▶ **1.5**

1 Firstly, academic reading. In school reading was mainly to start a discussion or to learn vocabulary or grammar. We didn't have to do much with the actual text. To give you an idea of what I mean, in academic situations you're always reading for a reason – for example, to write an essay, to give a presentation, to prepare for a test.

2 … This course really helps you to deal with these challenges. So to go back to what I was saying earlier, the reading needs to be used in the writing, and this is the other big area the course helped me with.

3 And also, you need to pay attention to your feedback you get from your tutor. Don't just look at the mark – look at the comments and see the areas your teachers want you to improve.

OK, let's move on and talk about work experience. It may seem a bit early to be talking about this now, at the start of your degree, but actually you do need to start thinking about it.

4 As you all know, there are lots of people graduating from university every year so you need to make yourself look different from everybody else.

5 So, to sum up, I would say don't just learn your subjects – develop other skills and don't worry if you're finding it hard. There's lots of help and support available.

Speaking

▶ **1.6**

Hi. My name's Ryo Hashimoto. Well, today I'd like to talk to you about my recent educational experience, and my aims for the future.

OK, so first let me tell you about where I've been studying. My first main aim was to get into a very good university in my home country, which is Japan. So I applied to Keio University in Tokyo, which is the capital of Japan, as you know.

So … that was my first choice, and I studied very hard, you know, late every evening, and most weekends. In Japan it's very competitive and you have to study very hard if you want to succeed. And … I'm pleased to say that I was offered a place at the university to study economics.

What I would really like to do is work in a large international company, like NTT, for example, or Mizuho Bank. And actually, this is my message to you today. Work hard and you can achieve success – anything you want, really.

OK, I'm making that sound, you know, quite easy. But in reality, it's not so simple, of course.

And this brings me on to my second main point. As I said, I was accepted by Keio University, but I needed to improve my English. In fact, I still need to improve my English, especially my writing. So before I was allowed to start my course at the Department of Economics, I had to improve my TOEFL score. And that's my second main aim – to improve my TOEFL score as well as my English.

Why is this important? Well, there are about thirty courses offered in English at Keio in Japan, but I would also like to study abroad, at one of the university's partner schools. They have a programme with the University of California, but they only accept a small number of students every year. My level of English was OK, but it was still below the entrance level for studying in California.

Anyway, what I want to say is, after I was accepted at Keio University, I still had to finish off my high school studies. I tried to do this by taking extra classes at *juku*. Jukus are private schools, where you can go after school and you pay for extra classes – in any subject, really. But for me it was English.

Unfortunately, that took up a lot of extra time, and of course I also had to concentrate on my main academic subjects. So … that didn't really work out for me.

Well, the end of my story is – I still haven't reached my target level yet. That's why I'm here.

I'd like to finish my presentation by saying again, 'work hard, and you can achieve success'. I know I haven't achieved my main ambitions yet, but I know that I will reach my goals and I will enter the Economics Department at Keio University next academic year. And go on to study abroad.

So … that's all. Thank you very much for listening.

Unit 2

Listening

▶ 2.1 Extract 1

So, as you would've seen from the lecture schedule, we're going to be looking first at the United Nations, or the 'UN' as it's usually known. Obviously, the UN is an international organization, and it operates in most countries around the world.

The UN is involved in a wide range of activities, but its main mission is to promote peace and security around the world. So, the aim of this lecture is really to give you an understanding of the UN from a number of different perspectives.

Now, as the name suggests, the United Nations is one of only a very few organizations with a truly global reach, from almost every perspective – political, economic, military, humanitarian, and so on. Historically, the UN can trace its development back to the two World Wars which took place in the 20th century, and we need to understand something about this historical background.

I'd like to begin with an overview of the structure of the UN, how it's organized, and after that we can move on to look at the purpose of the UN – in other words, what it's for and why we need it. And finally, we'll take a brief look at the history of the organization, and how such a historical institution remains relevant today.

▶ 2.2 Extract 2

OK, so let's start by looking at the structure of the United Nations. Now, the first point to note is the UN is made up of a group of international institutions. The best known of these is the central organization – the central United Nations system. Now, most of you will recognize the UN headquarters in New York.

… There are five main organs of the UN, five main divisions, if you like. But in this lecture we're going to look at only four of them – the Security Council, the General Assembly, the Secretariat, and the Economic and Social Council. We'll talk about the role of the International Court of Justice when we look at international law, later on in this semester.

So, firstly, as the name suggests, the purpose of the Security Council is to focus on security. It has five permanent member countries, and its main responsibility, essentially, is to maintain international peace and security. It has the power to issue directives and, if necessary, to send in peace-keeping forces to help reduce the risk of war in problem areas of the world. So the Security Council is the one organ which has some

military power. But the other organs of the UN really don't have that kind of power.

OK, so turning to the General Assembly – this is like the 'parliament' of the United Nations, the political arm, if you like. In political terms it carries a lot of weight. All the UN member states are represented in the General Assembly, and each member state has one vote. They vote on important matters related to international peace and security, and many other issues as well.

But whatever the General Assembly decides – on any issue – is basically a recommendation, it is not a binding decision. So this means they can't force any state, any country, to do anything. However, the General Assembly's recommendations are important. They are important indications of world opinion, and they represent the moral authority of the community of nations. And because of this the UN has moral authority. The General Assembly tries to ensure the governments of its member states treat their people well, that they behave in an ethical way, in other words.

Moving on now to the Secretariat. This is essentially administrative. It's led by the Secretary-General, who is normally a global figure of some importance – think of recent Secretary-Generals like Kofi Annan or Ban Ki-moon. As well as having an administrative role, the Secretariat carries out research. But it's mainly bureaucratic, and it doesn't have that much obvious political power. The Secretary-General, though, does have an important diplomatic role.

OK. The next organ is the Economic and Social Council – abbreviated to ECOSOC. ECOSOC is responsible for overseeing the activities of a large number of other institutions within the United Nations. It operates with the authority of the General Assembly, and its main purpose is to coordinate the economic and social work of the UN.

ECOSOC also oversees a large number of other institutions, such as the World Health Organization. They have their own budgets and their own heads, and so on … so financially and politically speaking, these institutions are independent. And they're big financial institutions – for example, the WHO budget for 2012–13 was approximately 2.5 billion dollars.

▶ 2.3 Extract 3

OK, now I'd like to talk about the history of the organization. So the United Nations was established just after the end of the Second World War, on the 24th of October, 1945. Historically, it was set up to replace the League of Nations, which itself was established just after the First World War, in 1919.

The aim of the League of Nations was to ensure that future wars were impossible. Now obviously, it failed in that objective, and a key reason why it failed was that it had no real power. Similarly, a key aim of the UN has always been to promote world peace. But unlike the League of Nations, it has the legitimacy to do so. In other words, it has legal authority, the legal power, to carry out that objective.

OK, so the UN started out in 1945 with 51 member countries. Today, nearly every state in the world is a member of the UN. And what's important about the UN, and one reason why it's more successful than the League of Nations, is that it has the UN Security Council. So, from a legal and a military perspective, the UN is much more powerful.

Now, as I suggested earlier, the Security Council gives the UN significant potential military power and reach. It's one of the UN's most important organs. The Security Council was initially made up of 11 states. After 1965 it had 15 states, and these include the five permanent members – China, France, Russia, the UK, and the United States. The other ten members are non-permanent members.

Now, as far as geography is concerned, the UN Security Council appears to cover a lot of the globe. But if you think about it, all of these countries are in the northern hemisphere. No southern hemisphere countries are represented permanently on the Security Council – no African, no Latin American countries, no countries from the South Pacific regions.

Speaking

◀)) 2.4 Extract 1

A So, erm, Dan … I mean, what do you think? Should governments be the ones who are responsible for managing pollution?

B Well, from my point of view, yes, they should. Definitely. Because it's a global problem – it affects everyone. But … you don't think so?

A Well, no … no, I think it's more about, um, individual responsibility. Individuals and companies … well, they all need to take responsibility for their own actions … you know, whatever they do that contributes to carbon emissions, or whatever.

B But why?

A Well, look, it just makes sense to me that the people who cause the pollution should be more responsible.

B Well, I think it makes more sense for governments to do it if …

◀)) 2.5 Extract 2

C Right, so what perspectives might there be on this topic? Apart from the environmental perspective, obviously.

D Well, I think just in that statement you've clearly got three groups. The government is the political perspective. Individuals, the general public – that's the social perspective. And then companies would have a commercial perspective.

C Yeah, yeah, that's right. OK, well … so what political perspective might there be on this idea?

D Well, politically you'd want some control on who managed it … and also how.

C Mm … Politically speaking, the responsibility would probably be put back onto companies and people, wouldn't it? I mean, for example, by creating new laws.

D Exactly, yes … so I would say from a political perspective it would become the responsibility of companies and individuals and not the government – through the creation of new laws.

C Yeah, I agree with that. OK, how about socially, the social perspective? I mean, don't people think that they pay their taxes, so basically the government should take care of it?

D That's true, but I think a lot of people are also quite green, you know. They're quite … environmentally-minded.

C Yes, but they still expect the government to have a role. I think socially speaking it's difficult to have just one perspective … you know, because everyone's different. I would say most people would see this as mainly the government's role, but not only the government's role.

D Yeah, that sounds about right. So it's mostly the government's responsibility, but not only the government's. And individuals should take some responsibility too. OK. So what about from a commercial perspective?

C Well ... No company likes to spend money unless it has to.

D Right. Companies aren't going to take responsibility unless the government makes them. So, commercially speaking there has to be a financial benefit for companies to be more ... green, I suppose. I think many companies would probably say it's the government's role and they'll only do what they have to within the law.

C Yeah, that's the key difference for me between the social and commercial perspectives. Individual people might take some responsibility, but companies won't take responsibility without a good reason ... or unless the law makes them.

D OK, so ... we think that it has to be mainly the government's responsibility. Because, as we said, commercially there's no profit to be made, so companies won't take responsibility.

C Yes. But I'd also add that society should, and probably does, take some responsibility.

◀)) 2.6 Extract 3

A So come on, then, Dan. What are your views on this issue? I mean, should university education be provided for free by the government?

B Er ... well, yeah. From my point of view, it should be. If you look at it from an economic perspective, a highly-educated country ... well, it usually has a strong economy. So it's probably going to benefit the whole of society to educate people for free. I mean, what do you think?

A In my view, it ... no, it shouldn't be free.

B Really?

A No. I think if you want to go to university you should be, well, you know, you should be prepared to pay for it. Otherwise it's just, look, it's far too expensive for the economy. Especially in this economic climate. Governments, they don't want to support free education.

B OK, I can see what you're saying, but in most countries people pay their taxes, so they should have a right to education, surely? I mean, the economy gets the benefit because people's incomes will be higher if they have a better education, so the government gets more income tax eventually, anyway.

A Mm ... I see what you mean, but ... I don't know. I'm not sure that's the case. I mean, I think it depends on, you know, the university and the subject you study. And anyway, look, some people go just for an education. Not everyone goes just so they can make money.

B But surely if they have to pay, that means only people with money will get to go to university. I mean, really, morally speaking is that right? Is it fair?

A Oh ... OK, perhaps we should look at this from a different perspective ...

Unit 3

Listening

▶ 3.1 Extract 1

So as we discussed last week, one of the first people to write about the role of management was the American, Frederick Taylor. And Taylor is thought of as one of the first management consultants. As we'll see from today's lecture, Taylor's ideas still apply to many different areas of management – they're still relevant today, in other words. However, not everyone takes the view that money is what motivates people to do a particular job.

In today's lecture, I'd like to look at a number of theories related to motivation and management. And I want to answer these three questions.

What are the things that motivate people? How have these different theories developed over time? And how have they influenced each other?

So ... First, we'll look in more detail at Taylor's idea that money is the key motivator in the workplace. Then, we'll move on to look at one of the most famous theories of motivation, which is Maslow's hierarchy of needs. Some of you may be already familiar with this. After that, we're going to see how Maslow's ideas influenced the work of Douglas McGregor in the 1960s. And then finally, I want to take a look at a slightly different view of motivation developed by McClelland and Burnham, which was all about power.

▶ 3.2 Extract 2

Frederick Taylor was, as you know, responsible for developing the theory of 'scientific management'. This idea was based on late 19th, early 20th century working practices, and it was all about increasing efficiency in the workplace – so, doing the same amount of work using less time and less money. Taylor's theory, as we've seen, was based on the idea that people are motivated mainly by money. Essentially, if you pay someone enough money, then they'll be willing to do any job. OK?

At first, very few people questioned this relatively early concept of motivation. However, as psychology, the study of psychology, started to become more accepted, more ideas about motivation started to emerge. And this happened right through the second half of the twentieth century.

So ... much later, in the 1940s and 1950s, you have the psychologist Abraham Maslow, the man most people probably associate with theories of motivation. In 1943 Maslow published a paper in which he divided motivation into five main areas in hierarchy ... a hierarchy of needs. This was followed a few years later by a book, *Motivation and Personality*. And we'll talk more about this in a moment. Now, Maslow's theory caused a lot of discussion and debate, and consequently a number of other theories emerged quite quickly afterwards.

One theory that soon followed Maslow was McGregor's theory of management styles. McGregor divided his theory of management into two groups, Theory X and Theory Y. Theory X was heavily influenced by the lower levels of Maslow's hierarchy and Theory Y was influenced by the higher levels of the hierarchy. Some time later, in the 1970s, McClelland and Burnham looked at motivation in a different way. Unlike McGregor, they didn't think about how a manager could motivate workers. Instead, they focused on what motivates the manager. And they concluded that managers are mainly motivated by power. I'll come back to this point later.

▶ 3.3 Extract 3

As we've already seen, perhaps the most famous theory of motivation is Maslow's theory of hierarchy of needs. Maslow's theory is usually shown in a pyramid ... like the one on the slide here and in your handout. Now, if you look at the labels on each level, these are quite broad, quite general ... so it may not be clear exactly what Maslow means. So let's look at each one in detail.

Firstly, at the bottom, you have the physiological needs, the essential things we need to survive, to live ... so things like food, water, a place to live. The basics. And in terms of work, this need is met by a person receiving a basic salary, their basic pay.

The next level up is called security needs, which is the need to feel safe and secure. So in terms of work this means things like job security and a pension.

Next we have belonging. Now, this can be understood as the need to feel part of a group – in other words, to have friends, and to feel close to people you work with, to your colleagues.

OK, moving up, number four is esteem. Esteem needs are connected to status – it's about being accepted and respected by other people. An obvious example of this at work is someone's job title – are they a 'manager', or are they a 'director'?

Finally, the highest level is self-actualization. This comes from a sense of achievement. To fulfil this need, people need to have a job that they find challenging, to feel they are achieving everything they are capable of ... although, of course, not everyone gets to this level.

Now, Maslow believed that the needs of each level had to be satisfied before a person could move up to the next level. So for example, if you take someone at work, their physiological needs like having a basic salary have to be met before they can start to think about security needs, such as having a pension plan.

Maslow also argued that people had to move from one level to the next level in the hierarchy. They couldn't miss a level. In other words, it's not possible to go straight from physiological needs to belonging needs. How that works is that, according to Maslow, as one need is met people start to feel that they want to fulfil the other needs. But not everyone needs to reach the top level. As I said, in terms of their work, some people may just be happy meeting the lower-level needs.

Speaking

◀)) 3.4 Extract 1

A OK, so we have five minutes to decide on the three most important qualities that make a good language learner. Does anyone have any ideas ...?

B Well, yes ... I think as far as I'm concerned, it's about focus. If you focus on the task, really focus, then you will, you know, you'll achieve results.

C All right, but what type of focus? Do you mean like focus on exams, or taking your lecture notes, or ... or what?

B No, not exactly, no. I mean that you have to focus on the big picture. Focus is when you have a clear idea what you want to achieve, and why. In other words – you know where you're going, and you're clear about what you need to do to get there.

A I see. And so you're saying that focus is the most important thing?

B Well, yes. Focus ... you know? Being committed to your goals.

A OK, right ... And what about you, Carina? What do you think makes a good language learner?

C Well, I would say motivation.

A Right ... Yes?

C And ... um, well, we were looking at that text earlier, it talks about two kinds of motivation, intrinsic motivation and extrinsic motivation.

A Can you explain what you mean by intrinsic and extrinsic motivation? It seems like they can be defined differently.

C OK, well, in very simple terms you could say, like, 'inside' and 'outside' motivation.

B Sorry, can you explain that?

A Yes, do you mean, like, inside your head?

C OK ... What I mean by intrinsic motivation is motivation that comes from inside you. So it has nothing to do with outside factors, or with what other people want from you. But ... motivation can also be extrinsic, which means it comes from outside. It's in the text, guys.

A OK ...

C So, if you really want to achieve something, let's say run a marathon, or, I don't know, learn Arabic or something ... if you're motivated enough, you'll do it. You will be successful, ultimately.

B So it's like focus, then. It's the same thing.

C Well, not exactly, because ... Look, to put it another way, if you're intrinsically motivated, then you'll do it because you really want to do it. And that will drive you to do it, even if it's really hard.

A And for extrinsic motivation, an example ...?

C Well, I think with extrinsic motivation there's often some kind of reward, like money or, like, higher status. And that's what motivates you.

Unit 4

Listening

▶ 4.1 Extract 1

So as I'm the first, I think maybe it's a good idea to start with a definition of an eco-city ... so that we all have the same definition, and we're all talking about the same thing. So, what is an eco-city?

Well, here are a few characteristics. An eco-city is a city that puts the environment first. It's sustainable – it uses energy sources in a sustainable way ... in other words, it aims for low energy use, and low emissions. That means not creating too many carbon emissions, putting CO_2 into the air.

Also, an eco-city is planned. It doesn't just happen. So, if you put these things together, you could say that an eco-city is a city which is planned to have low energy use and low emissions. It's environmentally friendly.

So, last week we talked about using contextualizing questions during our presentations, to help structure our talks. I've tried to use them all, so hopefully you'll find this presentation easy to follow.

OK. Firstly, *what* ... the 'what' question. In this case, what is an eco-city? And what is Tianjin, the particular eco-city I'm talking about? Then, it's *where* and *when* – so, where is it? And when did the project start? When did key decisions get made? Then *why* – the 'academic' question. Why was it planned in that way? Why did it happen? Next *how* – how does it work, how did it come about? And finally evaluation. Will it be effective or not? How significant is it? How influential is it? We need to think about questions like that.

▶ 4.2 Extract 2

So ... I've been reading about Tianjin eco-city. Tianjin is situated on the north-east coast of China. Actually, Tianjin itself is an old city, and today it's an increasingly important and fast-growing city.

So, what is Tianjin eco-city? Basically it's a modern city which is designed to be environmentally friendly, and to be as sustainable as possible. And also, to have a low impact on the environment around it.

Tianjin eco-city is situated a little bit outside of the main city. It takes about an hour to drive there, but if you use the new light railway system you can get there in about ten minutes.

So when did it start? Well, it's quite a new project. It started in 2007 when the Chinese prime minister at the time, Wen Jiabao, met with a senior minister from Singapore to discuss the building of a new sustainable but efficient city.

The reason for this was because there are so many pressures on the environment in a country like China ... Pollution is a big problem, and also the rapidly increasing demand for resources like food and energy. And land, of course – a lot of the countryside is being taken up with the development of new towns and cities. So new ideas, new solutions, are needed.

So how did it happen? Well, ... the way they did this was first to decide on the location and the piece of land. They then had to clean up the land, because it was waste land and quite polluted. And it was by the sea so it was also quite salty. After the clean-up, basically they made all the plans and they went ahead with the eco-city project.

There were a lot of challenges. For example, how to deal with the greenhouse gases like CO_2, carbon dioxide. All the buildings in Tianjin have very good insulation, so they use less energy, all the windows are double-glazed, and so on. The whole city has a percentage of its energy which must be zero-emission energy, like using solar power.

So, has all this been effective? Does it work? Actually, right now it's too early to say. But there are a lot of positive things about Tianjin eco-city. It has high-level political support, and this has been a really important factor in getting the project off the ground. Also, it has clear aims, and it has some really interesting and good ideas about how to achieve these aims. So I think you can say that the project is an effective, recent, ecological success.

▶ 4.3 Extract 3

OK, well, I want to tell you about Masdar, which is the city that I've been researching.

First of all, has anyone heard of Masdar City before? ... No? Well, maybe it isn't very well known yet, but actually it's a very important city. Basically, Masdar is a completely new, planned city. It's been described as an 'emerging cleantech cluster'.

What does that mean? Well, an 'emerging cleantech cluster' is a cluster – that means like a group, or a network, a cluster of say computers, it's a cluster of businesses or companies which are connected. And 'cleantech' means they're based around clean technology like carbon-neutral energy systems. So they don't cause dangerous emissions. And 'emerging' just means it's growing, it's happening now. Is that clear? Is that OK?

OK. So, as I said, Masdar is this new development for new and environmentally-based companies. It's located in the Middle East, near Abu Dhabi, which is the capital of the United Arab Emirates. It's about 17 kilometres south-east of the main city of Abu Dhabi, near Abu Dhabi international airport.

I said Masdar was a new development. It was created in 2006, but I think the interesting thing, the interesting question, is why was Masdar established.

Obviously it's in the middle of a major oil-producing region – the United Arab Emirates has over eight per cent of the world's total oil reserves. That's enough oil to last about another hundred years. But there are problems with this because, as we all know, the oil is going to run out one day. And the use of oil and other fuels is having a negative effect on the environment. Climate change, pollution – these are serious issues.

So ... Masdar was planned as this new kind of eco-city. It's not based on oil. It uses solar energy, and other renewable energy sources. It aims for zero emissions, and zero waste. They're managing the water supply, there are no cars, only public transport. And the city will be home to companies that specialize in environmentally-based products. Most of these companies are privately owned and they're there to make money. But the philosophy is for nature, for the environment, for a new clean technology. In other words, for a different kind of development.

So, how successful is it? Well, like Tianjin, it's still early days. But Masdar has attracted a lot of interest and investment. Many important new companies – and more importantly – talented employees, are working there now. So I think that it's already very successful, and is going to be even more successful in the future.

Speaking

▶ 4.4 Extract 1

In my presentation today I'm going to look at the background to urbanization across the world and in particular in China, where there's been a dramatic movement of the total population from the country to urban areas in recent years. I'll then move on to look at firstly the economic impacts, and secondly the environmental impacts, of urbanization in China.

OK, first I want to talk about urbanization in general, across the world. Since the beginning of the twentieth century, the world's urban population has increased massively. For instance, in 1900 it stood at just 220 million – at that time, this was 13 per cent of the total world population. By 1950, it had increased to 732 million, which was 29 per cent of the total world population. And in 2005, this had risen to 3.2 billion. So in 2005, 49 per cent of the total world population were living in urban areas. That's almost half the world's population living in major towns and cities. And according to the UN, this figure is likely to rise to 4.9 billion, or 60 per cent, by 2030. So nearly 5 billion urban residents.

However, it's clear that urbanization is not happening at the same rate across the world. So, if we look at the slide here we can see an overview of the main urban areas. The largest urban areas are still mainly in the developed countries. The population of the world's largest urban area, greater Tokyo, is currently around 35.6 million. But the newly industrialized countries are catching up very quickly – that's countries like Brazil, China, and India.

As you can see, in 1978, three-quarters of the US population, so 75 per cent, lived in towns and cities, but less than 20 per cent of China's population lived in urban areas. By 2011, America's urban population had increased slightly to 80 per cent of the total population. But it's now not really increasing. Over the same period, China's urban population increased to almost 50 per cent, almost half of the population. The size of the population in China also means that a small percentage increase is a large number in real terms. It's estimated that an extra 350 million people will be living in cities in China by 2030 – that would be a further 15 per cent increase.

So moving on to look at the economic impacts of urbanization. Now, you could say that urbanization has been one of the main drivers of economic growth in China, and it's likely to continue to move the country forward. In the next twenty years, it's predicted that around 50,000 new skyscrapers will be built, and that there will be around 200 million new urban jobs.

Urban populations consume more food, energy, and consumer goods than rural populations. For example, in China the urban population eats 60 per cent more meat than the rural population. Urban residents are also 25 per cent more likely to have a refrigerator than people in rural areas. All of this is positive in terms of future economic development.

OK, that was the economic impacts. Next I'd like to look at the environmental impact. There are obviously concerns about the negative effects of urbanization ... overcrowding in cities, pollution, people consuming more resources. But there are also positive aspects to urbanization from an environmental point of view.

Firstly, the birth rate among urban populations usually falls ... and in the longer term this will reduce population growth. Secondly, a fall in the rural population means fewer people using the land for farming, and over time this reduces the negative effects on the environment, and the total amount of land used by the human population.

However, the increased use of energy in urban areas, and the increase in pollution, means that cities tend to be warmer. City temperatures can be up to 1.3 degrees Celsius higher, and in the context of climate change, this can be seen as a problem.

So, in conclusion, I would say that the process of urbanization is going to continue. Currently, there are nearly four billion people living in towns and cities worldwide. There are environmental challenges, but also economic benefits. I think that if it's well managed, urbanization will lead to increased health and prosperity everywhere, especially in the developing world.

▶ 4.5 Extract 2

OK, first I want to talk about urbanization in general, across the world. Since the beginning of the twentieth century, the world's urban population has increased massively. For instance, in 1900 it stood at just 220 million – at that time, this was 13 per cent of the total world population. By 1950, it had increased to 732 million, which was 29 per cent of the total world population. And in 2005, this had risen to 3.2 billion. So in 2005, 49 per cent of the total world population were living in urban areas. That's almost half the world's population living in major towns and cities. And according to the UN, this figure is likely to rise to 4.9 billion, or 60 per cent, by 2030. So nearly 5 billion urban residents.

As you can see, in 1978, three-quarters of the US population, so 75 per cent, lived

in towns and cities, but less than 20 per cent of China's population lived in urban areas. By 2011, America's urban population had increased slightly to 80 per cent of the total population. But it's now not really increasing. Over the same period, China's urban population increased to almost 50 per cent, almost half of the population. The size of the population in China also means that a small percentage increase is a large number in real terms. It's estimated that an extra 350 million people will be living in cities in China by 2030 – that would be a further 15 per cent increase.

▶ 4.6

1 In my presentation today I'm going to look at the background to urbanization across the world and in particular in China ...
2 I'll then move on to look at firstly the economic impacts, and secondly the environmental impacts, of urbanization in China.
3 For instance, in 1900 it stood at just 220 million – at that time, this was 13 per cent of the total world population.
4 So, if we look at the slide here we can see an overview of the main urban areas.
5 As you can see, in 1978, three-quarters of the US population, so 75 per cent, lived in towns and cities, but less than 20 per cent of China's population lived in urban areas.
6 So moving on to look at the economic impacts of urbanization. Now, you could say that urbanization has been one of the main drivers of economic growth in China ...
7 For example, in China the urban population eats 60 per cent more meat than the rural population.
8 OK, that was the economic impacts. Next I'd like to look at the environmental impact.

Unit 5

Listening

▶ 5.1 Extract 1

In today's lecture we're going to be looking at the ethics of advertising to children. In particular, we'll look at the different views on how the advertising industry should be regulated when it comes to advertising aimed at children. Firstly, I want to consider some of the industry's arguments against regulations being put in place. So, why do they feel advertising doesn't need to be regulated? I'll then move on to look at some of the public health concerns, particularly in relation to the advertising of food and drink products. And then ... another position I want to look at is that of the parents, with a focus on 'pester power'. Do parents believe that television advertising really makes their children more demanding, especially in terms of asking them to buy particular products? And then finally, we'll look at the role of government and the steps that different governments around the world have taken to regulate advertising to children.

▶ 5.2 Extract 2

So firstly, why is the market ... children as a group... why is this market interesting to advertisers? Well, it's worth a lot of money, although it's not easy to give exact figures on the purchasing power of children ... even in just one country, never mind the world. But for example, in 2007 CBS reported that the

amount of money spent on advertising to children in the US was 17 billion dollars.

Most countries have controls on what can be advertised to children, and when, and how. One example of this is limiting the advertising of things like sweets, breakfast cereals, and fast food products. Obviously, this is because of the concerns about children's health, and in particular the rise in obesity. The argument is that advertising makes unhealthy foods more attractive. But the advertising industry doesn't necessarily agree that these regulations are needed. One common argument they put forward is that there's no evidence that advertising is a cause of childhood obesity. Another common argument from the advertising industry is that it has the right to free speech ... that as an organization, advertisers should have the same rights as any individual. Finally, they argue that the quality of children's television would be much lower if there was less money from advertising. And this is significant – according to a UNESCO-funded study, income from children's advertising has reached around 900 million dollars per year ... so it's a market that's worth almost a billion dollars.

▶ 5.3 Extract 3

In response to the industry's argument that there's actually no proof of a link between advertising and childhood obesity, a number of health organizations and doctors have come out strongly to argue against this. No one is claiming it's the only cause of obesity, obviously – changes in lifestyle, genetics, and diet in general are all major causes of obesity. However, many health professionals think it's an important factor. For example, the World Health Organization has judged that advertising is a probable cause of obesity. Unfortunately, it's very difficult to prove a clear cause and effect relationship, but it's still interesting that such respected organizations believe there is a relationship.

▶ 5.4 Extract 4

So moving on ... As I said earlier, it's quite difficult to estimate children's spending power, either direct or indirect. However, it's clear that children can influence parental spending. So how do parents feel about the effects of advertising on their children? Well, there's evidence that many parents feel very strongly about the way advertising influences the demands their children make on them. One study by the Australian consumer group CHOICE has shown that as many as 89 per cent of parents feel that advertising directly affects the demands that their children make for certain types of food. The same study has also highlighted the fact that 86 per cent of parents would be in favour of more government regulation of advertising. I should stress that this is only one study, but at the same time such high figures – 89 per cent and 86 per cent – suggest that the concern is widespread.

▶ 5.5 Extract 5

This brings me on to my next point, which is the role of government regulation. As we've seen, the advertising industry argues that it has the right to free speech, but there's also a widespread feeling that it's more important to protect the health of children. The World Health Organization has reported on the various positions taken by different governments. A number of European countries including Sweden, Norway, and Ireland, have banned advertising to children under the age of twelve, and also advertising during children's programmes on television. However, it's probably too soon to judge whether this has had any sort of impact ... on levels of obesity, for example.

OK ... so before we move on to the next section I'd just like you to think about the following questions.

Speaking

▶ 5.6 Extract 1

Welcome to my presentation this morning. I'm Jamila Khan and I'm going to be talking about *The power of social media*.

I've been interested in social media for a number of years, and recently I've been doing some research into this area. And when I say social media in this presentation, I'm mainly talking about Facebook and Twitter.

So first of all, I'd like to give you an idea of how powerful these social media have become. They're products of Web 2.0, part of the later development of the world wide web, basically after the year 2000. So let's look at how they started.

Firstly, Facebook ... Facebook was launched in 2004. If you've seen the film *The Social Network*, you'll know that it was originally set up as a networking site for students at Harvard University, in the United States. It expanded to other American universities and high schools ... and it was particularly useful when people were looking for jobs, because they could promote themselves in a more direct way.

Facebook currently has about one billion users worldwide. That figure is rising rapidly – but it's also falling. It's both rising and falling because there are always new people joining the network from around the world. But, at the same time, other users are leaving Facebook and cancelling their subscriptions, especially in places like the United States.

The United States was also where Twitter started. Twitter was set up in 2006 as a way of communicating for small groups of people. But obviously, it didn't stay small for long, and it currently it has over 200 million users worldwide.

So, these companies, Facebook and Twitter, are probably the most successful social media companies. They're integrated into smart phones and tablets and they're also being used more and more by businesses, as well as by individuals.

▶ 5.7 Extract 2

So, now I'd like to look at the purpose and the possibilities of social media.

Basically, there's been a change in the way social media are used since most of these companies were first set up. There's been a move from small local use ... like university students in the case of Facebook ... to the global mass-market use that we see today.

Secondly, social media like Facebook and Twitter allow businesses and individuals to network with each other and make useful contacts – so they have a professional role as well as a social role. Businesses can advertise themselves and their ideas ... or exchange information with anyone in the world. And obviously they make it possible for individuals to keep in contact socially ... with friends, family, former classmates, and colleagues. And also to make new friends, of course.

Next, what's interesting is that social media can often bypass the traditional media – newspapers, TV, radio ... Social media are much faster, much more direct. In the past, if

you wanted to say something, if you wanted to reach an audience or publicize an idea, you had to use the 'old media' – the newspapers, or TV. Now you can just do it yourself. You just Tweet your message and everyone who follows you will pick it up. Or put it on your Facebook wall.

And related to this, there have been some unexpected outcomes of using social media. Nobody thought in the early days how important they would be for social and political movements. I mean, think about the role social media have played in recent world events – that kind of activity would not have been possible a few years ago. And that's really exciting.

OK, let's look at social media in action – what are the advantages and what are the limitations?

So, first of all, most social media have low barriers of entry. They're easy to access, easy to use, and almost everyone can get their message out there.

And then there's equality. Social media are democratic – you don't have to be famous or rich or well-connected to use them. Everyone has the same access, everyone can have an equal say.

Also, there are no direct costs. Social media are free to use, and obviously this is attractive to businesses as well as individuals.

OK, I'm kind of contradicting myself here ... In theory, everybody can access social media. But in reality, they can't. People who are very poor, or don't have internet or mobile access, they're excluded, just as they're excluded from many other areas of modern life.

I said earlier that social media bypass other traditional media. They can also bypass governments, and government regulations. They have a global reach, and most governments find that they're almost impossible to regulate.

However, just because you're operating digitally, in the virtual world, that doesn't mean you're above the law. There are cases where users have got into trouble through Tweeting. Some users have even been convicted of crimes ... like the recent case where a student was sent to prison for writing racist Tweets about a public figure.

On the other hand, there is 'safety in numbers'. If one person is doing something, it might be considered to be wrong, but if a million people are doing it, what can anyone do about it, even the government? So, for example, if thousands of users are sharing some restricted information, how do you stop them? You can't prosecute them all. So this is another example of the power of social media.

There are other limitations, of course. There are some things you just can't do with social media. You still need real people, and real places, to meet up and do real things, obviously.

If you ask a 13-year-old what they want from social media, they'll probably say they want to socialize, to chat with their friends. Great – but what happens to real-life chatting? How does that help children develop socially?

And is someone you only know online really a 'friend'? Isn't it a bit sad that people – not just kids – prefer to communicate by text or Tweet rather than face to face?

So finally, I think we have to ask, what is the point of social media? How useful are they really? And how reliable? Are the advantages bigger than the disadvantages?

OK, so, I'd like to leave you with a few questions to think about.

Unit 6

Listening

▶ 6.1 Extract 1

So this is our first lecture in the module, *The Globalization of Business*. The main topic of today's lecture is the growth of the world economy, the global economy ... And in particular, we're going to focus on the way technology and capitalism have developed over the last two hundred years or so ... and how their development might be linked. What are the parallels? What are the connections?

Now ... The growth of technology and capitalism within the world economy ... OK, this is obviously a very broad theme to be starting out with. Essentially, we need to ask the key question: what are – or what were – the main causes of technological growth, and the growth of capitalism as an economic system? And we could also ask, is this growth a good thing? Who exactly has benefited from it, and who hasn't?

OK, so let's start by looking at the reasons behind the growth of the world economy over the past two to three hundred years. And in particular, the part played by the Industrial Revolution and the changes which led up to the Industrial Revolution.

▶ 6.2 Extract 2

To understand how the world economy came to grow so significantly and for such a long period of time, we have to go back in time – to the centuries leading up to the Industrial Revolution. During this period, there was a gradual move away from a mainly agricultural economy, where the majority of goods – tools, clothing, household items – were made individually, by hand. As technology advanced more quickly, new tools and other products were invented. And this enabled economic growth, which in turn led to further technological advances. So you had this momentum building up ... and these advances in technology and new inventions, this cycle of invention, if you will ... this was what led eventually to the Industrial Revolution.

Now, you might think of the Industrial Revolution as something that happened a long time ago – about two hundred to two hundred and fifty years ago, in fact. And in a sense you'd be right. However, one view is that the Industrial Revolution is not over. It's actually still going on – it's become permanent, a kind of permanent revolution. This is the view of Bowles, Edwards, and Roosevelt in their book *Understanding Capitalism*. You should be familiar with the first three chapters of this book, as it's on your reading list. The authors talk about what they call a 'permanent technological revolution'. And basically what they mean is, the Industrial Revolution is still going on.

So, if we look at the global economy today, the single most important cause of the growth in the world economy is the Industrial Revolution. And there are a number of reasons for this.

As I said earlier, in the late eighteenth and nineteenth centuries, technology developed rapidly in vital areas like agriculture and manufacturing. This early technological development didn't just stop – it continued, and it had very significant effects. There were improvements in areas like transport, both in shipping and land transport. In terms of shipping, for example, steam power replaced sail power. And in the industrial heartlands like Britain and America, you had a huge expansion of the railways and canals, which created a land transport network.

As we know, this process of technological growth and economic development continued into the twentieth century. Obviously one of the major changes was the expansion of the road network, highways, and the increase in the numbers of cars and trucks, especially after World War 2. But it wasn't just in transport, clearly – you have advances in other areas like medicine, healthcare, communications, and urbanization.

▶ **6.3 Extract 3**

In the twenty-first century, this growth has continued, especially in terms of new technologies. Since the year 2000, we've seen significant developments in key areas like computing, digital technology, and mobile communications ... smart phones are just one example of this.

Now, no one disputes this continued growth is real. What is more open to discussion is its impact, and in particular what it means for ordinary people. In the book I referred to earlier, Bowles, Edwards, and Roosevelt stress the improvements, what they describe as 'the significant increase in people's consumption standards'. In other words, people are buying and consuming more products and services ... they have more, they use more. And the authors see a direct link between these improvements in living standards and the growth of capitalism through the 20th century. Their argument is, and I'm quoting here from the same page, 'Wherever and whenever capitalism took hold, people's incomes and consumption levels began to rise in a sustained way'.

Now, they do offer some statistics to support this. For example, if we look at 'buying power' ... in other words, what people can buy with the money they have ... the buying power of Americans in 2002 was 32 times higher than it was in 1789. That works out at something like a 3,200 per cent increase over a period of 220 years. So basically, they're saying that these huge increases in living standards were brought about by the growth of industry and – effectively – by capitalism.

In fact, the authors are generally very positive about the benefits of sustained economic growth over this period. They call this an 'unprecedented growth in the availability of material goods' ... with improvements to people's diet, larger, more comfortable houses, ownership of cars and consumer goods, and so on. Now, I'd like you to think about all this for a moment, before we move on. So, spend a couple of minutes discussing this with the person next to you and decide if you agree that this industrial and technological growth is really a good thing.

▶ **6.4**

In fact, the authors are generally very positive about the benefits of sustained economic growth over this period. They call this an 'unprecedented growth in the availability of material goods' ... with improvements to people's diet, ... larger, more comfortable houses, ... ownership of cars and consumer goods ... and so on. Now, I'd like you to think about all this for a moment, before we move on. So spend a couple of minutes discussing this with the person next to you and decide if you agree that this industrial and technological growth is really a good thing.

▶ **6.5 Extract 4**

OK, ... I think you've probably worked out by now that there's more than one side to the story. Whether or not industrial and technological growth is a good thing is open to discussion and interpretation.

For the moment, in this part of the lecture, let's consider another, opposing political perspective – the Marxist perspective. I want to look at the Marxist perspective as it's presented in one of the other main textbooks on your reading list – *The Business Environment* by Wetherly and Otter. We'll be referring to this text frequently during the semester, and I'll indicate which chapters you need to be reading as we go along.

So, Wetherly and Otter. In Chapter 12, they look at the ways in which business has become more global, and they present a Marxist view of this process. As the authors point out, the political thinker and writer Karl Marx was associated with a radical view of capitalism. So we might expect a more critical stance than the one we looked at earlier, put forward by Bowles, Edwards, and Roosevelt.

OK, so in the context of the globalization of business, then ... the authors' first point is that Marx understood that capitalism led to growth, strong growth. In this sense he agreed with the views of Adam Smith, the eighteenth-century philosopher and political writer. Smith's view, essentially, was that the development of markets led to improvements in productivity, and therefore to economic growth – and because of this, he believed capitalism was a positive force, a force for good. But this is where Marx disagreed with Smith. Marx believed that the problem with capitalism, and with industrialization generally, was that it led to inequality – the system was basically unequal. Why? Because a small number of people controlled the wealth, while most of the population actually had very little in material terms. So essentially, the Marxist view is anti-capitalist – it sees the effect of capitalism as increasing poverty among the majority of the population.

Speaking

◀⫶ **6.6 Extract 1**

A So maybe we should just start by picking out a few of the main ideas.
B Yeah, OK ... It says in the text that there are currently about a billion cars in the world. I'm surprised it's not more, really. That's only one car for every seven people. Well, in the States it's at least one car per family and, well, often it's two or three.
A Yes, it's the same in Turkey as well. But I don't know what you can do about it. I mean, the problem is that cars improve everyone's lives. So ... as the text says, and I have to agree, cars aren't going to go away. We all depend on them so much.
B Exactly, yes. I don't see how you could convince someone to give up their car if they can afford it. I mean, everyone knows there are problems ... the text talks about, you know, using up oil supplies, pollution, traffic congestion. And I understand all that. You can't argue with the evidence. But I just think most people – me included – find it really difficult to step back and say, 'Actually, you know, cars are bad for the environment, I'm not going to use one any more'.
A I understand what you're saying, but I don't think it's as simple as shall I have a car or not, or how much I should use it. I mean, according to the text it's also about how

we think about the technology, and just having better systems, isn't it? If you look at paragraphs 2 and 3, it suggests a number of possible alternatives. Let me find it, wait a minute, um, ... yeah, here, it says, 'Vehicles need to change, as do the energy and transportation systems in which they are embedded'. I think that's pretty clear.
B I suppose so, but it seems to me that these ideas are for the developed world. In the developing world, you know, Africa or wherever, if someone can afford a car they're going to buy one, they, they're going to use it. I mean, wouldn't you? And a lot of governments in the developing world just don't have the resources, the money to develop the right kind of infrastructure. So I don't necessarily agree with that point.
A Yes ... OK, I see your point. But the authors also suggest that if we don't make these changes, we're all going to suffer ... economically, environmentally ...
B OK ... yeah ...
A And they argue that even if we make these changes there are still going to be big problems. I just think we have to take this really seriously.

◀⫶ **6.7 Extract 2**

A So, do you think the situation is really that bad?
B Well, if you look at the first paragraph, I think it's difficult to argue with the points. I mean, according to the text the number of cars is increasing, which means the problem will only get worse.
A I suppose so, but it seems to me that there are more serious threats to society than cars. I mean, over-population, water supply ... There are other things to worry about.
B I understand what you're saying, but isn't it all connected? I mean, the authors also suggest that there's a connection with climate change.
A But ... well, yes, I have to agree with that. But the text also says that we need a radical solution, we need to make big changes in the technology and the infrastructure. I don't necessarily agree with that point.

Unit 7

Listening

▶ **7.1 Extract 1**

So we're going to be talking about the development of cloud computing, which the *Wall Street Journal* has argued is just about the biggest creator of wealth in history. But not everyone thinks cloud computing is a good thing, and we'll look at some of the arguments for and against it in a minute. Um, but, to put the development of the cloud into some kind of context, it's useful to look at some of the early ideas behind the development of the internet itself.

As I'm sure you know, the internet has its origins in the American military, but the world wide web as we know it today is a much more recent phenomenon. There was a document called 'World Wide Web: A Proposal' which was written in 1990, by the British computer scientist Tim Berners-Lee and his colleague Robert Cailliau. And this document states that, 'Hypertext ... is a way to link and access information of various kinds as a web of nodes in which the user can browse at will'. In other words, the web is a variety of connection points, a network, that people can browse whenever they want. Now, the authors claimed in this document that a relatively small number of links was enough to get from A to B, from anywhere to anywhere.

So, essentially, the web has evolved in the same way as … well, for example, a food chain might develop in the natural world. Now, after a brief posting to a newsgroup in August 1991, it went global very, very quickly. In an article about the web, Tim Berners-Lee wrote 'collaborators welcome'. Now, so many people took up that invitation, that by 2009 there were 230 million websites and an average of six million new ones being added every month. So even looking at it from a different way, looking at the internet in a different way, it could be argued that it had already become the size of a cloud at that point.

▶ 7.2 Extract 2

So what is cloud computing? Well, the idea of cloud computing is similar to Berners-Lee and Cailliau's original business model, revised and expanded to take advantage of the growth of the world wide web. There's been a lot of interest in cloud computing in the media over the last few years, and a lot of people have written about its potential for the future. However, there's still some debate about what cloud computing is, exactly. For example, the science fiction writer William Gibson, who created the term *cyberspace*, has argued that its 'main usefulness lies in its vagueness'. In other words, the term 'cloud' is useful precisely because it's not exactly clear what the cloud is … and to try to define it too exactly would be impossible. And Larry Ellison, the co-founder of the computer company Oracle, has argued that cloud computing is simply a term to describe 'everything we already do'. Now, of course, both Gibson and Ellison are right. The cloud is everything the web does and so it has to be vague, otherwise it would be inaccurate. OK?

So, if we don't know exactly what cloud computing is, why is everyone so interested in it?

Well, for businesses there are a number of advantages. Firstly, cloud computing allows a computer user to have additional capacity beyond their existing capabilities. For example, they can get access to software, to data and extra storage space on a needs basis, when they need it. How does that work? Well, companies or individuals can get additional hard disk space by paying a fee for what they use. Now, that fee is normally much, much lower than the cost of buying, installing, and maintaining new hardware. So, as a result, a company can have a sophisticated IT infrastructure with minimal investment. And this also means they don't have to invest in expensive upgrades as well.

The second advantage is connected to the way that the hardware and the software are provided. Cloud computing is basically the delivery of a service rather than a product. So things like software, shared resources, and information are supplied to users' computers from a centralized source, via the internet. Think of it like electricity or gas, say, or other utilities like your water supply. What I mean by this is, at the moment most traditional standalone systems rarely use more than 20 per cent of their available capacity. So many users, especially businesses, are buying products that are much bigger than they really need. It's a bit like every street having their own electricity system … in other words, it's very inefficient.

So, a clear advantage of cloud computing is that it offers a much more efficient use of resources. For example, it allows different levels of use depending on how busy you are … so it's greener, because there's, there's less waste of resources … And there's normally automatic data protection, and backup, and recovery as part of the service.

So, there are clear advantages and clear economic benefits associated with cloud computing, as well as benefits in terms of efficiency and security. But there are also a number of disadvantages. Firstly, security again. The nature of cloud computing means that all security services are managed externally, so you're trusting a third party, someone you don't know, with your data, and quite possibly quite valuable data. How secure is that? For instance, cloud computing service providers, are able to control and monitor communication and data. In other words, they can access your confidential information whenever they want, and do what they want with it. There is something called the Cloud Security Alliance, which is an organization that promotes best practice for security assurances, but it's not a legal code. So the issue of security is a long way from being resolved.

Another disadvantage is that users can become too dependent on an external cloud service provider. Let's look at a couple of examples. Firstly, there's the obvious risk that the service provider could go out of business – cloud computing is like any other business, it faces the same economic challenges as any company. Secondly, cloud computing providers can have technical problems … and that means that your data may not be accessible when you need it. And while this can happen with any service model, in this case, with cloud computing, there's nothing the user can do to solve the problem.

A third issue is cost. You might think that this kind of service is always going to be cheaper, but it's actually not clear whether it will save users money longer term. Currently, there's a lot of competition for cloud services because it's not the normal model. But … one scenario is that as more and more companies change to this model, they'll become more dependent. And as a result, costs are likely to go up and the fees for additional services are also going to get higher. To put it another way, cloud models tend to make sense only when the user needs a limited range of services for a short period of time, or when their usage is minimal.

So, at the moment, cloud computing looks likely to become the normal model for many business users. However, there are certain risks attached around security and reliability. And also, depending on how the business model develops, it's still not clear whether it makes economic sense for the majority of companies.

▶ 7.3 Extract 2 Part 1

So what is cloud computing? Well, the idea of cloud computing is similar to Berners-Lee and Cailliau's original business model, revised and expanded to take advantage of the growth of the world wide web. There's been a lot of interest in cloud computing in the media over the last few years, and a lot of people have written about its potential for the future. However, there's still some debate about what cloud computing is, exactly. For example, the science fiction writer William Gibson, who created the term *cyberspace*, has argued that its 'main usefulness lies in its vagueness'. In other words, the term 'cloud' is useful precisely because it's not exactly clear what the cloud is … and to try to define it too exactly

would be impossible. And Larry Ellison, the co-founder of the computer company Oracle, has argued that cloud computing is simply a term to describe 'everything we already do'. Now, of course, both Gibson and Ellison are right. The cloud is everything the web does and so it has to be vague, otherwise it would be inaccurate. OK?

▶ 7.4 Extract 2 Part 2

So, if we don't know exactly what cloud computing is, why is everyone so interested in it?

Well, for businesses there are a number of advantages. Firstly, cloud computing allows a computer user to have additional capacity beyond their existing capabilities. For example, they can get access to software, to data and extra storage space on a needs basis, when they need it. How does that work? Well, companies or individuals can get additional hard disk space by paying a fee for what they use. Now, that fee is normally much, much lower than the cost of buying, installing, and maintaining new hardware. So, as a result, a company can have a sophisticated IT infrastructure with minimal investment. And this also means they don't have to invest in expensive upgrades as well.

The second advantage is connected to the way that the hardware and the software are provided. Cloud computing is basically the delivery of a service rather than a product. So things like software, shared resources, and information are supplied to users' computers from a centralized source, via the internet. Think of it like electricity or gas, say, or other utilities like your water supply. What I mean by this is, at the moment most traditional standalone systems rarely use more than 20 per cent of their available capacity. So many users, especially businesses, are buying products that are much bigger than they really need. It's a bit like every street having their own electricity system … in other words, it's very inefficient.

So, a clear advantage of cloud computing is that it offers a much more efficient use of resources. For example, it allows different levels of use depending on how busy you are … so it's greener, because there's, there's less waste of resources … And there's normally automatic data protection, and backup, and recovery as part of the service.

So, there are clear advantages and clear economic benefits associated with cloud computing, as well as benefits in terms of efficiency and security. But there are also a number of disadvantages. Firstly, security again. The nature of cloud computing means that all security services are managed externally, so you're trusting a third party, someone you don't know, with your data, and quite possibly quite valuable data. How secure is that? For instance, cloud computing service providers, are able to control and monitor communication and data. In other words, they can access your confidential information whenever they want, and do what they want with it. There is something called the Cloud Security Alliance, which is an organization that promotes best practice for security assurances, but it's not a legal code. So the issue of security is a long way from being resolved.

Another disadvantage is that users can become too dependent on an external cloud service provider. Let's look at a couple of examples. Firstly, there's the obvious risk that the service provider could go out of business – cloud computing is like any other business, it faces the same economic challenges as any company. Secondly, cloud computing providers can have technical problems ... and that means that your data may not be accessible when you need it. And while this can happen with any service model, in this case, with cloud computing, there's nothing the user can do to solve the problem.

A third issue is cost. You might think that this kind of service is always going to be cheaper, but it's actually not clear whether it will save users money longer term. Currently, there's a lot of competition for cloud services because it's not the normal model. But ... one scenario is that as more and more companies change to this model, they'll become more dependent. And as a result, costs are likely to go up and the fees for additional services are also going to get higher. To put it another way, cloud models tend to make sense only when the user needs a limited range of services for a short period of time, or when their usage is minimal.

So, at the moment, cloud computing looks likely to become the normal model for many business users. However, there are certain risks attached around security and reliability. And also, depending on how the business model develops, it's still not clear whether it makes economic sense for the majority of companies.

Speaking

🔊 **7.5 Extract 1**

A So, what did you think of Professor Chapman's presentation?

B Well, it just reminded me how much work I have to do. I'm not doing enough studying.

A Yes, well, it's the same for me. But I meant, you know, um, about the information on learning and assessments. All that stuff about how to study.

B I'm glad he talked about all that, it was interesting. I mean, he's right, we do need to manage our learning and our assignments more effectively. Yeah, I think it's good that he talked about it.

A Yes, I guess we already know that, but, um, ... what I found interesting was what he said about working together, and how we're expected to work together on the learning assignments ... so we depend on each other for our assessments. I think that's really important.

B I know. I read about it in the prospectus!

A Come on. You know what I mean. What I meant was ... basically we've got to work together and study together ...

C Hi.

B Oh, hello ... I didn't see you in the presentation.

C No, I couldn't make it this morning. I feel really bad about missing Professor Chapman's presentation. Erm ... could you maybe explain the main points ...?

B Of course. Actually, he said in the presentation that when you have to explain something to another student, you understand it better yourself.

A Yes, and it's true. In France, ... when I was at university in France ... it was very competitive. But actually we all worked together, we helped each other a lot.

C You mean, like, helping each other with the answers?

A No, no ... not that. What I'm trying to say is, in France we worked together a lot. We got together and shared our ideas. We helped each other with our work ... so, maybe we should do the same thing here. Maybe we should set up our own study network.

C OK, why not?

B OK, well, we've got half an hour now. Why don't we have a coffee and talk about how to do it?

🔊 **7.6 Extract 2**

B So, how do you actually work together? I mean, Professor Chapman was talking about study networks – study groups. How did they work for you in France?

A OK ... Well, we used to meet regularly, and work out how to do our assignments. What to read, what the texts mean. Quite difficult things, like what the tutor wanted us to do, and what ideas to use.

B That sounds interesting. Well, I think you're right. We should set up our own study network.

C Erm ... What is a study network, exactly?

A Well, basically, there's the work we all have to do individually ...

C OK ...

A ... So that means obviously our assignments and assessments. But there are a lot of opportunities to work in groups, too. For example, we have to do a group presentation this term, and there are online discussion groups ...

B Yes, so we need to look for these opportunities. And Professor Chapman said we'll get regular study quizzes ...

C That's good. We used to have pop quizzes, like a test in class. But they didn't tell us in advance. It was to check our learning.

B Mm ... that's interesting. So regular progress tests – is that what you mean?

C Yeah, progress tests, that's right.

A So, out of interest, do either of you normally study in groups, with other students? Or do you study alone?

C I like studying in groups, but ...

B I usually study on my own.

C That's what I was going to say. I think studying in groups is really useful, but I usually work on my own. Like you.

A OK, good. So, the next question is, do we really want to go ahead and set up a study network? Or do we want to join a study network that already exists?

B OK, well, first of all, Professor Chapman said that we have to 'maximize our study opportunities.'

C What does that mean?

B Well, basically what it means is that we have to take responsibility. So ... let's try to come up with some concrete ideas for our study network.

A OK. Let's start with some questions.

C I'll write them down.

A Thanks. So, first, what's our aim? What's the point of having a study network?

C Well, I think ...

A Hold on, let's just get the questions down first. Then we can think about the answers.

B What about resources? What do we need?

A OK, that's good.

B And who's going to join the network?

A Excellent ... How big will it be? How many people?

C And what are the responsibilities? How will the network be managed?

B I have another question. How does it all fit in with what we already do? We already have a lot of face-to-face learning ... you know, like lectures and seminars.

C What, you think it might be a waste of time?

B Well, no, but ... what I'm saying is, how does a study network add to all that? What's the extra value?

A Can we come back to resources? Remember what Professor Chapman said about resources ... that you should make sure

that they help you, and they don't ... erm, dictate what you do, he said.

B OK, fine. So ... what approach should we take? And, should we look for some kind of study network system that's already out there somewhere? Or should we try to work with what we've got?

C Yeah.

🔊 **7.7 Clips 1–5**

1

B I know. I read about it in the prospectus!

A Come on. You know what I mean. What I meant was ... basically we've got to work together and study together ...

2

A Yes, and it's true. In France, ... when I was at university in France ... it was very competitive. But actually we all worked together, we helped each other a lot.

C You mean, like, helping each other with the answers?

A No, no ...not that. What I'm trying to say is, in France we worked together a lot. We got together and shared our ideas. We helped each other with our work ... So, maybe we should do the same thing here. Maybe we should set up our own study network.

3

A ... So that means obviously our assignments and assessments. But there are a lot of opportunities to work in groups, too. For example, we have to do a group presentation this term, and there are online discussion groups ...

4

B OK, well, first of all, Professor Chapman said that we have to 'maximize our study opportunities.'

C What does that mean?

B Well, basically what it means is that we have to take responsibility. So ... let's try to come up with some concrete ideas for our study network.

5

B I have another question. How does it all fit in with what we already do? We already have a lot of face-to-face learning ... you know, like lectures and seminars.

C What, you think it might be a waste of time?

B Well, no, but ... What I'm saying is, how does a study network add to all that? What's the extra value?

Unit 8

Listening

▶ **8.1 Extract 1**

So today's lecture is on *Major construction projects: innovation and risk in airport design*. Now, at the centre of innovation is the idea of something new, and for architecture and construction projects, innovation has always been important. Without innovation, we just repeat what exists already, and we don't move forward. And to meet the needs of complex projects, such as those of a new airport, we need innovation ... new ideas, new techniques.

So today's lecture will focus on two recent projects, both major innovations in the construction of international airports. We'll be looking at, firstly, Chek Lap Kok airport in China – which is better known as Hong Kong airport – and also at the Terminal 5 development at London's Heathrow airport, one of the busiest airports in the world. I want to describe these projects briefly, and use them as examples to show why innovation is one of the main factors behind new infrastructure developments at airports generally … And I also want to show how innovative ideas can benefit the end users, in this case passengers and airport staff.

Now, when you start a major construction project, obviously you have to think about the risks involved, so I want to look at risk in relation to these two airport projects … to see what can go wrong, and look at why such projects don't always turn out as planned. We'll look at how, to be successful, they need not only physical resources – land, building materials – they also need effective management and innovative technology in the form of computer software. And this software has to be reliable. If it's not reliable, the whole project can be affected.

And then later in the lecture, I want to look at how we evaluate major construction projects … and why so many big projects overrun their budgets … and end up costing much more than was planned at the start.

▶ 8.2 Extract 2

So let's look first at Hong Kong's airport. I want to start by going back to the 1970s. At this time it was clear that the old airport in Hong Kong, Kai Tak, was running out of capacity. They needed to increase the size of the airport and build a second runway, but there was very little space.

The map on this slide shows the whole of Hong Kong, and on the right-hand side, you can see the old airport, Kai Tak – it's situated in the north-east of the city. The problem was that Kai Tak was in a very risky location … the planes had to fly low over the city to land. Because space was so limited, an innovative solution was needed. So a completely new site was chosen to build a replacement airport – the island known as Chek Lap Kok, here on the left of the slide, off the north coast of Lantau. And as you can probably see, it doesn't look very natural in shape compared with the other islands around it.

This is because Chek Lap Kok island presented a major engineering challenge. The island had to be levelled off, and new land had to be reclaimed back from the sea on its north coast. This kind of thing had been done before, in other parts of the world, but the preparation of Chek Lap Kok island for its new role as host to Hong Kong's airport was one of the largest construction projects of the 20th century. The architects Foster and Partners, from the UK, were chosen to design the project, and the whole project, including the levelling off of the island and the reclamation of land from the sea, was completed extremely quickly – in only six years. This is an extraordinary achievement. The new airport opened in 1998, about a year after the handover of Hong Kong to China in 1997.

▶ 8.3 Extract 3

Here's a plan of the airport. You should be able to make out the two runways, situated along each side of Chek Lap Kok island, north and south. And you'll also notice a very large area, well, two very large areas, actually … Near the top of the slide is the passenger terminal, on the east side, there. And the cargo area in the bottom half of the slide, is to the south. Back in 2010, the airport became the busiest cargo airport in the world, taking over from Memphis in the USA. It's obviously a major hub for the region – for mainland China, particularly the south, but also for other countries in the region.

The other area in the centre of the slide is currently not developed. As you can see, it's reserved for future airport expansion. During the design stage, in the 1980s, it was realized they would probably need to continue to expand, and in fact these plans, these expansion plans, are now quite far advanced.

OK, so let's turn to our other project. This is the project at Terminal 5 at London Heathrow. This was needed for similar reasons to the expansion at Hong Kong – growing demand and limited capacity.

Here on this map of London you can see Heathrow, situated on the left-hand side of the slide, to the west of the city near the M25, London's orbital motorway, in blue. There are other airports around London, including City airport to the east of the centre, but Heathrow is the largest airport, and there was pressure on it to expand.

So it was decided in the early 1980s that a new fifth terminal was needed at Heathrow. For many years it had just three terminals. Terminal 4 opened in 1986. But the need for a fifth terminal quickly became apparent. This was driven by British Airways, who are now based in Terminal 5. The British architectural firm, the Richard Rogers Partnership, was chosen to design the building, working with the engineering firm Arup, and other partners as well.

Here, you can see Terminal 5, on the left of the slide, in the western part of the airport. The terminal took a long time to complete. There was a long public consultation process and construction didn't start until 2002. And the new terminal opened in 2008. The terminal building is currently the largest single covered construction in the UK.

So what about innovation? Well, several innovative techniques were used in the construction process for Terminal 5. For example, conventional cranes couldn't be used because they would interfere with the airport's radar systems, so smaller cranes were used to build the roof on the ground and then it was lifted up into position in sections.

So you can see that innovation has played an important role in the development of both major projects. As I said, we'll examine the idea of innovation in more detail later on.

▶ 8.4 Extract 4

OK, these are two very successful and innovative projects. However, there were also serious problems with both projects, and these need to be considered alongside the success stories. When they opened, both Hong Kong airport and Heathrow Terminal 5 suffered from serious IT failures.

Now, I'd like to relate these failures to a number of questions raised by Professor Bent Flyvbjerg of the Said Business School at the University of Oxford. Flyvbjerg has identified a number of negative characteristics of major infrastructure projects. This slide outlines these characteristics, which I'd like to run through now.

First, Flyvbjerg argues that most major infrastructure projects involve risk. This is because they have long periods of preparation and planning. And also they're very complex. Put simply, in most projects like this, a lot of things can go wrong.

Second point. The technology and design of these projects are non-standard. They've been developed for one particular project. They may be innovative, but they're also unusual – so most of the time, they're not tried and tested.

Flyvbjerg's third point is that there are many different groups of people involved – the architects, construction companies, governments, shareholders, and so on. So there are often competing interests in terms of decision-making, and planning and management of the project.

Fourth, there is what Flyvbjerg calls 'lock in'. Now, by this he means that the main idea of the project is decided at a very early stage, and alternative choices and options often are not looked at or analysed. All the planning is focused on the chosen project and its design, so other alternatives, which may be better, are not considered.

Number five, the details and size of a project can also change. For example, technology may change or customers may come up with new requirements.

OK, point six. Statistical evidence shows that most projects don't take account of unplanned events. Now, obviously, unplanned events can't be predicted. But the point is, they're going to happen and project teams need to make sure they have extra time and money available in case something unexpected happens. This is known as contingency planning.

Flyvbjerg also refers to 'misinformation' – the wrong information, in other words. This is very common in big projects. And this misinformation is mainly about the costs, about the benefits, and about risks. For example, it may be in some people's interest to underestimate the cost of construction, and this can lead to problems.

So, all these factors that Flyvbjerg talks about can result in what he calls 'cost overruns' and 'benefit shortfalls'. What this means in simple terms is that more is promised, less is delivered, and the whole project costs more than was planned.

OK, I'd like now to look again at Hong Kong airport and Heathrow Terminal 5, and see how Flyvbjerg's points about risk apply to these two projects.

Speaking

◀)) 8.5 Extract 1

A It's pretty obvious really, isn't it? That a more innovative firm is going to be more successful.

B Well, I'm not so sure. I mean, there are a lot of innovative firms that have failed, that aren't really successful.

A So what you're saying is that the innovative firms aren't always the successful ones?

B Well, yes … I mean, you always hear about the successful ones like Apple and Microsoft … but there must be hundreds of others that fail, even though they're quite innovative. But then as the text says, companies that aren't aware of technological change, or aren't prepared for it, they're in a dangerous position.

A Yes, and if you're … you know, successfully innovative, it can put you in a good position. Like the text says, you can end up with a bigger market share. As you said, Apple are incredibly successful, and incredibly innovative. I mean, the products, the design, their brand … everything.

B Yeah, yeah, … And following on from that point, er, it can also help products or brands that aren't, you know, aren't selling so well. I mean, the text gives Lego as an example, but I also think of when BMW started producing the new Mini … and it suddenly became cool again.

A Yeah, and I think Apple is like that too. And another point the text raises is about globalization. The global organization is the easiest one for a company, I think.

B Do you mean it's the easiest kind of innovation for companies to take advantage of?

A Well, yeah, because the company doesn't have to be innovative – they just have to see what's there and take advantage of it. Do you see what I mean?

B I think so. You mean, someone else does the innovating so the company takes less of a risk.

A Yeah, exactly, a firm can have its head office in one location but have different parts of the business based anywhere. The last point ... erm, in the text ... about the size of a company. I think it's the most interesting. You know, that small firms now have a chance to compete with big firms. I think that's a really important point.

B Really? So what you're saying is ... being big is not an advantage any more?

A Well, no, not quite. But they at least have a chance to compete. A smaller firm selling a niche product can actually reach a lot of customers now, much more easily than in the past.

B Well, they're not really competing though, are they? I mean, if a big company wanted to sell the same product they could. So it's a bigger market but there's not really direct competition. Does that make sense?

A OK, so if I understand you correctly, you mean the company is more innovative, it's stronger, but it's still not competing?

B Exactly. Like it says in the text, innovations like the internet mean they can potentially sell to a lot more people.

🔊 8.6 Extract 2

B But it's common sense that spending money on Research and Development is an advantage to a firm, isn't it?

A Do you mean companies are going to be more successful the more they spend? I'm not sure I agree with that. That means that a lot of companies must waste a lot of money never really going anywhere. I mean, if it was that easy everyone would do it. Do you follow what I'm saying?

B Well, yes, I think so ... if I understand you correctly, you think a lot of money is invested and effectively it's wasted. They never get it back.

A Exactly. It's not that simple. If research equals success, equals profit, everyone would do it. As you said, a lot of the time there's no return on the investment.

🔊 8.7 Extract 3

C Companies that fall behind with technology are going to fail. It's obvious.

D Yes, technology helps companies operate much more globally than before.

E There are a lot of companies that were successful, but didn't recognize the importance of a new development.

C Well, Nokia were a top mobile company, but they fell behind because they didn't move quickly enough with good smart phones.

D Amazon was started in a garage and it's now one of the biggest book retailers in the world. Well, not just books, actually.

E A lot of telecoms companies had real problems because mobile phone companies took so much of the market.

🔊 8.8 Extract 4

C As you said earlier, there's a lot of companies that have failed because they've fallen behind with technological developments.

D Well, yeah, that's right. If you take the companies that sold music CDs, for example, selling online, you know, downloads ... that allowed them to not only sell to a bigger market but it also cut production costs massively ... and distribution.

C Yeah ...

E Yeah, and following on from that point there are also a lot of companies that were successful but just didn't recognize the importance of new developments. Some music companies are a classic example of that.

C Well, there are quite a few music shops that just don't exist any more ... on the high street or online. If they'd moved to downloads, you know, more quickly or whatever, they'd probably still be doing OK.

D You made an interesting point about companies not recognizing the importance of a new development quickly enough. I mean, well, Nokia is a classic example.

E Exactly, they were a brand leader but they just lost so much ground because they were too slow with smart phones.

Unit 9

Listening

▶️ 9.1 Extract 1

... Now, as we've seen, approaches to marketing a new product are quite varied, depending on the sector and the type of product. In this lecture I would like to focus on a particular area, which we could call high-value consumer electronics. So this is things like smart phones, MP3 players, tablet computers, laptops, notebooks, all kinds of personal devices ... So, innovative technology in a consumer context. As we know, this is a very competitive and fast-moving sector. Now, I want to look at two main areas. Firstly, how companies differentiate themselves, and their products, from their competitors' products. And then secondly, we're going to look at differentiation in terms of the consumer, the customer. So, who these products are targeted at, and the risks associated with each type of product, and each type of consumer. OK? So just to give you an example of what I want to talk about, let's take a look at some of the typical examples of high-value consumer products ...

▶️ 9.2 Extract 2

OK, now I'm sure you will recognize some of these products and their brand names. You probably own at least one of them, or a more up to date version. All of these products were released between 2001 and 2011. Now, you'll see that they're arranged in pairs ... and each pair, one of the products could be described as a revolutionary product and the other as a me-too product. So, in very basic terms, one is an original idea, something new and different, and the other is a copy.

If we take the Apple iPod, for example ... Now the iPod revolutionized the way people buy and listen to music. Apple released the iPod in 2001 and in 2006 Microsoft released their MP3 player, the Zune, as a direct competitor to the iPod. Some of you may not have heard of the Zune because Microsoft stopped producing new models in 2011. So why did a product from one of the most successful companies of all time, Microsoft, fail to gain market share? Both of these devices could play music and videos, both had similar features, and both had their own online store where users could buy videos and music. So ... so far, nothing particularly different. However, the iPod was generally considered to have a more attractive design than Zune. It was seen as stylish, modern, cool ... whereas, you know, many people disliked the design of Zune. Not everyone agrees, but some experts in the industry said that the Zune was actually technically superior, although it depends which individual features you're talking about. For example, the Zune had a bigger screen, which you'd think would be a positive feature. However, some users felt it was more pixelated so it didn't actually provide better viewing of movies ... even though the screen was bigger. Many features such as the navigation were considered equally good on both devices. So if the Zune was in many ways just as good as the iPod, and for some people was technically superior, why did it fail to gain market share? Well, it may be that it was simply five years too late. The iPod gained its market-leading position by being the first of its kind, by doing something new and different ...

▶️ 9.3 Extract 3

Before we continue, I'd just like to give you an overview of one of the most common methods of analysing consumer behaviour. You may have seen this diagram before – this is known as an adoption curve, or innovation curve, and it was developed by an American sociologist called Everett Rogers in 1962 ... and it's still used today. Basically, Rogers divided consumers into five main groups, called *innovators*, *early adopters*, *early majority*, *late majority*, and *laggards*. Now, *innovators* are the smallest group ... they're the first people to adopt a new, revolutionary product. Innovators are more adventurous than other consumers, more willing to take risks. They're often young, they have a high social status, and a good income. And the second-fastest group to adopt a new product are *early adopters*. They have similar characteristics to innovators, they're perhaps a little more careful, but they're open-minded and willing to try out new ideas. Then we come to the majority of consumers – these fall into two roughly equal groups. The *early majority* are careful consumers – they may take significantly longer than the innovators and early adopters to buy a revolutionary product, but they accept change probably more quickly than the average consumer. Then after the early majority, we have the *late majority* – they're more conservative and usually they'll adopt a revolutionary product when most people are using it. Late majority consumers are less interested in innovation and they're often more concerned about price – they may be more likely to buy a me-too product. And finally, we have the *laggards*, the last to adopt a new product. They're more traditional, they tend to be older and tend not to like change.

▶️ 9.4 Extract 4

So let's take a look at this issue of revolutionary products versus me-too products. The first thing to say is that not all me-too products fail to take market share in the way that the Microsoft Zune did. And obviously, Microsoft has been incredibly successful in other areas.

So how does being a revolutionary product compare with being a me-too product? Is it better or worse to be revolutionary?

Well, revolutionary products face a number of challenges that me-too products don't.

One reason is that it's much more difficult to communicate the benefits of a completely new product to consumers. So companies need to be more creative in communicating those benefits ... in persuading consumers that they need something they've never had. And Apple, of course, have been very successful at this. Me-too products, on the other hand, are usually entering an established market and competing with products that are already there. So what the manufacturer of a me-too product has to do is persuade consumers that their product is better than the others. That can also be difficult, but it's a very different kind of challenge.

There are risks for companies in launching both types of product. As we saw with the Rogers adoption curve, the people who are most likely to buy a revolutionary product are the innovators and the early adopters, followed by the early majority. Late majority consumers and laggards are much more likely to buy me-too products. Now, the risks for me-too products are not as high as for the revolutionary ones. It's much riskier to launch a revolutionary product because statistically only 2.5 per cent of consumers are likely to buy it at the start of its life cycle. If a revolutionary product reaches the later stages in this cycle, that's when other companies will try to gain market share through me-too products. For example, the iPod was arguably being used by the early or even late majority before Microsoft launched the Zune.

So where's the risk in being a revolutionary product? Well, quite simply, failure. It's easy to fail, and a lot of products do. There are studies that show that somewhere between 48 and 99 per cent of innovative products fail. For every iPhone there are hundreds of other products that fail and they fail for many reasons – lack of market, poor research, coming into the market too early or too late. In general, fewer me-too products fail, not least because they know that the market does exist.

In terms of pricing ... Well, in general, me-too products need to be cheaper than revolutionary ones. Companies have traditionally been able to set a high price for revolutionary products. After all, it's likely that their product is the only one in the market. But getting the price right can be difficult, and if it's too high people may be put off. Similarly, the companies offering me-too products have an equally hard decision. They often need to set a lower price than the market leader because they're trying to gain market share. But if they set the price too low, it may send the wrong message to consumers – they may question the quality or the functionality of the product.

The key to being successful as a me-too product is differentiation. A product needs to be different enough from its competitors to be interesting to consumers. A study by Cooper in 2000 found that a product that is clearly differentiated can gain as much as 50 per cent market share, while products that were seen as simply copying the market leading product gained less than 20 per cent market share. Cooper argued that me-too products need to analyse how revolutionary products fail to meet consumer needs, and then meet those needs, but do it better. So they have the double challenge of needing to be better, but also cheaper, than the competition.

So, what does this tell us? Well, revolutionary products need to be more creative in their marketing, they need to be able to handle risk and accept a higher rate of failure. A successful revolutionary product can gain a strong share of the market that can be difficult for me-too products to enter. However, by differentiating itself from the competition, and meeting customer needs better, a me-too product can gain significant market share.

Speaking

◀)) 9.5 Extract 1

Tutor So we're talking about the main factors that contribute to personal happiness. OK, so, Alex, could we start with you today?

Alex Er ... OK, thanks. Yes, well I read an article called 'Measuring the impact of major life events upon happiness' ... from the *International Journal of Epidemiology*. It's by two researchers called Dmitri Ballas and Danny Dorling from the University of Sheffield. So, their aim was to look at ways of measuring happiness in terms of what happened in people's lives. So what were the situations or events that affected whether or not people were happy. They looked at these mainly from an economic perspective. And the main context for their research is Britain, so it's only people living in Britain who were interviewed. The research took place in the 1990s, so it's presented as the state of British happiness at the end of the last century. OK?

All Yes, thanks, Alex ... Yes, thank you.

Alex OK, well, Ballas and Dorling based their research on a survey using questionnaires. These questionnaires were given out to 10,000 people ... living in Britain in the 1990s. And one of the questions on the survey is about happiness. So, Ballas and Dorling, these researchers, they categorized eighty ... that's eight zero ... eighty different types of life event into seven categories. And these categories were one, health-related events ... two, education ... three, employment ... four, leisure ... five, births and deaths... six, personal relationships, so friends, family, colleagues ... and seven, finance, including income. OK, and in the results, they found that two-thirds of the respondents reported no life-changing events during the last year, so no births and deaths, no major illnesses, or whatever. But out of the other 33 per cent, the biggest group was finance, at 6.49 per cent. So that's people who had some kind of change in their financial situation. And after that, the next largest category is personal relationships, with 6 per cent. So, anyway ... they analyse and discuss the results, and their main conclusions are quite clear. This is what they say, and I'm quoting: 'Our analysis suggests that in British society by the end of the 20th century, personal relationships were extremely important in terms of happiness. The analysis presented in this article suggests that what matters the most in British people's lives is to have good interpersonal relationships at home, and to be respected at work'.

Emily That's from the discussion section of the article?

Alex Yes. Erm, there's one more point I'd like to make. I won't go into too much detail but ... Ballas and Dorling looked at another piece of similar research. And this alternative research found that people's health is more important compared to other life events, including financial situation.

◀)) 9.6 Extract 2

Tutor Well, thank you very much for that, Alex. OK, let's move on to our next piece of research. So that was Emily next. Over to you, Emily.

Emily Thank you. Well, the article I read is by Rodríguez-Pose and Maslauskaite ... I think that's how you say it, yeah? ... OK. So the article is 'Can policy make us happier? Individual characteristics, socio-economic factors and life satisfaction in Central and Eastern Europe'. It was published in 2011. Well, first of all, the context. The focus of the research is Central and Eastern European countries. The article starts out by saying that ten years after the fall of the Berlin Wall in 1989 ... so around the year 2000 ... erm, the main characteristics which defined people in Central and Eastern European countries compared to Western Europeans was that they were poorer, and less happy. The article takes a mainly economic perspective, and they use data from EVS ... that's the European Values Study ... and Eurostat data. Anyway, in 2004 there were ten countries that joined the European Union, and these countries were mainly former communist countries. They were called the EU10. And during the period 1999 to 2008 the gross domestic product, the GDP of these ten countries, grew by an average of 400 per cent.

Alex That's very strong growth.

Emily Yes, but what's interesting is, during the same period levels of individual happiness stayed more or less the same – they increased by less than 15 per cent in most countries. The article says that the level of happiness has, and this is the quote, 'remained low or very low throughout the region in comparison with the EU as a whole'. This relates to the 'Easterlin paradox'...

Alex What's the Easterlin paradox?

Emily OK, this is an idea that comes from a paper published in 1974 by Richard Easterlin from the University of Southern California. And he argued that increased wealth doesn't result in increased happiness. But not everybody accepts his findings. Anyway, Stefan is going to talk about this later.

Alex OK, thanks.

Emily So moving on now to their research, Rodríguez-Pose and Maslauskaite found many of the factors that Alex has mentioned, and a few more. For example, individual income, gender, so there are differences between men and women ... erm, age, civil status, the number of children you have, employment conditions, level of education, and where you live. These are all possible factors which can affect happiness. Anyway, these researchers emphasize that income is 'among the most studied' factors, and they find that – and again I'm quoting from the article – 'wealthier people are, as a general rule, much happier'.

Alex But that's not what Easterlin says.

Emily No, that's right, these researchers say that Easterlin is not really correct. They find that Central and Eastern Europeans aren't significantly different from people in Western Europe. What the researchers find is that, here's the quote, 'people tend to be happier when they are healthy, earn more, are better educated, married and employed'.

Alex That's pretty clear.

Emily Yes. And also ... well, there has been strong economic growth, but it takes time for this to change people's levels of happiness. And economic factors can be negative as well – there's high unemployment, inflation, a lot of inequality between people ... these factors can bring down people's happiness.

Tutor Well, thank you very much, Emily. That was very interesting. And now we need to hear about Stefan's research. Thank you, Stefan ...

Unit 10

Listening

▶ 10.1 Extract 1

So this debate focuses on the motion 'Playing video games leads to increased levels of crime, including violence and antisocial behaviour'. Our two main speakers today are the journalist and social commentator, Suzanna Fiorella, who will be arguing in favour of the motion – that playing video games does lead to increased levels of crime ...

And speaking against the motion we have the psychologist and blogger Michael Connelly, who is an expert on the psychological and social effects of technology. Welcome to both of you.

There will be an opportunity for the audience to say what they think after we've heard from Suzanna and Michael. And it'll be interesting at the end to see whether you're convinced by their arguments and the supporting evidence that you've heard.

So, let's start with arguments in favour of the motion ... Suzanna Fiorella.

▶ 10.2 Extract 2

Thank you. I'd like to start by asking two questions. What are video games for? And what are the effects on the people who play them?

In answer to the first question ... well, actually there are a number of possible answers. From a commercial perspective, you could say that video games are a product. They're there to make money for the companies that produce them, and they do this very successfully.

But of course, there's more to it than that. We live in an age when people work fewer hours than at any time in the past, and therefore have much more leisure time. Children and young people in particular have a lot of free time. Playing video games fills some of that time for many of these people, whereas in the past they may have spent that time working or studying, reading or playing sport. I'll come back to this point later, but I think what it tells us is that video games exist mainly to fill up people's time. Apart from that, they don't make a useful contribution to people's lives. Indeed, as I'm about to argue, most of the effects they have on people, especially younger people, are negative. And at the extreme end of 'negative', video games can lead to crime.

So, this brings us to the second question. What are the effects? I have to say first of all that there's no absolutely clear answer to this question. The evidence is not as strong as, say, the evidence for the negative effects of smoking on health. But there appears to be evidence, quite convincing evidence, to suggest that many of the effects of playing video games are negative. And

that potentially, they can lead to antisocial attitudes and behaviour, even criminal activity.

Let's look at some of these points now. My first point is that playing video games is not a productive activity. I said that video games exist, erm, essentially, to fill up leisure time, and they certainly take up a great deal of time for the people who play them. But while they're playing, they're not producing anything useful, they're not achieving anything. They're not being sociable, building friendships and networks, and they're not out there learning new skills and doing new things. So game-playing is clearly unproductive. From that point of view, it's a complete a waste of time.

Moving on to my second point. You could argue that game-playing improves players' cognitive skills ... their ability to think and react. But research has shown that any improvement in cognitive skills is very limited, as Sims and Mayer found in 2002. In other words, if you play a game where you have to manipulate an object, you might be able to manipulate a similar object more effectively in real life, but you probably won't be able to transfer this skill to other kinds of objects and contexts.

My third point is important, and it goes like this. It's widely believed that playing violent video games can lead to violence in real life. Admittedly, this can be a difficult point to prove, but there is research to suggest that after playing violent and aggressive video games, people may behave in an aggressive way. And if more people are behaving aggressively, this has a negative effect on society generally. Aggression becomes more common in society as a whole.

Bensley and Van Eenwynk found evidence of this in their 2001 analysis of 28 research studies. It applied particularly to younger children, aged from four to eight years old. Another piece of research links video-games halls in South-East Asia with recruitment for criminal gangs. These video-games halls are one place where established gang members can find new members. This research is by Jon Vagg, published in *the British Journal of Criminology*.

Another related point is the research that has been done into antisocial effects on children. The work of Gentile and others found 'increased levels' of video-game playing were linked to antisocial effects in children, even children who weren't previously behaving in an aggressive way. This suggests that playing video games is linked to antisocial behaviour, which may include violent behaviour. So, it would seem that there is some evidence to suggest that antisocial behaviour can lead to violent behaviour, and then to criminal activity.

One last point. Playing video games can, like other activities, be addictive. The more you play, the more you want to play. I've seen children play games literally for hours, and the next day they want to go back and spend even more time doing the same thing. And if you try to stop them, they get moody or angry. I'm sure that many of you have seen similar examples of this kind of effect. And addiction is, of course, linked to criminality – addicts often behave aggressively when they don't get their 'fix'. And in extreme cases some commit crimes to fuel their addictions.

So, video-gaming and criminality – in my view, they're closely linked.

▶ 10.3 Extract 3

Chair Thank you very much, Suzanna. Well, some important points there, and lots to think about. I know that Michael has a number of points that he would like to make, but I'm going to ask him first to respond to what Suzanna has said.

Michael Thank you ... Yes, as you say, Suzanna raises a number of interesting points. What I'd like to do, I think, is respond to these points one by one. Now, I've read the same research as Suzanna, and I think it's interesting that we don't agree on the evidence.

So firstly, the point about game-playing being an unproductive activity – a 'waste of time', I believe were the words you used. Now, this may be a widely held opinion, but to be convincing it needs more evidence. Also, if playing computer games is a waste of time, then you might as well say that watching television is a waste of time, reading magazines is a waste of time, chatting to your friends online is a waste of time. Maybe they are, but there doesn't seem to be any evidence for this. It's just an opinion. So you could also say that all these activities are perfectly valid and useful.

OK, Suzanna's second point, that players' cognitive skills are only improved in a very limited way. Now, there's actually very little evidence for this. Other research seems to support the idea that gaming can have a significant effect on cognitive ability. For example, there's an article published by a team of researchers from the Psychology Department at the University of Illinois. The title of this is 'The effects of video game playing on attention, memory, and executive control'. And the authors found some very important cognitive differences between expert game-players and non-gamers. Now, there's no doubt that expert game-players performed better in certain areas – they track objects more effectively, they identify changes to objects, their reaction times are faster, and they can switch more quickly from one task to another.

Now, I could give you more examples, but let's move on to Suzanna's third point – that playing violent video games can lead to violence in real life, to a more aggressive society. I think we have to be careful here. As Suzanna said, a lot of people believe this to be true. But I don't agree with the interpretation of the research done by Bensley and Van Eenwynk. I don't think it's as simple as you suggest, Suzanna. Yes, they did find that playing an aggressive video game was often followed by aggressive behaviour, but this behaviour was very brief. And more importantly, the research only identified this behaviour in children aged four years to eight years, not in older children. In other words, it's not certain whether the effect is the same in other groups of gamers of different ages.

Also, the research done by Jon Vagg doesn't conclude that playing video games leads to violent behaviour. What he is actually saying is that some gang members go to places like gaming halls to find the kind of people who might be persuaded to join their gang. This is not the same thing. It's not playing video games that leads to gang culture, it's the places where young people play the games. This is like saying that drug dealers try to sell their drugs to people in cafés and bars – so going to cafés and bars leads to drug use. Now, we must be careful about working out causes and effects – a context shouldn't be mistaken for a cause.

Suzanna said that playing video games is linked to antisocial behaviour in children. I'd like to say that I think this is her strongest point. There's definitely plenty of evidence to support this view, although the evidence is not consistent. The piece of research Suzanna quoted is quite convincing, although there's other research which has found that antisocial effects in children are not significant. But as I say, there's quite a substantial body of evidence which suggests a possible link between playing video games and a degree of antisocial behaviour.

And moving on to Suzanna's fifth point now … I'm sorry, but this point is really not very convincing. Think about what she said. 'I've seen children play for hours'. Well, I've seen a lot of interesting things too, but that doesn't make them scientific facts. Kids get moody when they can't do what they want – now, is that really news? Do kids who don't play video games not get moody? This is just personal experience. Maybe playing video games can be addictive, but where's the evidence? Another point … 'addiction is linked to criminality'. I don't think so. It's a big step from playing a video game to committing a crime. If you're going to make claims like these, you must provide real evidence, not just a generalization with no support.

Suzanna, I know that you'll want to come back at me on all of this, but let me just say a couple more things, if I may …

▶ 10.4 Extract 4

1 Indeed, as I'm about to argue, most of the effects they have on people, especially younger people, are negative. And at the extreme end of 'negative', video games can lead to crime.
2 Admittedly, this can be a difficult point to prove, but there is research to suggest that after playing violent and aggressive video games, people may behave in an aggressive way.
3 I said that video games exist, erm, essentially, to fill up leisure time … and they certainly take up a great deal of time for the people who play them.
4 So game-playing is clearly unproductive. From that point of view, it's a complete a waste of time.
5 This suggests that playing video games is linked to antisocial behaviour, which may include violent behaviour.
6 So, it would seem that there is some evidence to suggest that antisocial behaviour can lead to violent behaviour, and then to criminal activity.
7 Maybe they are – but there doesn't seem to be any evidence for this. It's just an opinion. So you could also say that all these activities are perfectly valid and useful.
8 If you're going to make claims like these, you must provide real evidence, not just a generalization with no support.

Speaking

◀》 10.5 Extract 1

A So what do you think? What choices does he have?
B Well, he could leave his job, look for something else.
A I suppose that's one option. Quitting his job might be a good idea. Or he could do something less drastic. For example, he could just speak to his boss. I mean … what else do you think he could do?
B Erm … he could just carry on and hope it'll be OK.
A You mean do nothing?
B Yeah, exactly.
A OK, so he basically has three options. He can leave his job, he can talk to his superiors, or he can do nothing and pretend it's not happening.
B Basically, yes. So what are the advantages and disadvantages of each of these ideas?

◀》 10.6 Extract 2

B Well, the first option certainly deals with the problem from a personal perspective, but … well, what about the other people involved?
A What do you mean?
B Well arguably, that could put other people at risk. They could lose their jobs too, if the situation comes to light. The company might lose a lot of business.
A You think so?
B Definitely. What happens when they find that people haven't been doing their jobs properly? Or what if someone's taking money out of the company?
A True. OK, so personally it would mean he'd be better off because he'd be out of the situation … but it might not be the right decision ethically.
B And actually it might not be the right decision personally. It's his first job, he's not very experienced. It won't look good if he moves on too quickly.
A Well, OK, what about the idea of speaking to his bosses?
B I'm not sure. He could lose his job because he's not being a team player. I mean, generally speaking, companies expect everyone to be a team player. And also, if he's the one who brings up the problem, that could be a bad thing for him. You know … if he's seen as a whistle-blower.
A Yes, I see what you mean. But it could have the effect of getting his bosses to provide more staff. They might not realize how bad it is.
B That could be the case, but I doubt it. I think they might be more likely to blame Bruce.
A OK, well … I suppose it could be argued that the last option is preferable.
B What, just do nothing? You think that's an option?
A Yes, arguably, if he manages to cope and the client's happy he might get promoted.
B Mm, possibly.
A Then it would be someone else's problem, not his.
B I don't know … I mean, what if he can't cope? He could still lose his job and people would think it was his fault. Surely it's better to quit than be fired? I still think quitting could be his best option.

Unit 11

Listening

▶ 11.1 Extract 1

As the wealth of a country's population grows, so too does their standard of living. They have more money, they eat better, they have nicer homes, their health improves. All of this is a good thing, of course. But the downside of this – and it's obvious when you think about it – is that at the same time, their energy consumption goes up. As a country's overall standard of living improves, and its material wealth increases, so too does the burden on that country's resources in terms of energy use. The consumption of energy increases in parallel with a rise in the wealth of a population.

And make no mistake. Along with the need to maintain a sustainable water supply, this is the key issue facing the world's governments today – how to deal with rising demand for energy, when conventional sources are already under pressure, and in some cases in danger of running out.

For many years the highest consumers of energy globally have been in the developed world, principally Europe and North America, and increasingly now in the Middle East. However, in recent years, we've seen the emergence of other major economies, in particular Brazilian, Russian, Chinese, and Indian economies. Several of these – China and Russia in particular – are energy-rich, with extensive supplies of their own.

The development of these newly industrialized economies places increasing pressure on the world's energy supplies, particularly oil and gas. Just under three billion of the world's seven billion inhabitants live in these four countries. And they're getting richer, and they're consuming more. Over the next few decades, the world is going to face increasing challenges in terms of fulfilling the growing demand for energy.

This is clearly a global issue, but the solutions – partly, at least – lie with individual countries. And this is what I want to concentrate on today.

Currently, the world's largest consumer of energy is China. And China itself acknowledges that there are a number of problems with its own energy infrastructure. The system is far from perfect. However, not only are the Chinese authorities looking to address these issues within China, they are also responding to them in a way that could further enhance their economic growth.

So, in what ways is China looking to resolve these issues? What solutions are they currently implementing?

◀》 11.2

World energy supply is considered by some analysts to be a threat to world peace. It's likely that there'll be a shortage of fossil fuels in the future, and any drop in world energy supplies could cause a crisis on a scale never seen before. One issue to overcome is that modern life is dependent on high energy consumption. Many countries are looking to improve the energy efficiency of homes and offices. For example, the Chinese government hopes to address the issue by introducing a range of solutions. One option is to update and modernize power plants. Additionally, alternative sources such as wind, solar, and biofuels are being explored. However, there has been a recent dispute about the use of biofuels as an alternative energy source.

▶ 11.3 Extract 2

Now, as I said, China is the world's biggest energy consumer and its energy consumption has grown dramatically, in line with a similar growth in its economy. Between 2005 and 2010 China's demand for energy went up nearly 50 per cent in response to this rapid economic expansion – a very substantial increase, clearly. And consequently, over a similar period of time, a large number of power plants were built in order to meet this increased demand. A number of these older power plants are now quite inefficient and

China wants to close them down and replace them with more energy-efficient plants. Many small and medium-sized power plants can also be quite inefficient … and there are issues around pollution here too.

The Chinese government has a plan to replace these smaller plants with larger, more energy-efficient, coal-fired power stations such as the one in Beihua, which is Asia's largest coal-fired power station. Now, while this solution may not address the fundamental issue of increased energy consumption overall, or the longer-term environmental impact, it does improve energy production in the short-term.

In the long term, China recognizes the need to limit its energy use and intends to put a cap on energy growth. An energy cap, therefore, is a maximum limit placed on the amount of energy used. The annual growth in energy consumption has been around 8 per cent on average. In 2010, the rate of energy consumption was 3.25 billion tonnes of coal, or the equivalent, per year. China acknowledges that the demand for energy is still going to increase over the coming decades … but none the less, they've set a cap of just over four billion tonnes of coal, or the equivalent, per year. This would reduce energy consumption, or the level of increase in energy consumption each year, to below five per cent. However, it still means the annual consumption will be higher than at present. And it would still make China one of the largest, if not the largest, energy consumer in the world.

Now, as we know, China has rapidly become one of the world's most important economies, dominating the production of a huge range of goods and achieving economic growth rates in excess of 10 per cent year on year. So it's perhaps not surprising, therefore, that China is once again approaching this new challenge in an entrepreneurial way.

As I mentioned earlier, on a micro level, China has decided to shut down its less efficient power plants and replace them with new, more energy-efficient facilities. However, on the macro level, China aims to use climate change to encourage the development of emerging technologies as well. Like many other countries, they plan to invest in new energy technologies such as wave power, wind power, and solar energy … energy from the sun.

In terms of transportation, China has also seen significant growth in the number of cars on the road and therefore they're looking at the large-scale development of electric vehicles – more energy-efficient, less polluting, and not reliant on oil. And in terms of agriculture, food production, China is also investing in biotechnology with the aim of developing more energy-efficient food crops.

The question is, of course, will these newer technologies be able to make up for the proposed reduction in the use of conventional energy sources? These are all fairly small-scale technologies. At the moment, there are concerns about efficiency, about cost, and whether it will be possible to make them work on a larger scale.

[…] When China began its process of reform, and adopted a more open economic policy, one of the things it did was to create a number of special economic zones. These were specific areas of the country that were given the job of pushing forward China's economic growth. In other words, China was looking for local solutions to a national problem, or a national issue. And in the same way, China is now looking for local solutions to the national and international issue of energy consumption, of energy-efficiency.

So the government has selected five provinces and eight cities around the country to be the first to introduce low-carbon development. Each province and city is being encouraged to create plans for medium- and long-term development aimed at reducing energy use in their local area. The government intends to support low-carbon innovations in these areas … special industrial parks, residential communities, and specific products and services … so it's putting a lot of money and resources into the initiative.

One example of this is Tianjin eco-city in the north-east of the country. This is an innovative approach, and it has worked for China in the past. However, some critics have suggested that too many resources will be concentrated in certain areas, and that other parts of the country will fall behind as a result.

Speaking

🔊)) **11.4 Extract 1**

We all know that our main sources of energy, coal, oil and gas, the so-called fossil fuels … they take millions of years to develop, and at some point in the future they are going to run out. So we have to think about this now. What happens when the oil runs out? When there's no more coal, no more gas? Where do we get our energy from?

So this presentation is about some of the possible solutions to the future of energy supplies. We need to think about alternatives, about renewable sources of energy – and as we know, there are a number of these. Some countries, like Denmark for example, have already set a target of being completely independent of fossil fuels by 2050. How this can be achieved is still not clear. But there's a lot of research that suggests that there aren't really any technological or economic reasons for not making this change.

So today we're going to look at three of the solutions, three ways to generate renewable energy. What we want to do is to show that there are concerns about all of these solutions … but these concerns, these ideas, are not actually a problem, because the technologies are developing and improving all the time.

OK, we only have a few minutes, so each part of the presentation will be quite short. So firstly, Louisa's going to talk about solar energy, and the idea that it's too expensive. Then Yakut is going to look at wind power, and the concern that it's unreliable. And finally, I'll talk about a third possible solution, marine energy, energy from the sea, and the idea that it's too expensive and difficult to produce.

But I should say that these are only some of the possible solutions – there isn't time to talk about all of them. So … over to you, Louisa.

🔊)) **11.5 Extract 2**

So, the solution I want to talk about is solar power. And just to be clear, this means solar panels, the ones you can see on the roof of buildings, or out in the countryside, in big groups. A lot of people think that solar panels are expensive and not a very efficient way of creating energy. In the past this was probably true. But because of changes in technology, solar panels have become much more efficient and cheaper, more cost-effective.

For example, a few years ago most solar panels could only capture around 10 per cent of the sun's energy and convert this into electricity. But because of changes to the materials used to make the solar panels, there have been dramatic improvements in the cost and efficiency of using this system. Researchers in the United States have been working on photovoltaics, photovoltaic cells. These convert the sun's energy directly into electricity. And today they can capture and convert nearer to 35 per cent of the sun's energy.

There have also been improvements to the way energy is stored. For example, in battery design, in particular, a lithium-ion energy storage unit that's much more efficient than traditional batteries.

What this means is, solar panels are now able to generate substantially more electricity than in the past, and to store it more efficiently. So solar energy is becoming a lot cheaper. So the belief that solar power is an expensive source of renewable energy is rapidly changing, due to technological developments that have improved both costs and efficiency.

OK, now I'd like to hand over to Yakut to talk about the next solution.

🔊)) **11.6 Extract 3**

Thanks, Louisa. So what I want to look at is wind power. People have been using wind power in different ways for thousands of years, and it's actually one of the most efficient ways of generating electricity. The main problem is the belief that wind power is too unreliable. The wind doesn't blow all the time, it blows at different speeds, in different directions, you don't know when it's going to blow … you can't rely on it. There are other concerns too, large groups of wind turbines change the landscape, they're a danger to birds … but unreliability is the main concern.

Where the wind turbines are located is important, obviously. For example, offshore wind farms … in other words, in the sea … often have a more reliable supply of wind. But what is really important is to connect wind farms together in a larger network. This is the real solution to making wind energy reliable. We need to connect the wind farms in all the different locations to a national grid, a national energy network, that can store and distribute electricity efficiently across the whole region. It has been argued by some researchers that as much as 30 per cent of our total energy needs could be met by wind power – with the right structure.

So, as Andrews and Jelley say in their book, *Energy Science*, if we can improve storage and distribution methods, then wind energy could make a significant contribution to the supply of carbon-free electricity. OK, so I'll hand over to Kris for the last part.

🔊)) **11.7 Extract 4**

OK, so lastly, I'm going to look at wave energy, or marine energy as it's sometimes called.

The main concern about wave energy, as with any new technology, is cost. The initial costs are very high. This means that the running costs, the costs of actually producing electricity, need to be low in order for wave energy to be competitive. Another concern is that the equipment has to be tough enough to stand up to conditions at sea in all weathers.

As with solar and wind power, the more investment a sector receives, the more quickly the costs come down. It's likely to take ten to twenty years to develop the technology enough for it to be competitive. However, the Sustainable Energy Research Group from Southampton University in the UK have predicted that there is likely to be a reduction in costs over the next twenty years of up to 60 per cent. They also say that the potential market for wave power is larger than the market for wind and solar power combined. So while the costs may be high at the moment, they'll eventually come down. This could make wave energy much more competitive in the longer term.

So, to sum up ... all three of the solutions we've looked at – solar, wind, and wave power – all of these solutions may have been thought of as inefficient and/or expensive in the past. But over the last ten to fifteen years environmental needs and political support have created a growing market. Now, there's an increasing amount of evidence to suggest that they will all become increasingly important sources of energy production over the next ten to twenty years.

11.8 Extract 5

1 What I'm saying is that environmental and economic considerations need to be balanced.
2 What is now possible, but expensive, is to capture and store CO_2.
3 What I'd like to emphasize are the difficulties involved in dealing with nuclear waste.
4 Where 1,200 new wind turbines a week can be situated is hard to see.

Unit 12

Listening

12.1 Extract 1

In today's lecture we're going to develop the general theme of progress by looking at a key area of human progress. This is urbanization, the gradual movement of human populations away from a rural existence in the countryside, to living in towns and cities. And our title today is *The effects of urbanization on human health.*

Progress, as we saw last week, suggests improvement, the idea of things getting better ... and it tends to be associated with things like economic growth, industrialization, and urbanization. Well, these things are of course in many ways very positive, but as I'm about to argue, rapid growth such as we see around us today in many parts of the world can have serious consequences. And not all of them are positive.

The area I'm going to focus on today is urbanization, and in particular the impacts of the urban lifestyle, the urban climate, on human health. What are the effects on human health of living in a city? Obviously it depends on what kind of urban environment we're talking about ... not all cities are the same. Living in, living in Vancouver or Copenhagen and living in ... I don't know, let's say Jakarta or Kolkata ... is clearly not the same thing, but there will be similar effects, none the less. Now these effects, these impacts, can be positive, negative, or broadly neutral. But actually, when we talk about 'impacts', they tend to be more negative than positive.

So, what are the main impacts of the urban climate on human health? Broadly speaking, there are two main issues which influence people's health in cities. These are heat stress during summer conditions, and air pollution. Heat stress in particular is a major factor, mainly due to the 'urban heat island' effect.

Now, the urban heat island effect refers to a situation where the areas around large urban centres, or cities, are measurably hotter than the surrounding countryside and agricultural areas. Urban centres are hotter because firstly they're built up, rather than natural. They have more buildings and roads and fewer green spaces ... rather than vegetation which releases moisture into the atmosphere. So, in very broad terms, you could say that rural areas are cooler and wetter, built-up areas are hotter and drier. Secondly, urban areas release heat into the atmosphere – they release heat in the form of the energy from buildings, from heating and air-conditioning. And heat is also created by people, and by traffic, of course. For these reasons urban areas are hotter, causing what is known as the urban heat island effect.

Let me give you an example. The summer of 2003 was the hottest summer in Europe for many centuries, possibly since the year 1500. It resulted in large numbers of heat-related deaths across much of western Europe, particularly in big cities where temperatures were higher. Since then, this whole issue has become a particularly important topic in science and government policy.

12.2 Extract 2

I'd now like to look at the topic of bio-climate in some more detail. Bio-climate is an important factor for human health. Bio-climate involves and brings together all the meteorological variables, the different factors which affect the temperature of the human body. So, things like air temperature and air humidity ... the amount of moisture in the air ... also wind speed, short wave solar radiation from the sun, and long wave terrestrial emissions, heat from the earth itself. All of these variables influence our body temperature.

The normally accepted body temperature for a healthy human is 37 degrees Celsius. What this means is that humans have to keep a body temperature of 37 in all climates – under all climatic conditions. So there is very little room for variation. Therefore, too much heat, or thermal stress, can lead to negative effects on human health, very quickly.

It is quite likely that in some parts of the world summer temperatures will increase due to global warming. This is going to be a particular problem in urban areas. And heat waves like the one in Europe in 2003 will be normal rather than exceptional.

So, how does heat work in relation to the human body? Well, there are several processes going on. We produce energy constantly, as a result of digesting our food and through activities like walking and running. This energy has to be balanced in order to keep the body temperature constant, at 37 degrees. Basically, in cooler air, we lose heat energy because we need to use more energy to keep warm. And in warm air we gain heat energy.

Humans release energy in a number of ways, such as sweating, and breathing deeply. Breathing deeply produces a lot of humidity, a lot of moisture, and this leads to a significant loss of energy from the body. We can do this at any temperature, including tropical temperatures, but as the humidity in the surrounding air increases, the process becomes less effective. The result is an increase in people suffering from heat stress.

Two local environmental factors directly affect body temperature. These are wind and sun. Any wind speed will help to keep your body temperature down – the higher the wind speed, the stronger the cooling effect, normally. On the other hand, if you stay too long in the sun, you're exposed to solar radiation, which means you're receiving more heat energy compared with being in the shade.

So heat stress is related to summer weather conditions without high wind speed, with high air temperatures and high humidity, and also surrounded by the warm surfaces of walls and roads. And it's pretty clear that you'll find most of these conditions in an urban environment rather than a rural one. Another factor is that night-time temperatures tend to be much higher in cities than outside. These conditions are not ideal for achieving a good sleep and recovery.

12.3 Extract 1

In this presentation, I want to look at the argument that economic growth is the best way of measuring progress, the progress of a society. I think most people agree that if the economy is growing, then things are generally improving for that society. However, there are a number of arguments against this idea that economic growth is the best measure of progress for all societies. And that's what I want to talk about first.

One of the main arguments is that if you have goods or services that are not sold, not exchanged for money, then these goods or services don't have any economic value. For example, when people produce their own food, or take care of someone who is sick, or look after an old person in their own home, no economic value is placed on this. Or in societies where there's a system of exchanging goods, of exchanging services, where no money changes hands, then these transactions aren't measured. So in cases like these you have a kind of 'hidden economy' which can't be measured.

OK, let's think about it in relation to the aims of a society. In most societies high levels of employment, where most people have a job, is a sign of progress. However, economic growth doesn't automatically mean high employment. For example, when the economy is growing you often have technological advances taking place ... and these technological advances can actually reduce employment, especially in areas like manufacturing or agriculture. If technology starts to do the work that was previously done by people, then obviously more people will be unemployed, without a job. And this has a negative effect, because there are fewer people spending money keeping the economy growing. And low levels of employment also have other effects ... on people's health, on their psychological well-being, educational opportunities, levels of crime, and so on.

Another issue to think about is that economic growth is usually measured in gross domestic product, or GDP. GDP is the total value of all goods and services, in all sectors, produced by a country in one year. But the problem with using GDP as a measure of progress is that it doesn't show how much money people earn in comparison to each other ... who is rich and who is poor, basically. So you can have a situation, for a small percentage of the people, where their income is increasing drastically ... but for most other people there's very little increase in their income, and their living standards. So growth doesn't mean that everyone is getting richer, only that some people are getting richer. In fact, there are signs in some societies where the gap between the rich and the poor is increasing. So even in countries with a high GDP, it's very possible for many people to still be living in poverty.

One more point about GDP ... GDP focuses on the short term. It doesn't take into account, like, that resources such as oil or gas are finite. There's a limited supply and one day they're going to run out. GDP only provides a short-term view. So you could argue that it doesn't actually help measure progress at all.

🔊 12.4

A So, ... do you think economic growth is a good measure of progress?

B Well, it's a good question. I suppose it depends what you mean by progress.

A OK, well let's not get into that. I mean, we're talking about things generally getting better, aren't we?

B OK, well then ... From what Matt was saying, it seems that economic growth isn't a good indicator of progress, but ... I'm not sure I agree. I mean, if the economy's doing well, isn't that a good thing?

A But what about the fact that it might not be an accurate measure? There was the example that not all goods and services are sold, so ... I think arguably there's a lot of economic activity going on that can't be measured, because we don't know about it.

B Yeah ... I know what you're saying, but ... in a sense we can't expect to measure everything. I would argue that it still gives us a good indication of ... well, you know, how well things are progressing.

A Perhaps, but then as we heard, it also doesn't mean we know who's benefiting. We don't know anything about the distribution of wealth, and if incomes are going up right across society. Some people could still be on low incomes.

B That's true to a certain extent, I suppose. But then, presumably the argument is that rich people will be paying higher taxes and that money can be used by the government ... well, you know, for the good of everyone.

A Well, only in countries where there is taxation. There's also the argument that unemployment can be higher when the economy is doing well because of technological developments, technological progress, you know. And there's also the point about GDP being a short-term measure.

B I'm sorry, but I just don't see the logic in those arguments. OK, it appears that there might not always be very high employment, but ... surely unemployment would be higher in an economy that's performing badly? And also ... well, nothing's really a good long-term indicator, is it?

A So you mean low economic growth leads to high unemployment?

B Yes. And also, erm ... an indication of good performance now tends not to be a reliable indicator of future performance.

A I see what you're saying, but for me the basic measure is just wrong. As Matt said, GDP doesn't reflect individual wealth and it doesn't include all aspects of goods and services.

▶ 12.5 Extract 2

So, I'm saying that economic growth alone is not a good way to measure progress in any society. We also need to consider other social and environmental factors. I want to argue that the two most important factors related to progress are education and health. Whether you view progress in economic or social terms, the two key factors in achieving it are having a good standard of education, and a healthy population.

Firstly, education. In most societies, education allows people to improve their lives. It helps them get better access to jobs, to earn better salaries, and to achieve their own economic goals. As a result, they contribute to the economy by spending money and paying taxes. Improving people's knowledge and skills – through education – means you have a better educated workforce, and this supports economic growth. From a social perspective, education gives people more opportunities to work in a wide range of professions. It gives them more choice, more control over their working lives, and over their future. And also, you could argue that education leads to a more creative society – people who have knowledge and ideas, and want to improve things. And let's not forget that improvements in education are also connected to improvements in health generally.

So, health is also closely linked to education, and to the economic and social factors associated with progress. From an economic perspective, obviously, if people are healthy then they're able to work, to find productive employment. This factor has real economic benefits. Over time, it raises income levels and leads to a reduction in poverty ... because if you have a productive workforce, people who are earning money, then as I said before, you're putting more money into the economy. So improvements in health mean people are able to participate better in all areas of society. And also, there's a direct connection, between education and health. People who are better educated are able to make better decisions about their health, what food they eat, how much they drink or smoke, and so on. So you could say that education allows people to be healthier, they live longer, they have a better quality of life.

So ... both education and health, in the past, were seen as positive effects of economic growth. However, I think you could argue that the cause and effect relationship is actually the other way around. A well-educated and healthy population is likely to lead to economic growth, rather than the opposite. So it could be argued that increased access to education, improvements in health care, and healthier lifestyles, are actually better indicators of progress than economic growth.

Oxford source material used in this course

The reading, writing, and speaking skills modules of *Oxford EAP* include extracts from the following source material published by Oxford University Press. For more information about any of these titles, please visit: **www.oup.com**.

pages 013, 014, 020, 041-042
IB Psychology: Course Companion

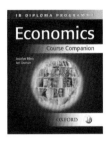

pages 026-027
IB Economics Companion

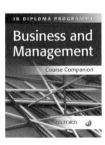

pages 038, 114
IB Business and Management Course Companion

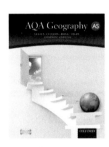

page 055
AQA Geography

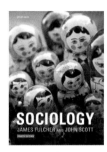

pages 069-070, 124
Sociology 4th edition

page 080
Two Billion Cars: Driving Towards Sustainability

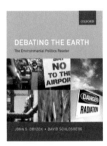

page 083
Debating the Earth: The Environmental Politics Reader

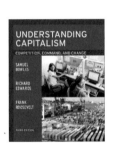

pages 087, 198
Understanding Capitalism: Competition, Command, and Change

pages 097-098
Online Marketing: A Customer-Led Approach

pages 111
The Business Environment 2nd Edition

page 115
Introduction to Business Management 8th Edition

pages 124-125
Media and Journalism 2nd Edition

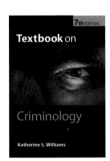

page 139
Textbook on Criminology 6th edition

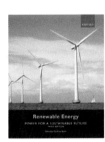

page 153
Renewable Energy: Power for a Sustained Future 2nd Edition

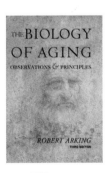

page 167
The Biology of Aging: Observations and Principles

page 202
AS & A level Psychology Through Diagrams

page 202
Business Ethics 4th Edition

page 204
A Cubic Mile of Oil

OXFORD
UNIVERSITY PRESS

Great Clarendon Street, Oxford, OX2 6DP, United Kingdom

Oxford University Press is a department of the University of Oxford.
It furthers the University's objective of excellence in research, scholarship,
and education by publishing worldwide. Oxford is a registered trade
mark of Oxford University Press in the UK and in certain other countries

ACKNOWLEDGEMENTS

*The authors and publisher are grateful to those who have given permission to reproduce
the following extracts and adaptations of copyright material:* p.13, 14, 41, 43, 48
Extract from *IB Psychology: Course Companion* by Crane, J. and Hannibal, J. (Oxford
University Press, 2009), copyright © Oxford University Press. Reproduced
by permission of Oxford University Press; p.26, 28 Extract from *IB Economics
Companion* by Blink, J. and Dorton, I. (Oxford University Press, 2007), copyright
© Oxford University Press. Reproduced by permission of Oxford University
Press; p.38,114 Extract from *IB Diploma Programme- Business and Management
Course Companion* by Clark, p., Golden, p., O'Dea, M., Weiner, J. & Woolrich, p.
(Oxford University Press, 2009), copyright © Clark, p., Golden, p., O'Dea, M.,
Weiner, J. & Woolrich, p. Reproduced by permission of Oxford University Press;
p.55 Extract from *AS Geography for AQA* by Ross, S., Digley, B., Chapman, R., and
Cowling, D. (Oxford University Press, 2011), copyright © Oxford University
Press. Reproduced by permission of Oxford University Press; p.68,70, 124
Extract from *Sociology 4th Edition* by Fulcher, J. & Scott, J. © Oxford University
Press 2005. Reprinted by permission of Oxford University Press; p.80, 205
Extract from *Two Billion Cars: Driving Towards Sustainability* by Sperling, D. &
Gordon, D. © Oxford University Press 2009. Reprinted by permission of Oxford
University Press, USA; p.83 Extract from *Plan B: Rescuing a Planet Under Stress
and a Civilization in Trouble* (Earth Policy Institute, 2003), 3-19. Reproduced by
permission; p.87, 205 Extract from *Understanding Capitalism* by Bowles, S.,
Edwards, R., and Roosevelt, F. © Oxford University Press 2005. Reproduced
by permission of Oxford University Press, USA; p.97, 98 Extract from *Online
Marketing: A Customer-led Approach* by Gay, R. et al. © Oxford University Press
2007. Reproduced by permission of Oxford University Press; p.108, 144, 207
Extract from *The International Business Environment* by Hamilton, L. © Oxford
University Press 2009. Reproduced by permission of Oxford University Press;
p.110, 204, 206 Extract from *The Business Environment: Themes & Issues 2nd Edition*
by Wetherly, p. & Otter, D. © Oxford University Press. Reproduced by permission
of Oxford University Press; p.115 Extract from *Introduction to Business Management
8th Edition* by du Toit, G.S., Erasmus, B.J., & Syrydom, J.W. © Oxford University
Press Southern Africa 2010. Reproduced by permission; p.125 Reproduced by
permission of Oxford University Press Australia & New Zealand, from *Media
and Journalism, Second Edition*, by Jason Bainbridge, Nicola Goc & Liz Tynan,
2011, Oxford University Press; p.134 Extract from *AS & A level Psychology through
Diagrams* by Hill, G. (Oxford University Press, 1998), copyright (C) Grahame Hill
1998, 2001. Reproduced by permission of Oxford University Press; p.136, 208
Reproduced by permission of Oxford University Press Australia & New Zealand,
from *Business Ethics, Fourth Edition*, by Damian Grace and Stephen Cohen, 2009,
Oxford University Press; p.139 Extract from *Textbook on Criminology, 7th Edition*
by Williams, K. © Oxford University Press 2012. Reproduced by permission of
Oxford University Press; p.150, 208 Extract from *A Cubic Mile of Oil* by Crane,
H.D. et al. © Oxford University Press 2010. Reproduced by permission of Oxford
University Press, USA; p.153 Extract from *Renewable Energy* edited by G. Boyle.
© Oxford University Press 1996. Reproduced by permission of Oxford University
Press; p.166 Extract from *The Biology of Aging: Observations & Principles 3rd Edition*
by Arking, R. © Oxford University Press 2006. Reproduced by permission of
Oxford University Press, USA; p.174 Extract from *Urban Ecology: Patterns, Processes
and Applications* edited by Niemela, J. et al. © Oxford University Press 2011.
Reproduced by permission of Oxford University Press; p.187 Extract from *The
Globalization of World Politics 4th Edition* by Baylis, J.S., & Owens, O. © Oxford
University Press 2007. Reprinted by permission of Oxford University Press.

*The publisher is grateful to the following for their permission to reproduce photographs and
illustrative material:* Alamy Images pp.66 (iPhone screen detail/Jakob Kamender),
101 (Call centre/David Pearson), 120 (Apple iPhone/Adrian Lyon), 120 (Smartphone
Google Maps satellite navigation/Ian Dagnall), 120 (iPod/Pillyphotos),
133 (Fingerprint scanning technology/Johan Swanepoel), 167 (African girl/Irene
Abdou), 167 (Senior man/Radius Images), 170 (Deforestation/Martin Shields);
Corbis pp.13 (Advanced Maths student/Peter M. Fisher), 15 (Quarter Final England
vs Italy, Euro 2012/Sergey Dolzhenko/epa), 19 (MRI scan of brain/CNRI/Science
Photo Library), 21 (Human Rights Council/Salvatore Di Nolfi/epa), 24 (River Jiu in
Lupeni/Michael St. Maur Sheil), 31 (Lab researcher/Andrew Brookes), 41 (London
Marathon/Ricky Leaver/Loop Images), 50 (Financial Square at the TEDA/(C) Lo Mak/
Redlink), 80 (Imported cars), 83 (Hands holding rice/Radius Images), 92 (Robert
Cailliau at CERN/Pallava Bagla), 92 (Tim Berners-Lee/Andrew Brusso), 97 (Campus
Party Europe/Britta Pedersen/dpa), 105 (Dubai International Airport/Gavin Hellier/
JAI), 152 (Spillway of a dam/Richard Gross), 152 (Cleansing department, Hamberg/
Christian Charisius/dpa), 152 (Solar panels/Jake Wyman), 152 (Wind turbines/
Marco Cristofori), 152 (Nuclear power plant/Larry Lee Photography), 158 (Cows/
Sam Wirzba/AgStock Images), 161 (Woman travelling by train/Jesco Tscholitsch);
Getty Images pp.7 (Business presentation/Clerkenwell), 22 (United Nations
building/Tetra Images), 35 (USA Pro Challenge/Garrett W. Ellwood), 43 (Sprint/
Enrico Calderoni/Aflo), 46 (Professor and university students/Clerkenwell), 49 (Rice
fields, China/Thomas Kokta), 54 (Drought/Eco Images), 59 (Morning traffic/J/J
Images - J Morrill Photo), 61 (Satellite receiver/VisionsofAmerica/Joe Sohm),
63 (Times Square/Mitchell Funk), 75 (Climbers descending mountain/Buena Vista
Images), 77 (Crowds in New York/Mitchell Funk), 82 (Water shortage/Hannah
McNeish/AFP), 91 (Nanpu Bridge, Shanghai/Wei Fang), 94 (Study group with tutor/
René Mansi), 94 (Teen girl doing homework/Ron Levine), 111 (Nanobot working in
artery/Fredrik Skoid), 119 (Bottles on production line/Jean-Christophe Verhaegen/
AFP), 120 (E-readers/Daniel Acker/Bloomberg via Getty Images), 123 (Mother and
son at picnic/Douglas Menuez), 125 (Edward R. Murrow, of CBS News/CBS via
Getty images), 130 (Woman using laptop/Nomurasa), 134 (Playing video game/
Karen Moskowitz), 137 (Advertising/Hector Mata/AFP), 139 (Remand cell block/
Diana Mayfield), 147 (Wave/Cavataio Vince), 152 (Corn field/Philippe Huguen/
AFP), 165 (Indian schoolchildren/Anna Henly); LAVA p.50; Reuters Pictures
pp.26 (Employees at clothing factory/Reuters/Jason Lee), 26 (Traders in New York
Mercatile Exchange/Reuters/Lucas Jackson), 27 (Women working in factory/
Reuters/Akintunde Akinleye); Rex Features p.120 (MP3 player technology/David
Howells); Oxford University Press covers on page 223.

Lecturer and presenter portraits by: Mark Bassett pp.8 (all), 11, 23, 36, 51 (both), 52, 65,
66, 78, 93, 107, 121, 134 (man and woman), 148, 162, 164;

Illustrations by: Peter Bull p.106 (all); Oxford University Press p.55 taken from AQA
Geography, by Simon Ross, Bob Digby, Russell Chapman, Dan Cowling, (March
2011); Richard Ponsford pp.53 (both), 80 (graph), 120, 204.

Cover photograph by: Gareth Boden.

Design by: Richard Ponsford

*The authors and publisher would like to thank the following individuals and institutions for
their advice and assistance in developing the material for this course:* Michael Abberton
(NCUK), Sean Ahern (Isis Group, Greenwich, UK), Fiona Aish (Target English),
Alex Anderson (St Giles International, Brighton), Kenneth Anderson (University
of Edinburgh), Lisa Bishop (Isis Group, Greenwich, UK), Margo Blythman
(University of the Arts, London), Dr Charles Boyle (University of Oxford), Rupert
Brown (University of Cambridge), Carrick Cameron, James Chantry (University
of York), Sarah Cooper (South Thames College, London), Tracey Costley (King's
College, London), Leslie Cox (University of Salford), Eowyn Crisfield (Intercollege,
Netherlands), Alister Drury (Leeds English Language School), Diarmud Fogarty
(Manchester Metropolitan University), Sarah Gartland (Roehampton University),
Teresa Goff-Lindsay (Windesheim Honours College, Netherlands), Sandra
Haywood (University of Nottingham), Laura Hebden (freelance, Netherlands),
Alice Henderson (Université de Savoie, France), Maggie Holmes (York St John
University), Andy Hoodith (Manchester Metropolitan University), Phil Horspool
(University of Leicester), Barbara Howarth (University of Glasgow), Paul Hullock
(University of East Anglia), David Jay (freelance, UK), Dr Meaghan Kowalsky
(Leeds English Language School), Ricky Lowes (University of Plymouth), Patrick
McMahon (University of Plymouth), Janet Milne (Erasmus University, Rotterdam,
Netherlands), Dr Elizabeth Molt (Hogeschool Rotterdam, Netherlands), Tessa
Moore (University of Nottingham), Simon Mumford, Clive Newton (University
of Liverpool), Shirley Norton (London School of English), Henrietta Pocock
(University of Loughborough), Lynne Robinson, David Sawtell (English in Chester),
Becky Smith (freelance, UK), Alison Standring (London School of Economics),
Wendy Sturrock (freelance, Netherlands), Allyson White (University of Cardiff),
Patricia White (freelance, UK), Anneli Williams (University of Glasgow). *Bellerby's
College, Brighton:* Adam Bradley, Mandy Bright, Sarah Brooker, David Rowson,
Gordon Watts. *Bellerby's College, Oxford:* Steve Antoniou, Juliette Calow, Jackie Eadie,
Penny Ponton, Suzannah Lambe, David Mackenzie, Idaly Mackenzie, Kieran
Suchet. *International Study Centre, University of Sussex:* Robert Cooper, Kath Gilmore,
Joanna Lee, Jo Odgers, Tom Ottway, Peter Ryley, Victoria Stephenson, Jennifer
Wain. *King's Colleges Oxford:* Jan Akbar, Sarah Bacon, Nick Davids, Jeanette Lindsay-
Clarke, Nick Row, Nick Thorner. *University College London Language Centre:* Jon Butt,
Angela Cooper, Rhod Fiorini, Hayley Gewer, Kate Tranter, Julie Willis.

Special thanks to: Richard Storton. Edward de Chazal would particularly like to
thank his family, especially Martha, and his co-author Louis Rogers, for their help
and support. Louis Rogers would particularly like to thank his family, especially
Cathy, and his co-author Edward de Chazal, for their help and support.

*Although every effort has been made to trace and contact copyright holders before publication,
this has not been possible in some cases. We apologise for any apparent infringement of
copyright and, if notified, the publisher will be pleased to rectify any errors or omissions at the
earliest possible opportunity.*